Organizational Culture in Action

Offering students and practitioners an applied approach to the subject, Organizational Culture in Action (OCA) walks them through a six-step model for analyzing an organization's culture. The application of the model provides insight into positive communication practices to improve organizational ethics and effectiveness. The authors review relevant theory while integrating a constitutive approach to studying organizational culture and communication. Practical guides for multiple data collection methods are provided, and the workbook format is full of interactive tools that engage students and reinforce learning.

Based on feedback from professionals, students, and colleagues, the 4th edition includes the following substantive developments:

- Development and integration of the Model for Positive Communication by engaging Dr. Julien Mirivel, co-founder of the Positive Communication Network, as a co-author.
- A clear commitment and focus on the role and goal of the OCA in *fostering the co-creation of positive organizations by developing implications through the analysis of enacted elements that both shape and are shaped by communication.*
- An improved applied focus by stating "Mental Shifts in Chapter 1," which is carried throughout the book
- All chapters are updated with recent literature and case studies.
- The latest applied research is integrated into units on diversity, change, leadership, and effectiveness in relation to positive organizational communication.
- Cases, examples, and applications relevant to crisis, Generative AI, employee engagement, virtual organizations, conflict management, and public relations are provided.
- Pedagogical guides to aid in qualitative analysis and ways to utilize research literature in the final report.
- Clarification of cultural analysis used throughout the book by: a) reformatting Chapter 1 with an inclusion of a visual of the model; and b) revising the wording of the six steps in the model.
- Colleagues and alumni serving and guiding the development of cases and reviewing positive practices in chapters on diversity and change.
- Online resources, including guides for auto-ethnography and coding.

Professionals come away equipped to apply cultural insights into fostering inclusiveness in relation to diversity, supporting organizational change, making leadership more dynamic, understanding the link between ethics and culture, and achieving personal and professional growth.

Gerald W. C. Driskill—University of Arkansas, Little Rock

Julien C. Mirivel—University of Arkansas, Little Rock

As a new faculty member building a course on people-centered organizational cultures, *Organizational Culture in Action* was a perfect fit. The workbook provides a guided tour to build knowledge and make application. This book is a must for anyone in leadership roles—operational, consultant, or HR—seeking to make a positive culture change.

Dr. S. Lynee Willett, DBA, SPHR, sHRBP, Assistant Professor—University of Wisconsin-Stout

This excellent book offers a variety of deep conceptual tools to understand what makes organizations tick. The authors' masterful hands-on approach equips readers with insights into how organizational cultures are created, how we can navigate them more skillfully, and how we might shape culture positively and as a result.

Dr. Alex Lyon, Professor, SUNY, Brockport

Driskill and Mirivel have updated a pivotal work for understanding organizations and their cultures based in recent and wide-ranging research. There is no better way to understand how communication works in organizations. They provide practical exercises and useful advice for exploring key aspects of organizational culture.

Dr. John Meyer, Professor of Communication Studies, University of Southern Mississippi

While maintaining an academic focus the text offers a unique contribution through the practical exercise and checks on learning designed to stimulate and engage the reader. The format makes it an ideal companion for individuals or groups who are undertaking a cultural analysis in organizations, or for the purpose of corporate training and development.

Dr. Nicholas Jackson, University of Leeds, UK

Organizational culture remains one of the most compelling explanations for why people do what they do in the workplace. In this essential edition, Professors Driskill and Mirivel weave together the latest insights on culture analysis, positive communication, and ethics to offer a crucial guide for today's leaders. They make complex ideas accessible while delivering profound, actionable wisdom. I recommend this book to leaders and aspiring leaders who understand that culture is not just an abstract concept—it is a foundation of success.

Ryan S. Bisel, Ph.D. Professor of Organizational Communication, Dept. of Communication University of Oklahoma

Organizational Culture in Action

A Cultural Analysis Workbook

Fourth Edition

Gerald W. C. Driskill and Julien C. Mirivel

Routledge
Taylor & Francis Group
NEW YORK AND LONDON

Designed cover image: Getty Images

Fourth edition published 2026
by Routledge
605 Third Avenue, New York, NY 10158

and by Routledge
4 Park Square, Milton Park, Abingdon, Oxon, OX14 4RN

Routledge is an imprint of the Taylor & Francis Group, an informa business

First edition published by Sage Publications, Inc. 2005
Third edition published by Routledge 2019

ISBN: 978-1-032-77333-9 (hbk)
ISBN: 978-1-032-77332-2 (pbk)
ISBN: 978-1-003-48252-9 (ebk)

DOI: 10.4324/9781003482529

Typeset in Bembo
by Apex CoVantage, LLC

Access the Instructor and Student Resources: www.routledge.com/9781032773322

To Angela Laird Brenton, who had the vision in the 1980s to develop a cultural analysis course to serve students decades before this book or others had been written. To her passion as an educator and a leader, and her love for her husband, Keith, and children Matthew and Laura, who gave her time and space to serve others, and her mother, Harriet Laird, who served as her perpetual role model and encourager. Angela will always be missed, yet her faith and love, even in the midst of her battle with cancer, remain an inspiration.

To Angela, Eli and Katie, Lily, Ella, Abigail, and Elijah, who give smiles, hugs, and laughter to remind me what matters most. To Daryll Patton, for modeling perseverance as part of our family. My parents, Ferne and Lawrence Driskill, who I cherish as models of love and faith through the bitter-sweet of life. And to my new co-author, friend, and colleague, Dr. Julien Mirivel.

To Meg, Hugo, John Luke, and Claire, who give me the most joy and meaning. To my friend, colleague, and co-author, Gerald, for inviting me to join in the writing and for always having a kind word and a positive approach to life and people. And to all the faculty in the Department of Applied Communication at UA Little Rock for the way we live our mission.

Contents

About the Authors

Dr. Gerald W. C. Driskill

Dr. Driskill is a professor in the Department of Applied Communication at the University of Arkansas at Little Rock. He teaches undergraduate and graduate courses in organizational communication, theory, and intercultural communication and leads workshops on leadership and communication. His community-engaged research focuses on cultures of collaboration bridging ethnic and organizational boundaries. He serves with the Little Rock Congregations Study, is the author of *Organizational Culture in Action* (4th Ed), and continues to write both fiction and non-fiction stories as well.

Julien C. Mirivel

Dr. Mirivel is a professor in the Department of Applied Communication at the University of Arkansas at Little Rock. He is the author of four additional books on positive communication: *The Art of Positive Communication: Theory and Practice*, *How Communication Scholars Think and Act: A Lifespan Perspective*, *Communication and Community* (with Kristen Christman) and *Positive Communication for Leaders: Proven Strategies for Inspiring Unity and Effecting Change* (with Alex Lyon). Dr. Mirivel has delivered hundreds of keynotes, training, and workshops on how to communicate effectively. He is a TEDx speaker whose mission is to inspire individuals and groups to communicate more positively at work and at home, as well as the Founder of the Positive Communication Network. His work has been featured in FastCompany, CEOWorld Magazine, HR Morning, and more. For more information and resources, please visit julienmirivel.com.

Preface to the Fourth Edition

As I welcome Dr. Julien Mirivel as a second author, together we want to continue to pay our debt. In 1984, Angi Brenton, Ph.D., introduced a course on organizational culture to the graduate students in the Masters of Interpersonal and Organizational Communication at the University of Arkansas at Little Rock. Her students came from a wide array of organizations (high tech to medical to industry) and positions in those organizations (management to HRD to entry-level employees). This same array of students continued to participate in this course when Gerald Driskill, Ph.D., began to teach the course in 1994. Over time, our approach to working with these students resulted in this application-focused workbook.

Fast forward to 2018, when I was faced with the impossible task of revision without Angi. Dr. Brenton, a colleague and friend, died at the age of 60 on May 8, 2013, after a courageous but brief battle with cancer. In one of her last posts, she let her friends know that their prayers had been answered as she went on to write about the good she saw going on both in and around her. Those words remain with me in this revision process. Her passion for ideas, for life, for serving, and difference-making is what continues to motivate me and other colleagues to engage in co-creating better social worlds.

This passion finds its way into this book. In this 4th edition, along with my new co-author, Dr. Julien Mirivel, we maintain our shared voice through the use of "we" and included some of her original examples to represent the way Angi's ideas, passion, and presence continue to be part of this book. Former students and colleagues established the Angie Laird Brenton Memorial Scholarship in her honor.

Students continue to comment on the practical and powerful nature of the approach outlined in this workbook. In this fourth edition, we maintained the original hands-on approach to learning to "read" organizational cultures and using that cultural knowledge to develop formal and informal leadership curiosity and commitment to growth. The insights for managing change, supporting diversity, improving ethics, and unleashing creativity are developed through a clear focus on best practices. This workbook, with additional guides from faculty currently using this book, also serves as an introduction to qualitative research methods, introducing students to field observation, interviewing, qualitative surveys, content analysis, and other methods of textual analysis.

What has changed? Students, professionals, and colleagues challenge us to take several major steps.

- A development of and foregrounding of positive communication practices in each application chapter.
- An introduction to the Positive Communication Network founded by Dr. Julien Mirivel.
- Integration of "mental shifts" in the opening chapter and throughout the book.

- Online connections, including links to
  - Interviews conducted by Dr. Alex Lyon, The Communication Coach.
  - Opportunity to connect with the Positive Communication Network.
  - Options to connect via LinkedIn.
  - Additional "Rehearsals," including surveys and interpretation guides.
- A redefining of the OCA model focused on co-creating better social worlds grounded in our connectedness.
- Attention to AI (and Generative AI) from student input and recent research on AI and ethics.
- Chapter one uses the first FAQ to review the OCA model with an image. This change was in response to a working professional student who said, "I didn't really get it until seeing the image at the end of the book."
- Rewording of the six steps to clarify the intent of each step.
- Recent research on diversity, ethics, effectiveness, change, leadership that amplifies the thread of ethics.
- Development of the theatre metaphor to capture this approach to seeing ourselves as "enacting culture" each day.
- Diversity Chapter updates on theory and research, including a new online survey to gauge progress with attentiveness to recent shifts away from DEI efforts in some organizations and in the current political climate.
- New "Rehearsal" Activities that prompt reflection at the opening of chapters as well as others now online.
- Additional online tools to guide students in data analysis.

We continue to be convinced that the application of this text can help leaders shorten their learning curves and avoid costly mistakes while understanding the power of strategic symbolic managerial performances in co-creating highly ethical and effective organizations. It could help the new MBA choose a company consistent with her values. It will reinforce to the training and development director the importance of storytelling in organizational socialization. It will equip those seeking organizational change to understand ways in which change is actually constituted in communicative practices.

We all participate in multiple organizations, and that participation demands the art and skill of determining the communicative practices that shape more ethical and effective organizations and organizing practices. May you find yourself reading, interacting with others, and completing various activities designed to equip you to lead with confidence and purpose and to see yourself as co-creating not only better organizations but communities and social worlds.

Acknowledgments

Those who made this workbook a reality easily come to mind. For any names we omitted, we accept the blame and ask your forgiveness.

- To a mentor, colleague, and friend during my KU days and beyond, Dr. Cal Downs.
- To my new co-author, Dr. Julien Mirivel, for joining me on this 4th Ed. with his passion for excellence and his leadership with the founding of the Positive Communication Network.
- To you, the colleague, student, and/or practitioner, for what you will contribute to the organizations you serve and to the dialogue over improving life in organizations.
- To several colleagues, Dr. Eleana Gabor who provided online and text resources, including feedback on application chapters and the need to attend to "just cultures" in contrast to toxic cultures. Plus, Dr. Lynne Willett, whose dissertation on introducing change provided needed insights along with edits on this chapter. She also provided online resources and gained permission to include a student's voice on AI in the chapter on Leadership. In addition, for continued formative feedback from Dr. Evangelina Holvino for taking a call and sharing updates on our diversity model and to Dr. Bernado Ferdman for his continued contributions to DEI research and theory.
- A special thanks continues from the 3rd edition to Drs. Linda Putnam and Dr. Ryan Bisel, whose detailed feedback on the theory framework and treatments on the change and ethics chapters were meaningful and significant. Plus, an added appreciation to Dr. Bisel for connecting me with his former students and their work on totalistic organizations.
- Early reviewers of various drafts who developed this project: John Gribas, John Myer, Jon Camp, and Phil Clampitt.
- Gratitude for Melissa Johnston, an alumni of our MA program who gave her time to learn more about First Orion's culture.
- Applause to 35 years of graduate program alumni who provided rich feedback. Extra thanks to those who shaped the first editions of the book: Melissa Johnston, Debbie West, Robert Mock, Michelle Young, Pat Sweeden, Patricia Hawkins-Sweeden, Jane Martin, Sherrie Sandor, Cheryl Johnston, Elaine Wooten, Martha Lowry, Tracy Pleasants, Wanda Culbreath, Hope Coleman, Brenda Winston, Lisa Rawn, and Michael Strobel; and to recent students who patiently worked with me Gerald on new ideas in the third edition-Rosa Boast, Amare-Brianna Beuch, Chris Elsworth, Rania Elbahey, Frankye Jimenez, Michael (Jacob) Nesbit, Michelle Scroggins, Bonnie Ward, and Karen Willson. Then to students in recent classes who shared amazing ideas to make this workbook more accessible: Kalidash Adhikari, Cathy Beynon, Odette Cooh, Robin Freeman, Savannah Gann, Sara Windsor, Savanah Brinkley, Geneva Galloway, Kelley Gulley, Cari Karugireyo, Stephanie Lee, Erin Maxwell, Robert O'Connor, Jennifer Smith, Lauren Sutherland, and Marquita Williams.

- Current and former faculty in the Applied Communication Department who motivate excellence in the scholarship of integrating teaching, research, and service: Mike Hemphill, Linda Pledger, Carol Thompson, Rob Ulmer, Alex Lyon, Kristin McIntyre, Julien Mirivel, Avinash Thombre, Ryan Fuller, April Chatham-Carpenter, Bailey Oliver-Blackburn, Katie Halford, and emeritus faculty: Alan Ward, Jerry Butler, John Gray, and Ralph Eubanks.
- Writers and colleagues who have shaped and enriched our thinking with their contributions to the study of organizational communication: Chuck Bantz, Kevin Barge, Ryan Bisel, Lee Bolman, George Cheney, Charles Conrad, Francois Cooren, Terry Deal, Stan Deetz, Eric Eisenberg, Buddy Goodall, Evangelina Holvino, Allan Kennedy, Joanne Keyton, Joann Martin, Bob McPhee, Robert D. McPhee, Gareth Morgan, Nick O'Donnell-Trujillo, Barbara O'Keefe, Gerald Pepper, Mike Pacanowsky, Barnett and Kim Pearce, Linda Putnam, M. Scott Poole, Patti Riley, Linda Smircich, Karl Weick, and Pamela Zaug.

Part I

Cultural Analysis Planning

Chapter 1

Introduction

Setting the Stage

Organizations are more than the places we work. They include places that carry us from the cradle to the grave. The "Organizational Culture in Action" (OCA) model is introduced as a valuable tool grounded in constitutive theories of communication with three goals: 1) provide tools and techniques to make mental shifts in the way we think and enact organizational culture and communication; 2) illustrate ways you can co-create positive, meaningful, purposeful, and ethical performances; and 3) guide you in leading an effective cultural analysis either as a leader within your organization or as a consultant and/or informally as a member. Responses to frequently asked questions introduce "mental shifts" designed to improve our conduct of cultural analysis. Closing rehearsals guide you in selecting an organization and understanding the value of the theatre/acting metaphor.

Objectives

- Reflect on the pervasiveness of organizations in our lives.
- State the goal of cultural analysis.
- Apply guides for selecting an organization for analysis.

Stage Terms

Organizations	Organizational culture	Dramatism
Organizational communication	Cultural analysis	Organizational performance

> I was backstage, not as an actor, but as an observer. I looked up in awe at the myriad of lights and ropes. I glanced around at the props and backdrops. Each seemed to be holding their breath in anticipation of their role in the performance. All was silent. The deep purple folds of the still-drawn curtains prompted an unbidden thought. Panics seized control of my imagination: What if the curtains were opened and I was really on stage? What if I was no longer an observer but a full participant? What role would I play? Could I play? Should I play?

Cradle to Grave

- You run into a hospital anxious about the life of a loved one, nearing the end. Your mind flashes back to entering the same hospital to welcome your first child into the world.
- You re-arrange your desk for the first time in your new job, excited and anxious about how you will adjust and if you can do the work expected of you.

DOI: 10.4324/9781003482529-2

- A member of your team says, "I know you can do better leading." You know they are right, but you are not sure where to begin.
- You want to speak up about a bad decision being made by upper management, but you fear more harm than good coming from saying something. Is silence an option?
- Your HR team asks you to lead a cultural analysis project focused on diversity and change. You are not sure you trust AI, nor are you sure you can trust the motives of your leaders.
- The funeral home director welcomes you. For a brief moment, you realize life is bookended by organizations.

What statements would you add to these varied challenges? The preceding list is far from exhaustive. Our lives are lived out in a web of diverse organizations. We have all played, laughed, cried, worked and/or consulted with, and dreamed and been bored in hospitals, daycares, schools, businesses, non-profits, prisons, houses of worship, universities, and nursing homes. Consider further the following from a 2020 survey:

- We spend one-third of our lives, or about 90,000 hours, at work.
- Nine in ten employees say workplace stress affects their mental health.
- Four in five employees feel emotionally drained from their work (an early sign of burnout).
- Three in five employees are not receiving adequate support from supervisors to help manage stress (Adams, Reinert, Fritze, & Nguyen, 2021).

At the same time, people develop meaningful friendships and experience joy, connection, and meaning at work. These varied experiences have inspired us and, at times, left us broken by dysfunctional and unethical practices. As managers, students, employees, customers, volunteers, consultants, members, and patients, we all have tragic and comic stories to tell. Use Rehearsal 1.1 to reflect on a positive as well as a negative memory in an organization.

Rehearsal 1.1

Directions: Briefly describe a positive and a negative organizational memory.

The point is clear—we cannot escape our inextricable connection with organizations—the varied stages on which we live out our lives. Like you, we know something of the moment of panic when called on to perform: lead a meeting, address a conflict, confront or admit to an ethical failure, make a presentation, or have a difficult conversation. In such moments, we may not be aware of the way the lights, the props, and our assumptions about our audience shape and constrain our performances. In fact, the opening lines about being backstage as a panicked observer capture a real moment. Gerald was backstage at a theater with a colleague. Along with a colleague, he was about to facilitate a communication training that happened to be taking place on stage. As we walked onto the stage, a larger reality struck home—organizational performances are part of our everyday lives. We may know when to show up; however, we may or may not be aware of unspoken relationship scripts and the impact of the props—place, history, and rituals. In fact, we rarely see the big picture of how all the various aspects of the stage impact us. In this fourth edition, we continue to value and be honored by feedback from students, working professionals, and colleagues, as well as recent research. This feedback has resulted in three practical objectives. Each objective is connected to concepts, learning activities, and cultural analysis tools:

1. Make mental shifts in the way we think and enact organizational culture.
2. Conduct a formal or informal cultural analysis as an organizational leader, consultant, and/or participant.
3. Co-create positive (ethical, effective, learning) organizations.

> *Organizations are places that carry us from cradle to grave by shaping our sense of ethics, identity, role, and meaning in life.*

Organizations are no more and no less than a significant stage for human drama. Our research on cultures in hospitals, engineering firms, non-profits, banks, airlines, phone companies, schools, and day care centers and our service and training experiences in hospitals, prisons, state agencies, multinationals, and nursing homes have all underscored our conviction that organizations are far more than the places where we work and make money. Organizations carry us from "the cradle to the grave" by shaping our sense of ethics, identity, role, and meaning in life.

In this chapter, we respond to FAQ by first introducing the OCA model (Organizational Culture in Action). This model flows from our passion for developing *a cultural analysis process that fosters the co-creation of highly ethical and effective organizations.* We believe such an effort to be fundamental to us all as participants in the human drama. In order to create better lives for all, we accept that organizations can range from highly positive and ethical to highly toxic and unethical. Thus, we do not relegate ethics to an individual chapter or sidebar, as Dr. Meisenbach (2017), an organizational scholar, laments, is so often the case. Instead, ethics are woven into each phase of the analysis process. Because of this focus, a cultural analysis holds promise for surfacing practices that may clarify or distort, accurately represent or misrepresent, and fully involve or marginalize the interests of various stakeholders.

After introducing the OCA model, we respond to other questions on core concepts ranging from the goals of an analysis to how we define organizations. Each question includes the challenge to make a "mental shift" in how we think about and engage in this process. We end this opening chapter by reviewing the criteria for selecting an organization. We provide online Rehearsals for making mental shifts and applying the theatre/drama metaphor.

FAQs on Cultural Analysis

Over the years, students and practitioners have made us aware of the need to shift the way they think about and engage in the process of exploring organizational culture. We refer to these as "mental shifts." As you reflect on these "mental shifts," you should gain a clearer sense of our approach.

1. What Is the OCA Model?

Let's begin with you. Afterall, this book was created and continues to be revised due to requests from working professionals, students, and leaders with a curiosity about organizational culture. Perhaps you want to conduct a formal cultural analysis. You are asking, *how*? Perhaps you seek insights to navigate and improve a culture. Again, you are asking, *how*? The OCA model seeks to answer the question of "how"? The OCA model serves to ***foster the co-creation of positive organizations by developing implications through the analysis of enacted elements that both shape and are shaped by communication***.

What, then, does this co-creation of positive organizations look like? A former student asked us to begin the book with an image that captured this process. Indeed, we now end this first FAQ with that image. The rest of this book unpacks this definition and guides you in applying this six-step model. First, however, key phrases in the definition merit an initial explanation:

a. "Positive organizations"—Perhaps, like us, when you hear the word "positive," you might think in terms of somehow avoiding thinking what is "bad"—that is, wearing rose-colored glasses. A line from a song might come to mind, "Don't worry, be happy (or positive, it "will all be ok"). We invite you to join a network of scholars and practitioners (www.positivecommunication.net/) who are thinking differently about "positive." The focus on positive communication includes:

   - A shift from a problem orientation that focuses on what is going wrong to one that identifies practices that are and/or can co-create healthy, supportive, learning, highly ethical organizations.
   - Commitments to excellence, bringing out people's best, and a long-term investment in others (Mirivel & Lyon, 2023).

> *Mental shift 1: From a problem orientation that focuses on what is going wrong to one that identifies practices that are and/or can co-create healthy, supportive, learning, highly ethical organizations.*

b. "Constituted in enacted elements"—We explore "constituted" in greater detail in Chapter 3 as part of the second phase of the model and "enacted elements" in Chapter 4 in the third phase of the model. In brief, unlike approaches to culture that think of variables or ways to reveal a culture, OCA follows an established organizational framework, the Communicative Constitution of Organization (CCO; McPhee & Zaug, 2009). This framework holds a pragmatic value due to its focus on everyday organizational processes. By processes, consider the value of reflecting on stories and rituals in your organization. Such reflections using the model prompt questions like, *What are we creating in these stories or rituals? Should they be adjusted or replaced to ensure we are co-creating a more ethical and effective organization?* For example, this process might cause you to be aware of a formal ritual (e.g., a weekly department meeting) or an informal one (a hallway chat). The idea then of "constituted" is that these "enacted elements" shape or create the culture and that the culture then shapes these elements. For example, you might hear a story during the informal hallway chat that the new supervisor has no tolerance for disagreements in weekly meetings. You find yourself in a meeting being quiet about a discrepancy in a financial report. You then share that moment with a colleague who, like you, is challenged about how to respond to possible future moments. The point? The OCA model has value in that it explores what is being created in taken-for-granted interactions and discerns then-practical implications for growth and development.

c. "Social worlds"—Organizations are complex systems with intertwined relational networks; thus, our analysis process is also about multiple interrelated levels: a) micro or the individual level; b) meso or the group level; c) macro or the organizational level; d) community or the surrounding society; and e) cultural or the larger national level. For example, you might notice how a meeting begins with a question about a "high and low" experienced by team members. This meso- or group-level ritual has the power to shape a network of care and compassion that is about more than productivity and likely has an influence on other levels. Our shared concern and passion for exploring organizational culture is grounded in the awareness that not only do we spend significant time in organizations, but that our organizations are embedded in networks that shape and are shaped by one another (i.e., friends, families, other organizations, our communities, nations). Furthermore, our organizations are more than just places we work. They also represent the places where we carry out our aspirations, ideals, and hopes for bettering life.

d. "Co-created"—Consistent with CCO theorizing, co-creation is not just about individuals but what we do or fail to do together. This focus of co-creation is what we do or do not do in our interactions with others. It thus also involves the presence or absence of ethical discourse. More specifically, we encourage reflection on our varied social worlds concerning practices or aspects of day-to-day individual, group, and organizational level interactions, often taken for granted, such as greetings, questions, disclosure, and affirmation (c.f., Mirivel, 2014; Mirivel & Lyon, 2023). The significance of these interactions is also substantiated by research ranging from identifying communication practices that encourage ethical dialogue (Anderson, Baxter, & Cissna, 2009) and engaging in participatory decision-making (Deetz & Brown, 2004) to democratizing practices (Gergen, Gergen, & Barrett, 2004) and applying a model of organizational moral learning to co-create highly ethical organizations (Bisel, 2018).

To that end, the OCA model relies on three questions focused on co-creating better social worlds. These questions, informed by the Coordinated Management of Meaning (CMM) theory (Pearce, 2007), guide our process:

1. *What kind of culture is being co-created?* Here, the goal is to enhance our ability to collect and interpret data ethically. The third phase of the model explores the data collection and interpretation process.
2. *What kind of culture should we co-create?* The goal is to determine and co-create positive communication goals based on the data you have collected. In prior editions, we used the phrase "want to co-create." We changed the language to fit what we trust is an obvious rationale. What we want to co-create may or may not include careful ethical reflection and co-creation. The sixth and final phase of the model focuses on different application contexts, such as ethics, diversity, leadership, and change.
3. *What forms of communication will co-create the culture we seek to create?*

In conjunction with the final phase of the model, we provide final chapters on co-creating organizational and professional development plans grounded in positive communication practices. We stress that the culture creation and change process does not happen in isolation.

If you want to gain a clear picture of the cultural analysis process, we turn to an analogy Dr. Angela Brenton introduced in the early editions of this book. Perhaps, as you engage in this process you can identify a different, more meaningful analogy that will help you grasp the overall process.

Angi's Analogy: A Jigsaw Puzzle. The point of this analogy is to understand the tensions between seeing parts versus the whole and to appreciate the impact the process has on the person doing the analysis. First, it is often difficult to get a sense of the big picture when you are looking at individual pieces. Only after you have assembled a number of segments can you start to get an idea of the picture the puzzle will create. Second, it takes both dark and bright pieces in most cases to assemble a complete puzzle. I recently read a story of a young girl who secretly stole pieces of a puzzle her family was assembling and hid them under the sofa cushion because they were so ugly. In frustration, her family began to despair of ever being able to put the puzzle together because so many pieces were missing. Only when the girl provided the dark pieces could the entire picture be revealed. Sometimes, in our cultural analysis, it is tempting to linger on the positive stories and upbeat images. They rarely form the complete picture. Sometimes, you must provide the dark elements to understand the complete culture (c.f., Mumby, 1993; Deetz, 1992). Third, the process of putting together the puzzle is often as important as the finished product. The mental exercise of seeing connections, developing creativity, and growing in patience and discipline will develop the puzzle builder, even if the particular puzzle is not a particularly useful one. Finally, though, unlike puzzles, which have a set order and only one way for all of the parts to fit together, cultural analysis is a complex and interpretive pursuit. Four different people sitting around a table would see the picture from different perspectives and develop similar but varying pictures, and each of those constructions would have degrees of validity and usefulness for understanding the organization.

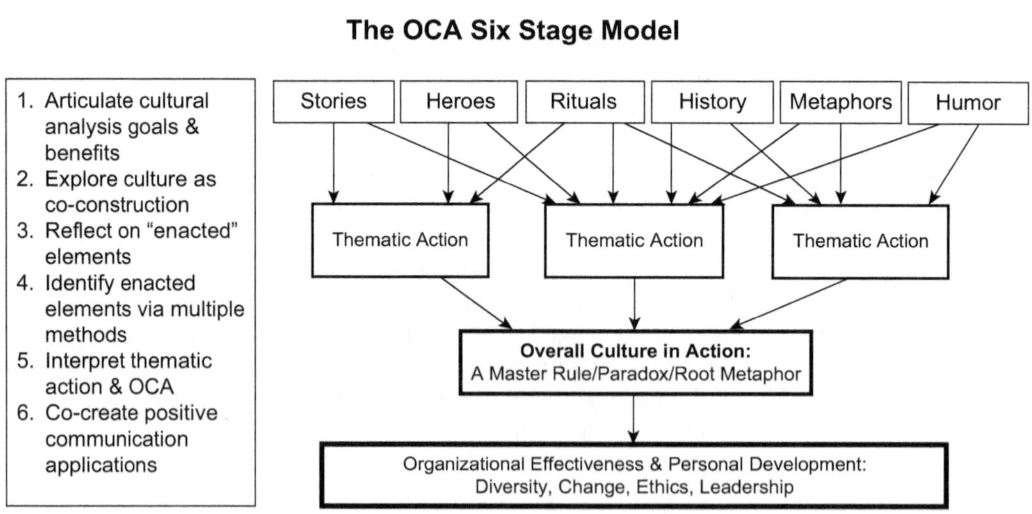

Figure 1.1 The OCA Six Stage Model

2. What Are the Goals and Benefits of the Cultural Analysis Process?

The first step of the model (Chapter 2) responds to this question in greater detail. Overall, consider this statement as a way to capture the overarching goal and benefits: *a cultural analysis provides insight for improving positive communication practices that result in meaningful personal, professional, and organizational culture development and growth.* To take it a step further, consider the following comments about benefits from students and practitioners.

At the Organizational Level, the Impact is Evident

- I now see the connections between culture and employee engagement.
- My analysis aiding in the creation of a communication plan related to diversity.
- This process aided us in improving recruitment and retention practices.
- Insights were gained for leading change and overall effectiveness that impacts stakeholders beyond the organization.
- The cultural data helped me reflect on organizational ethics and leadership.

At a Personal and Professional Level, Example Comments Include

- I have learned that in any organization, change must start with me.
- I got my last job because the interviewer was intrigued by my answers about organizational culture and how quickly I could "read" the organization.
- I have improved my ability to apply theory to the real world—including places I volunteer.
- I saved myself a lot of time and energy by deciding during an interview process that I didn't fit the culture. Even though the salary was great, I would have become frustrated quickly.

We are confident that one or more of these benefits and/or others will apply to your own growth and development and to the organization. The OCA model, whether used formally or informally, is designed to aid us all in being more competent organizational actors. Furthermore, this process is not about finding problems. Rather, the overarching goal in describing the culture is to discern positive communication applications. As such, you will be engaged in an analysis that resonates with recent work flowing from the "Positive Communication Network" (Mirivel & Fuller, 2024). This network has its mission—to promote "foster a community dedicated to creating better social worlds for all through positive communication research, education, and practice." These applications are grounded in our interdisciplinary approach, discussed further in Chapters 2 and 3, which promises insight into organizational diversity, crisis communication, leadership, ethics, conflict management, leadership, change, and overall effectiveness. Complete Rehearsal 1.2 as an initial reflection on your own personal and professional goals. Chapter 2 provides a rehearsal focused on the goals and benefits of the organization you study.

> *Mental shift 2: From the value of engaging in cultural analysis as only organizational and professional to also personal and community.*

Rehearsal 1.2 Your Professional Cultural Analysis Goals and Benefits

Purpose: Reflect on and identify possible goals and benefits of a cultural analysis tied to your personal/professional goals. Be sure to return to this rehearsal after completing Chapter 2 in light of the benefits focused on the organization you will analyze.

Check any of the following goals and benefits that describe your primary reasons for conducting an organizational cultural analysis:

______ Learn cultural analysis skills for work as a consultant
______ Gain insight into another type of organization for career development
______ Gain insight to aid an organization in areas such as ethics, change, diversity
______ Develop insight as a new employee to move up in your organization
______ Learn to use cultural data to be a more effective leader in your own organization
______ Identify ways to improve the way you serve in a community organization
______ Learn about an organizational culture different (or similar) to your own to aid in developing your professional network
______ Other reason: ______________________________

3. What Is an Organization?

We all know what organizations are, right? Pause now. Write your own definition of organization. Ok, now continue reading. We invited you to write your own first because definitions matter. Textbooks tend to introduce definitions and then move on, leaving them buried in the opening chapter. We contend that how we think about organizations, communication, and culture are grounded in unconscious lived experiences or dominant logics (White, 2021). For all of us to get at the importance of how we think about organizations, see what the following definitions share in common with and/or how they differ with each other and your own.

- "[A]n organization consists of the organizing activities of its members" (Pepper, 1995, p. 17).
- Organizations involve "five critical features—the existence of a social collectivity, organizational and individual goals, coordinating activity, organizational structure, and the embedding of the organization with an environment of other organizations" (Miller & Barbour, 2015, p. 11).
- A "dynamic system of organizational members, influenced by external stakeholders, who communicate within and across organizational structures in a purposeful and ordered way to achieve a superordinate goal" (Keyton, 2005, p. 10).
- "[A] social interaction system, influenced by prevailing economic and legal institutional practices, and including coordinated action and interaction within and across a socially constructed system boundary, manifestly directed toward a privileged set of outcomes" (McPhee & Zaug, 2009, p. 28)

Two questions for you to consider. First, *did you notice what is shared in common across definitions?* Phrases or words like "goals" or "outcomes are included," along with a focus on "coordinating." In addition, the way organizations are embedded in or influenced by other organizations or stakeholders. Second, *did you notice the added phrase in the final definition?* Perhaps you have not fully considered the notion of a "privileged" set of outcomes. Beyond outcomes tied to profits or products, organizations engage in processes that impact people and our planet, as well as processes that give or fail to give participants and their communities a voice on matters that impact their lives. As we stress throughout the book, then, ethics are part of all of our lived experiences. What, then, is the definition we will carry throughout or work together in cultural analysis?

> *Mental shift 3: From organizations as buildings and businesses to a complex communication system that constitutes social reality in ethical and unethical ways.*

Over the past three decades, we have continued to reflect with students and colleagues on an evolving definition that draws our attention to what we need to see, think about, and ultimately study in the cultural analysis process. In this edition, we have done more to stress outcomes. We define organizations as

- A complex communication system of interactional social processes that both reflect and constitute social reality in ethical and unethical ways.

Like the other definitions, we invite you to push back against the natural tendency to hold an image of people in a building working toward some shared set of goals. The image of a building or container misses key ideas that we will explore throughout the analysis process.

Our definition, influenced by reflecting on the previous definition along with McPhee and Zaug (2009) (c.f., McPhee, 2015) and the Coordinated Management of Meaning (CMM) theory (Pearce, 2007), draws attention to: a) *complex communication systems*-we are all engaged in intertwined networks. The borders between our home lives, the places we volunteer or worship, gather with friends, and work are interwoven with legal, political, and national and local cultures; and b) *reflects and constitutes social reality*-our lives or woven together like a web-we are constrained by this web but we also participate in creating the web; c) *ethical and unethical*—our unavoidable interdependence involves our sense of what should or should not be happen.

4. What Is Organizational Communication?

In the same way as what has already been stated, take time now to pause and jot down your definition of organizational communication before reviewing the following ones. Did you pause? Great! Now consider these varied definitions introduced across several decades—what is present and/or absent in each of them? How do they mirror your own? Add to your own?

- "The social act of humans who collaborate, through the use of symbols, to manage and/or control the internal and external environments" (Cummings, Long, & Lewis, 1988. p. 14).
- The "collective and interactive process of generating and interpreting messages" (Stohl, 1995, p. 4).
- "[T]he process of creating, exchanging, interpreting (correctly or incorrectly), and storing messages within a system of human interrelationships" (Modaff & Butler, 2022, p. 5).

- "[T]he interaction required to direct a group toward a shared goal" (LeGreco, Eisenberg, Tretheway, & Goodall, 2024, p. 4).

The preceding definitions represent colleagues who have and continue to shape our thinking. With them, we again stress that how we think about organizational communication matters. We trust, like the definition of communication, that you see a focus on connectivity ("collaborate," "collective," and "interrelationships.") What about our definition? First, let us set the stage for why we are inviting you to consider a mental shift. Over the years, we have asked professionals in formal classrooms and in training settings to define communication and/or organizational communication. The dominant theme across definitions is on information sending/receiving or exchange or sometimes expressing emotion. Yet, the image we tend to see is that of a building, a grouping of people working together toward a goal (or not). In fact, notice how the second definition focuses on "generating and interpreting" messages. Yet, in reading further about her use of the term "collective," Stohl's definition is developed in a way to set the stage for our own.

> Our personal lives and our view of the world are intricately interwoven with our work relations . . . networks of understanding are created through coordinated activities and relationships that permeate organizational boundaries.
>
> (p. 4)

Her ideas, combined with others, inspired our definition and a mental shift.

Mental shift 4: From organizational communication as information exchange to co-creation of relational networks that create and constrain ethical and effective processes and goals.

The goal here is not about memorizing a definition but rather to challenge our thinking about organizational communication, how it works, and how our interactions are mutually connected (Barbour, Jacocks, & Wesner, 2013; Edwards & Shepherd, 2007; O'Keefe, 1988). For instance, the focus on message exchange directs our attention to message quality or clarity, which is important, but insufficient. For example, a message about a change in how performance reviews will happen might outline the reasons and nature of the change. However, what might be missed might be who decided the change had to happen and the fact that who conducts the reviews will also change. What this creates is lowered trust despite efforts at clarity. Thus, we invite you to reflect on a definition foregrounding four foundational ideas central to the OCA model and to improving life in organizations. As you review our definition, reflect on what it has in common and then what it adds to the other definitions.

- *The co-creation of intertwined relational networks through symbolic actions that create and constrain ethical and effective processes, goals, and outcomes.*

What did you notice in this definition that might aid in understanding organizational culture? Reflect with us on four distinctive elements.

- **Communication creates.** As stressed earlier, communication is more than sharing information to reach a goal, more than strategy, and more than generating and interpreting messages. Communication is constitutive—it creates and recreates our identities, relationships, organizations, and cultures. Viewed from this perspective, an organization is a dynamic system that is evolving and changing on the basis of complex interactive processes within and between people. In turn, these organizations (and identities, relationships, and cultures) shape communication. For example, something as simple as greeting rituals impacts the extent to which values such as trust are built (Mirivel, 2014).

- **Inescapable ethics**. This focus entails more than individual decision-making about what is right and wrong. From a CCO perspective, "ethics are constituted in communication" (McClellan & Sanders, 2013, p. 259). As such, our individual choices, both intentional and unintentional, make and shape organizations and, in turn, are shaped by organizing practices. For instance, Kuhn and Ashcraft (2003) highlight the constitutive, or meaning-making, role of organizational practices that create justifications for unethical behaviors. They highlight the ironic practices at Enron, where stated values of "respect, integrity, and communication" were marginalized due to a "rank and yank" system of employee evaluation in which profits were primary (Kuhn & Ashcraft, 2003, p. 44). On a subtler level, any of us might unconsciously pick up on phrases such as "well, that is how we do things around here" and find ourselves using these same words when engaged in false reporting behaviors. Thus, our role throughout the cultural analysis process should involve discerning ways to co-create positive and ethical practices and structures.
- **Boundaries are not clear-cut**. Communication defines and constitutes both the "what" and "where" of these boundaries. For instance, we are part of multiple organizations (civic, social, religious, corporations, etc.). These organizations and ways of working interact and function in complex ways: multinational hybrids, virtual organizations, global outsourcing, gig employees, and inter-organizational collaborations created by non-profits. For example, in an exploration of the connected nature of societal and organizational discourse, Meisenbach and Feldner (2019) identified hero narratives in the reality television series "Undercover Boss." They found that a surface reading of the two ideal bosses echoed corporate propaganda by the way they provided "an admirable response to economic problems." However, a critical reading captured how narratives "hide larger inequities" (p. 417).
- **Membership, like boundaries, is fuzzy.** For example, who counts as a member of a professional sports team? Only the athletes, cheerleaders, and coaches? Team physicians, who may be members of a medical practice but travel with the team on weekends? What about the die-hard fans who come to every game and may have a 50-year history of following a team? These same questions could be asked of a multinational in terms of their interactions with other organizations and their respective communities. So, while leaders should always consider "stakeholders," not just "stockholders," the fuzziness of membership goes further. Our interconnectedness stresses that our organizational interactions impact far more than easily defined members or employees.

In summary, viewing organizational communication as relational networks co-created and recreated in and through communication reminds us of the challenges faced as we seek to analyze organizational culture. Organizations are multi-layered and multi-faceted, consisting of individuals and groups connected across space and time with shared and competing interests.

5. What Is Organizational Culture?

Like the question on goals and benefits, we view this question as central to the OCA model, and thus, it is covered in the second stage of the model, "Reframe the Concept of Culture."

Nonetheless, we see value in providing an initial response. First, though, consider Googling this question. Let AI answer the question. Of course, you may select to write your own answer or simply give up due to the myriad of conflicting definitions across business leaders, academia, and consultants. Ok, do one or the other. What did you find? Perhaps, like us, you may ask: Is it even possible or needed to find the right or best definition? Who cares; culture just is, right? Pause, drum beat. We are about to say what "AI" never revealed.

Culture does not exist. Let that statement sink in. Culture does not exist. *How is it possible that such a statement is made, given the title of the book?* Given AI? All the books?

How would we respond to the Harvard Business Review articles? "[T]here is universal agreement that [culture] exists" (Watkins, 2013). I mean, do we have a problem with Harvard? You may have guessed the reason we say, "culture does not exist." When we say, "culture does not exist," we are simply reminding all of us that culture is a construct. As a construct, it is a way of making sense of our world, our groups, our clans, and our organizations. In fact, there was a time when that word was not used to talk about organizations. Hear that again. At one point, the word "culture" was <u>not part of how we talked</u> about organizations. *From whence did this construct arise for use in organizations?*

The construct was co-opted from cultural anthropologists who first introduced culture as an application to organizations in about 1951. It would take about 30 years for it to catch on in the business and consulting world. The rest, as we say, is history. You may ask then, *Why should we care that it is a construct—a sense-making tool?*

Fair question. The short two-part answer is that, first, there is <u>no consensus</u> on how to define organizational culture. One meta-analysis of 40 years of research concluded that not only is there no consensus on defining culture, but also there are, at best, inconsistent and inconclusive results from low- to moderate-quality research linking culture to productivity. In one case, the researchers simply renamed what they had called "organizational effectiveness" as culture, and in another, three questions of leaders were used to measure culture (Barends & Rousseau, 2022). The main limitation of such a study is what is called construct validity; that is, are we truly measuring what we claim to measure? And second, culture, defining and measuring culture is complex. Messy. In Chapter 3, we capture three main approaches to defining culture with a focus on the final one that informs the OCA model:

- Culture as a ***variable***—an aspect or aspects of culture, such as values, is studied and then linked to a change that is claimed to influence an outcome like productivity.
- Culture as a ***root metaphor***—culture *is* the organization. Varied elements of the culture, such as rituals or history, may be studied to *reveal* the culture and give clues on how to interpret it and perhaps improve it.
- Culture as ***co-construction***—culture shapes and is shaped by communication. Like a spider in a web, culture is seen as the webs of significance that we have spun for ourselves (Geertz, 1973), and those webs shape future interactions. This way of thinking about culture is the one informing the OCA model.

Mental shift 5: From organizational culture as a variable or a metaphor to culture as constituted in everyday communication practices that shape and are also shaped by culture.

Thus, we define ***organizational culture as everyday interconnected communication practices that shape and reflect the ways things get done across the organization.*** We invite you to make this mental shift because if we focus on a select variable, such as values or engagement levels, we miss other aspects of the culture. If we explore culture as a root metaphor, we miss the co-construction process. This focus on co-construction captures what is being created or "enacted" between us (White, 2017, p. 47) that gets at "how things get done around here" (Collins, 2001, p. 76; c.f., Gallop, n.d.). This mental shift holds out the possibility that together, we can become a true ensemble cast by coordinating our actions more effectively and ethically with others.

6. What Is the Value of Using a Dramatic/Theater Metaphor?

Short answer—it works. It keeps me aware that life is always on stage, always about what we are creating together in our varied roles. Just what are we creating? A comedy? Tragedy? A fairy tale? A different question may help you see the value of this metaphor. Have you heard this famous line before? "All the world's a stage, and all the men and women merely players. They have their exits and their entrances; And one man in his time plays many parts." Our guess is that many of you recall Shakespeare or perhaps the fear of memorization. Few of us recall that it is from the play *As you like it*. And perhaps, like us, you may not recall that it is the opening of a speech about the seven stages of life and ends with these lines about the final stage—"That ends this strange eventful history, Is second childishness and mere oblivion; Sans teeth, sans eyes, sans taste, sans everything" (Shakespeare, 1564–1616, As You Like It, Brushell (Ed.), 1954, p. 42).

Our response, then, about the value and purpose of the theatre metaphor is best captured by the famous playwright. This speech captures and claims, as we do, that we need to see our shared human drama. We need to be sure not to miss how our entrances and exits, and the stages between, are inextricably linked to organizations. Our hellos and goodbyes and all that happens in between matter, for they are what make life, life.

Nonetheless, we find variation in the extent to which those engaging in cultural analysis connect with the metaphor of drama or theater. Some have had experiences like Gerald mentioned in the opening—the idea of being on stage only produces anxiety. Few of us have done more than attend a theatrical performance. So, why maintain this metaphor? We recognize the need to see the limits of metaphor, such as imprecision and the tendency to focus on similarities (Putnam & Boys, 2006). Nonetheless, we argue that organizational communication viewed through the lens of dramatism has much to offer. The use of this metaphor has a long history, from Aristotle to Kenneth Burke (1972) to more contemporary writers (Boje, Luhman, & Cunliffe, 2023). We see value in understanding organizations through a drama/theater lens, whether through Goffman's (1959, 1974) metaphor approach or Burke's (1972) take as literal take—life itself as drama or theater.

Mental shift 6: From seeing our role as just one actor on the stage to daily enactments with others that create and recreate the culture.

The lens of theater or drama illuminates organizational life in at least three ways:

- *Viewing members of an organization as actors provides insight into their scripts.*

Actors on stage must coordinate their actions with others—some tightly scripted and traditional; others, improvised and informal. Like dramatic genres, organizational performances can be categorized by themes or archetypes. For instance, some organizations are highly controlled, with the emphasis on the role of a leader (a director or a star), while others are ensemble casts lacking a lead character. We may gain insight as well as to the extent themes of "victimage" or "scapegoating" emerge in the way members talk (Burke's (1972). To what extent do actors see themselves as having agency or control over day-to-day events? To return to the behind-stage moment, the fear of being on stage challenges us. We see value in being challenged to step up, engage, and improve our sense of agency in what we bring to the stage with others.

- *Viewing organizations as engaged in performances draws attention to the complexity of our interactions.* Pacanowsky and O'Donnell-Trujillo (1982) write about organizational communication as performance and note that organizational performances have four characteristics: they are interactive, contextual, episodic, and improvisational. Some performances are episodic on an interpersonal level—with two employees enacting an episode to determine power or credibility in their relationship. Others are larger organizational performances with a company trying to recover credibility after a crisis. As you conduct a cultural analysis, you will be challenged to listen in on performances. For instance, you might hear an employee story (episode) about what one co-worker said to another (interactive) about recent layoffs (contextual) as they discussed the various ways organizational members are responding (improvisational) to management mandates.
- *The "ventriloquistic" nature of communication is foregrounded* (Cooren, Matte, Benoit-Barné, & Brummans, 2013). The idea of viewing communication as ventriloquism involves recalling what may be missed when seeing such an act on stage. You may recall seeing a human standing on the stage with a puppet in their lap or on a stand. The puppet appears to be speaking. The ventriloquist is not moving their lips (at least the good ones do not). Even if you do not know how to speak through a puppet, the analogy of ventriloquism to everyday communication involves seeing what is missed when looking at the puppet. At first, it might seem like the ventriloquist is in charge—he is doing the talking for the puppet. We, too, may sense that the ventriloquist is the one making decisions about how the puppet communicates. Yet, the identity or type of puppet shapes what the ventriloquist is allowed to say. For example, in the Broadway production of "The Lion King," the actor holding the puppet depicting the character of *Timon* had to stay true to the character of this light-hearted "meerkat." In the same way, we may think of ourselves as doing or saying what we choose to say. Yet, the nature of our requests, the ideas we present, who we speak with and how we speak, as well as the ethical claims we make, are shaped by the "puppet" or, in the case of a cultural analysis, the power of shared logics embedded in enacted elements. In Chapter 4, we will note how "who" is doing the acting is not limited to what people say and do. An element of culture like a ritual, metaphor, or artifact (i.e., the type of puppet) is also co-creating the organization (Cooren, Kuhn, Cornelissen, & Clark, 2011). For example, in one engineering firm, office cubicles, a significant non-verbal

> symbol, were installed with lower walls that, in turn, reduced privacy. In addition, no one was given a permanent cubicle. Thus, an implicit norm meant that no one displayed personal artifacts such as pictures. This use of non-verbal space also impacted who talked to whom as well as when and how they interacted. The "puppets" or the cubicles created opportunities for interaction but shaped the employees. In the same way, ventriloquists are constrained by their puppets. The challenge is to be aware of the culture/puppet shaping forces—the rituals we engage in, the stories we share. Such awareness will aid us in co-creating more ethical and effective organizations.

In summary, if asked why we encourage the use of the drama or theater metaphor, our response is that this metaphor not only carries a rich history from Aristotle to Shakespeare to the present, but more importantly, it provides a valuable way for us to see ourselves and our organizations. This metaphor foregrounds members as actors, introduces the ventriloquistic nature of communication, and enriches and complicates our understanding of our communicative performances in organizations. Or, to return to Shakespeare's words, "All the world's a stage, and all the men and women merely players. They have their exits and their entrances; And one man in his time plays many parts."

7. How Do I Select an Organization for a Cultural Analysis?

There are a variety of factors to consider when selecting an organization. First and foremost, much depends on your goals for a cultural analysis. We return to a discussion of goals and benefits in the next chapter. An initial consideration should be given where you will take on the role of an insider or an outsider. In Table 1.1, the relative advantage of each role is not intended to paint a black/white list of criteria. Rather, you should consider the options in terms of a continuum. In other words, give thought to your knowledge and experience with an organization should be weighed. For example, in your own workplace, you may be new to the organization and/or industry; thus, your knowledge of the culture and

Table 1.1 Organization Insider or Outsider

Insider advantages	*Insider Disadvantages*
Ease of access Personal communication insights Potential value to your own organization Time—ease of data collection	Lack of perceived freedom for analysis Bias due to being enmeshed in the culture; start with hidden assumptions Too familiar, thus "see less," ask fewer questions People don't explain things to you the same way they would to an outsider
Outsider Advantages	*Outsider Disadvantages*
Insights for career development Insights for "newcomer" socialization Less familiar, thus "see more" See the more obvious layers of the culture	May misinterpret cultural data Access to the organization Time outside of the job to collect data Oversimplifications

ability to work with the culture is far different from someone with extensive knowledge or experience. On the other hand, outside of the workplace, you may be a relative insider as a volunteer for the Arthritis Foundation or a religious organization. You may also be somewhat of an insider due to weekly visits to a favorite restaurant or health club. Farther down the continuum toward being an outsider, you may have never worked for General Motors, but you have worked for another major auto company and thus know some of the basic aspects of this industry. You may have read widely about a given industry but have yet to visit an actual site. And then there are organizations that are completely alien to your world—you have heard of high-tech companies but have not read about, visited, or studied one. The key to examining the pros and cons of the "insider" versus "outsider" perspective is more complex, and perhaps your decision ultimately comes down to your immediate and/or long-range goals for developing your ability to conduct an analysis. We have found value, as have our students and workshop participants, in engaging in a cultural analysis with goals ranging from "becoming a consultant" to "learning the ropes as a newcomer" to "enhancing the way one serves in the community." Regardless of your decision, the OCA model will guide you in gaining valuable experience that goes far beyond completing tasks. The final mental shift aids us in keeping a bigger purpose in mind as we have the opportunity to co-create better social worlds.

Rehearsal 1.3 Applying the Drama Metaphor

Purpose: Identify the value and limits of the theatre metaphor.

1. What value do you see in using the theatre/drama metaphor to reflect on organizational life and communication?

2. What limits or possible cautions should we consider when using this metaphor?

Mental shift 7: From cultural analysis goals as just completing a task to gaining positive communication insights for co-creating better social worlds.

Other considerations (in addition to outsider/insider) might guide your choice of organization as well. What contacts do you have that might provide access to an organization to analyze? What organizations might provide especially interesting sites to study for your personal or professional development? Organizations are particularly interesting sites at some stages, such as the start-up of new organizations at which culture is being formed or major organizational transitions such as downsizing or leadership changes at which culture is being modified (see Rehearsal 1.4).

Rehearsal 1.4 Identifying an Organization

Purpose: Identify organizations that you might make the focus of an analysis.

Steps:

1. Review the pluses and minuses of being an insider versus an outsider in the cultural analysis process in Table 1.1.
2. Consider an organization you might serve as an outsider/consultant and then list the top three reasons it would be advantageous to the organization for you to serve in this role.

Organization: ______________________________

____

____

3. Consider an organization you might serve as an insider and then list the top three reasons it would be advantageous to the organization for you to serve in this role.

Organization: ______________________________

____

____

Once you have determined an organization, you should have confidence in proposing a cultural analysis to a potential organization (see Rehearsal 2.3). The final report has significant value to the organization (see Rehearsal 14.2). If hired to conduct this type of study for an organization, it would involve a major fee. In addition, as we will explore throughout this process, the benefits to the one conducting the analysis are also significant (see Rehearsal 14.1).

8. How Is This Workbook Structured?

The workbook is organized around the six major steps or processes of the OCA models. The chapters, regardless of the steps being explored, share in common the following features:

- *Stage Terms:* At the start of each chapter, we list important terms and concepts covered in the chapter. The reader may want to pay special attention to definitions and explanations of these terms contained in the chapter.
- *Connections:* In sections labeled "Connections," we assist the reader in making connections between theories, constructs, and organizational practice by extended examples.
- *Rehearsals:* Case studies and other activities are designed for hands-on experience. We incorporated activities that we have found enriching for workshop participants and students. You will find these activities in Rehearsal boxes in the workbook as well as at the ends of most chapters.

The Six Steps Include

1. *Articulate cultural analysis goals and benefits.* Both at the informal and formal level, a cultural analysis has value. The application chapters on diversity, ethics, change, leadership, and effectiveness capture significant ways to introduce positive benefits.
2. *Explore culture as co-construction.* The concept of culture needs to be understood beyond the popular business literature on improving corporate culture. Understanding the richness of this concept will further enrich your ability to clearly articulate the value of a cultural analysis as well as enhance your ability to navigate the remaining four steps.
3. *Reflect on enacted elements of the culture.* We review research on and examples of elements such as stories, rules, and heroes. The importance of being aware of these elements is that each one provides a different vantage point on the often-hidden aspects of discursive and organizing practices that constitute culture.
4. *Identify enacted elements via multiple methods.* Multiple methods, whether gathering data at a formal or informal level, are critical for validity. Thus, guides for observations, surveys, and interviews are introduced.
5. *Interpret thematic action and the culture in action.* Culture analysis does not claim to be objective. Instead, the goal is to provide a credible interpretation. You will be guided to explore enacted elements to discern patterns of thematic action (i.e., organizing processes) and overall culture in action; the master plot, if you will.
6. *Co-create positive communication applications.* Like any good play, a cultural analysis should inspire new insights. However, this process is not linear; application insights may occur at any step in the process. In the final section of the text, you will be guided to explore your data in light of one or more of the five application chapters: diversity, ethics, change, leadership, and effectiveness. The application chapters, along with online resources, provide cultural analysis tools to aid in exploring conflict management and crisis communication.

In all, the value of an analysis is tied back to various application arenas, including organizational effectiveness, diversity, change management, leadership, and ethics. In addition, we provide ancillary materials for additional cultural analysis tools to aid in exploring conflict management and crisis.

We encourage you to develop your ability to stay engaged in the first phase of the model by communicating with the organization you study about the value of this process in Rehearsal 2.3. To that end, the next section provides your first "Connections" to prompt further reflection and application.

Connections: Reflection

The opening lines described a moment when Gerald was conducting a workshop. The workshop was being held back stage when the previously mentioned thought struck him. "What if I was literally about to be on stage?" Like the majority reading this book, being backstage is perhaps a rare experience, but being on an actual stage is even rarer. The thought of being on stage is not one most of us entertain as an option. If we do, we perhaps wonder as Gerald did: What if I forget my lines? Can I really pull off this character? Will the show even mean anything to others? These questions, we contend, should also compel us to be more reflective as daily participants in varied organizations.

This workbook will have the greatest value if you are willing to shift from going through the motions of acting on stage to active reflection. We contend that effective and ethical leadership requires space and time for such reflection. In our work, we have learned again and again the need to spend regular, if not daily, times in which we pause to reflect on the larger questions. Earlier in this chapter, we introduced three big questions to guide such reflection: 1) *What kind of culture is being co-created*? 2) *What kind of culture should we co-create*? and 3) *What forms of communication will co-create the culture we want*?

These questions assume both interpretive and critical approaches to organizational culture. By interpretive, we mean a focus on exploring meaning-making processes, and thus a focus not simply on upper management viewpoints but on the perspective of organizational members. The approach has an inherent concern for ethics in everyday communication by attending to "marginalization, misrepresentation, or distortion of some interests over others" (McClellan & Sanders, 2013, p. 255). As such, we have stressed that ethical concerns should involve what we are creating on the stage, not just in the analysis process but in our daily application. We find Bisel's (2018) claim compelling—ethics training and education tends to focus more on some past event or imagined future ("there and then" talk) rather than the present, "here and now" talk, which is "more personal, emotional, messy, and context-sensitive" with "real consequences for those involved in the conversation" (Bisel, 2018, p. 102).

Our hope is the OCA model will aid us in becoming more mindful of the "here and now."

These three questions encourage us, then, to not just move through our lives reacting to others, carrying on with business as usual, perhaps talking about the past or future, but to reflect and then participate in the present moment by co-creating more ethical and effective organizations. Competent leadership in organizations involves going backstage; that is, active reflection on the cultural forces that shape communication practices and the way our communication practices shape culture. The steps previewed in the next chapter reflect a process that we all participate in each day. For instance, we consciously and unconsciously decide what, how, and when to communicate in our organizations; we decide what changes in organizational practices we can and/or should encourage or discourage; we determine what changes we believe we are empowered or powerless to introduce. Perhaps most critical of all, we make decisions about whether to reflect on our communication or remain somewhat unconscious of our roles. In all, we share in common taken-for-granted communication behavior, including our interpretation of the culture.

We can always improve both the quality of the data we collect as well as our communication performances in response to these data.

These daily taken-for-granted interpretive processes are based on our informal "data collection" about our organizations (e.g., norms, what is allowed, what is expected, how to communicate, and with whom to communicate). Based on our interpretations, we act and react. Before reading this book, you may never have considered yourself someone who collected and used cultural data or thought of yourself as an actor on an organizational stage. However, consider the following scenarios and then add your own and share it with a colleague, mentor, or friend.

- You heard a story about a recent firing and wondered if all the details were true but are not sure of who to ask or if you should even ask.
- You were hired as a minority employee and now wonder how to move forward in an organization.

- You read a staff development handbook and were left wondering why no one seemed to engage in the practices outlined.
- You heard during a performance evaluation that no one else was having trouble with clients like you are and found yourself wondering if you were really that bad.
- ____

When faced with the mysteries or uncertainties embedded in these types of scenarios, we may become more aware of an organization's unspoken or unwritten rules and values. Rehearsal 1.5 prompts reflection on past experiences to enhance your current efforts at conducting a cultural analysis.

In summary, this workbook assumes that we can always improve the quality of the data we collect, the accuracy of our interpretations, and, as a result, our organizational communication performances. As you apply the OCA model, we hope you will be reminded of what we observe each time we cover this material in the classroom, a training, or a consultation—how and why we communicate in our organizations matters. To extend Shakespeare's well-worn analogy, "All the world's a stage" (Shakespeare, 1954, p. 42), our challenge is to be on the stage not merely as players or actors but also as co-directors and producers. In these varied roles, our communication practices shape not only the culture of our organizations but all of our social worlds. That we are and will shape and influence is inescapable. The question again and again before us is profound: *What kinds of social worlds are we shaping each day, in and through each interaction?* We invite you to take on the same challenge we are committed to each day when the curtains are opened. We seek to keep co-creating better social worlds through positive communication.

Rehearsal 1.5 Method Acting and Getting Real About Cultural Analysis

Purpose: Reflect on your expectations concerning the process of conducting a cultural analysis in order to identify beliefs that may help or hinder your progress.

Overview: Method acting is a term that captures a major approach to training actors (Vineberg, 1991). At the core of this method is an active observation of the real and genuine emotion (or mining the real experiences of the actor or actress). Strasberg (1987), the major U.S. proponent of this method, notes that the procedures for developing an actor's capacity are "equally, if not more, necessary for the layman" (p. 201). This activity is designed to apply method acting concepts to the cultural analysis process. In short, the more you are real with your own reactions and emotions concerning the process, the more you will be able to overcome hurdles to make it a valuable experience.

Steps:

1. Briefly list two or three of your own initial reactions to this first chapter. What was clear? Unclear? What appeared promising for your own application? What emotions, if any, did this chapter evoke in you?

2. Have you had a previous positive experience with cultural analysis in which you gained insight into what "made an organization tick" or how to be more effective in an organization? What happened? What was your reaction?

3. Have you had a previous negative or confusing experience with cultural analysis? Perhaps you discovered information about an organization that was disappointing. Or perhaps you were baffled by why something happened in an organization. What happened? What was your reaction?

4. What will need to happen for you to have a positive, fulfilling experience in learning about conducting a cultural analysis? In particular, what concerns do you have? Questions?

Summary

1. The Organizational Culture in Action (OCA model) seeks to foster the co-creation of positive organizations by capturing their unique qualities as constituted in enacted elements such as rituals, stories, and history that both shape and are shaped by communication.
2. This cultural analysis process applies constructivist theories, such as the Communicative Constitutive of Organization (CCO).
3. The OCA model: a) provides tools and techniques to make mental shifts in the way we think and enact organizational culture and communication; b) identifies ways you can co-create positive, meaningful, purposeful, and ethical performances; c) guides you in leading an effective cultural analysis within your organization as an insider or outsider or informally as a member.

4. The OCA model is based on seven "mental shifts" foundational to the application (see the online Rehearsal) to support the challenge involved in making these shifts.
    - Mental shift 1: From a problem orientation that focuses on what is going wrong to one that identifies practices that are and/or can co-create healthy, supportive, learning, highly ethical organizations.
    - Mental shift 2: From the value of engaging in cultural analysis as only organizational and professional to also personal and community.
    - Mental shift 3: From organizations as buildings and businesses to intertwined networks that co-create our social worlds for better or worse.
    - Mental shift 4: From organizational communication as information exchange to co-creation of relational networks that create and constrain ethical and effective processes and goals.
    - Mental shift 5: From culture as a variable or a metaphor to culture as constituted in everyday communication practices that shape and are also shaped by culture.
    - Mental shift 6: From cultural analysis as attending to our role as just one actor on the stage to daily enactments with others that create and recreate the culture.
    - Mental shift 7: From cultural analysis goals as just completing a task to gaining positive communication insights for improving our social worlds.
5. The goal of this process is to learn how to conduct a cultural analysis and apply this analysis to critical aspects of organizational life such as diversity, ethics, leadership, and change, as well as to your own professional development,
6. This workbook will help you understand the concept of culture as well as the basics of data collection, interpretation, and application. Pay attention to the key organizing features of the book: *Stage Terms* to introduce relevant theories and concepts; *Connections* to aid your understanding of concepts; and *Rehearsals*, both within the chapters and at the end of chapters, to aid you in application.
7. You should have taken the first step in selecting an organization for a cultural analysis based on your purposes for conducting the analysis as well as the pros and cons of being an insider versus an outsider.

Discussion Questions

1. Discuss the broad array of organizations of which you are a member.
2. What impacts do organizations have on your life?
3. What do you see as the benefits of a cultural analysis?
4. How are organizations like theater? How does thinking this way provide insight?
5. Reflect on the way a cultural analysis is defined. What do you understand about this process based on the definition?
6. As you reflect on the possible benefits of cultural analysis, what are your initial goals?

References

Adams, T., Reinert, M., Fritze, D., & Nguyen, T. (2021). *Mind the workplace, mental health America.* Retrieved from https://mhanational.org/sites/default/files/Mind%20the%20Workplace%20-%20MHA%20Workplace%20Health%20Survey%202021%202.12.21.pdf

Anderson, R., Baxter, L., & Cissna, K. (Eds.). (2009). *Dialogue: Theorizing difference in communication studies.* Thousand Oaks, CA: Sage.

Barbour, J., Jacocks, C., & Wesner, K. (2013). The message design logics of organizational change. *Communication Monographs, 80*, 354–378. https://doi.org/10.1080/03637751.2013.788251

Barends, E., & Rousseau, D. (2022). Organizational culture and performance: An evidence review. In *Scientific summary*. London: Chartered Institute of Personnel and Development. Retrieved from www.cipd.org/en/knowledge/evidence-reviews/evidence-culture-climate

Bisel, R. (2018). *Organizational moral learning: A communication approach*. New York: Routledge.

Boje, D. M., Luhman, J. T., & Cunliffe, A. L. (2003). A dialectic perspective on the organization theatre metaphor. *American Communication Journal, 6(2)*, 1.

Burke, K. (1972). *Dramatism and development*. Barre, MA: Clark University Press.

Collins, J. (2001). *Good to great: Why some companies make the leap and others don't*. New York: Harper Collins.

Cooren, F., Kuhn, T., Cornelissen, J., & Clark, T. (2011). Communication, organizing and organization: An overview and introduction to the special issue. *Organization Studies, 32(9)*, 1149–1170. https://doi.org/10.1177/0170840611410836

Cooren, F., Matte, F., Benoit-Barné, C., & Brummans, B. M. (2013). Communication as ventriloquism: A grounded-in-action approach to the study of organizational tensions. *Communication Monographs, 80(3)*, 255–277. https://doi.org/10.1080/03637751.2013.788255

Cummings, H., Long, L., & Lewis, M. (1988). *Manageing communication in organizations: An introduction* (2nd ed.). Scottsdale, AZ: Gorsuch Scarisbrick.

Deetz, S. (1992). *Democracy in an age of corporate colonization*. Albany: SUNY Press.

Deetz, S., & Brown, D. (2004). Conceptualizing involvement, participation and workplace decision processes: A communication theory perspective. In D. Tourish & O. Hargie (Eds.), *Key issues in organizational communication* (pp. 172–187). London: Routledge.

Edwards, A. P., & Shepherd, G. J. (2007). An investigation of the relationship between implicit personal theories of communication and community behavior. *Communication Studies, 58*, 359–375. https://doi.org/10.1080/10510970701648574

Gallop. (n.d.). *Fortune 500 employee engagement tools*. Retrieved from https://q12.gallup.com/

Geertz, C. (1973). *The interpretation of cultures*. New York: Basic Books.

Gergen, K., Gergen, M., & Barrett, F. (2004). Dialogue: Life and death of the organization. In D. Grant, C. Hardy, C. Oswick, & L. Putnam (Eds.), *The Sage handbook of organizational discourse* (pp. 39–59). Thousand Oaks, CA: Sage.

Goffman, E. (1959). *The presentation of self in everyday life*. Hammondsworth, UK: Penguin Books.

Goffman, E. (1974). *Frame analysis*. New York: Harper Books.

Keyton, J. (2005). *Communication and organizational culture*. Thousand Oaks, CA: Sage.

Kuhn, T., & Ashcraft, K. (2003). Corporate scandal and the theory of the firm: Formulating the contributions of organizational communication studies. *Management Communication Quarterly, 17*, 20–57. https://doi.org/10.1177/0893318903253421

LeGreco, M., Eisenberg, E., Tretheway, A., & Goodall, H. (2024). *Organizational communication: Balancing creativity and constraint* (9th ed.). New York: St. Martin's.

McClellan, J. G., & Sanders, M. L. (2013). (Re)organizing organizational communication pedagogy: Attending to the salient qualities of a communicative approach to organization. *Review of Communication, 13(4)*, 249–268. https://doi.org/10.1080/15358593.2014.886334

McPhee, R. D. (2015). Agency and the four flows. *Management Communication Quarterly, 29(3)*, 487–492. https://doi.org/10.1177/0893318915584826

McPhee, R. D., & Zaug, P. (2009). The communicative constitution of organization: A framework for explanation. In L. L. Putnam & A. M. Nicotera (Eds.), *Building theories of organization: The constitutive role of communication* (pp. 21–48). New York: Routledge.

Meisenbach, R. J. (2017). Integrating ethics and responsibility into organizational communication research: Issues and new directions. *Management Communication Quarterly, 31(1)*. https://doi.org/10.1177/0893318916676891

Meisenbach, R. J., & Feldner, S. B. (2019). Constructing the ideal worker identity: The rhetorical construction of discursive resources in *undercover boss*. *Western Journal of Communication, 83(4)*, 403–422. https://doi.org/10.1080/10570314.2019.1566564

Miller, K., & Barbour, J. (2015). *Organizational communication: Approaches and processes* (7th ed.). Stamford, CT: Cengage Learning.

Mirivel, J. C. (2014). *The art of positive communication: Theory and practice*. New York: Peter Lang.

Mirivel, J. C., & Fuller, R. P. (2024). A world of possibilities: Introducing positive communication scholarship to inspire better business and organizational communication research. *International Journal of Business Communication, 61(4)*, 743–759. https://doi.org/10.1177/23294884241264268

Mirivel, J., & Lyon, A. (2023). *Positive communication for leaders: Proven strategies for inspiring unity and effecting change*. New York: Rowen & Littlefield.

Modaff, D. P., & Butler, J. A. (2022). *Organizational communication: Foundations, challenges, and misunderstandings* (5th ed.). Cognella.

Mumby, D. (1993). *Narrative and social control*. Newbury Park, CA: Sage.

O'Keefe, B. J. (1988). The logic of message design: Individual differences in reasoning about communication. *Communication Monographs, 55*, 80–103. https://doi.org/10.1080/03637758809376159

Pacanowsky, M., & O'Donnell-Trujillo, N. (1982). Communication and organizational cultures. *Western Journal of Speech Communication, 46*, 115–130. https://doi.org/10.1080/10570318209374072

Pearce, W. (2007). *Making social worlds: A communication perspective*. Malden, MA: Blackwell Publishing.

Pepper, G. (1995). *Communicating in organizations: A cultural approach*. New York: McGraw-Hill.

Putnam, L., & Boys, S. (2006). Revisiting metaphors of organizational communication. In S. R. Clegg, C. Hardy, T. B. Lawrence, & W. Nord (Eds.), *The Sage handbook of organizational studies* (2nd ed., pp. 541–576). London: Sage.

Shakespeare, W. (1954). *As you like it*. (S. Burchell, Ed.). New Haven, CT: Yale University Press.

Stohl, C. (1995). *Organizational communication: Connectedness in action*. Newbury Park, CA: Sage.

Strasberg, L. (1987). *A dream of passion: The development of the method*. Boston, MA: Little, Brown.

Vineberg, S. (1991). *Method actors: Three generations of an American acting style*. New York: Schirmer Books.

Watkins, M. (2013). What is organizational culture? And why should we care?. *Harvard Business Review*. Retrieved from https://hbr.org/2013/05/what-is-organizational-culture

White, D. (2017). *Rethinking culture: Embodied cognition and the origin of culture in organizations*. New York: Routledge.

White, D. (2021). *Disrupting corporate culture: How cognitive science alters accepted beliefs about culture and culture change and its impact on leaders and change agents*. New York: Routledge.

Chapter 2

The Significance of the Stage

The Goals and Benefits of Cultural Analysis

To set the stage for this first step in the OCA model, options for articulating goals are first reviewed. We begin with the overarching goal—to provide insight for improving positive communication practices that result in meaningful personal, professional, and organizational culture development and growth. We then review specific ways to focus on your goals. By reflecting on the Google CEO's cornerstone of "culture eats strategy for breakfast," Nine benefits of the culture analysis process are introduced to aid you in making a case to engage with your organization.

1. Articulate cultural analysis goals and benefits
2. Explore culture as co-construction
3. Reflect on enacted elements
4. Identify enacted elements via multiple methods
5. Interpret thematic action and OCA
6. Co-create positive communication applications

Step One: Articulate the Goals and Benefits of a Cultural Analysis

Objectives

- Explore the varied goals for a cultural analysis.
- State ways a cultural analysis adds value to an organization.
- Explain the "Communicative Constitutive of Organization" as a framework for a cultural analysis.

Stage Terms

Construct	Constitutive	Social constructionism
Culture	Structuration	Coordinated Management of Meaning

DOI: 10.4324/9781003482529-3

The following quote reflects the chapter's aims:

> Culture eats strategy for breakfast.
>
> Laszlo Bock, *Work Rules!: Insights from Inside Google That Will Transform How You Live and Lead*

The Tales We Could Tell

This morning, I (Julien) entered the building to prepare for class. A few minutes before class, I changed what I wore to put on a Kurta, an Indian article of clothing my colleague and friend Avinash gave me. Avinash arrived, and together, we walked to class. Today, he was my guest, and both of us are wearing a Kurta to introduce students to intercultural communication. On the way to class, we swing by another classroom. Avinash beams with joy as he waves "hello" to our colleague and chair of the department, April, who is also about to teach. She moves toward us and says, "We need to take a picture!" Sure enough. We pose for the picture and smile. Then, we entered our classroom. What does this moment reveal about the culture of the department and the characters on stage?

We all have stories from our experiences in organizations. Julien's opening story reflects the power of culture co-created through an informal and then the development of a formal mission statement about 40 years after the department began. To provide context, our department is a montage of culturally, nationally, religiously, and personality diverse faculty and staff. Yet, over time, the values co-created by the founding members coalesced into a formal mission statement that keeps us on a path of learning and growth. This mission, "fostering the co-construction of better social worlds through positive communication," continues to challenge and inspire us. Beyond informing and reflecting on faculty teaching, research, and local and global community-engaged service, this mission is one our students share and our alumni discuss with co-workers and family (Driskill, Chatham-Carpenter, & McIntyre, 2018). Indeed, we concur with the opening quote. Our departmental culture does "eat strategy for breakfast" in that it is the lens, the filter, the inspiration, and the drive through which we make decisions, prioritize resources, and develop student learning-focused strategies.

Like you, we all have stories to tell from varied organizations ranging from small businesses and community organizations to multinational corporations, as well as nonprofits and congregations with local and global impact. Our stories reveal the good, such as what was already shared by Julien, but also the bad and the ugly of organizational life. They prompt laughter and tears, meaning and confusion, love and hate, hope and fear. In all, while perhaps rarely said, organizational life is messy—complex and simple, filled with the best and worst we bring to the stage. In short, our organizations are us.

We have all been told and listened to stories mirroring this range of experiences. From mundane frustrations over time schedules to anguish in dealing with a difficult boss, co-worker, employee, and/or customer to fears over a change, one common theme is how we are all confronted with major communication challenges.

- How do I respond to a change? A request? A co-worker who hates our boss?
- How do I deal with a sense of not fitting in or not seeing value in the work I do?
- How do I talk to others about changes that need to happen? My stressors at home?
- What do I do with this gut feeling that my supervisor is asking me to be unethical?

In order to gain perspective on our experiences while shedding light on the good, bad, and ugly found in our stories, this workbook takes you through a six-step model for conducting an analysis. In this chapter, we focus on the first step of the OCA model: "Articulate cultural analysis goals and benefits." Before discussing goals and benefits, we introduce our personal hopes for you in this process before moving to Rehearsals focused on goals and benefits.

Any Hope of Change?

Hope is one of those four-letter words that are too easily tossed out.

- *Hope you get to feeling better.*
- *I hope you can make it to _____.*
- *I hope this project goes well.*

Hope, at the same time, is what we may cling to when overwhelmed, frustrated, and challenged. Such difficult moments are, at times, part of our lives in organizations. Before we turn to benefits, it is fair to acknowledge a potential obstacle to working together on cultural analysis. Put simply—class work and discussions of theory have not always created hope—and have not assisted us with the difficulties listed previously, such as a conflict in ethics, personality, and adjusting to change.

It is not uncommon to hear the following complaint against theory: "I don't see how this theory helps my life now!" In the midst of reading, reflecting, and theorizing about organizational communication and cultural analysis, we have been asked fair and challenging questions:

- Is all of this work of analysis really worth it?
- Can I really apply the cultural information I'm learning?
- Can a cultural analysis help me bring change to my organization?
- Is it realistic to expect change in myself or in the organization?

Our answer to each of the preceding questions is "YES!" We have seen changes not only in our own communication practices but also in our organizations and those we serve as a result of applying the OCA model. In fact, in each revision of this book, colleagues, alumni serving in organizations, and current students continue to push us toward making theory practical. Before moving to specific benefits, here are a few that we keep hearing:

- Increased understanding of the role of culture in everyday professional life.
- Developing skills and techniques to improve your communication and impact.
- Grounded reflection to lead the organization toward an aspiring and positive vision.

As you review these benefits, know we are also realists. At times, we have avoided change. Resisted change. We have not always accepted that developing new habits involves failure and a community of support. Growth involves "mental shifts" or new ways of thinking. Such shifts do not come easily. Habitual ways of acting and reacting may seem impossible to change. Ingrained habits in any area, whether it is nail-biting, reactions in conflict, a golf slice or tennis serve, or asking better questions, do not come easily. Often, in the change process, we may get worse before we get better because the new behavior seems unnatural. Our old responses are unconscious, and in contrast, we must think constantly about a new behavior. Only in time does the new behavior fade into the comfortable, taken-for-granted. In spite of these challenges, positive change is possible. An insight from the theatre motif helps here. The basic premise of method acting is to create a performance that seems natural and unpracticed despite the many hours of practice and preparation. Strasberg (1987) writes,

> The preparation of every art must be conscious—you must know how and what you are going to do. Don't trust your inspiration. . . . Then being trained in the method to the best of your ability. Conscious preparation, unconscious result.
>
> (p. 79)

Thus, a major workbook theme is that challenges create an opportunity for positive change. We can all grow. Gerald recalls learning a new grip to improve his tennis serve. Over time, it became natural (and the number of aces grew). We can both recall learning to shift from overreacting to an idea to paraphrasing (e.g., "Let me first be sure I am getting what you are feeling and saying . . ."). As you move through this book, we invite you to consider ways of strengthening your learning, making it stick, and putting into practice what you are learning.

1. *Engage in meaningful personal reflection.* John Dewey, in his model of experiential learning, stressed that we do not learn from experience, but rather we learn from reflecting on experience. Research also shows that the act of writing with pen and paper will lead to much better retention of learning (Van der Weel & Van der Meer, 2023). Consider joining us then in a habit—as you move through the cultural analysis process, take notes and perhaps journal daily or weekly about your discoveries and applications.
2. *Own this workbook by writing all over it.* Make comments in the margins.
3. *Complete the Rehearsals* that not only prepare you for conducting the analysis but also give you an opportunity to reflect on ways to develop your positive communication practices.

As you engage in this journey, we realize the process is not always easy. We like to use a particular mantra when we hear or feel something is "hard." "We do hard." "We do hard." "We do hard." Hard does not mean bad or impossible, but rather accepting and doing what it takes to respond to the challenges involved in a worthwhile undertaking. Perhaps what matters most is finding yourself engaged by a goal, a bigger purpose for being part of an analysis that inspires you and others.

Cultural Analysis Goals

In a book that continues to shape our thinking, Daniel Pink introduces three factors that create "Drive" or motivation: *mastery*—opportunities for growth; *autonomy*—a sense of options over what you do or how you do it; and *purpose*—a sense of goals, direction, and meaning. The OCA model includes all three of these elements. Thus, as we review potential goals for your analysis, our intent is for you to engage in co-creating purposes or goals that involve ***choice***—deciding on a goal and sense of ***purpose*** that matters to you and the organization you study. Goals, then, combined with the value of the study that also ensure opportunities for personal, professional, and organizational ***growth/mastery*** and development. After discussing the overall OCA goal, we move to options you may explore, whether you are engaging in a formal (i.e., student, consultant) or informal analysis (e.g., auto-ethnography).

The overarching goal of a cultural analysis is to ***provide insight for improving positive communication practices that result in meaningful personal, professional, and organizational culture development and growth.*** This goal implies a question: What am I doing, formally and informally, to participate in co-creating better organizations? Better organizations that participate in creating better social worlds? For example, on an informal level, we consider times when we or others in our organization have developed creative openings for work meetings. These openings might involve sharing a personal growth story or a best moment in training or a classroom. A simple ritual, yet one that has a powerful impact in terms of developing trust, connection, and inspiration. Thus, as you consider particular goals for using the model, we invite you to engage in considering professional development as well as organizational development goals and strategies. In fact, Chapter 14 provides a space for developing both of these. Our purpose in this section is to consider two types of goals.

Overall Culture Analysis: You can explore with your contact the goal of interpreting the overall culture of an organization or unit in the organization. That is, you may decide that the goal would be to capture the unique enacted elements such as history, stories, and rituals to gain insight into what is being created in their communicative practices. When might an overall analysis be merited? You might ask the following questions with your contact (or for yourself as an insider):

- Has the leadership engaged in a cultural analysis of their organization? If yes, what was the goal? Outcome? What was done? What helped? Is there a copy of the report? If they have never taken this step or years have passed since that time, then a case could be made for this overall focus. Much like a health checkup has merit, even if you sense all is well, an overall analysis promises practical insights into the health of an organization.
- What does leadership think members would say about the culture? What would members, as well as leaders, consider cultural strengths? Are they aware of any areas of concern?
- What types of changes have occurred recently? Anticipated changes? How might an overall cultural analysis aid in navigating changes?

These, in other questions introduced in Rehearsal 2.1 on cultural analysis goals, may suggest the need to further explore the goals and values of an overall analysis of the culture. Alternatively, their responses and/or your knowledge of the organization might provide an exploration of a more focused analysis.

Identifying a Focus Area: Gerald's first organizational communication analysis as a student back in 1984. He began with a simple question: *Which focus or goal might be of greater value to your organization at this time?* He went on to list options. In much the same way, this workbook is designed to give you options. On the one hand, an overall analysis has value for insights ranging from internal and external communication. On the other hand, discussing the option of an overall analysis might bring to the surface the need to focus on a specific area. Thus, as you explore goals, consider this question: *To what extent do you see value in making the goal of this analysis centered around one of the following areas that mirror our application chapters*:

- Diversity (e.g., checking progress, current initiatives)
- Change (e.g., downsizing, conflicts, crisis)
- Ethics (e.g., current and/or past challenges, lack of clarity on ethical norms)
- Leadership (e.g., recent changes, down/up information flow)

We capture reflections on these and other questions in Rehearsal 2.3 on benefits. Thus, while a general analysis includes data collection that touches on the previously mentioned areas, an organization may prefer to focus on one. It is fair to ask what you might be asking and/or your contact might be asking at this juncture: What about even more specific areas like performance reviews or onboarding practices? Gerald recalls studying the way national cultural differences were being managed in an engineering firm. At the same time, he was asked to review their performance review process. As you might imagine, the two were intertwined, and thus, both were of value. Yet, to the question of focusing on a given practice, like a performance review, a credible understanding of the culture is about looking at enacted elements, not just one. Thus, if asked to explore a formal ritual, such as a performance review, we would want to be sure to look at other enacted elements, such as onboarding, training, and professional development practices, in light of what happens in a performance review. For example, if one part of the performance review focused on the effectiveness of an employee's conflict management, we would want to explore the extent to which there are training rituals, onboarding practices, as well as leadership modeling aimed at creating a culture of ethical and productive conflict management. Across the goal of a general or a more focused analysis, the OCA model seeks to keep before us the identification of what enacted elements are creating.

Rehearsal 2.1 Exploring Cultural Analysis Goals

Purpose: Explore and then identify the analysis goal(s).

Steps:

- Arrange a meeting with individuals/leaders most likely to be the decision-makers. Indicate that the goal is to explore their interest and the analysis goals.
- Utilize the following questions to guide this initial exploration:

1. What has this organization's experience been with assessments, analyses of communication, or culture?
    a. What was done? What was valued? Not valued?
    b. What was the impact?
2. Do you see an overall analysis as best or one focused on a specific area? If specific, who of the following areas might be of value:
    a. Diversity (e.g., checking progress, current initiatives)
    b. Change (e.g., downsizing, conflicts, crisis)
    c. Ethics (e.g., the extent to which members give voice to ethical concerns)
    d. Leadership (e.g., recent changes, down/up information flow)
3. What do you see as our next steps?
4. Who else needs to be involved in this decision?
5. What questions do you have and/or anticipate others having?
6. What would you like to see in a final report?

Close: I look forward to working with you. Once we finalize the next steps, I will develop a proposal that summarizes goals, benefits, and our process as well.

As indicated in the Rehearsal 2.1, it is not uncommon for a discussion of goals and benefits to intertwine. This opening section on goals and the following one on benefits are intended to prepare you for these discussions with the intent to lay the groundwork for a formal proposal, which we provide guides for in Chapter 3. If you are engaged in autoethnography, the intent is the same in that we would want you to discern goals and benefits for yourself and the organization.

Cultural Analysis Benefits

Depending on your role and the organization, a discussion of benefits will vary widely. Consider these sharp contrasts:

- We would love to have you on board. Whether part of a class project or hired to conduct the analysis, we get it. We need to pay attention to culture. It is what we do here. How do we get started?
- Well, we know you want to do this project, but to be honest, the timing is not great, and it is a hard sale around here. The last time we had someone do a project like this, the report landed on a shelf.

We would like to say that these are made-up scenarios. In fact, they do represent extremes, from a contact in an organization that is quickly on board, and, in truth, the last one could have included a detail that is more extreme. One faculty member was hired by a multinational to make sense of three consulting reports sitting on the shelf. Therefore, as we discuss goals and benefits, you will need to tailor these in light of the organization (c.f. Rehearsal 2.3); these broader and often less known or obvious benefits to more specific ones. In fact, one place to begin may be with a question. The question we are responding to in this chapter is one you might be asking: *Just what is the value or the benefit of a cultural analysis?* Our responses will vary depending on the person and the organization, but we might begin with the following—A cultural analysis has numerous benefits. We counted ten! Before moving to specific benefits, we discuss the first one, "Insight into what we take for granted," in more detail. In the closing "Connections" section, we take you to the tenth benefit—*Using Metaphors To See & Ask Better Questions* (Hint: Have you ever considered how atoms, rivers, and Lego people could help us ask better questions?)

1. **Insight into what we take for granted.**

Consider Moments Like These

- You join your first Zoom meeting as a new member and are caught off guard by the way the opening 20 minutes is spent responding to questions about their personal lives.
- You keep seeing the way one team member arrives early and greets and talks to all team members before the meeting.
- You overhear co-workers at the coffee pot sharing stories about their families.

We begin with these seemingly mundane examples to introduce some of the early work on organizational culture in the 1980's. Pacanowsky and O'Donnell-Trujillo (1982) introduced communication scholars to the concept of organizational culture, although the notion of interpretive studies emerged in the social sciences in the 1970s. Their basic premise was that organizations needed to be studied as cultures of interest for their own sake: as places where we "gossip, joke, knife one another, initiate romantic involvements, cue new employees to ways of doing the least amount of work that still avoids hassles from a supervisor, talk sports, arrange picnics" (p. 116). Their contention is a simple yet profound one—so much more is going on in our organizations than "getting the job done." For instance, the explicit link between cultural competence and the metaphor of acting is foregrounded in their classic article, "Organizational Communication as Cultural Performance" (Pacanowsky & O'Donnell-Trujillo, 1983). They indicate the benefit of paying attention to varied performances, their function, and what is being created in these "performances" that may be overlooked or taken for granted. A few examples include:

- **Enacting rituals**. Consider all the functions and all that is created in company picnics, retirement parties, board meetings, and coffee room chats. A cultural analysis has the benefit of understanding not just the surface or stated function (e.g., having a cup of coffee or celebrating a retiring employee) but other functions (e.g., learning about what is happening back home, laughter and tears over shared memories of life together).
- **Storytelling**. What might be learned if data involved hearing more than corporate stories put on the web page? What might be learned if personal and collegial stories surfaced as well? Listening to diverse stories lets us know what is being created (or not created) and lived out in the organization.
- **Communication and Politics**. Here, the authors again encourage attention to the taken-for-granted, not some national or party affiliation. For example, the role of "showing personal strength" (p. 142) attends to the subtle ways managers and employees exert influence (e.g., "squeezing a budget" to maintain a favorite program, assuming rights over certain documents, files, or processes, creating allies).

Other areas could be explored, such as "enculturation processes" (e.g., learning the ropes) and "communication and sociality" (e.g., talk focused on courtesies, pleasantries, humor). All of these indicate the value of paying attention to what is taken for granted, the informal cultural and communicative practices (Pacanowsky & O'Donnell-Trujillo, 1983, pp. 140–144).

Attending to what is taken for granted suggests other more specific benefits.

Rehearsal 2.2 Taken-for-Granted

Purpose: Discern taken for granted communication practices.

1. Identify a "taken-for-granted" practice in your organization.

2. How was/is this practice created through interaction?

3. How does it constrain and or create new future interactions?

____

____

____

Before turning to five additional benefits, Rehearsal 2.2 provides an opportunity to reflect on varied interaction patterns that you might have taken for granted.

2. **Ways to improve external communication or public relations.** Cultural meanings represented in member language, stories, and humor are critical to effective external communication related to image, vision, and strategy (Hatch & Schultz, 1997).
3. **Insight into socialization processes.** A typology of stories might be used to determine the effectiveness of current formal and informal onboard, acculturation processes (Brown, 1990).
4. **Develop awareness of contradictory communication patterns.** What stories could you tell of management dictates that make little sense? For example, imagine research showing a contradiction between maternity leave and organizational policy. Women who secured their leave also undermined their image as competent employees (Buzzanell et al., 2017; c.f., Boren & Johnson, 2013). Scott Adams (1996), the creator of the *Dilbert* cartoon, captures the irony in such moments. He illustrates a business plan as having two steps: a) "gather information"; and b) "ignore it" (p. 162). Yet, despite the humor of *Dilbert* characters dealing with meaningless (or harmful and unjust) business practices, none of us likes to be in those roles.

   The next five cultural analysis benefits mirror the closing application chapters.
5. **Understand and improve diversity practices** (Chapter 9), including an understanding of the relationship between ethnic and national cultures in light of organizational communication patterns and norms.
6. **Enhance change processes** (Chapter 10) by uncovering cultural strengths and potential areas for growth, conflict management, crisis response, and external communication.
7. **Empower members to integrate ethical practices** (Chapter 11) into organizational processes relevant to internal and external communication in relation to conflict management, crisis response, short versus long-term sustainability, power and decision-making, and concerns for the environment.
8. **Encourage positive leadership communication** (Chapter 12) to ethically co-construct symbolic resources such as stories and rituals that shape meaning and purpose, what is valued, ethical practices, and readiness to grow through change, conflict, and crisis events.
9. **Attend overall organizational effectiveness** (Chapter 13) through cultural practices connected with hiring, onboarding, retention, public relations, development and training, crisis response, conflict management, and strategic planning.

In summary, this review of benefits captures an array of entry points—some you and/or your organizational contact(s) may have already considered; others perhaps useful to introduce after reflection on Rehearsal 2.3.

Rehearsal 2.3 Cultural Analysis Benefits

Purpose: Identify the primary benefits of an analysis for your organization or the organization you have decided to study. Since goals and benefits are often discussed at the same time, we recommend completing this along with 2.2 before entering a formal discussion.

Steps:

1. Review the preceding benefits in light of what you consider to be more relevant to your organization.
2. Consider possible problems you currently perceive in the organization and describe how a cultural analysis would help you better identify solutions to these problems. Or, you might reflect on current changes being considered or implemented and ways a cultural analysis would help in the process of change management.
3. Write down the top *three potential benefits* of an analysis of your own organization or of the organization you are considering as a focus for an analysis.

Connections: Using Metaphors to See and Ask Better Questions

Consider if any of the following experiences are ones you have had:

- You take a picture of autumn colors, and in looking at the picture, you see what you missed when looking without the camera lens—the way the light reflected off the water, the deep reflection of a majestic oak turned gold and red in the fall.
- You hold a camera up to take a picture of part of a cave wall. You are told you cannot see what is there, but your camera will do it for you. The picture reveals an ancient drawing your naked eye could not see.
- You hear talk about life in the organization as being like a family, a prison, or working as a cog in a machine, a role in a play.

Each of the preceding scenarios has been experienced by most, if not all, of us. What is our point? We know something about the value of finding a different way of seeing. Gerald still recalls seeing an empty cave wall during a scout trip. Then, using his camera stick figure, horses and people appeared.

What is the point of these examples? Theory can function metaphorically as a way of seeing. Theories hold implicit metaphors or ways of seeing (Morgan, 2006). Metaphors are foundational to our learning and development—a fundamental mechanism of our mind as we learn by seeing one thing in comparison to another (Lakoff & Johnson, 1980).

As a way to add another benefit, join us in "Gedankenexperiment" (German for "thought experiment"). Three theory-based metaphors inform the OCA model. Each provides an opportunity to experiment and see the value added to cultural analysis in a novel way. In what follows, we label each section with the metaphor and then name the theory informing the OCA model.

Atoms Plus More: Communicative Constitutive of Organization

The "Communicative Constitutive of Organization" (CCO) is a phrase used to capture a diverse collection of theories and approaches to the study of organizational communication (Novak, 2016). *What specifically is meant by the term "constitutive"?* This term is used not only in the communication field but also in chemistry, politics, and genetics (American Heritage Dictionary, 2017). These varied usages present an array of images with questions that aid us in seeing.

a. Atoms-Chemistry: Defined as what makes a "thing what it is" (e.g., a physical property determined by the arrangement of atoms). An atom is not defined by its nucleus but by all that spins around it. The particles. Consider questions like:
   - What might we see if we viewed organizational communication like an atom?
   - How would our understanding of the culture change if we took our eye off what may be assumed to be the core of such stated values and goals?
   - What if we looked for what actually defines the culture (the atom)?
b. Politics: Defined as what has the power to "institute, establish or enact" (e.g., political power to appoint a position or create and/or enact a policy, procedure, or law). Thus, questions like:
   - What do you notice when members talk about decisions?
   - How do things get done and why? Do members reference history?
   - If a policy manual is referenced, what is known about how that manual was created? Contested areas?
   - What is not being said about how influence happens? Differences negotiated?
c. Genetics: Defined as the controlling mechanism (e.g., DNA controlling the synthesis of a protein regardless of the organism). Questions might include:
   - What might a newcomer soon or eventually learn about where and how decisions are made? The "room" where "it" happens?
   - What are the spoken and unspoken forces that create and/or resist change?
   - Tell me a story about recent changes? How was it talked about? Where?

All About Rivers: Structuration

The term *structuration* (Giddens, 1979) captures two ideas: a) we are constrained by structures (i.e., social norms, organizational decision-making hierarchies); and b) we participate in maintaining, changing, and defending these structures in an ongoing process (Poole, 1992; Poole, Seibold, & McPhee, 1986). For example, each time I follow a management directive, while I may feel constrained by the directive, my submission to the directive adds to the power of such directives in the future. What image or images have occurred to you as you consider structuration? One image we introduced earlier might be that of a river. Does the bank of the river or the river itself determine the flow and direction of the water? You got it. Both. A river is constrained by the banks in terms of width and direction of flow, yet at the same time, the river influences width and direction through processes such as erosion. This image prompts questions that seek to attend to the river and the banks:

- What communication norms guide the flow of the organization?
- How is membership negotiated? Daily activities coordinated?
- What stories are told about the way conflicts are managed?
- What happens when a member brings up a concern about ethics?

Lego People: The Coordinated Management of Meaning

A third and final theory that underlies the OCA model is the Coordinated Management of Meaning (CMM). This theory assumes that our interactions with one another create our most basic understandings of life (Berger & Luckmann, 1966; Leeds-Hurwitz, 2016). CMM seeks to be a practical theory that provides tools intended to improve the quality of our lives in and outside of organizations (Pearce, 2007). This idea of co-construction, as introduced in Chapter 1, foregrounds the assumption that communication is substantial, weighty, and consequential. CMM practitioners ask the same reflexive questions we ask: a) What are we creating in our communication? b) What should we create? and c) What forms of communication will create what we want to create? Yet, to go beyond these broad questions, consider a CMM metaphor of Lego people made of Legos. These Lego people come together to build something out of Legos. Lego blocks represent various symbolic resources we share in common (language, rules, rituals, etc.). However, these blocks do not just create norms for running a meeting, but the blocks co-create us—they shape our identity. Symbol use and abuse also construct our relationships, organizations, and cultures. What questions are prompted by this image?

- How are members made aware of options/expectations for managing a conflict?
- What stories are told about constructive responses to change? Crises?
- What stories are told about leaders? Do they include stories of admitting to failures? Of modeling growth (finding new Legos)?

Summary

This chapter opens with a quote by Laslo Bock (2015), former CEO of Google. In his book *Work Rules*, he tells the story of his being hired by Google. The person scheduled to interview him stressed that he should not show up in a suit, "or they will think you do not understand their culture if you show up in one" (p. 4). He speaks of the tens of thousands who visit Google headquarters asking, "What is the culture all about?" (p. 8). Bock devoted a chapter to Google's cultural cornerstones entitled "Culture Eats Strategy for Breakfast." This phrase captures the significance and value of a cultural analysis.

Indeed, the continued use of this construct means it is not merely a fad. Culture, as a construct, continues to appear in the popular (Goodpasture, 2007; Taylor, 2015; Hetrick, 2023). and research literature (Daher, 2016; Gailliard & Davis, 2017; Gibbs, Boyraz, Sivunen, & Nordbäck, 2021; Smith, 2024; Walker & Aritz, 2015). Culture, though not always foregrounded in the jargon of an organization or in popular books, is something organizational leaders, researchers, consultants, and members recognize as important. As a way to recap this chapter:

1. We focused on the first step or phase of the OCA model—Articulate cultural analysis goals and benefits
2. The overarching goal of a cultural analysis is to provide insight for improving positive communication practices that result in meaningful personal, professional, and organizational culture development and growth.
3. You have the option of having a goal to provide an overall analysis of an organization (or unit in an organization or determining a focus area such as diversity, change, ethics, or leadership).
4. Ten benefits of studying organizational culture include:
    1. Insight into what we take for granted.
    2. Ways to improve external communication or public relations.
    3. Insight into socialization processes.
    4. Develop awareness of contradictory communication patterns.
    5. Understand and improve diversity practices.
    6. Enhance change processes.
    7. Empower members to integrate ethical practices.
    8. Encourage positive leadership communication.
    9. Attend overall organizational effectiveness.
    10. Using metaphors to see and ask better questions.
5. Rehearsals were provided to explore goals as well as benefits.

Discussion Questions

1. What would you say to a CEO about the possible goals of a cultural analysis?
2. How would you discuss the benefits of letting you study the culture of their organization?
3. What are the options for a more focused analysis? What are the benefits of such a focus?
4. What benefit would an analysis provide for improving internal as well as external communication?
5. Which metaphor or way of seeing organization provided the most practical insight for you?
6. What is clear about the six major phases of the cultural analysis process? What would you like clarified?

References

Adams, S. (1996). *The dilbert principle.* New York: HarperCollins.

APA. (2017). *American heritage dictionary* (5th ed.). Boston, MA: Houghton Mifflin Harcourt Publishing Company.

Berger, P. L., & Luckmann, T. (1966). *The social construction of reality: A treatise in the sociology of knowledge.* Garden City: Anchor Books.

Bock, L. (2015). *Work rules.* New York: Twelve Hachette Book Group.

Boren, J. P., & Johnson, S. L. (2013). Examining the relationships among peer resentment messages overheard, state guilt, and employees' perceived ability to use work/family policies. *Southern Communication Journal, 78*(2), 128–145. https://doi.org/10.1080/1041794X.2012.736008

Brown, M. H. (1990). Defining stories in organizations: Characteristics and functions. In J. A. Anderson (Ed.), *Communication yearbook* (Vol. 13, pp. 162–190). Newbury Park, CA: Sage.

Buzzanell, P., et al. (2017). Standpoints of maternity leave: Discourses of temporality and ability. *Women' Studies in Communication, 40(1)*, 67–90. https://doi.org/10.1080/07491409.2015.1113451

Daher, N. (2016). The relationships between organizational culture and organizational innovation. *International Journal of Business & Public Administration, 13(2)*, 1–15. https://doi.org/10.1108/01437720510597667

Driskill, G. W., Chatham-Carpenter, A., & McIntyre, K. (2018). The power of a mission: Transformations of a department culture through social constructionist principles. *Journal of Innovation in Higher Education*. https://doi.org/10.1007/s10755-018-9449-8. Retrieved from https://rdcu.be/bbNYo

Gailliard, B. M., & Davis, C. W. (2017). To be known, accepted, and involved: Investigating organizational assimilation in christian churches. *Southern Communication Journal, 82(3)*, 117–128. https://doi.org/10.1080/1041794X.2017.1315451

Gibbs, J. L., Boyraz, M., Sivunen, A., & Nordbäck, E. (2021). Exploring the discursive construction of subgroups in global virtual teams. *Journal of Applied Communication Research, 49(1)*, 86–108. https://doi.org/10.1080/00909882.2020.1851745

Giddens, A. (1979). *Central problems in social theory*. London, England: Macmillan.

Goodpasture, K. E. (2007). *Conscience and corporate culture*. Malden, MA: Blackwell Publishing.

Hatch, M. J., & Schultz, M. (1997). Relations between organizational culture, identity and image. *European Journal of Marketing, 31(5)*, 356–365. Retrieved from https://0-search-proquest-com.library.ualr.edu/docview/237024416?accountid=14482

Hetrick, S. (2023). *Toxic organizational cultures and leadership: How to build and sustain a healthy workplace*. New York: Routledge.

Lakoff, G., & Johnson, M. (1980). *Metaphors we live by*. University of Chicago Press.

Leeds-Hurwitz, W. (2016). Social construction. In *Oxford bibliographies*. Oxford: Oxford University Press. https://doi.org/10.1093.OBO.97801997568410106

Morgan, G. (2006). *Images of organization* (updated ed.). Newbury Park, CA: Sage.

Novak, D. R. (2016). Democratic work at an organization-society boundary. *Management Communication Quarterly, 30(2)*, 218–244. https://doi.org/10.1177/0893318915622455

Pacanowsky, M., & O'Donnell-Trujillo, N. (1982). Communication and organizational cultures. *Western Journal of Speech Communication, 46*, 115–130. https://doi.org/10.1080/10570318209374072

Pacanowsky, M., & O'Donnell-Trujillo, N. (1983). Organizational communication as cultural performance. *Communication Monographs, 50*, 126–147. https://doi.org/10.1080/03637758309390158

Pearce, W. (2007). *Making social worlds: A communication perspective*. Malden, MA: Blackwell Publishing.

Poole, M. S. (1992). Structuration and the group communication process. In L. Samovar & R. Cathcart (Eds.), *Small group communication: A reader* (6th ed.). Dubuque, IA: William C. Brown.

Poole, M. S., Seibold, D., & McPhee, R. (1986). A structurational approach to theory-building in group decision-making research. In R. Hirokawa & M. Poole (Eds.), *Communication and group decision making* (pp. 79–108). Newbury Park, CA: Sage.

Smith, W. R. (2024). "No dig, no ride": The communicative constitution and consequences of imperfect authoritative texts in fluid collective organizing. *Management Communication Quarterly, 38(1)*, 147–170. https://doi.org/10.1177/08933189231173076

Strasberg, L. (1987). *A dream of passion: The development of the method*. Boston, MA: Little, Brown.

Taylor, C. (2015). *Walking the talk: Building a culture for success*. New York: Random House.

Van der Weel, F. R. R., & Van der Meer, A. L. H. (2023). Handwriting but not typewriting leads to widespread brain connectivity: A high-density EEG study with implications for the classroom. *Frontiers in Psychology, 14*, 1219945. https://doi.org/10.3389/fpsyg.2023.1219945

Walker, R. C., & Aritz, J. (2015). Women doing leadership: Leadership styles and organizational culture. *International Journal of Business Communication, 52(4)*, 452–478. https://doi.org/10.1177/2329488415598429

Part II

Cultural Analysis Basics

Chapter 3

Constructing the Set

The Concept of Culture

The second step of the OCA model, "Explore culture as co-construction," focuses on understanding three dominant ways of studying organizational culture. These approaches, "culture as a variable," "culture as a root metaphor," and "culture as a discursive construction," each provide insight into organizational culture. However, the "culture as discursive construction" or co-construction is foregrounded as beneficial due to the way communication is viewed as constitutive of organizing and organizations. The OCA model provides a framework to ***foster the co-creation of positive organizations by developing implications through the analysis of enacted elements that both shape and are shaped by communication.*** We hold five assumptions about culture and communication when advocating this framework. The concepts of "levels of culture" and "images of organization" are introduced as ways to further understand the construct of culture. Guidelines are provided for writing a cultural analysis proposal.

1. Articulate cultural analysis goals and benefits
2. Explore culture as co-construction
3. Reflect on enacted elements
4. Identify enacted elements via multiple methods
5. Interpret thematic action and OCA
6. Co-create positive communication applications

Step Two: Explore Culture as Co-Construction

Objectives

- Explain the concept of culture in light of three approaches.
- Discuss the value of using a "culture as discursive construction" approach.
- Explain the implications of understanding the three "levels" of organizational culture for your analysis.
- Describe the OCA framework.

Stage Terms

Culture as a variable	Culture as a root metaphor	Metaphors of organizing
Levels of culture	Culture as a discursive construction	

DOI: 10.4324/9781003482529-5

The following quote from Gertz, an anthropologist, reflects the chapter's aims:

> Man is an animal suspended in webs of significance he himself has spun, I take culture to be those webs.
>
> (Geertz, *The Interpretation of Cultures*, 1973, p. 5)

Good News, Bad News

To enhance our performances on the stage, we have to be clear about what play we are performing. Yet, set construction will be determined not only by the play but also by the director's, as well as the actor's, interpretation of the work. In the world of cultural analysis, a number of options exist for what we may attempt in a cultural analysis in terms of focus, scope, and purpose. In this section on "Cultural Analysis Basics," we provide two chapters. In this chapter, we focus on the second step of the OCA model, "Explore culture as construction," and then in Chapter 4, we cover the third step, "Reflect on enacted elements of culture." Combined, these chapters prepare you for the third step of data collection processes aimed at co-creating ethical and effective cultures.

How do we define "culture"? Why does it matter? Imagine the lights dimming, the curtain going up, and you see two actors standing on a stage. Nothing is on the stage. No walls. No doors. No pictures. No chairs. No music is playing. Most of us would either think something was wrong or perhaps we might turn to the friend next to us and comment, "I expected this. I mean, this is supposed to be very postmodern. The lack of a set is like life sometimes. The void is the set." Perhaps no one is smiling when reading such a dark or postmodern comment, but the point is this—*How we think about and define culture is all about drawing our attention to what we take for granted.* Culture is more than the set. Culture is more than values, rituals, or communication norms. Culture is more than what leaders attempt to change. So, again, how do we define culture?

The good news is that culture can be defined in a way that is helpful to our organizations. The bad news is that we may not be aware of how we define the term, which results in different outcomes of data collection, analysis, and application. The examples that follow span 50 years of varied efforts at defining *organizational culture.*

- "Culture is a system of shared symbols" (Geertz, 1973).
- Culture is the way things are done in the organization (Deal & Kennedy, 1982, 2000).
- Culture is "a pattern of shared basic assumptions that was learned by a group as it solved problems of external adaptation and internal integration, that has worked well enough to be considered valid, and therefore, to be taught to new members as the correct way to perceive, think, and feel in relation to these problems" (Schein, 2004, p. 17).
- "Organizational culture is the set(s) of artifacts, values, and assumptions that emerge from the interactions of organizational members" (Keyton, 2005).
- Culture is shared knowledge (p. 74) or shared dominant logics (White, 2021).
- "How we do things around here" (Gallop, n.d.).

The differences in definitions betray important assumptions about what to study when analyzing culture as well as the implications for introducing change. *However, popular literature on organizational culture may not make the differences clear, and consultants and leaders may not realize the importance of these differences.* In the following section, we argue for the value of exploring culture as co-construction. We review and provide images for three major approaches: a) culture as variable, b) culture as a metaphor, but then focus on c) culture as co-construction. Our intent is not to dismiss the value of the first two approaches. Rather, we make a case for the OCA model that relies on "culture as construction."This focus reflects *the mental shift away from culture as a variable or a metaphor to culture as constituted in everyday communication practices that shape and are also shaped by culture.* As such, this approach aids in listening to what is being created in the organization you study. In that listening process, you then move toward agreements on data collection methods that will provide communication insights for co-creating a positive culture.

The Concept of Culture

Varied approaches and categorization systems of how to define and study culture have emerged. We provide one such categorization system via three images: a) "culture as a variable"; b) culture as root metaphor"; but focus on the third image, "discursive constructions" (Putnam & Fairhurst, 2015, p. 386). This final image informs the OCA model. Understanding these approaches will aid you in checking their assumptions and discerning their relative merits (Bisel, Messersmith, & Keyton, 2010. We conclude this chapter by providing "Connections" focused on writing a proposal using the OCA model

Culture as a Variable

The culture-as-a-variable approach focuses on causality. Culture is thought to be able to predict and thus cause certain outcomes. You might view culture as variable "X" (values, norms, etc.) that is influencing variable "Y" (productivity, for example). This focus on culture as an "object" assumes "(a) culture is measurable, (b) culture produces discourse, (c) cultures can be managed, (d) changes in the culture will result in changes to communicative activities" (Bisel et al., 2010, p. 349). Within the cultural as a variable approach, we need to reflect on two major categories: culture as an internal variable and as an external variable

CULTURE AS AN INTERNAL VARIABLE

The relationship between culture and communication is complex due to the fact that culture is not an easily defined internal variable. For example, try to answer the question, *"What makes a culture 'good' or 'strong?'"* You will find that the answers are not easily placed in a formula. Based on the variable approach, a leader who does not have a clear understanding of the complexity of culture might say something like: "If we could just get our culture stronger, our productivity would go up." However, several cultural profiles provide meaningful frameworks (e.g., Denison Organizational Culture Survey Cameron and Quin's Organizational Culture Assessment Instrument (2011) operationalizes culture in light of four major value tensions grounded in decades of research with thousands of organizations. Positive cultures are spaces in which people experience "positive meaning," "positive climate," "positive relationships," and "positive communication."The authors do well indicating that they do not claim to have the only way to define and study culture. They do see the need to attend to shifts and changes. In fact, we return to this focus on inherit values tensions in our chapter on interpretation and on leading change.

Nonetheless, caution is in order with models that use language such as "strong vs. weak." The assumption is that "culture profiles that impede performance are 'bad' or 'weak' and need to be changed, whereas culture profiles that enhance performance are 'strong' and need to be fostered" (Barends & Rousseau, 2022, p. 7). As we will note in later chapters on ethics and effectiveness, a culture can be "strong" in the wrong direction or "weak" in a positive direction. Furthermore, potential problems arise when a leader attempts to strengthen the culture without a clear sense of what is to be strengthened: Consistency of performance evaluations?

Creating connectivity through rituals of play? Ensuring that values are shared? We concur with White (2021), who stresses that treating values as the key issue is problematic in five ways:

- "Values mean different things to different people" (e.g., worth moral right, social vs. racial equality, etc.), and, in some cultures, the word cannot be translated (p. 22).
- "Values are expectations, not behaviors," thus "similar values can lead to different behaviors" (e.g., a value at the societal or organizational level, such as individualism–collectivism, indicates how one should live, but the variation on how one lives it out vary; pp. 22–23).
- "Values need to be already socialized to be adopted," which means more diverse, larger organizations will face greater challenges in finding convergence (p. 23).
- "Some values are compensations for deeper cultural forces" (p. 23), which means that values are not integrated or simple. For example, the value of equality does not mean equality in measures of wealth or treatment in the US healthcare system.
- "Values cannot be instilled by telling people what to value" (p. 25), which unfortunately, is the assumption by leaders who may make concerted efforts to create shared values. For example, social responsibility may be found on a web page and part of giving back to the community, yet what is shared organization-wide is mediated by varied life experiences and contexts such that perhaps only one department or a cross-section of members share this value.

Beyond the problems of treating values as a key variable, two other major issues are present.

1. *Confusing causation with correlation.* Research in this tradition makes claims about a particular aspect of culture causing a change in productivity, satisfaction, or engagement. Yet, the reality is that the relationship might be reversed. Recall that productivity or "what works" forms shared cultural logics, and thus, a change in productivity may well bring a change to culture. To make valid use of findings in this arena, we need to see that correlation does not equal causation.
2. *Leadership focused efforts to change culture may not be best or ethical.* A leader-centric approach to change, as we will explore in Chapter 12, misses the reality that culture emerges from interactions over long periods of time. Pepper (2008) offers an interesting example of PLH Technologies, an organization that spent millions to build a new corporate headquarters that would reinforce and display an organizational culture of openness, modernity, and fun. The new structure, with its open floor plan, walking tracks, picnic areas, and glass walls, was perceived and used by employees much differently from the executives' plan. It actually inhibited open communication and was seen as counter to organizational values.

In summary, as the preceding example illustrates, the complexity and challenge of treating culture as an internal variable is evident. Consultants and researchers are, therefore, interested in exploring aspects of culture (e.g., leadership values, norms, structures) that predict organizational survival and effectiveness (Collins, 2001; Deal & Kennedy, 1982; Peters & Waterman, 1982). In contrast, the external variable focus explores the influence of national culture.

CULTURE AS AN EXTERNAL VARIABLE

The variable approach is also evidenced in comparative or cross-cultural management research that takes into account culture as an external variable. As an external variable, culture is seen as a map for navigating differences across organizations and differences in national cultures. This approach tends to focus on ways to tap into national cultural differences to improve productivity or competitiveness (Harris, Moran, & Moran, 2007; Ouchi, 1981). For example, Mexican organizations have been compared with US-based organizations in their orientation to time and relationships (Condon, 1997). In this comparison, the variable of national culture is used to explain why, for example, Mexicans tend to give priority to talk surrounding relationships, whereas the US norm is to have a greater task focus. Hofstede (2003), in a similar vein, has done extensive research on five underlying value assumptions that differentiate workers in one national culture from another. He considers these value assumptions, these ways of thinking, feeling, and acting as a "software of the mind" and thus central to exploring communication behaviors (Hofstede, Hofstede, & Minkov, 2010, p. 5). A web-based resource has been developed that provides country scores from over 50 countries and three regions (Hofstede, n.d.). For example, cross-cultural comparisons depict the US culture as highly individualistic in comparison to countries in South America and in the East. Given the widespread recognition of international economic interdependence, the importance of understanding national cultural influences will only increase. In fact, "over three-quarters of all US companies conduct business internationally" (LeGreco, Eisenberg, Tretheway, & Goodall, 2024, p. 15).

Understanding the relationship of national culture to organizational culture is an important, and often overlooked, aspect of organizational culture analysis. For instance, US value dimensions such as short-term orientation played a role in the 2008 global financial crisis. This research will be explored further in the chapter on ethics (Hofstede, 2009). Beyond the financial crisis, there is no doubt that the deepest unconscious assumptions we bring to our work life are often rooted in our cultural socialization. As Figure 3.1 summarizes, researchers have focused on cross-cultural organizational studies. This approach, when considering its merits, focuses on the controlling and static features of culture that shape communication and thus help visualize its impact. On the other hand, a focus on variables may tend to shift attention away from ethics and individual responsibility, as well as the role of communication in shaping culture (Bisel, Messersmith, & Keyton, 2010). Furthermore, treating culture as an internal or external variable may tempt us to believe that it can be manipulated or changed to produce certain outcomes. These strengths and weaknesses should be considered in the context of two other approaches.

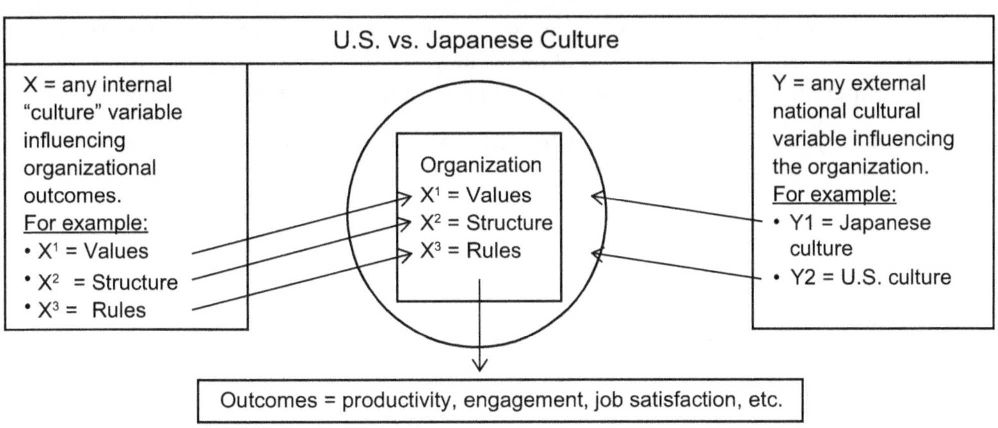

Figure 3.1 Culture as a Variable

CULTURE AS A ROOT METAPHOR

This second major approach to the study of culture focuses on how organizational members create a culture and how the culture affects members. Culture, as such, is more about a process than a product or variable. The core idea of this approach is that culture is something an organization "is" versus culture as something an organization "has." Thus, for example, if someone were researching or consulting with a Wall Street investment firm, consultants using the variable approach might determine how cultural practices, such as values or rituals, influence productivity and seek to bring changes as needed. In contrast, a scholar or consultant operating from a root metaphor concept of culture might attempt to develop a deeper understanding of the relationship between cultural values or rituals and these problems. Yet, as you might infer from the examples, both see the pragmatic value of understanding culture. There are three major research traditions within the root metaphor approach. Researchers in these traditions formulate or focus on different aspects of culture.

1. *Culture as shared cognition.* In this tradition, the beliefs or assumptions of the members of the culture are the focus of the inquiry (Schall, 1983). Researchers examine how employees think and what patterns of logic are shared among organization members. Researchers, for example, might describe assumptive differences between members of the same organization who come from different national cultures (Auer-Rizzi & Berry, 2000; Driskill & Downs, 1995; Heldal, Sjøvold, & Stålsett, 2020).
2. *Culture as systems of shared symbols.* This research places a focus on the actual language, non-verbal, and other organizational symbols (Eisenberg & Riley, 1988; Geertz, 1973; Smircich, 1983). A consultant or researcher using this approach might observe and record interaction patterns to understand and describe the way members use language to manage conflicts or build friendships (Jameson, 2001). In addition, such an approach may focus on discourses or underlying scripts that members may not always consciously enact. For example, in a not-for-profit organization, one study revealed how language embedded in rituals tended to minimize the experiences of lower-class participants in favor of the middle class (Lawless, 2015).
3. *Culture as the expression of unconscious processes.* This focus involves an exploration of the way symbols reflect the underlying beliefs and assumptions of the members. Such research might explore the deeper unconscious meaning of a common metaphor used in the organization or the underlying archetype that predominates the lives of the members (Jung, 1964; Levi-Strauss, 1967). For instance, Forbes (2002) explores the way women's discourse reveals underlying dominant masculine values. Schein's Organizational Culture Model (2004) is perhaps the best example that captures these three levels of culture:
   - Underlying assumptions and beliefs (that may be conscious or unconscious).
   - Norms and values about appropriate attitudes and behaviors (that may be espoused or real).
   - Artifacts that may reflect these (for example, symbols and language).

A visual depiction of the metaphor approach (Figure 3.2) captures the contrast with the variable approach (Figure 3.1). The internal variable approach assumes that culture is one element of an organization that can be studied and used to make predictions about organizational effectiveness. In the same vein, the external variable approach addresses culture as a force outside the organization, such as the norms of the larger national culture (e.g., Japanese vs. US culture). In

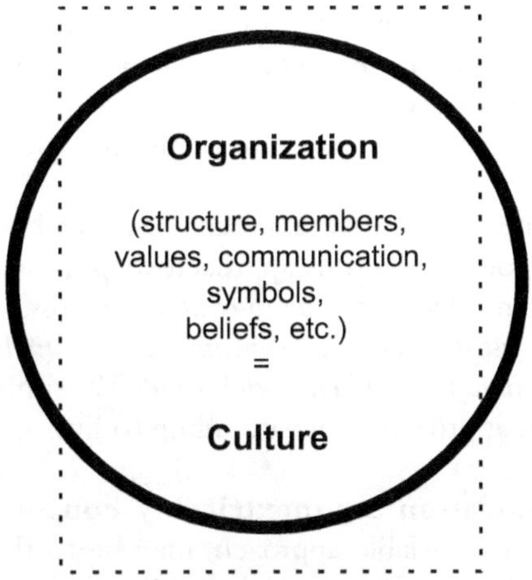

Figure 3.2 Culture as a Root Metaphor

contrast, the root metaphor approach assumes that the organization is the culture and therefore, depending on how culture is defined, various aspects of the culture may be explored. Thus, the root metaphor approach sees the role of communication in shaping the culture, and does not treat culture as static but dynamic and present. As such, individual choice and attentiveness to ethics may be more appreciated. On the other hand, present, rather than past, communication may be stressed along with a tendency to overlook the impact of such material constraints as place and structure (Bisel, Messersmith, & Keyton, 2010). As we turn to the final approach, it may be useful to capture the variable approach as viewing culture as an "object," whereas the metaphor approach focuses on culture as "in process" or "becoming." The final approach introduces the notice of culture as "grounded in action" (Fairhurst & Putnam, 2004). Put differently, as we will stress from a positive communication framework, we need to attend to what is being enacted or how organizational members are "acting into" or co-creating culture.

Culture as Discursive Construction

We see merits in the preceding approaches. In fact, in previous editions of this book, we relied on the "culture as root metaphor" approach. Our current work introduces a third option that is more consistent with the constructivist approaches introduced in prior editions (i.e., Structuration, CMM, CCO). This third approach, "culture as discursive construction," challenges the assumptions of the other perspectives in relation to communication and culture. This approach views culture as "grounded in action" by treating communication and structure as mutually constitutive (Fairhurst & Putnam, 2004). Put differently, past interactions create culture that then shapes present interactions. This notion of "grounded in action" is consistent with the CCO framework introduced in Chapters 1 and 2. Recall the idea of "constitutive" from Chapter 2 with varied images of political power to institute, the role of DNA in controlling synthesis, or the determinative role of how atoms are structured. Each image is meant to convey that communication is more than information sharing. Culture then is more than a variable shaped by communication and is more than the organization itself (metaphor). It is continually shaped by and shaping communicative action. As such, this approach challenges us to ***attend to both individual choice in shaping culture as well as the controlling or constraining influence of culture***. There may, however, be a tendency to overemphasize the power of past interactions and then give too much attention to communication over culture (Bisel, Messersmith, & Keyton, 2010).

In our effort to apply the constitutive approach, we need to be aware of these relative strengths and weaknesses. Nonetheless, this approach shapes the definition of our model for cultural analysis. The OCA model *fosters the co-creation* of positive organizations by *capturing their unique qualities as constituted in enacted elements such as rituals, stories, and history that both shape and are shaped by communication and our social worlds*. We summarize five assumptions that indicate the strengths of this approach while attending to limits.

- **Culture and communication are inextricably constitutive of one another.** The tendency, especially with a variable approach, may be to think in terms of using communication to shape a culture. Or, we might think in terms of certain types of cultures as shaping communication. Instead, consistent with CCO, we concur with Shepherd's (1999) statement about how a constitutive view "demands that we reverse the causal direction typical in our theories: Individuals don't make communication so much as individuals are made by communication; goals don't drive discourse so much as discourse drives goals" (p. 163). To this we would add, the individuals (and organization and culture) "made by communication" are then shaped by communication patterns and the goals driven by "discourse" then, in turn, shape the discourse, and thus the organization and culture. We used the web metaphor in the opening FAQs chapter—the spider spins the webs, and then the web constrains their movement (and what they catch). Unless? Unless the spider realizes they have options for creating different webs. Put differently, what determines the course of a river, the water, or the banks?
- **Culture creation, maintenance, and modification are both top-down and bottom-up.** Leaders cannot unilaterally create or enforce organizational values and artifacts; however, they can be quite influential by what they focus on, what they reward, and how they model positive communication. Organization members must buy-in and be genuinely involved for cultural change to occur. Any member of the organization may serve as an impetus for change.
- **Cultural knowledge can counter managerial manipulation.** Critical theorists characterize culture as "unobtrusive control" of employees (Deetz, 1992; Lyon, 2008; Mumby, 1997, 2015). For example, one might argue that gaining employee identification with corporate values or other related efforts aimed at "employee engagement" may actually undermine employee best interests by encouraging over-commitment through unconsciously accepted norms of working overtime. Promoting conscious awareness of cultural and communicative processes among all organization members equips them to act in ethical ways for overall organizational effectiveness. While cultures can be constraining, as we discussed in the previous chapter in describing structuration theory, they can also be the means of empowering members for creativity and change.
- **Credible culture-based interpretation requires thick description** (Geertz, 1973). Thick description is about gaining information about context. For example, we all read various texts (e-mails, newsletters), make observations (in meetings, at business lunches), and engage in conversations. Our tendency may be to develop "thin" cultural interpretations and implications based on a few interactions, a bias toward how a meeting was run, etc. Thus, we provide guides for engaging in thick descriptions with both qualitative

(depth) and quantitative (breadth) measures (see Chapters 5–7). The goal is to improve our everyday informal and formal cultural analysis. As such, we improve our chances of avoiding a tendency to overemphasize communication over culture or vice versa.

- **Organizational cultures are both enduring and dynamic.** We acknowledge the "ambiguous and unmanageable" aspects of organizing (Cameron & Quinn, 2011, p. 26). While organizational change is not easy or fast, it is possible. The OCA framework asserts that cultures are created in communication, and then, in turn, these same cultures both create and constrain our ability to introduce change. The analysis process is about gaining insight into ethical change processes while recognizing the complexity of this process.

This approach is hard to capture in an image. As referenced earlier, we might visualize DNA in a cell or perhaps Lego people building with Legos. Also, consider Bisel, Messersmith, and Keyton's (2010) contrasting approaches in terms of a gyroscope metaphor. Here, consistent with the other images using simple line drawing, notice how the half arrows of culture and communication are reflexively connected and thus constitute varied organizing processes, which in turn construct and are constructed by what we experience as the organization. See Figure 3.3.

The culture as a discursive construction approach is carried throughout the remaining chapters to guide the cultural analysis process. In Chapter 4, we introduce "enacted elements" as foundational to the study of culture and communication. Identifying multiple enacted elements encourages a valid and credible analysis as opposed to an exploration of a single feature of the culture. The focus on multiple and mixed data collection methods (i.e., observation, organizational texts, in-depth interviews) does not preclude you from using other types of quantitative data (e.g., quantitative surveys inclusive of closed- and open-ended questions). Indeed, gaining an overall sense of the level of member engagement via a quantitative survey, if combined with other data, can be helpful. Culture as a discursive construction does suggest that culture is not a concept that can be captured through brief surveys. Beginning in Chapter 5, we present research skills aimed at sharpening what you do throughout your day—observe, read, talk to others, and ask questions.

Our approach has a bottom line of enhancing personal, professional, and organizational performances. We will do this by developing awareness of various cultural elements (Chapter 4), sharpening your ability to collect and interpret data about these elements (Chapters 5–8), and then guiding you in developing positive communication application of insights from the

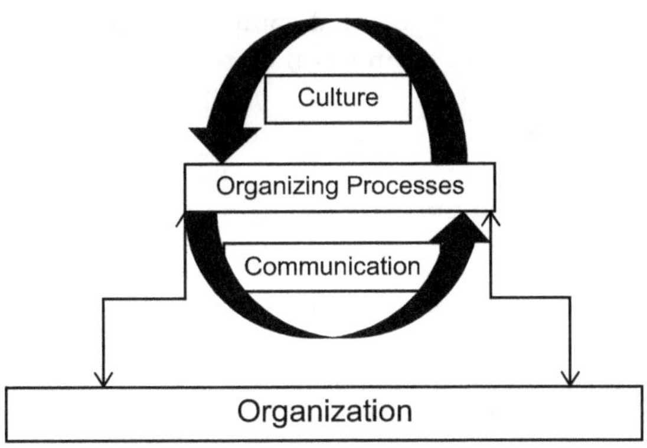

Figure 3.3 Culture as Discursive Construction

cultural analysis (Chapters 9–14). This process has been proven valuable, in our experience and that of our students and clients, for improving our understanding of organizations and our ability to lead and serve. Our hope is that the cultural analysis process will assist all of us in our efforts to be better observers, interpreters, and, thus, organizational participants who not only survive but thrive in the organizations that greet us at birth and carry us to the grave.

Connections: Definitions, Levels, and Metaphors

In order to make a meaningful application of the varied definitions, we invite you to reflect not only on the definitions provided but also on your own and that of the organization you study (Rehearsal 3.1). We then turn to prompt connections with the notion of levels of culture introduced earlier as well as the value of reflecting on the power of metaphor in thinking about organizational culture analysis.

Definitions

The three major contrasting approaches to the study of culture suggest three practical connections: a) first, definitions matter; b) definitions guide analysis; and c) definitions determine what we pay attention to and ignore. Therefore, it is important to reflect on two questions based on these approaches. In particular, these questions and example answers should be kept in mind as you discern the assumptions the organization holds about your analysis process.

1. *How will you define culture in your analysis process?*
   - As a variable?
     - Internal? External?
   - As a root metaphor?
     - Shared beliefs? Shared symbols? Unconscious processes?
   - As a discursive construction?
     - How are rules, rituals, symbols, and history constituting organizing processes?
2. *How will the results be used?* For example:
   - Change culture by manipulating certain elements of culture (internal variable).
   - Assist multinationals via cross-cultural comparisons (external variable).
   - Determine the way surface elements (i.e., rituals, roles) play in revealing values or assumptions (root metaphor).
   - Make unconscious processes part of our consciousness (root metaphor).
   - Learn how varied communicative practices are creating the culture and how culture is shaping the same communicative practices (discursive construction).

These basic questions, if bypassed, can lead to misunderstandings and frustrations. For example, imagine if a consultant held a root metaphor approach to culture and thus sought to surface values or cultural assumptions based on identifying rituals or rules. Then, imagine a disappointed organizational leader who unconsciously held a variable approach and thus expected recommendations based on identifying cultural elements as variables (e.g., a value or ritual) that would impact productivity. The OCA model is based on a "culture as discursive construction" approach. In this approach, as noted earlier, we focus on capturing cultural elements that constitute the culture in order to interpret thematic action and an overall characterization of the culture in order to develop practical and positive communication implications. Thus, take time to complete Rehearsal 3.1 as a way to engage with and learn about expectations from organizational leaders. At the same time, you can explore the best ways to discuss the value of an approach focused on culture as construction.

Rehearsal 3.1 How Do You Define Culture?

Purpose: Identify your own definition and that of the organization you study in light of the three ways of viewing culture.

Directions: Based on the review of the three perspectives mentioned earlier, answer the following questions:

1. How do you define the term *culture*?

2. What definition of culture is most commonly held in your own organization?

3. How would you describe the value of a "culture as discursive function" approach?

Levels of Culture

As you connected with leadership about definitions and expectations tied to cultural analysis, you might have learned that their responses actually took on a more complex, nuanced set of ideas. Thus, we invite you to reflect further on how culture can be viewed as having different levels. Schein (2004) describes organizational culture as consisting of three levels:

- Artifacts and creations such as technology, art, and behavior patterns such as daily norms for work and communication (what we describe in this text as enacted elements of culture).

- Values held collectively by the group.
- Basic assumptions held by group members concerning their relationship to the environment; the nature of reality, time, and space; the nature of human nature and activity; and the nature of human relationships.

Schein (2004), from a "culture as root metaphor approach," explains that the deepest levels of culture, basic assumptions, operate at the preconscious level and affect our behavior without our critical awareness. We are likely to be more aware of our values and can observe our artifacts and processes, but often, we do not understand their connections to our values and assumptions.

To illustrate Schein's levels, you might observe an organizational ritual in a factory of workers clocking in and out as they begin and end their workday. You might also observe rewards given to teams that produce the most at the end of a day or week. To fully understand the cultural meaning of that behavior, discerning values would involve going beyond attending to espoused values on the web page or in company documents (e.g., value statements about excellence, diversity, and community involvement). The goal would be to learn about enacted values by listening to members talk and what they do (e.g., rewards for efficiency and speed and accountability as part of being maximally productive). Going deeper, unspoken, basic assumptions would need to be inferred from the first two levels (e.g., time is money, extrinsic motivation matters most, etc.).

How do Schein's levels of culture relate to the OCA model's constructivist perspective? As we will explore in the following chapters, attending to varied enacted elements, such as history and communication norms, constitute organizing processes that allow us to draw inferences about the others' levels. The key distinction is to see how they are reflectively linked to one another—one is not causing the other, but they are part of an on-going cultural co-construction process.

An intercultural context example can aid in seeing this co-construction process. In one service project in a small Mexican town, Gerald was waiting, along with several Mexican friends, for an appointment with the small-town city mayor. His friends, aware of US norms on time, kept apologizing for what became an over 30-minute "delay." Relational time, however, was a norm Gerald knew about and paused to explain, "Let's enjoy this time to visit." In fact, when they finally entered the mayor's office, the mayor was not only responding to the questions they introduced but his responses were delayed at times by multiple phone calls and requests from his secretary. In this example, assumptions about time and human activity were being constituted in an interaction. The norms shaped the interaction but the interaction continued to reify the norms.

Metaphors—Ways of Seeing

A third way to understand cultures, in addition to definitions and levels, is through metaphors. Morgan (2006), as introduced in Chapter 2, presents eight images of organizations as a way to improve insight and understanding. Since its first publication in 1986, his book *Images of Organization* has been translated into 14 languages and cited over 15,000 times (Putnam, Örtenblad, & Trehan, 2017). He introduced these metaphors as ways of seeing that are implicit in organizational theory: machines, organism, brain, culture, political systems, psychic prison, flux and transformation, and instruments of domination. Bolman and Deal (2017) take a similar approach but focus on four specific metaphors or frames for viewing organizations.

Each frame (structural, political, human resource, and symbolic) represents a way of viewing organizations. The structural frame focuses on organizational charts, work processes, and role definitions. Leaders operating within this frame will tend more readily to see organizational problems and possible solutions in terms of role uncertainty versus role clarity. The political frame focuses on the use of power in organizations and how interactions are structured to maintain or challenge power. Decision-making, from this frame, would involve attentiveness to who and how power was distributed. The human resource frame directs attention to the needs and motivation of members. A leader relying on this frame would assume that organizing processes are best improved through various efforts to focus on member needs, such as training and engagement. The symbolic frame focuses more on vision and inspiration. Leading from this perspective, somewhat akin to the OCA model, views the organization as the enactment of symbols, stories, and performances that create meaning for employees. Rehearsal 3.2 provides an opportunity to gain insights into metaphors that may be implicit or explicit in your organization. This rehearsal may also be useful for reflecting on your analysis, as metaphors can be one way to interpret the overall culture of the organization (i.e., see Chapter 8 for examples).

Rehearsal 3.2 Playing with Metaphors

Purpose: Reflect on insights gained from identifying metaphors for organizing.

1. What is a metaphor you would use to describe your organization? When have you heard this metaphor used or implied?

2. What are the implications, both positive and negative, of this metaphor? What value might there be in reflecting on a metaphor that was not part of the communication practices of this organization?

3. What value might there be in reflecting on a metaphor that was not part of the communication practices of this organization?

The value of reflecting on images or metaphors should be clear: Metaphors capture the assumptions we hold about ways to think and thus frame the questions that guide our analysis of organizations. In fact, we will return to these four metaphors in our application chapter on Leadership (Chapter 12), where we discuss these approaches as a way to enhance communication competence.

Metaphors may also be one way to get to the unconscious level of assumptions that Schein (2004) describes as the deeper layers of culture. Metaphors correspondingly provide clues to alternative ways to think about how we manage our communication behavior. For example, an image of an organization as a prison captures the reality of certain political restraints in an organization. Members of an organization or unit in such an organization might say things like, "I feel trapped here" or "We don't hear much besides where to move next, never why." Such comments reflect the constraints members of this culture see in their organization. Leaders seeking to work with employees operating with this image of the organization may run into difficulty if they try to deny these perceptions. Saying, "You have no reason to feel trapped," would do little to change things. Instead, the challenge for leaders and employees in this situation would be to explore the aspects of the culture that are influencing these perceptions (e.g., history, toxic communication norms, rituals). The core challenge is to remember that we live by the images we hold; thus, we are both constrained and enabled by what we view as possible or impossible in our communication behavior.

The cultural analysis process can serve to make us aware of the dominant images held in an organization as well as the images we hold. These images or metaphors influence our everyday communication behavior. ***Cultural analysis captures images of organizations that can be obstacles as well as provide opportunities to become better problem solvers and leaders***. For example, if we became aware of an excessive focus on the structure of an organization (e.g., rigid machine-like roles and routines), we might present to organizational leaders the value of other metaphors or ways of thinking about their organization. A shift to include reflection on the political frame/metaphor), might be more likely to reflect on structures in terms of how communication roles need to be clarified to improve collaboration as well as exploring communication norms about why and how decisions are being made.

Metaphors matter, and a cultural analysis can help reveal the implicit metaphors influencing the way we communicate and coordinate our behaviors. Part of the power and value of a cultural analysis comes from the fact that organizational members not only create but also maintain and transform organizational meanings and expectations. Thus, the challenge is how to use insights from analysis to shift from a sole focus on constraints and problems to identify and enact constructive, positive communication behaviors. Such a shift is made more likely if we understand and reflect on the implicit and explicit metaphors constituting daily organizing and communicative practices. Chapter 4 further explores metaphors as one of the enacted elements of a cultural analysis.

Connection: Writing a Cultural Analysis Proposal

Depending on your purposes, you may or may not need to create a formal proposal. For those who need to take this step, we have provided an example to guide you. If you gain permission to conduct an analysis, you may still use the template provided later to guide you in responding to common questions. Furthermore, this example provides reminders about the importance of protecting participants via confidentiality. In some cases, you may be in a university context where full Institutional Review Board (IRB) approval is required. We discuss this process further in the introductory section to Step Three. In addition, note the importance of gaining agreement on sharing a summary of the results with participants. Some organizations may want to share the full report, but regardless, we find a major obstacle to an effective analysis is the prior experiences of participants who gave time in the past for interviews or surveys but never heard about the findings. Thus, we encourage you to review the example that follows and adapt it based on your focus and method as a guide for completing Rehearsal 3.3, "Writing a Cultural Analysis Proposal." In addition, we provide an example proposal at the end of the chapter in Table 3.1.

Rehearsal 3.3 Writing a Cultural Analysis Proposal

Purpose: Develop a formal proposal for conducting a cultural analysis in an organization.

Steps:

1. Identify the person (CEO, HRD manager, etc.) whom you know to be the person to contact concerning the analysis. It might be useful to have some informal visits first, before sending the formal proposal.
2. Develop a one- to two-page proposal in which you:
    - Identify who you are and your relationship to the organization.
    - Review the goal of a cultural analysis in light of the OCA model (i.e., a focus on capturing the unique qualities of an organization as constituted in elements of culture such as rituals, stories, and history that both shape and are shaped by communication that has significance for organizational and interpersonal ethics, effectiveness, and development).
    - Discuss the advantages or value of the analysis—be specific and, when possible, connect it with relevant issues within the organization (i.e., if you know turnover has been high, you could discuss the way an analysis often uncovers socialization practices).
    - Gain agreement on confidentiality of individual responses or identifying data collected during the cultural analysis.
    - Gain agreement on a process for sharing findings.
3. Have a trusted colleague critique or review your proposal before sending it.
4. Schedule an interview to discuss your proposal.

Note: A formal letter of permission is required for your project, even if you are studying your own organization. If conducting an autoethnography, your faculty member may still ask you to develop a proposal to gain experience.

Summary

We can easily get tangled in the web of culture if we do not pause to understand it. A failure to pay attention to how the set is constructed and how the construct culture is defined can lead to problems. A practitioner, for example, might pick up a cultural survey, measure an aspect of the culture, and then assume changes suggested by the survey will result in a payoff for the company. Although well intended, such efforts may fail because of a lack of understanding of what is being measured. Thus, we again encourage the *mental shift from culture as a variable or a metaphor to culture as constituted in everyday communication practices that shape and are also shaped by culture*. Several major ideas were introduced to encourage this mental shift and to lay the foundation for the rest of this workbook:

1. The second phase of the OCA model invites us to "explore culture as co-construction." To encourage this exploration, three major approaches with images were described: a) culture as variable; b) culture as a metaphor; and c) culture as co-construction.
2. Culture can be understood as consisting of three levels: artifacts and creations such as technology, art, and behavior patterns, values held collectively by the group, and basic assumptions held by group members.
3. The dominant images or metaphors (prisons, structures, etc.) that are held by members of the organization influence their communication behaviors, for example, the way problems and solutions are identified.
4. Culture is often complex and thus not easily captured through surveys. Therefore, we outline a process involving options for a combination of qualitative and quantitative data collection methods to improve the validity of the process of cultural analysis.
5. Our goal is to guide you in the "how to" of conducting an analysis as well as the "how to" of applying insights for improving such important aspects of organizational life as managing change and ethics.

Discussion Questions

1. Which definition of culture in this chapter most intrigued you? Prompted reflection? Why?
2. Take a position pro or con on the following statement: The leader is the most significant influence on the culture of an organization.
3. How does national culture influence organizational culture? Do all US companies have some similarities? What is the influence of national cultures on multinational companies?
4. How does viewing organizations as culture aid you in understanding organizations of which you are a part?
5. How can cultural knowledge empower organizational members?

Table 3.1 Example Proposal

To: Chief Executive Officer
From: Your name

Overview

This proposal seeks permission to conduct a cultural analysis of your company. An organization's culture is revealed by the values, history, stories, heroes, and other communicative practices that make an organization a unique place to work. As such, this analysis will have implications for overall organizational and professional effectiveness. Findings may provide insights into diversity, ethics, leadership, and change, as well as employee engagement.

What Is Involved in a Cultural Analysis?

We would need permission to interview __ members of your organization in confidential interviews, preferably during work hours. Each interview would last 45–60 minutes. Interviews would include the following types of questions:

- What is it like to work here?
- What is one memory you have of being proud to be part of this organization?
- What types of individuals get ahead here? Why?
- Does the organization give any employee awards or recognition? For what?
- What types of events does the company sponsor for employees?
- What is different about working here than working at another similar organization?
- What does a new employee need to learn to fit in here?
- What type of individual would not be happy working here?
- What is a story that illustrates what this company is like at its best? Worst?

We would also need permission to "walk around and observe"—to see how offices are configured and decorated, what visitors to the organization encounter, how routine tasks are done, and how employees work and interact with one another. If we could have the opportunity to observe representative meetings or events during the period of the study, that would also be helpful in understanding the culture. We would also do analysis of the website, written publications, memos, and e-mails that are generally available to employees of the organization. The time period of the study would be approximately four weeks.

Deliverable Product

Upon conclusion of the study, you will receive a written report summarizing what we learned about your organizational culture and its communication implications for your company. You will also have an option for an oral presentation of results to whatever groups(s) you may choose within the organization. We encourage sharing findings, an area of action coming from the analysis, with those involved.

What Are the Benefits to My Organization?

A cultural analysis can probe whether values are widely shared among employees and whether organizational practices support organizational values and priorities. For example, one company we studied was attempting to make a transition to a team-based culture, yet we discovered that all awards and benefits were based on individual accomplishment. Cultural information can also be of value in employee recruitment, selection, orientation, and engagement. Knowing the current culture is vital in promoting successful organizational change attempts, as well as in promoting values of ethics and diversity within the organization. Cultural knowledge is also vital to effective leadership.

Considerations

1. Employees need to be promised confidentiality in order to feel comfortable in offering candid information in the interviews. This means that the source of information will not be revealed at any point in the report or oral presentation.
2. Our study and report of your organization are offered for your benefit, and we promise to maintain the confidentiality of the information we collect. We would seek your permission if we ever chose to publish any information from the study, and the identity of your company would be protected from any external use if you agreed.
3. It is important that employees receive feedback from the results process. Therefore, we ask that clients inform participants in advance that an executive summary of results will be provided to all for discussion and determination of implications.

Consultant

Attach a brief bio stressing your professional and academic experience. If you are a student, you might emphasize that your work is overseen by your professor and include a brief bio from your professor as well.

References

Auer-Rizzi, W., & Berry, M. (2000). Business vs. cultural frames of reference in group decision making: Interactions among Austrian, Finnish, and Swedish business students. *Journal of Business Communication, 37*(*3*), 264–292. https://doi.org/10.1177/002194360003700304

Barends, E., & Rousseau, D. (2022). Organizational culture and performance: An evidence review. In *Scientific summary*. London: Chartered Institute of Personnel and Development. Retrieved from www.cipd.org/en/knowledge/evidence-reviews/evidence-culture-climate

Bisel, R. S., Messersmith, A. S., & Keyton, J. (2010). Understanding organizational culture and communication through a gyroscope metaphor. *Journal of Management Education, 34*(*3*), 342–366. https://doi.org/10.1177/1052562909340879

Bolman, L., & Deal, T. (2017). *Reframing organizations* (7th ed.). San Francisco: Jossey-Bass.

Cameron, K. S., & Quinn, R. E. (2011). *Diagnosing and changing organizational culture: Based on the competing values framework* (3rd ed.). San Francisco: Jossey-Bass.

Collins, J. (2001). *Good to great: Why some companies make the leap and others don't.* New York: Harper Collins.

Condon, J. (1997). *Good neighbors: Communicating with the Mexicans* (2nd ed.). Yarmouth, ME: Intercultural Press.

Deal, T., & Kennedy, A. (1982). *Corporate cultures.* New York: Addison-Wesley.

Deal, T., & Kennedy, A. (2000). *Corporate cultures.* Cambridge, MA: Perseus.

Deetz, S. (1992). *Democracy in an age of corporate colonization.* Albany: SUNY Press.

Driskill, G., & Downs, C. (1995). Hidden differences in competent communication: A case study of Asian Indians in a bi-national organization. *International Journal of Intercultural Relations, 19(4)*, 505–522. https://doi.org/10.1016/0147-1767(95)00031

Eisenberg, E., & Riley, P. (1988). Organizational symbols and sense-making. In G. M. Goldhaber & G. A. Barnett (Eds.), *Handbook of organizational communication* (pp. 131–158). Norwood, NJ: Ablex.

Fairhurst, G. T., & Putnam, L. (2004). Organizations as discursive constructions. *Communication Theory, 14*, 5–26.

Forbes, D. A. (2002). Internalized masculinity and women's discourse: A critical analysis of the (re) production of masculinity in organizations. *Communication Quarterly, 50*, 269–291. https://doi.org/10.1080/01463370209385664

Gallop. (n.d.). *Fortune 500 employee engagement tools.* Retrieved from https://q12.gallup.com/

Geertz, C. (1973). *The interpretation of cultures.* New York: Basic Books.

Harris, P., Moran, R., & Moran, S. (2007). *Managing cultural differences: Global leadership strategies for the 21st century* (7th ed.). Houston, TX: Gulf Professional.

Heldal, F., Sjøvold, E., & Stålsett, K. (2020). Shared cognition in intercultural teams: Collaborating without understanding each other. *Team Performance Management, 26(3/4)*, 211–226. https://doi.org/10.1108/TPM-06-2019-0051

Hofstede, G. (2003). *Culture's consequences: Comparing values, behaviors, institutions and organizations across nations.* Newbury Park, CA: Sage.

Hofstede, G. (2009). American culture and the 2008 financial crisis. *European Business Review, 21*, 307–312. https://doi.org/10.1108/09555340910970418

Hofstede, G. (n.d.). *Country comparison.* Retrieved from www.hofstede-insights.com/country-comparison/

Hofstede, G., Hofstede, G., & Minkov, M. (2010). *Cultures and organizations: Software of the mind* (3rd ed.). New York: McGraw-Hill.

Jameson, D. (2001). Narrative discourse and management action. *Journal of Business Communication, 38*, 476–511. https://doi.org/10.1177/002194360103800404

Jung, C. (1964). *Man and his symbols.* London: Aldus Books.

Keyton, J. (2005). *Communication and organizational culture.* Thousand Oaks: Sage.

Lawless, B. (2015). Performing identity in "transforming poverty partnerships": An extension of critical discourse analysis. *Howard Journal of Communications, 26(3)*, 275–291. https://doi.org/10.1080/10646175.2015.1049758

LeGreco, M., Eisenberg, E., Tretheway, A., & Goodall, H. (2024). *Organizational communication: Balancing creativity and constraint* (9th ed.). New York: St. Martin's.

Levi-Strauss, C. (1967). *The scope of anthropology.* New York: Jonathan Cape.

Lyon, A. (2008). The mis/recognition of Enron executives' competence as cultural and social capital. *Communication Studies, 59*, 371–387. https://doi.org/10.1080/10510970802467411

Morgan, G. (2006). *Images of organization* (updated ed.). Newbury Park, CA: Sage.

Mumby, D. K. (1997). The problem of hegemony: Rereading Gramsci for organizational studies. *Western Journal of Communication, 61*, 343–375. https://doi.org/10.1080/10570319709374585

Mumby, D. K. (2015). Organizing power. *Review of Communication, 15(1)*, 19–38. https://doi.org/10.1080/15358593.2015.1015245

Ouchi, W. (1981). *Theory Z.* Reading, MA: Addison-Wesley.

Pepper, G. L. (2008). The physical organization as equivocal message. *Journal of Applied Communication Research, 36(3)*, 318–338. https://doi.org/10.1080/00909880802104882

Peters, T., & Waterman, R. (1982). *In search of excellence.* New York: Harper & Row.

Putnam, L. L., & Fairhurst, G. T. (2015). Revisiting "organizations as discursive constructions": 10 years later. *Communication Theory, 25(4)*, 375–392. https://doi.org/10.1111/comt.12074

Putnam, L. L., Örtenblad, A., & Trehan, K. (2017). Introduction: From theory to application of metaphor in organizational analysis. In A. Örtenblad, K. Trehan, & L. L. Putnam (Eds.), *Exploring Morgan's metaphors: Theory, research, and practice in organizational studies* (pp. 2–14). Thousand Oaks, CA. Sage Publications.

Schall, M. (1983). A communication-rules approach to organizational culture. *Administrative Science Quarterly*, *28*, 557–581. https://doi.org/10.1177/0893318991004004002

Schein, E. (2004). *Organizational culture and leadership* (3rd ed.). San Francisco: Jossey-Bass.

Shepherd, G. J. (1999). Advances in communication theory: A critical review. *Journal of Communication*, *49*, 156–164. https://doi.org/10.1111/j.1460-2466.1999.tb02810.x

Smircich, L. (1983). Concepts of culture and organizational analysis. *Administrative Science Quarterly*, *28*, 339–358. https://doi.org/10.1111/j.1460-2466.1999.tb02810.x

White, D. (2021). *Disrupting corporate culture: How cognitive science alters accepted beliefs about culture and culture change and its impact on leaders and change agents*. New York: Routledge.

Chapter 4

Understanding Roles

Cultural Elements

The third step of the OCA model, "reflect on enacted cultural elements," prepares the researcher, consultant, leader, and/or student to understand and discern various types of elements as they "enact" or constitute the culture. Five principles are foundational to the next step on data collection. Each principle encourages reflection by stressing how enacted elements: a) are not all consciously held or enacted; b) are part of a larger continuing story; c) are embedded in one another; d) appear in both official and unofficial sources, e) vary in how widely shared they are across the organization. Four major categories are then reviewed: a) symbolic; b) role; c) interactive; and d) context. Definitions, examples, and ways to identity are provided. Concerning ethics, a lack of attention to what is created via elements means that communicative behaviors that cause harm and/or fail to co-create good fall under the radar screen. The need also exists to attend to the way elements—convey multiple meanings, including ethical and unethical motives.

1. Articulate cultural analysis goals and benefits
2. Explore culture as co-construction
3. Reflect on enacted elements
4. Identify enacted elements via multiple methods
5. Interpret thematic action and OCA
6. Co-create positive communication applications

Step Three: Identify Core Cultural Elements

Objectives

- Explain five principles for understanding enacted elements.
- Reflect on 14 different enacted elements.

Stage Terms: Enacted Elements of Culture

Values	Language	Heroes	Rules	History
Symbols	Metaphors	Outlaws	Humor	Place
Stories	Artifacts	Rituals	Communication style	

DOI: 10.4324/9781003482529-6

The burglars came in the back door at about midnight. They knew the layout of the restaurant and went right to the office and demanded money from the safe. When I first saw them, I was with the area manager by the dishwasher, about 30 feet from the office. They each wore a ski mask and held 2-foot iron pipes. I still recall the command: "Everybody get down and stay where you are." I hit the floor with other employees closing the restaurant. We waited, and in a few minutes, we heard laughter and then a scuffle. I craned my neck and saw the district manager, who happened to be in town to evaluate our restaurant, picking up one of the burglars while trying to pull off his mask. I did not hear what was said next, but in a few minutes, both burglars were running for the back door, and all that we heard was the district manager's laughter. I do not recall the district manager's name, but I do recall the look on his face when we let him know that it had not been a joke and that he had just thwarted a burglary.

The Making of a Legend?

What stories stand out in your mind from past experiences in organizations? What stories do you have to tell from your first memories after leaving the cradle? When do you first recall a parent coming home from work? Attending your first school? Showing up for your first job? What of stories that involve birthdays, weddings, anniversaries, and funerals? We all have cradle-to-grave stories.

The preceding story grew from an event in 1978 when Gerald worked as a restaurant manager. (Yes, we know, pre-internet—no Twitter or Snapchat, or AI to capture images). The story was repeated often in the coming weeks, and no doubt, the legend of the brave area manager spread to other restaurants in the chain. You may have similar stories. We hope not. Indeed, we close this chapter by returning to another similar story. This story of the legendary area manager illustrates the fact that stories are one of the most common means of sharing and shaping organization culture. They are rich with information about informal and unstated rules and about roles such as heroes and villains. In fact, we will return to the potentially dark side of this story later. Yet, beyond the idea of shaping culture, we encourage exploration of how culture itself is constituted in the weaving of such stories with other discourse, such as communication rules or norms tied to valued behaviors in a given position or role. The analogue to method acting provides an added connection.

A widely accepted approach to actor training provides insight on roles (Strasberg, 1987). An effective performance grows from becoming a true ensemble, an acting troupe that has such intimate communication with one another and with the set (props, etc.) that where one scene begins and another ends, where one player's lines end and another's begin are almost indistinguishable. In short, the audience gets the sense that the actors are part of a whole (Vineberg, 1991). What does this analogy say about our roles in an organization? ***Effective and ethical organizational members learn to pay attention to more than their own individual roles.*** This chapter will introduce you to varied enacted elements that shape and serve as resources for effective individual, team, and organizational role performances.

The term *enacted elements of culture* may be defined as *interwoven discursive forms that are constitutive of the organizational culture.* Put differently, elements of culture are what create and then are shaped by the culture. They are the everyday "scripts" we enact and "stages" that shape those enactments. For example, an employee repeats a story about something that "can't be talked about in meetings." He then enacts this norm of "not talking" about those topics in a meeting. In doing so, he recreates this pattern. The focus on the word "enacted" is a way to stress that the

OCA model is not treating elements such as values or rituals from a "culture as variable" perspective. The culture as a variable approach would focus on predicting ways to make changes in one element to impact employee engagement or productivity, for instance. Nor does this model assume a "culture as root metaphor" approach with a focus on elements revealing culture. As stressed in earlier chapters, the variable and metaphor approaches can be of value.

In contrast, this shift to "enacted elements" assumes a view of culture and organizations congruent with a constructivist view of communication. Consistent with other social constructivist theories introduced earlier (e.g., CCO, Structuration, and CMM), the OCA model stresses that rather than variables, or revealing and concealing, these elements "enact" or create culture and then, in turn, are shaped by the culture. In particular, a CCO perspective challenges us to "consider how multiple levels and processes of communication create and are created by ethics" (Meisenbach, 2016, p. 150).

We return to this challenge in Chapter 8 on interpretation and in application Chapters (9–13), yet here, it is important to be mindful of how some of these enacted elements clearly involve human choice or agency while others do not. For instance, when stories are introduced, one can easily imagine being in a crisis response meeting. You are aware of the history of a prior, poorly handled crisis and thus make a decision to tell a story about how we need to learn from this past incident about the high cost of not reflecting on ethics. Conversely, ethical action is easily seen in a decision not to tell a story if it is understood to be a rumor or malicious gossip. Still, other elements, such as "place," make discerning ethical responsibility more challenging. It may be difficult, for instance, to discern individual or group-level ethical responsibilities regarding the place their physical building is located. For instance, what response should leadership take if they learn their property was purchased decades before by forcing out minorities with a low-cost purchase? Current members may not even be aware of that history. In a similar vein, patterns of communication may have been inherited that limit input from various units or positions. Current members may not even be aware of when, why, or how those norms were established. These challenges, however, underscore the value of this process even further.

The bottom line of this chapter is that an awareness of and reflection on multiple elements, whether consciously held or having unconscious influence, is central to improving our ability to gain a credible and ethical understanding of a culture. Thus, before moving to the next step in the model focused on data collection, we invite you to reflect with us on these elements. Indeed, perhaps the biggest challenge we all face is to see ourselves and our enactment and/or lack of enactment of varied elements in terms of what we are creating. We proceed in this chapter by first exploring five guides for understanding and analyzing enacted elements. A review of and a way to identify levels and types of elements is provided. We conclude with a "Connection" on the role of ambiguity in studying these enacted elements. You will also find Rehearsals that encourage you to explore web sites as well as activities that provide a closer look at stories and metaphors. This chapter functions as a prelude to the coming section focused on data collection. Thus, these Rehearsals are meant to prepare you for identifying elements you will use in your analysis.

> *Reliance on one element of culture to draw inferences about effective or ethical communication behaviors is a source of communication problems for organizations.*

Reflecting on Enacted Elements of Culture

Researchers define and discuss varied elements of culture (Bolman & Deal, 2008; Pacanowsky & O'Donnell-Trujillo, 1983). The elements discussed in the following are not an exhaustive treatment but provide sufficient direction to develop a credible interpretation of the culture. Five guiding principles should be kept in mind as we discuss these elements. As we introduce these guides and then move to descriptions of the various elements, we again invite you to make a mental shift *from culture as a variable or a metaphor to culture as constituted in everyday communication practices that shape and are also shaped by culture.*

1. ***Elements of culture are not all consciously held or enacted.*** As we introduced in Chapter 3, Schein (2004) foregrounds three "layers" of organizational culture—artifacts, values, and assumptions. Schein, relying on the "culture as a root metaphor" approach, uses the term "artifacts" more broadly than we do in this text to refer to all the objects, rituals, and interactions that characterize the uniqueness of an organization. "Artifacts" are observable, and values may be inferred from observation of organizational processes. He then depicts "assumptions" at a deeper level and forms the source for values and artifacts. Important from our perspective is that we tend to be unconscious of our enactments of these elements. I may, for example, as a newcomer, express a concern about the lack of questions asked during a meeting. My concern may (or may not) prompt others to consider meeting norms that leave out questions. However, from a CCO perspective, it is important to attend to multiple elements via multiple methods (as we note in the next step) that go beyond what participants may be aware of in their self-reporting. In the example of the lack of questions, this single report from one meeting may or may not reveal individuals not speaking up as an issue. If, as several theorists note,

   > [If] we only accept that human interactants have the ability to make a difference in the ways situations unfold, we run the risk of dismissing or downplaying the ways in which our clinging to principles, values, interests, [aspects of] ideologies, norms, and experiences defines who and how we are.
   >
   > (Cooren, Matte, Benoit-Barné, & Brummans, 2013, p. 273)

   For instance, returning to the opening story, consider what is not told, what all those hearing and telling the story were not even conscious of in the telling. Consider the dark side that even made the story possible. It is conceivable that no one was aware of the lack of training rituals devoted to safety. Perhaps someone in the past commented on it, but no action was taken to address the limited lighting or security near the back door that encouraged the entry of the would-be robbers. Thus, it is an error to hear a story and then draw an inference about the culture in the absence of other elements collected through observation, such as a ritual or an artifact, that provide contextual clues to the culture in action that is out of our immediate awareness.
2. ***Enacted elements are part of a larger continuing story.*** As we described in Chapter 2, from a constructivist perspective underlying the OCA analysis process, organizational culture is continually being created and recreated through communication. Depending on the time frame of your project, some of you may have access to a very narrow slice of organization life. However, even relying on a brief slice of time, if done well, captures more than just what is being communicatively accomplished at the moment. As we will continue to stress, data from micro-level elements, such as daily dyadic interactions or communication

during a meso or group rituals, should be combined with macro or organizational and cultural level elements, such as references made to policies or history. In doing so, you gain an understanding not just of "here and now" moments of a given interaction but also the "then and there" elements that have an on-going force or influence in organizing processes. For instance, consider all that is involved in a new member adjusting to their role. The process is not simply a matter of formal onboarding (e.g., policies, history, and stated values). Perhaps more important are the questions they ask or fail to ask and/or are invited to ask when they are confused or unclear about something. Consider the influence of the coffee chat with an old-timer telling stories of "how things really work around here." The old-timers' access to history (a macro element) is part of the communicative processes that constitute the culture (Cooren & Fairhurst, 2009).

Thus, even in an analysis constrained by a few weeks of data collection time, it will allow you to gain communication insights. On a professional level, you will become more attuned to enacted elements of culture that continually shape and are shaped by organizing processes. Recall from our discussion of the value of this process (Chapter 2) that increased mindfulness of these varied processes may aid us in the way we organize in relation to ethics and diversity and change leadership.

3. ***Enacted elements are embedded in one another.*** The opening story, as already indicated, contains potential information about organizational heroes, rules, and values. A full description of a ritual, such as a holiday party, will often contain information about organizational language, rules, heroes, and other cultural elements. Or, in the same vein, communication rules may be inferred from an interview designed to gain information about metaphors or stories. One enacted element of culture, humor, will likely emerge across elements. For instance, stories told about an organizational hero might include his self-effacing humor, often evidenced in formal rituals such as recognition ceremonies and "state of the organization" speeches. Those participating in these varied rituals would quickly notice that new leaders followed this same pattern of humor. In one organization, we observed an informal communication rule embedded in stories told that could be worded as follows—"leaders should laugh at themselves and be intentional in doing so at organization-wide gatherings." This sort of embedding, attending to such moments, gives clues to communicative practices that constitute the culture and reveal values being created and assumptions held. For instance, one might learn from additional observation and interviews that an actual value, not simply an espoused one, is recreated in these varied elements, such as humility and a willingness to not take oneself "too seriously" as a way to negotiate member identity and for coordinating times of stressful decision-making.
4. ***Enacted elements appear in both official and unofficial sources.*** What is one short cut not to take if you are formally or informally reflecting on enacted elements? We imagine you guessed it. Avoid thinking you are understanding the culture if all you do is reflect on official sources: the mission statement, an annual report, and the CEO's state-of-the-company address. You may gain insights, yet the key is to reflect on elements from unofficial sources as well. For instance, listen for comments made about the mission from someone on the security or sales team. Tune into stories told around the coffee machine. What do you hear in pre-meeting talk? As you might imagine, there may be times when the aspiration values of top management are not necessarily the values of the members of the organization. In fact, asking about what is "valued" is not the best way to learn about values. Consider creative, unobtrusive ways to reflect on cultural data, such as simply asking: "What do you like about working here?" In fact, this type of question surfaced in an informal discussion at a high-tech company. The HR team was charged by the founder and CEO to launch the

organization by engaging employees at another high-tech organization founded by the same leader. She was asked to find out "What they liked about working there" and then "What could we have done better?" The intent way to identify practices that would then co-create cornerstone values of the new organization. The implication for reflection on enacted elements is to be sure to gain information not only across official and unofficial sources but also with questions that avoid employing formal language, such as values, to questions that still capture something about the culture in action.

5. ***Enacted elements vary in how widely shared they are across the organization.*** As you read this principle, perhaps you thought something like, "Do you mean not always unified? And, well, if they are not widely shared, isn't that for sure a problem?" The short answer is "not necessarily." Or, as is so often the case, the best answer is "it depends." A particular element, such as a story, may have more relevance in one unit than another. Even a value set, like "efficiency," may vary in strength from the Production versus the HR department. Yet, it is fair to ask, "Doesn't a lack of shared elements, such as values, suggest a 'weak' culture?" We are glad you asked. Allow a sneak peek of two chapters.

First, in Chapter 10 on "Change," we explore Martin's (2002) four major perspectives about ways to view the elements of culture in terms of degree of unity. She argues that these perspectives provide a way to interpret a culture and lead change. In short, not all cultures are "good" because they are unified. Also, check out the online resource that captures these perspectives in terms of a "jungle" metaphor. Second, in Chapter 13, "Effectiveness," common misunderstandings about "strong" vs. "weak" cultures are introduced. In brief, as a prelude, we note that "strong" may not be good, and "weak" may not be bad. For instance, unity around an informal communication rule that discourages upward dissent or flow of information may be widely shared and strong in one sense but not in a positive one. However, this principle we are stressing at this point is about reflecting on varied elements and withholding or bracketing initial interpretation. It is not an easy task, as we will discuss further in Step 4 on data collection and Step 5 on Interpretation. *Why, then, do we need to reflect on how shared an element of culture happens to be?*

The degree of shared culture is especially relevant when considering new forms of organizations. For example, "virtual" organizations have become commonplace in which members rarely interact face to face and enact their culture in cyberspace (Blithe, 2014; Weber & Kim, 2015). Even in these virtual organizations, culture emerges from interactions as groups develop norms about posting or as members develop power and status through their interactions. Another recent trend in organizations is outsourcing key functions such as security, training, catering, accounting, or customer service (Kalaignanam & Varadarajan, 2012). Key organization functions are performed by employees who are not members of the company. How do values get transmitted to such "quasi-employees?" Does such outsourcing weaken organizational culture? Another hybrid organizational form is the multinational organization. Consider organizations like Adobe, First Orion, and Google, with offices across the globe. The actual culture of the organization may vary based on the influence of the national culture and the communication practices of the headquarters. For instance, Gerald learned of one organization that provided HR support via personnel recruiting and hiring. Employees had adjusted to working virtually three days a week and thus in the office only on Tuesdays and Thursdays. The CEO, sensing a loss of connection (and perhaps trust in virtual workers), opted to make a shift to requiring Wednesday as an office day along with common hours. Due to commute times and clients in different time zones, there was an immediate fall-out and potential loss of staff. This and other similar challenges to norms indicate that all such organizational forms present especially interesting challenges for cultural study. The key here is to reflect on the extent to which various elements are shared. While all enacted elements are not covered in Table 4.1, reflect on those listed and others that come to your mind.

In summary, enacted elements: a) are not all consciously held or enacted; b) are part of a larger continuing story; c) are embedded in one another; d) appear in both official and unofficial sources; and e) vary in how widely shared they are across the organization. We also end this chapter with discussion questions to aid in application. In the following section, you will gain a clearer understanding and way to reflect on 14 different enacted elements of culture, some of which we take for granted or have not considered.

Enacted Elements of Culture

Glance over the major elements with examples in Table 4.2 before going any further. As you do, see if you have your own examples. Reflect on any that you had not considered before.

Table 4.1 Widely vs. Narrowly Shared Elements

Widely Shared Elements	*Narrowly Shared Elements*
Values talked about across the entire organization	Values limited to top management or certain units
Elements of culture retain consistent meanings	Elements retain inconsistent meanings
Similar stories about history and heroes are told	Varied stories about history and heroes are told
Formal rituals engage the whole organization	Formal rituals engage certain units
Metaphors are shared in common	Metaphors vary across units
Shared history diffused across the organization	History is limited to a few units

Table 4.2 Categories of Enacted Elements of Culture

Category	*Element*	*Examples*
Master Element	• **Values**	• People first
Symbolic Elements	• **Symbols** • **Stories** • **Language** • **Metaphors** • **Artifacts**	• Starbucks Mermaid • Founder's story • We "do hard" • A three-ring circus • Family pictures in offices
Role Elements	• **Heroes** • **Outlaws**	• Founding leader • Innovator against norms
Interactive Elements	• **Rituals** • **Informal and formal comm. rules** • **Humor** • **Communication style**	• Coffee chat, Picnics • Pre-meeting talks; Mandatory reporting • Was that dumb or what? • If it is not in writing, then . . .
Context Elements	• **History** • **Place**	• Back in the day when • Race relations matter here because . . .

Our guess is that before reviewing the table, most every element is one that you knew about or at least recognized. Stories, humor, rituals, and history are easily part of our enacting repertoire. Perhaps, like us, outlaws and metaphors are not often considered. However, even those we recognize most may be taken for granted. To aid in this step of deepening our knowledge and awareness, we provide definitions, examples, and options for identifying each element. An in-depth discussion of identification is provided in data collection in the chapters on methods.

Tipton and Kupritz (2017) provide additional guides and activities for teaching and exploring elements of culture and debriefing what you learn. Their guides can be useful to both the student and the practitioner. We include a Rehearsal at the end of the section to provide further practice in identifying elements. Becoming adept at identifying each of these elements will give you a framework for your formal data collection, discussed in the next section. Again, recall that the idea is to attend to more than surface or obvious enacted elements, such as norms in a meeting. Pay attention as well to informal conversations and observations that may only pick up on stories, informal rituals, and communication norms. The process outlined here requires intentionality, with the result being a more credible and ethical set of data from which to develop interpretation and communication applications. We return to Martin's (2002) model in Chapter 10 on change leadership.

We have divided 14 enacted elements into five categories: master element (values); symbolic elements (symbols, stories, language, metaphors, artifacts); role elements (heroes, outlaws); interactive elements (rituals, rules, humor, and communication style); and context variables (history and place).

Values

Definition: **The common beliefs and priorities of a group of people. Values are qualities that define a group or organization to its members.** In Schein's (2004) model (see Chapter 3), values are the second level of culture, underlying the surface layer or all observable manifestations of culture or enacted elements. Yet, we argue that values, like other enacted elements, such as heroes or language, do more than provide a clue to the core of culture (basic assumptions), but they are also created through interaction (i.e., communication rules, rituals). When organization members share values, they form a strong force for motivating the performance of employees. Tompkins and Cheney (1985) refer to this motivating force of values as "unobtrusive control." Employees don't need close supervision or an elaborate set of rules to regulate their behavior if they have strongly internalized the values of the organization. Yet, recall from a culture a "discursive construction" approach, identifying a shared value involves attending to the organizing functions of varied elements. For example, Enron, at its zenith, held collective values of boldness, risk-taking, and innovation. These values became embedded in its rituals and defined the practices of the heroes of the organization (Seeger & Ulmer, 2003; Ulmer, Sellnow, & Seeger, 2015). In contrast, building bridges with universities and congregations co-creates a value of compassion through varied rituals of community service to broken, discouraged, and scarred individuals (Glazier, Driskill, & Kirk, 2020).

Examples: Creativity, risk-taking, cooperation, customer service, work hard-play hard, accountability.

Identification: Value statements may be written in conjunction with a mission statement. However, as you collect formal value statements, be sure also to learn about values that are seen, not just heard (practiced vs. merely espoused). Inferences about values can be drawn from what the organization rewards formally or informally, by the types of individuals who are drawn to the organization, from everyday rituals, and from stories. Values may also be inferred from almost any of the other elements (e.g., stories and rituals). As such, values are considered a master element typically created through multiple cultural elements and thus a key to interpreting the culture (Meyer, 1995, 1997).

What is an example of a value shared by members of your organization?

____

____

Symbolic Enacted Elements

The four cultural elements we categorize as "symbolic enacted elements" have in common their focus on language, nonverbal symbols, and meaning. They are all significant in interpreting organizational culture because they represent an important value or meaning in the culture. The cultural elements include symbols, stories, language, metaphors, and artifacts.

Symbols

Definition: **Physical objects or icons that may formally represent the organization yet informally constitute varied organizing processes.** Organizations may develop logos to represent themselves to their public. Great thought and expense may go into choosing a logo that conveys how the organization wishes to be portrayed. Other symbols can be analyzed as well, such as varied images in corporate newsletters, annual reports, and Web pages. However, like formally espoused values, an analysis should not focus on symbols intended to draw attention to some representational image of the culture. Informal symbolic enacted elements, such as building architecture, the floor plan of an office, and the function of open or closed doors, are integral to the idea of cultures as discursive constructions, as noted in the following examples.

Examples: Open doors, signs, floor space, uniforms, logos, uniforms, colors, etc. One former client of Angi's started out with values of equality and a lack of corporate hierarchy. These values led to a corporate headquarters in which it was impossible to distinguish the office of the CEO from the office of a mid-level computer programmer. The indistinguishable offices served as an important icon representing a key value of equality within the company. At the same time, such physical symbols constituted the way members saw themselves and the communicative expectations of one another in terms of giving voice to varied employees. Physical facilities are another example of significant symbols (e.g., building(s), layout of rooms, furniture, parking lots, vehicles, pictures, signs, plaques, uniforms). For instance, Pepper (2008) examined employees' negative reactions to a new building designed to enhance openness and creativity. In use, the open building design actually inhibited open communication because of a lack of privacy, and in a depressed economy (not anticipated when the building was planned), the expensive building was seen as a lack of concern for employee jobs when layoffs occurred. Finally, the organizational Web site is a rich, modern artifact that can yield a wealth of organizational symbolism. It has become the contemporary version of the corporate handbook or newsletter. Not only the content of the website but also the visual layout, the navigation logic, and the security, or lack thereof, yield information about organizational culture.

Identification: Researchers have developed elaborate classification systems to study symbols (Axley, 1984). As with other elements of culture, it is important to probe the meaning and importance of a symbol to members of the organization. Often, a symbol that might be interpreted in one way by outsiders has a very different meaning internally. It is also important, as just discussed, to distinguish between "official" and "unofficial" organizational symbols.

What symbols might you identify in your organization? Which unofficial symbols function to constitute the organization?

Stories

Definition: **Narratives that organization members tell and newcomers hear. They are often a primary form of socialization for new organization members.** When you hear the same story or type of story from many different individuals in an organization, it likely has cultural significance. In short, stories are not simply about telling about an event but also a way in which organizing processes are created, decision-making norms and member expectations conveyed. Stories may be told that feature the storyteller or some other organizational member as a main character. The stories may be about personal lives or perhaps just about work. Stories are often disseminated organization-wide to encourage members to accept a certain value or rule. Stories may contain explicit "morals" or lessons, while other stories are subtle and allow the listener to draw conclusions. Stories may take on fantasy or mythic qualities if they begin to deal with larger-than-life characters and do not seem to be situated in time (like fairy tales, sagas, or legends).

In a classic review of types of stories, Pacanowsky (1988) suggests three types of narratives that dramatize organizational life:

a. *Corporate stories*—Carry the ideology of management and reinforce company policy.
b. *Personal stories*—Those that members tell about themselves, often defining how they would like to be seen within the organization.
c. *Collegial stories*—These are positive and negative anecdotes told about others in the organization.

Examples: Stories told about the past, present, or future; stories told for image (corporate or personal) management; socialization stories told by colleagues; exit stories; hero stories; etc. One particular type of story may be prompted when something goes wrong. As an employee in retail selling paint, Gerald recalls a cautionary tale told by his manager after he created a minor accident by not following procedure. He blew up a "fire engine red" paint. Yes, his face and shirt changed color. The manager used the occasion, with other employees gathered around, to tell about a different, but not so funny, major accident that cost the company thousands of dollars. Employees, both recent hires and old-timers, heard a story constituting a company value on following procedure. As a consultant in one hospital setting, Angi heard a wide variety of stories about status differences. All the stories had different main characters and different inferences drawn. One story might be about racial differences. Another might be about insensitive doctors being unresponsive to the needs of staff. Yet the story type of status differences was strong in the culture. In the university setting, Julien has heard stories of how colleagues manage conflict. A colleague might say to another, "close the door." This statement signals a desire to work through a conflict. In fact, one faculty member, when he first engaged in this practice, shared that his colleague said with a laugh, "Well, I am glad we finally get to really talk."

Identification: Stories may be elicited in a direct fashion: "Tell me about the stories a newcomer is likely to hear around this place. What are the stories about? What stories, if any, would you hear about personal lives? Work situations?" Yes, we encourage you to consider an indirect approach, as will be discussed in Part III on data collection. The indirect approach is often the most valid way to gain cultural information. Thus, you may simply hear statements during an informal discussion or narratives presented during a formal interview. Stories in these settings may begin with statements like, "Let me tell you what happened when . . ." or "That reminds me of a time . . ." or "The boss often repeats . . ." At times, you can elicit stories by asking for an example when interviewees discuss a value or characteristic of the organization. You should be aware that conclusions you draw from a story as an outsider might be quite different from the implications of the story for an insider. Especially interesting are "story types" that you begin to discover in an organization (c.f., Brown, 1990; Meyer, 1995; Smith & Keyton, 2001). Because stories often have multiple elements embedded in them (heroes, values, etc.), Rehearsal 4.2 provides a way to explore your own organizational stories in light of varied functions.

Write down the main ideas of a story you have heard in your organization that has symbolic significance.

___

___

Language/Nonverbal

Definition: **The particular vocabulary or terms (argot, jargon, etc.) used by members of the organization, as well as the specialized nonverbal gestures, signs, and so on, that provide clues to important aspects of the culture** (Brenton, 1993). Language distinguishes insiders from outsiders and thus helps define cultural boundaries. The specific terms used by a group, as well as grammar and message construction, are also a means for drawing inferences about a group's metaphors and values.

Examples: A university that stresses its "business plan" or "margin" or talks about its students as "customers" may have adopted a business metaphor. This type of language may be a sign of "mission drift," where economics has taken more centrality than education as the mission of the institution. Again, the key is to view language use not simply as a conveyor of information but as practices that constitute the organization.

Identification: Brenton (1993) used critical linguistic analysis to analyze a cultural conflict in a church, looking at language features such as passive or active sentence construction, specificity versus abstraction, pronoun references, and how often certain word types appeared in a text. Scott (2013), in a cultural analysis utilizing "Structuration Theory," identified the use of phrases like "meeting them halfway" or "communicating through the roof" that captured expectations for interaction and, as such, values held and rules for interaction.

Give an example of language that is significant in differentiating an insider from an outsider in your organization:

___

___

Metaphors

Definition: **Figures of speech in which one thing is seen through the lens of another; in which two objects, individuals, or events are implicitly or explicitly compared to one another.**

Examples: We are a . . . team, family, circus, machine, growing plants. The metaphor of "family" is perhaps one most often heard. A small company may describe itself as a family because of close relationships among organization members. The metaphor is consistent with the values of caring, nurturing, and permanent commitments. The values embedded in the metaphor are also found in patterns of rituals, informal rules, heroes, and communication networks that profoundly affect how the company does business. While the metaphor may have great utility, it will pose limits for the company during financial stress. How do you lay off a family member? Why should the bottom line take precedence over the best health care insurance possible when providing for the family? It also may be challenged during times of corporate growth and change. While the family metaphor may work well in a small to medium-sized organization, it quickly becomes unwieldy when the company grows larger. Smith and Eisenberg (1987), in their now classic study of Disneyland, discuss the changes from the perspective of a root metaphor. Conflicts between management and employees surfaced as management relied more on a drama metaphor tied to profit and business while employees focused more on a family metaphor. Furthermore, it is important to listen for nuanced metaphors. Thus, asking members of the organization (or reading between the lines) might help you discern what "type of family" they have in mind (i.e., close-knit, blended, dysfunctional, etc.).

One of our students studied a temporary employment agency that characterized itself as a "pride of lions." All the managers were male, and the agents who processed orders and served employees were female. For some of the employees, the metaphor captured role division and gender status differences within the agency, as well as values of interdependence and competitiveness of the environment. In another analysis across organizations, metaphors surfaced as a primary means for describing the experience of workplace bullying (Tracy, Lungen-Sandvik, & Alberts, 2006). Metaphors, as these examples reflect, promise to provide a rich array of cultural meanings. In fact, Holger, Gross, Hartman, and Cunliffe (2008) argue that metaphor is a key ingredient in language and, as such, is foundational in holding the culture of an organization together.

Identification: Naturally occurring metaphors, which emerge from language patterns, are generally more valid in cultural analysis than artificially generated ones (Smith & Keyton, 2001). An artificially generated metaphor might be elicited by a question such as, "If this company were an animal, what would it be?" One can infer metaphors from language patterns, heroes, rituals, or other enacted elements. For example, if employees use terms such as "battle plan," "chain of command," "search and destroy," and "war games," it would be fair to assume that the culture is influenced by a military metaphor. Metaphors offer insight into rules and values. In the military metaphor example, you would expect to find values and norms of loyalty, obedience to orders, and respect for hierarchical positions within the organization. Rehearsal 4.3 provides direction on using metaphors to initiate the analysis process.

What metaphor(s) symbolize(s) your organizational culture?

____

____

Artifacts

Definition: **"phenomena that you would see, hear, and feel when you encounter a new group with an unfamiliar culture"** (Schein & Schein, 2016, p. 17). As such, they may constitute values or other enacted elements such as history and heroes.

Examples: logos, workout equipment, ping pong tables, office layout, artistic creations such as pictures, wall hangings, statues; clothing, manners of address, and emotional displays; its myths and stories told about the organization; its published lists of values; and its observable rituals and ceremonies

Identification: As what Schein and Schein (2016) consider the first level of culture, artifacts may represent role elements, such as pictures of the founder or of the first corporate headquarters. As such, this element may be embedded in ways the organization consciously tries to build on its history, legends, and heroes through rituals that include displays of values with images. For instance, imagine in the context of a healthcare organization tapestries displaying caregivers administering care. Alone, such an artifact takes on added meaning when you learn that the hero in the picture is from the early days of the organization known for compassionate hospice care.

What artifact(s) are present that constitute your organizational culture?

____

____

Role Enacted Elements

Although some authors, such as Deal and Kennedy (1982, 2000), identify a large number of cultural roles, such as a high priest, storyteller, and cabal member, we have found two roles especially helpful in understanding cultures. These two roles are heroes and outlaws.

Heroes

Definition: **Individuals or groups who are respected by a large number of individuals within the organization because they embody group values.**

Examples: Stories, rituals, and an examination of history reveal the continuing influence of founder-heroes such as Sam Walton and Walt Disney. Stories about Sam Walton still abound among Wal-Mart employees—from his driving a beat-up pickup truck to leading cheers with associates at Wal-Mart stores. A hero may also be someone other than a founder or a CEO, though. For example, in one church organization, an 85-year-old church secretary named Helen was widely cited by members as "the heart of the church" and "the custodian of all church stories, history, and procedures." Church leaders had come and gone over the years while Helen had remained. Her mentoring of new members, her structuring of church services, and her much-sought approval demonstrated her influence over church practices. One member told a story of a minister who didn't stay long once he earned Helen's ire. A critical time in any organization is the transition after the death or retirement of a hero. In most cases, the hero's influence remains through prominently displayed pictures and symbols, much-repeated stories, and influence on leadership succession processes. If new heroes fail to emerge over time, however, the organization may drift from its values and history.

Identification: The "hero" may or may not have high formal status within the organization. It is surprising how often you find quick consensus, however, when you begin asking individuals questions such as, "Who is a hero here?" "Who is an organization member you most respect?" "Who embodies this organization at its best?" Within most organizational stories, heroes are easily found. Heroes reveal a great deal about communication rules and cultural values.

Who is a hero in your organization, and why?

Outlaws

Definition: **Individuals who seem to be paradoxes in the organization, who defy organizational practices or values yet remain as valued members of the organization because they exemplify counter-cultural values that the organization wishes to cultivate.**

Examples: Angi belonged to one of the largest Rotary clubs in the United States, with more than 500 members. Most Tuesdays at lunch, one can look over a sea of sameness of American button-down business leaders. The shade of the tie may vary here or there, and the color of the suit may range from charcoal to navy, but the homogeneity is obvious—as are the informal rules of interaction: polite conversation. No rocking the boat with a political conversation, raised voices, or divisive topics. That is until you see Rollie—usually dressed in a Ducks Unlimited sweatshirt and always carrying one of his trademark hand-carved walking sticks. Any time he gets the microphone, which is frequently, he may "Call the Hogs" (an Arkansas football cheer), call the ducks, or tell everyone about his latest political protégé. Why has he gained almost legendary status when he follows almost none of the rules typical of the culture? Maybe because he embodies the spontaneity, fun, honesty, and bravado that many of the business leaders would like to emulate.

Identification: In interviews, you might ask a question like, "Who is someone in this organization who is different, who doesn't follow all the rules but is still valued?" You can also simply observe organizational interaction. Outlaws are usually easy to spot because they are dressed differently and interact with others in noticeably different ways than most organization members. Like heroes, outlaws reveal a great deal about communication rules and cultural values. They may embody subtle subordinate values missed in other elements. Outlaws are particularly interesting to identify and study. If they are expelled from the organization, the reasons for their expulsion tell a great deal about organizational norms and values. If they are allowed to remain in the organization, it may be because they embody important counterculture values (such as creativity in a traditional culture) that the organization wants to support. It is also interesting to discover times of cultural change when a former outlaw becomes a hero or when an outlaw who was previously tolerated in an organization is expelled or disciplined.

Who is someone who seems to break all the rules in your organization yet is allowed to remain a valued member? Why?

Interactive Cultural Enacted Elements

The four cultural elements we have identified as "interactive" exist in interactions between members of the organization. They are a clear example of the theory of structuration explained in Chapter 2. They are created through interaction, yet can also constrain the improvisation of actors within the culture. These elements are rituals, rules, humor, and organizational communication style and are explained in what follows.

Rituals

Definition: **Rituals are planned and unplanned events that are carried out through social interaction with explicit or implicit purposes and that have multiple social consequences** (Trice & Beyer, 1985). More than an event, though, from one CCO perspective, rituals may "display agency" or serve as "actants" that "make the organization present and thus display agency among organizational members" (Koschmann & McDonald, 2015, p. 235). The power of ritual is their role in enacting, beyond any one individual, an "authoritative text," a "manifestation of the organization that is 'read' in such a way that it becomes an official interpretation for most organizational members" (Koschmann & McDonald, 2015, p. 236). In other words, rituals have power because they capture and recreate norms and values in and beyond corporate documents and policies. Their significance is further underscored by varied types.

Six basic types of rituals (or rites) include passage, integration, enhancement, degradation, renewal, and conflict reduction (Trice & Beyer, 1985, 1993). Theorists argue that these various rituals are concerned with a) transformation, or the shifting of the social positions or statuses of organizational actors; and b) stability, or "the maintenance of a communal set of cultural beliefs and values" (Islam & Zyphur, 2009, p. 125). They also stress that other groups beyond management initiate and maintain them. In addition, nine interdependent functions of rituals include: 1) provide meaning; 2) manage anxiety; 3) exemplify and reinforce the social order; 4) communicate important values; 5) enhance group solidarity; 6) include and exclude; 7) signal commitment; 8) manage work structure; and 9) prescribe and reinforce significant events (Smith & Stewart, 2011).

Rituals form a rich source of data from which to mine inferences about other enacted elements of culture, such as symbols, values, rules, and cultural heroes. Trice and Beyer (1985, 1993) claim that rites are the richest and deepest sources of cultural understanding, containing the most symbolic impact. They go on to encourage attention to rites and rituals because leaders typically conduct or sponsor them without being aware of their significance. We attend to their significance in the method's chapter on observation (Rehearsal 6.1), applying the six types of rituals listed previously. We encourage you to begin an initial reflection on rituals in your organization in the space that follows.

Examples: Informal office gatherings, award and retirement ceremonies, coffee room talk, performance reviews, holiday parties, and collective bargaining. Rituals may have embedded in them routine behaviors that may include gossip, humor, play, language, rules, and values. For instance, play might be a routine expectation at a retreat. Yet, what members count as play, in contrast to work, serves critically important functions. For instance, play may function to save face, socialize, convey membership, and gain perspective on negative or tragic organizational events (Bolman & Deal, 2008; Meyer, 1997, 2000). In a similar way, play may encourage flexibility and adaptation. In addition, as you attend to the obvious, such as a business meeting, be sure to capture what happens prior to such events. Mirivel and Tracy (2005) captured several forms of pre-meeting talk. For instance, "small talk" focuses on relationship building, but other less obvious forms, such as "shop talk," involve discussions "about people, events, and issues that link to the workplace" (p. 16). Furthermore, attend to routine behaviors at the end of the meeting. In one virtual organization, as a way to discern support for decisions made, the person leading the meeting would ask for a "fist of five" as a way to elicit communication. Then, everyone held up the number of fingers to indicate their level of support (Scott, 2013). In short, be sure to attend to communication formal and informal ritualized interactions before, during, and after the formal ritual.

Notice as well that rituals are dynamic. They change and might evolve over time. In our own department, for example, instead of meeting face-to-face, we responded to the pandemic by moving our meetings completely virtually. We still hold on to this format to honor faculty who live further away. But, to create opportunities for small talk, sharing, and engagement, every faculty meeting begins with an important ritual: "Connect Time." Often driven by questions like "What are you grateful for today?" or "A favorite teaching moment," every faculty member is given the opportunity to share a personal story. This ritual exemplifies and constitutes values embodied in our mission, which is "to foster the co-creation of better social worlds through positive communication." As our department evolves, it is possible that this ritual will change, as well as others integrated that have yet to be developed.

Identification: One way to identify formal and informal rituals, beyond observing them, is to ask about the events that characterize the organization. For instance, are family picnics or Friday afternoon happy hours common? Or are members rewarded, either formally or informally? Does the organization have rites for recognizing stakeholders outside of the organization (community members, volunteers)? Once you have identified rituals, you can probe for values, rules, roles, networks, and heroes. For example, you might ask questions like: What signs of status are apparent from interactions? How do employees do their work? How do they greet strangers/customers/visitors? How do they interact in meetings?

What is a ritual in your organization? What does it tell you about the culture?

Informal and Formal Rules

Definition: **Informal organizational norms tell what behavior is preferred, permitted, required, or prohibited in organizational life.** Organization and logic that provides for behavior production (Sigman, 1980).

Examples: How to talk and when to talk during a meeting, interaction norms during performance reviews, greeting expectations, conflict management norms, etc. When Angi began as an assistant professor years ago, several colleagues took care to share a story about an assistant professor who, as legend had it, was denied tenure the year after he refused a request by the dean to chair the college United Way effort. She was left to deduce her own conclusions about organizational norms from the story. Was it expected that all employees would be active in United Way because of a strong community engagement? Was it prohibited for a junior faculty member to deny a request from the dean? Another example of the significance of informal or unconsciously held rules can be found by looking at decision-making processes. Jabs (2005) explored informal rules in the context of decisions surrounding the Challenger space shuttle disaster. One of the four rules she identified was: "subordinates (often engineers) should limit their input according to the interest level and receptivity of the managerial" (p. 286). In the context of gossip in a virtual organization, members had developed the norm of a "bookend" of asking colleagues to keep what they shared confidential (Blithe, 2014, p. 64). These examples support the importance of identifying informal rules both for aiding individuals adjusting to a new culture as well as to significant decision-making processes. These information rules may, indeed, provide clues to unethical and/or harmful patterns of interaction.

Identification: Uncovering the complex, often unconscious ways of thinking in an organization that makes some actions obligatory, some permissible, some discouraged, and some prohibited is challenging. You may find rules for behavior listed in an employee handbook (no smoking, etc.). However, informal cultural rules are rarely explicitly stated. Because rules operate in the unconscious, taken-for-granted realm, organizational members might not be able to identify rules if they are asked a direct question. Yet, in a story about a hero or an outlaw, you may learn what types of behaviors are encouraged or discouraged. You also can uncover rules in field observations of interactions among culture members. When you observe regularities of behavior over time and across actors, the regularity is generally produced by informal cultural rules. Who calls whom by first names or formal titles? Do people arrive early or late for meetings? Who is exempt from the "corporate uniform" and why? What distinguishes those who get promotions and honors from those who do not? What are common threads among those who are fired or voluntarily choose to leave the organization? It is important, once you identify the regularity, to ask organizational members to explain it. Their underlying logic is the key element in identifying the cultural norm or rule. Informal cultural rules are embodiments of organizational values and a direct outgrowth of organizational metaphors (Schall, 1983).

How might you then word an inferred rule based on observation? It can be useful to consider two different types of rules. First, a regulative rule has to do with the logic following an "if-then" pattern. For example, "If interacting before a meeting, then ask questions about events outside of work." Or, "If engaged in a performance review, then be prepared to discuss specific growth plans." Regulative rules suggest a certain implicit "ought" or contextual force to act in certain ways. A second type of communication rule is a constitutive or meaning-making rule. This type of rule clues you into the way meanings are being constructed. For example, pre-meeting exchanges about non-work events may be interpreted as valuing people for more than just what they do at work, or discussing growth plans in a review process might be interpreted as valuing a process of inviting others to support co-created goals. Like regulative rules, it is important to recognize that rules are learned and may not always be shared by all. One person, for instance, may interpret the pre-meeting talk as a waste of time and either keep those views to himself or seek support from others to interpret them in this way. For example, in one organization, one regulative rule was: "If a colleague makes a demeaning comment about you, you should respond in kind." The implicit meaning-making rule was to treat such an interaction as a playful speech act. However, in time, a few members had conversations about the possible harm caused by demeaning comments, even if meant as humorous. Thus, this practice disappeared, at least in formal workplace conversations. Also, while these examples are positive in nature, we recognize that rules are not always positive. As indicated previously, communication rules might form that create a sense of obligation not to share information, not confront unethical behaviors, etc.

What are informal norms at your organization that may not be written down but still have a strong effect on behaviors?

____

____

Humor

Definition: **Humor has been defined as "the capacity to perceive actions as funny, respond to an amusing stimulus, or create something that elicits amusement"** (Meyer, 2015, p. 1). Humor, as we have all experienced, may enhance our relationship or create division and confusion. (Meyer, 2000) indicates two uniting functions of humor—"mutual identification and clarification of positions and values" as well as two dividing functions—"enforcement of norms and differentiation of acceptable versus unacceptable behaviors" (p. 310). As such, the significance of humor in co-creating cultural patterns merits our attention.

Examples: Humor may surface then in informal communication rules. One organization's CEO maintains the norm of making sure members of his team laugh at themselves by offering self-effacing humor and being able to "take a joke." His view was that leaders may take themselves too seriously without such signs of humility. Humor may also surface in stories that function to unite. So, stories may also be told of shared events, even tragic ones, that trigger laughter at the antics of those who survived despite failures. Humor may also, then, divide by someone implicitly inviting you to laugh at a colleague or a boss. As such, supervisors should take care in creating division and reducing trust between groups (Ramsey & Meyer, 2024; Wolfgruber, 2023). In addition, humor may surface in irony or satire. Research on irony indicates it is a marker for and toward encouraging change (Sillince & Barker, 2012). For example, in an analysis of discourse related to ethnic diversity in churches, irony was a resource for change as a participant co-created an ironic moment. The moment occurred when someone noted the impossibility of integration of churches until heaven, and yet this statement was ironically made in a building that hosted a multiethnic church (Driskill, Arjannikova, & Meyer, 2014; For instance, the role of "situational irony" based in incongruities has also been explored in the context of the international relief organization, "Doctors without Borders." The authors identified situational ironies in such statements as "a hospital director" opposing "a humanitarian organization's health programs" or "humanitarian aid workers . . . almost forced to participate in a program that appears to go against their own organization's medical standards" (Cooren, Matte, Benoit-Barné, & Brummans, 2013, p. 260).

Identification: Discerning what "counts" as humor may be challenging, given the inevitable role of ambiguity (Meyer, 2015). Yes, laughter at a meeting may be a sign of humor, but as we all know, some types of humor may not elicit laughter. In other words, they can be "funny-ha-ha" moments, but humor may also be about "funny-ah-ha" moments when we may not laugh out loud but gain perspective that is simultaneously funny and enlightening.

Listening closely then for laughter or incongruous statements can help mark humor. The key—do not take "light" moments, times when the mood is lightened by a humorous anecdote, as unimportant. For instance, the presence or absence of laughter can be indicative of the warmth and experience between members of the organization. Recently, Julien has been undergoing physical therapy to heal from an injury. Almost twice a week, he goes to the local clinic to work on drills, exercises, and treatment. While doing the activity, he has noticed that at every single appointment, as the sessions unfold with clients, the physical therapists find ways of laughing together. They make jokes, challenge each other, or simply share a story. But in spite of the context in which suffering and pain are likely, the physical therapists are cultivating a warm environment driven by play, good-natured humor, and social support for one another. The presence of humor, in so many ways, really matters for both the therapists who are fostering their relationship and also for what he says to clients who are on the journey to recovery.

What are the norms in your organization related to humor? What exactly counts as humor? How is it functioning (e.g., release stress, control, maintain structure, teach a lesson, suggest the need for change?)

Organizational Communication Style

Definition: **A collective preference by organization members for certain channels of communication. Usually, organizations fall into three "styles": oral/interpersonal, written/formal documentation, and electronic.**

Examples: One major aspect of culture involves the collective communication patterns and preferences of the group. Some prefer **face-to-face communication in an oral tradition**. They value personal contact and may not "count" that they have received a message until someone has talked to them about it. A typical comment might be, "I saw some memo about that, but no one has actually talked to me about it yet." Cultural socialization and history are conveyed through stories and interactions. A fatal flaw in such a culture would be offering feedback or praise to a group through a memo versus a more personal contact. Change must be achieved by face-to-face appeals and coalition building.

A written culture, on the other hand, places emphasis on standardization of procedure and formal documentary evidence. This communication culture is most prevalent in bureaucratic organizations or in organizations with a high proclivity toward legal actions or grievances. In this culture, oral communication does not "count." A comment in a meeting must be followed by a formal written proposal. A request is not considered effective until it is put into writing. An affirmation would seem incomplete unless it is formalized in writing with copies to all affected parties.

A hybrid of the written culture is the **electronic communication culture**. In this culture, speed and ease of communication are highly valued, perhaps because the pace of change is intensified in highly competitive and fast-moving fields. Furthermore, the growth of "virtual" organizations may mean employees who only make contact with each other electronically, perhaps with quarterly or annual face-to-face meetings. Organization members are expected to be accessible through e-mail, text, voice mail, google hangouts, chat, and/or cell phone at any given time. In this culture, a faux pas might be sending a message by "snail" mail instead of by a more rapid channel, insisting on a paper copy instead of an electronic communication, or failing to check messages frequently. Challenges within this culture include information overload, improperly targeted messages, and "flaming," in which anger is more easily expressed in impersonal channels. The key is to discern the types of formal and informal rules that have emerged in terms of communication format, timing, etc. For instance, one study showed national culture differences between the on-line communication norms of French and Moroccan nationals (Moroccia, 2012). As such, your analysis should attend not simply to the style but to the communicative norms associated with that style.

Angi consulted with a company in the midst of cultural change. Along with changes in organizational structure, a change in communication style had gone almost unnoticed. The organization, before the round of changes, had a strong oral/interpersonal communication culture but now had shifted to an electronic communication style. Soon, employees no longer knew who was in charge of what and whom to call when emergencies arose. Complaints abounded about the difficulty of navigation, impersonality, and competition among branches. Most of these arose out of grief over losing a comfortable and efficient culture of communication without it being replaced by a clear strategy for how electronic means could serve the same functions as the previous communication culture.

Identification: You can ask organization members in interviews how most people communicate with one another. You can also observe face-to-face interactions, meeting schedules, the inbox (how many paper transactions), and the average number of emails per day.

What is the communication style of your organization? How do you know?

____

____

Context Enacted Elements

The two elements we classify as context elements, history and place, recognize that organizational culture is shaped by its placement in space and time. An organization located in India will develop different values and norms from one located in France. An organization located in New York City will have a different climate from one formed in Plains, Georgia. Organizations also do not exist in a time vacuum. Their history is vital for understanding how the organization was founded and how it has changed. It is hard to understand present organizational patterns without grounding cultural understanding in the organization's history.

History

Definition: **History involves knowledge of the purposes of its founding and how it has evolved over the years; it also involves knowing information about the founders of the organization.** Learning the history of an organization—the time period at which it was formed, the purposes for which it was formed, and the personality of the individual(s) who founded it—can offer great insight into persisting organizational patterns or resistance to change. The insights gleaned from history are valuable even when organizations have changed dramatically from their initial beginnings.

Examples: Stories by founders, crisis events that shaped values and practices, past mergers, etc. One of Angi's clients was a large university hospital with roots as a charity hospital for indigent patients. Even though it has now grown into an internationally recognized medical center, the value of offering universal access to health care remains. Understanding the historical value of access to care explains the tensions that result from serving different patient populations.

History reveals the continuing influence of a founder such as Sam Walton or Walt Disney. It is enlightening to determine how much organizational members know about organizational history. For example, a cultural analysis process was performed in a publishing group that started on a shoestring. Each employee we interviewed, and even recent hires, could tell about the early days when writers signed on with no salary and just a promise of future profit sharing. Most could tell about the first winter in a warehouse so cold that writers draped a stray cat across their shoulders for warmth as they sat before a typewriter. History was a vibrant part of the culture because the publishing group did not want to leave behind the value of passionate dedication to creativity. In organizations drifting away from founding values, members often know little about history. In contrast, a founder's values may guide the response of an organization facing a crisis (Ulmer, 2001).

Identification: History, like the other elements, is often embedded in stories of heroes or the founding of the organization. Rituals that capture certain common organizational memories are also important places to gain a sense of the history of a place. Artifacts, such as pictures of the founder or pictures of earlier corporate headquarters, also show that an organization consciously tries to build on its history.

What do you know about your organization's history? How does your knowledge affect your present behavior in the organization?

Rehearsal 4.1 Exploring Websites: Applying Principles

Purpose: Identify enacted elements that can be assessed from a company Website in tangent with identifying unofficial sources to discern espoused vs. actual culture and the degree culture is shared.

Steps:

1. Identify two different company or organization Websites. We encourage you to select organizations of interest to you in terms of consulting, career development, or benchmarking.
2. Identify as many different elements of culture as possible based on Table 4.2.
3. State the unofficial sources you might explore to determine the extent to which these are espoused as corporate-only level elements.
4. Indicate how you would assess the extent to which these are shared.
5. How would you determine how widely shared they are across the organization?

Place

Definition: **the complex environment in which an organization resides, whether it is a community, a state, a nation, or a multinational context.**

Example: Organizations are products of their environments, as well as entities that shape their environments—the same duality of creativity and constraint discussed earlier in structuration theory.

For example, one university leader's inaugural speech to various stakeholders stressed the need to address race relations because of the location of their organization. Place then also gave rise to enacted elements in this university, as evidenced by the stories and rituals that developed. Attending to "place" involves a complexity born of the growth of new economies. For instance, as part of the creative economy, employees such as university professors, software developers, medical researchers, information engineers, and others have highly portable careers. They can choose to live and work where they want. They tend to live in environments characterized by technology infrastructure, diversity, and rich cultural life, and the companies follow (Florida, 2002). Add to this list the development of the "gig" economy. A 2023 survey of 3,000 US professionals indicated that 38% of labor participants (64 million) engaged in freelance work, which is 4 million more than the previous year (Freelance Forward, 2023). Research on "place" tied to the "gig" economy would require learning about the ethical downside of workers without traditional workplace protections (e.g., sick days, health and safety precautions) (Zipperer et al., 2022).

Identification: This element challenges the researcher to move beyond observation of the internal environment to consider the impact of "place," which may be included in varied stories, history, and statements made related to values. What are the characteristics of the external environment? Big city or small? Homogeneous or diverse? History of race relations? Traditional or cutting edge? Prosperous or struggling? How does the environment contribute to the organization's culture? How does the organization contribute to its environment?

How does the physical environment in which your organization is located affect the organizational culture?

Take a moment to read your reflections about the enacted elements. What is your writing teaching you about your organization? What is to be done or not done? How can you best support the culture? How could you be an effective (and positive) change agent?

Connections: What About Ambiguity?

Enacted elements of culture may be viewed as the primary roles in the organizational culture drama. From your reading of the different elements and reflection on your experiences in organizations, did you notice instances when a rule, story, or ritual was complex, multifaceted, layered, or ambiguous in its meaning? For instance, in the burglar story at the beginning of the chapter, the moral of the story might be that even a great manager can make a nearly deadly mistake. Or conversely, it might be that the moral is about bravery in that this manager saved the day by recognizing that these burglars were a joke and not to be taken seriously. The meaning of the tale and its significance to the company depends on who retells it and for what purposes. Is it, for instance, told at an orientation on safety, or is it told at a picnic in which the virtues of brave managers are extolled? Part of its value and richness in embodying and shaping the culture is because of this very ambiguity. After defining and stressing the significance of ambiguity, we turn to its varied, too easily overlooked functions.

The Significance of Ambiguity

The notion of ambiguity in meaning is critical to interpreting and applying cultural data. Smith and Eisenberg (1987) (c.f., Meyer, 2009; Meyerson & Martin, 1987; Morgan, 2006) have drawn attention to the role of strategic ambiguity in organizational communication. Strategic ambiguity is being deliberately unclear or nonspecific for a strategic purpose. Common assumptions about organizational communication often deal with clarity and certainty about messages and meanings. This is especially true in popular literature about organizational culture. Leaders are encouraged to send clear and specific messages about values and expectations. However, the importance and existence of ambiguity should not be overlooked. Another way to think about ambiguity is to consider the value of being able to look at something in a different way. If all communication were clear and certain, there would be no room for adjustments, change, and alternative perspectives.

Functions of Ambiguity

Have you ever considered times when you saw value in a vague statement? Perhaps it was used to avoid a conflict (i.e., "Perhaps you are right, let's move on to talk about . . .") or to encourage unity in the midst of difference ("What matters now is we all care about . . ."). In particular, consider the following functions:

a. Creating unity in the midst of organizational change. Eisenberg (1984) points out that strategic ambiguity allows for "unified diversity" in which different groups within an organization can feel a common commitment to an abstract value (e.g., unity or collaboration) in which each can read its own connotations. Such unity would break down with more specifically drawn goals. For instance, consider the contrasting calls to action: "We have to agree that we will . . ."
b. Using ambiguity in a ritual to introduce a problem. Rituals may be exploited by those wishing to initiate change. For instance, Brenton (1993) studied the ritual of "going forward" at the end of a church service e. One member, in conflict with the leadership, utilized this ritual to confess his problems and sins in dealing with a particular issue. His confession was within the rules of this ritual; however, he also tapped into ambiguity by implicating leadership failures and challenging their authority. This moment proved to be a catalyst for change.
c. Resist change. Meyer (2009) found the use of ambiguous terms such as "unity" allowed for continuity in worship styles in a church setting. Leaders in his case study worked against those seeking change by claiming the value of "unity."
d. Risk and Crisis. Firefighter's daily talk includes ambiguous terms that help them downplay the level of risk in certain aspects of their job (Scott & Tretheway, 2008). In the context of crisis management, leaders use ambiguity in ways that privilege financial stakeholders. For instance, in the context of the tobacco industry, they argue that biased and incomplete information is used in strategically ambiguous ways and thus fails to provide stakeholders with "significant choice"—complete and relevant information to make decisions free from coercion (Ulmer & Sellnow, 1997).

In all, the concept of ambiguity connects with the notion of culture as a resource. In other words, ambiguity is not all bad. Indeed, ambiguity is used unethically and may create a source of confusion or "action paralysis," yet it can be a resource for innovation (Martin, 1992, p. 134) and for organizational renewal (Ulmer, Sellnow, & Seeger, 2015). The competent leader taps ambiguity to advance ethical performance goals. We need not be trapped in the web of culture. Instead, tapping into cultural resources develops and enacts meanings important for effective and ethical leadership.

Summary

We hope none of you have had to "hit the floor" during an attempted robbery. Tragically, it would not be the last such moment in Gerald's time in restaurants. Fast forward to about 1997. While dining out, his wife and friends had to hit the floor as armed robbers entered the restaurant. This time, there was no laughter. Only a gunshot and sirens. Later, we joined in group counseling to hear and learn to respond to a therapist's words, "Be kind to yourself. Be gentle." "Be kind to yourself. Be gentle."

Such moments remind us again of our interconnectedness in varied organizations from "cradle to grave." Our stories, the unique and taken-for-granted ones, the tragic, comic, and too-good-to-be true ones, are included in listening for and attending to enacted elements of culture.

Although we observe and participate in varied enacted elements every day, until now, you may not have recognized their significance in creating culture. While we may not formally reflect on implied rules or see a coffee break routine as an important ritual, we nevertheless learn, respond to, and enact cultures every day. This awareness can aid in co-creating more ethical and effective cultures that co-create better social worlds. Specifically, we learned that enacted elements: a) are not all consciously held or enacted; b) are part of a larger continuing story; c) are embedded in one another; d) appear in both official and unofficial sources, e) vary in how widely shared they are across the organization. In addition, the richness and challenge of cultural elements is their ambiguity and, therefore, their ability to convey multiple meanings simultaneously—meanings that may have ethical or unethical motives.

You have gained an awareness of cultural elements and insight into how to identify them systematically. The next task is to refine your ability to gather in-depth information about each of these elements before interpreting and applying their meaning. Thus, the next section introduces the third step, using multiple methods to collect cultural data via enacted elements.

Rehearsal 4.2 Getting More From Our Stories

Purpose: Review six major functions of stories before engaging in a practice analysis of stories from your experiences in organizations.

Rationale: The role of narratives or stories in understanding our organizational communication experiences is common both in and outside academia (Fisher, 1987; Kirkwood, 1983, 1985, 1992), including the use of stories to improve daycare communication practices (Meyer & Driskill, 1997). Stories range from mundane first job memories to ethical dilemmas to examples of the way a change in management practice can reshape an entire work environment as well as how we are shaped by our response to positive and negative experiences.

Directions:

1. Review the following six functions of stories:

    - *Life review or life construction.* Stories begin early in life. The standard question, "So, what did you do at school today?" is an invitation to create a story—to piece together events in a way that will make sense to us and to others. To be human is to be a storyteller.
    - *Passing on values and norms.* Rather than simply saying, "That is not how we do things around here," a member might socialize with a new member by telling about the fate of someone who did things right (or wrong).
    - *Creating a virtual shared reality.* Bormann (1969) writes about narrative functioning to create community among strangers.
    - *Exploration of your own communication practices.* Each story can reveal the cultural constraints and resources you perceive (e.g., your ethics, reactions to authority, relationships with coworkers, and response to change).
    - *Empower changes in their group or organization.* Counter-narratives function to provide missing, inaccurate, incomplete, and/or damaged social constructions (Papa, Singhal, & Papa, 2006). For instance, a story could capture a shift from a sole focus on short-term profits. For example, counternarratives surface in the healthcare context (Harter, 2009; Harter et al., 2006).
    - *Analyze culture.* Stories say something about the context of the stories. That context includes both the broader national culture as well as the immediate organizational culture (e.g., Driskill, 1995; Driskill & Downs, 1995).

2. Make a list of four to six organizations that you have belonged to and/or currently belong to.
3. Review this list, and then, based on your memories of events in the previously mentioned organizations, write down four organizational experiences (stories of any type) that come to your mind. Do not take time to analyze or write details. Instead, jot down a phrase in two lines or less that captures the event. If you draw blanks before you reach four experiences, review your list of ten organizations and ask: "Now, what experiences first come to my mind when I think about my time with organization 'X'?" Put down the first stories that come to mind.
4. Reflect on the following questions concerning the stories you recalled:

    - What themes predominated in your organizational stories?
    - Do you have stories of success as well as failure?
    - Do you have stories that you would still rather not talk about?
    - Are there situations that still perplex you?
    - Do you have stories that still excite and motivate you? Did you find examples of counter-narratives?

Rehearsal 4.3 A Game of Metaphors

Purpose: Discern the significance of applying a metaphor to enhance awareness of life in your organization.

Rationale: We act out "cultural" scripts of what we view as appropriate and effective communication (Fairhurst, 2011; Fairhurst & Sarr, 1996). Even in an era of film, videos, and reels, it is hard to see our own performances, our ways of responding to organizational structures. We have neither the eyes nor the objectivity of an outsider for viewing our own actions. A metaphor game can help gain some perspective. Let us illustrate.

If someone were to ask Gerald what it is like to work at the university, one answer would be that it is like being on a "team of circus clowns." The metaphor refers to a department that maintains a sense of humor amid the constant coordination needed to adjust to continuous changes. Angi, in a past role as an administrator at a Christian university, might use the metaphor of a Japanese Kabuki theater—thick masks often concealing personal identities and feelings, with a high degree of drama and traditional ritual.

Directions:

1. Identify a metaphor or analogy that comes to mind that best captures one of your own organizations. Perhaps you can think of more than one metaphor. These metaphors, as we will see, provide a rich source of insight. For example, Gerald's circus metaphor suggests the expectation of being able to take a joke and other roles of humor associated with workload pressures. The circus clown metaphor also suggests that if you cannot laugh at yourself, your own mistakes and limits, as others laugh with you, then you will not be viewed as an effective member of the organization.
2. After you identify one or more metaphors, reflect on the following questions:
   - What does the metaphor reveal about what is permitted in the organization?
   - What does the metaphor reveal about what is prohibited in the organization?
   - How widely held is the metaphor (i.e., across departments, roles, etc.)?
   - What does the metaphor suggest about organizational values?

Discussion Questions

1. What does it mean to say that an organization is "constituted" in various elements of culture?
2. Which of the elements do you view as most likely not to be consciously held or enacted (Principle #1).
3. How would you explain the importance of recognizing that these enacted elements are part of a larger continuing story? (Principle #2) How can you be sure the "chapter" or time frame you study best captures that larger story?
4. Reflect on an enacted element that is likely to have more than one element embedded in it. (Principle #3) Give an example. What insight do you draw from this awareness?

5. What formal as well as informal sources of cultural elements do you tend to pay the most attention to each day? (Principle #4) How might reflecting on your current tendency aid you in being more effective in future reflections?
6. What stories and/or humor did you hear when you first became part of an organization? What did they tell you about the culture? How widely shared were they? (Principle #5).

References

Axley, S. (1984). Managerial and organizational communication in terms of the conduit metaphor. *Academy of Management Review, 9*, 428–437. https://doi.org/10.1177/0893318991004003005

Blithe, S. J. (2014). Creating the water cooler: Virtual workers' discursive practices of gossip. *Qualitative Research Reports in Communication, 15(1)*, 59–65. https://doi.org/10.1080/17459435.2014.955593

Bolman, L., & Deal, T. (2008). *Reframing organizations* (4th ed.). San Francisco: Jossey-Bass.

Bormann, E. (1969). *Interpersonal communication in the modern organization.* Englewood Cliffs, NJ: Prentice Hall.

Brenton, A. (1993). Demystifying the magic of language: Critical linguistic case analysis of legitimization of authority. *Journal of Applied Communication Research, 21*, 227–244. https://doi.org/10.1080/00909889309365369

Brown, M. H. (1990). Defining stories in organizations: Characteristics and functions. In J. A. Anderson (Ed.), *Communication yearbook* (Vol. 13, pp. 162–190). Newbury Park, CA: Sage.

Cooren, F., & Fairhurst, G. (2009). Dislocation and stabilization: How to scale up from interactions to organizations. In L. L. Putnam & A. M. Nicotera (Eds.), *Building theories of organization: The constitutive role of communication* (pp. 117–152). New York: Routledge.

Cooren, F., Matte, F., Benoit-Barné, C., & Brummans, B. M. (2013). Communication as ventriloquism: A grounded-in-action approach to the study of organizational tensions. *Communication Monographs, 80(3)*, 255–277. https://doi.org/10.1080/03637751.2013.788255

Deal, T., & Kennedy, A. (1982). *Corporate cultures.* New York: Addison-Wesley.

Deal, T., & Kennedy, A. (2000). *Corporate cultures.* Cambridge, MA: Perseus.

Driskill, G. W. (1995). Managing cultural differences: A rules analysis in a bi-cultural organization. *Howard Journal of Communications, 5(4)*, 353–379. https://doi.org/10.1080/10646179509361676

Driskill, G. W., Arjannikova, A., & Meyer, J. (2014). A dialectic analysis of a community forum on faith: The "most segregated" or separated hour? *Journal of Applied Communication Research, 42(4)*, 477–496. https://doi.org/10.1080/00909882.2014.880938

Driskill, G. W., & Downs, C. (1995). Hidden differences in competent communication: A case study of Asian Indians in a bi-national organization. *International Journal of Intercultural Relations, 19(4)*, 505–522. https://doi.org/10.1016/0147-1767(95)00031-3

Eisenberg, E. M. (1984). Ambiguity as strategy in organizational communication. *Communication Monographs, 51(3)*, 227. https://doi.org/10.1080/03637758409390197

Fairhurst, G. (2011). *The power of framing: Creating the language of leadership.* San Francisco: Jossey-Bass.

Fairhurst, G., & Sarr, R. (1996). *The art of framing: Managing the language of leadership.* San Francisco: Jossey-Bass.

Fisher, W. (1987). *Human communication as narration: Toward a philosophy of reason, value, and action.* Columbia: University of South Carolina Press.

Florida, R. (2002). *The rise of the creative class and how it's transforming work, leisure, community, and everyday life.* New York: Basic Books.

Freelance Forward 2023, Future of Work Insights. (December 12, 2023). Retrieved from www.upwork.com/research/freelance-forward-2023-research-report

Glazier, R., Driskill, G., & Kirk, L. (2020). Connecting with community and facilitating learning through the little rock congregations study. *Metropolitan Universities Journal.* Special Issue: The Intersection of Faith and Community Engagement at Urban Institutions, *31(3)*. https://doi.org/10.18060/23990

Harter, L. M. (2009). Narratives as dialogic, contested, and aesthetic performances. *Journal of Applied Communication Research, 37(2)*, 140–150. https://doi.org/10.1080/00909880902792255

Harter, L. M., Scott, J., Novak, D., Leeman, M., & Morris, J. (2006). Freedom through flight: Performing a counter-narrative of disability. *Journal of Applied Communication Research, 34*, 3–29. https://doi.org/10.1080/00909880500420192

Holger, R., Gross, M., Hartman, J., & Cunliffe, A. (2008). Meaning in organizational communication: Why metaphor is the cake, not the icing. *Management Communication Quarterly, 21*, 393–412. https://doi.org/10.1177/0893318907309929

Islam, G., & Zyphur, M. (2009). Rituals in organizations: A review and expansion of current theory. *Group & Organization Management, 34(1)*, 114–139. https://doi.org/10.1177/1059601108329717

Jabs, L. B. (2005). Communication rules and organizational decision-making. *Journal of Business Communication, 42*, 265–288. https://doi.org/10.1080/00909880500420192

Kalaignanam, K., & Varadarajan, R. (2012). Offshore outsourcing of customer relationship management: Conceptual model and propositions. *Journal of the Academy of Marketing Science, 40(2)*, 347–363. https://doi.org/10.1007/s11747-011-0291-0

Kirkwood, W. (1983). Story-telling and self-confrontation: Parables as communication strategies. *Quarterly Journal of Speech, 69*, 56–74. https://doi.org/10.1080/00335638309383635

Kirkwood, W. (1985). Parables as metaphors and examples. *Quarterly Journal of Speech, 71*, 422–440. https://doi.org/10.1080/00335638509383746

Kirkwood, W. (1992). Narrative and the rhetoric of possibility. *Communication Monographs, 59*, 30–47. https://doi.org/10.1080/03637759209376247

Koschmann, M. A., & McDonald, J. (2015). Organizational rituals, communication, and the question of agency. *Management Communication Quarterly, 29(2)*, 229–256. https://doi.org/10.1177/0893318915572386

Martin, J. (1992). *Cultures in organizations: Three perspectives*. New York: Oxford University Press.

Martin, J. (2002). *Organizational culture: Mapping the Terrain*. London: Sage Publications.

Meisenbach, R. (2016). Integrating ethics and responsibility into organizational communication research: Issues and new directions. *Management Communication Quarterly, 31(1)*. https://doi.org/10.1177/0893318916676891

Meyer, J. (1995). Tell me a story: Eliciting organizational values from narratives. *Communication Quarterly, 43*, 210–224. https://doi.org/10.1080/01463379509369970

Meyer, J. (1997). Humor in member narratives: Uniting and dividing at work. *Western Journal of Communication, 61*, 188–208. https://doi.org/10.1080/10570319709374571

Meyer, J. (2000). Humor as a double-edged sword: Four functions of humor in communication. *Communication Theory, 10(3)*, 310–331. https://doi.org/10.1111/j.1468-2885.2000.tb00194.x

Meyer, J. (2009). Unity in response to mystery: Uniting diverse views to plan worship. *Journal of Communication & Religion, 32*, 62–92.

Meyer, J. (2015). *Understanding humor through communication: Why be funny anyway?* Lanham, MD: Lexington, Books.

Meyer, J., & Driskill, G. (1997). Children and relationship development: Communication strategies in a day care center. *Communication Reports, 10*, 75–85. https://doi.org/10.1080/08934219709367661

Meyerson, D., & Martin, J. (1987). Cultural change: An integration of three different views. *Journal of Management Studies, 24*, 625–647. https://doi.org/10.1111/j.1467-6486.1987.tb00466.x

Mirivel, J. C., & Tracy, K. (2005). Pre-meeting talk: An organizationally crucial form of talk. *Research on Language and Social Interaction, 32*, 1–34. https://doi.org/10.1002/9781444303094

Morgan, G. (2006). *Images of organization* (updated ed.). Newbury Park, CA: Sage.

Moroccia, M. (2012). The internet, intercultural communication and cultural variation. *Language and Intercultural Communication, 12(4)*, 353–368. https://doi.org/10.1080/14708477.2012.722101

Pacanowsky, M. (1988). Communication in the empowering organization. In J. Anderson (Ed.), *Communication yearbook* (Vol. 11, pp. 356–379). Newbury Park, CA: Sage.

Pacanowsky, M., & O'Donnell-Trujillo, N. (1983). Organizational communication as cultural performance. *Communication Monographs, 50*, 126–147. https://doi.org/10.1080/03637758309390158

Papa, M., Singhal, A., & Papa, W. (2006). *Organizing for social change: Dialectic journey of theory and praxis*. New Delhi, India: Sage.

Pepper, G. (2008). The physical organization as equivocal message. *Journal of Applied Communication Research, 36*, 318–338. https://doi.org/10.1080/00909880802104882

Ramsey, M. C., & Meyer, J. C. (2025). Uniting and dividing: An examination of supervisors' humor use as a predictor of subordinate dissent expression. *Communication Reports, 38(TBA)*, TBA. https://doi.org/10.1080/08934215.2024.2432328

Schall, M. (1983). A communication-rules approach to organizational culture. *Administrative Science Quarterly, 28*, 557–581. https://doi.org/10.1177/089331899100400400 2

Schein, E., & Schein, P. (2016). *Organizational culture and leadership* (5th ed.). San Francisco: Jossey-Bass.

Scott, C., & Trethewey, A. (2008). Organizational discourse and the appraisal of occupational hazards: Interpretive repertoires, heedful interrelating, and identity at work. *Journal of Applied Communication Research, 36*, 298–317. https://doi.org/10.1080/00909880802172137

Scott, M. E. (2013). "Communicate through the roof": A case study analysis of the communicative rules and resources of an effective global virtual team. *Communication Quarterly, 61(3)*, 301–318. https://doi.org/10.1080/01463373.2013.776987

Seeger, M., & Ulmer, R. (2003). Explaining Enron: Communication and responsible leadership. *Management Communication Quarterly, 17(1)*, 58–84. https://doi.org/10.1177/0893318903253436

Sigman, S. J. (1980). On communication rules from a social perspective. *Human Communication Research*, 7, 37–51. https://doi.org/10.1111/j.1468-2958.1980.tb00549.x

Sillince, J., & Barker, J. (2012). A tropological theory of institutionalization. *Organization Studies, 33*, 7–38. https://doi.org/10.1177/0170840611425735

Smith, A., & Stewart, B. (2011). Organizational rituals: Features, functions and mechanisms. *International Journal of Management Reviews, 13(2)*, 113–133. https://doi.org/10.1111/j.1468-2370.2010.00288.x

Smith, F., & Keyton, J. (2001). Organizational storytelling: Metaphors for relational power and identity struggles. *Management Communication Quarterly, 15*, 149–183. https://doi.org/10.1177/0893318901152001

Smith, R., & Eisenberg, E. (1987). Conflict at Disneyland: A root-metaphor analysis. *Communication Monographs, 54*, 365–380. https://doi.org/10.1080/03637758709390239

Strasberg, L. (1987). *A dream of passion: The development of the method*. Boston: Little, Brown.

Tipton, W., & Kupritz, V. (2017). Using the outdoor scavenger hunt to teach theories of organizational communication. *Communication Teacher, 31(2)*, 79–84. https://doi.org/10.1080/17404622.2017.1285411

Tompkins, P. K., & Cheney, G. (1985). Communication and unobtrusive control in contemporary organizations. In R. D. McPhee & P. K. Tompkins (Eds.), *Organizational communication: Traditional themes and new directions*. Newbury Park, CA: Sage.

Tracy, S., Lutgen-Sandvick, P., & Alberts, J. (2006). Nightmares, demons, and slaves: Exploring the painful metaphors of workplace bullying. *Management Communication Quarterly, 20*, 148–185. https://doi.org/10.1177/0893318906291980

Trice, H. M., & Beyer, J. (1985). Using six organizational rites to change cultures. In R. H. Kilmann, M. J. Saxton, & R. Serpa (Eds.), *Gaining control of the corporate culture* (pp. 370–399). San Francisco: Jossey-Bass.

Trice, H. M., & Beyer, J. (1993). *The cultures of work organizations*. Englewood Cliffs, NJ: Prentice Hall.

Ulmer, R. R. (2001). Effective crisis management through established stakeholder relationships. *Management Communication Quarterly, 14(4)*, 590–615. https://doi.org/10.1177/0893318901144003

Ulmer, R. R., & Sellnow, T. L. (1997). Strategic ambiguity and the ethic of significant choice in the tobacco industry's crisis communication. *Communication Studies, 48*, 215–233. https://doi.org/10.1080/10510979709368502

Ulmer, R. R., Sellnow, T. L., & Seeger, M. (2015). *Effective crisis communication: Moving from crisis to opportunity* (3rd ed.). Thousand Oaks, CA: Sage Publications.

Vineberg, S. (1991). *Method actors: Three generations of an American acting style*. New York: Schirmer Books.

Weber, M. S., & Kim, H. (2015). Virtuality, technology use, and engagement within organizations. *Journal of Applied Communication Research, 43*(4), 385–407. https://doi.org/10.1080/00909882.2015.1083604

Wolfgruber, D. (2023). I'm only joking! (?) the role of disparaging humor in the communicative constitution of inclusion/exclusion in organizations. *Equality, Diversity and Inclusion*. https://doi.org/10.1108/edi-08-2022-0223

Zipperer, B., McNicholas, C., Poydock, Schneider, M., & Harknett, K. (June 1, 2022). National survey of gig workers paints a picture of poor working conditions, low pay. *Economic Policy Institute*. Retrieved from www.epi.org/publication/gig-worker-survey/

Part III

Cultural Data Collection and Interpretation

An Introduction to Step Four

Method Acting

1. Articulate cultural analysis goals and benefits
2. Explore culture as co-construction
3. Reflect on enacted elements
4. Identify enacted elements via multiple methods
5. Interpret thematic action and OCA
6. Co-create positive communication applications

Step 4: Collect Data on Elements Via Multiple Methods

Objectives

- Explain the importance of using multiple data collection methods.
- Discuss the utility of three qualitative methods for identifying the cultural elements.
- Implement a plan for protecting human participants in a cultural analysis.

Stage Terms

Ethnography	Triangulation	Institutional Review Board

The Meeting

You walk into a meeting, and before you sit down, you notice that all the seats are taken except the one next to the boss. Your heartbeat races as you wonder what you've missed already. You are the new kid in the office. What a way to start. You swallow hard as everyone stops talking. You quickly but quietly sit down. You place your folder in front of you and glance at your watch, finding that you are hardly one minute late. The boss begins talking about second-quarter earnings, and as she talks, you glance around the room. Your mind shifts to the folder and concerns you had about the earnings statement. The boss seems not to be commenting on any of those issues. You see one of your colleagues, hired just months before you, gazing out the window, apparently paying little attention. You shuffle a few papers in front of you to prepare for any questions you might be asked and then notice several other partners in the firm engaged in writing notes or glancing at their laptops. "No one seems to respect the boss" is the first thought that comes to mind. The boss finishes

DOI: 10.4324/9781003482529-7

what appears to be a tirade against poor time management on everyone's part and then asks for comments and questions. You think it strange that she says nothing about the rude behavior of her subordinates. Silence ensues, and while you want to ask a question about discrepancies you observed in the earnings statement, you see almost everyone glancing at their watches, and thus, you decide to be silent. The boss calls the meeting to an end about 15 minutes after it started.

An Introduction to Cultural Analysis Methods

If you were the main character in the meeting story, you would be drawing inferences from the meeting you observed. Is it usual for employees to be early for meetings? How much did you really miss by being one minute late? Why is no one paying attention or asking questions? Are all meetings this short? While we all observe and make sense of interactions, we are rarely equipped for a more systemic, valid process for interpreting. For instance, beyond the meeting example, we likely engage in reading various texts (e.g., e-mails, policy documents, etc.), yet our process of discerning cultural patterns from texts may not be well developed. Furthermore, while we each have experiences with conversations and interviews, we may not be well adept at asking questions that provide insight to the culture.

It is fair to ask, "So, what is the real concern? We hired consultants and researchers for such work, right?" While it is true that not everyone serves in these formal roles, the question of concern is perhaps best addressed by returning to the aforementioned scenario.

Let's call the new employee, Mike. After the meeting, Mike, who was not even a minute late, talks with a co-worker, Jill, who explains that being early is the norm. Jill goes on to say, "I know the meeting may seem confusing, but just hang in there, and you will catch on." Mike wants to ask more questions but does not know where to begin. He is mostly concerned, not only about his credibility but about the discrepancies left unaddressed in the earnings statements. Mike has only been around for a couple of weeks. He has interacted with others, but this is his first time to be faced with this sort of challenge. What might guide him toward the next step? What questions should he ask? Who should he talk with next? And, we ask, what cultural data might guide him?

We argue that the process outlined in the coming chapters will sharpen his ability to gather cultural data to move him forward in ethical and effective ways. Thus, whether your goal for this analysis process is a formal one involving weeks or even months of data collection as part of a consultation or a class or consulting project, or a less formal and less involved process exploring a particular application such as ethics, conflict management, diversity, or change leadership, this unit is intended to sharpen your cultural data collection abilities to guide positive communication applications. Recalling our model, the OCA framework focuses on ***fostering the co-creation of positive organizations by developing implications through the analysis of enacted elements that both shape and are shaped by communication***. This framework is intended to aid, even in an informal way, an individual like Mike, in discerning communicative options. In short, we argue that improved use of data collection can aid us in becoming better characters in the stories we are living and creating with others.

What specifically do we want to accomplish in this "Introduction to Step Three: Collect data on enacted elements via multiple methods?"

Recall that the analysis process is guided by three big three questions. In this part of the book, Steps Four and Five, we formally respond to the first question: *What kind of culture is being co-created*? In order to answer this question, we seek to enhance our ability to ethically collect and interpret data. Thus, Part III explores the data collection and interpretation process. We will first provide background on the role of ethnography in a cultural analysis, including a brief overview of the major methods discussed in the following three chapters. Next, we provide a table to suggest ways to use specific methods to identify various elements of culture. Third, we provide a "Connections" section to encourage reflection on the significance of using more than one method in a systematic way. We conclude by responding to three FAQs, including questions about protecting human participants and the institutional review board process.

Ethnographic Methods

Method actors use a variety of tactics to provide a credible interpretation of their roles and the script of the play. They have as their "essential task the reproduction of recognizable reality—on stage (or screen), based on an acute observation of the world" (Vineberg, 1991, p. 6). In a similar vein, anthropologists who immerse themselves in a foreign culture rely on three primary methods of data gathering and analysis: systematic observation, conversational interviews, and systematic analysis of various oral and written texts. Such qualitative techniques are often grouped under the heading of "ethnomethodology" or "ethnography." Goodall (1989) defines ethnography as "representing in words what you have lived through as a person when your stated purpose was to study a culture" (p. xxiii). A professional ethnographer might spend years attempting to integrate herself into the culture to fully understand it. During those years, she would repeat many iterations of observing regularities, asking natives of the culture for their interpretations of the patterns of behavior she observed or their tacit knowledge of the culture, and analyzing field notes, interview transcripts, and cultural artifacts. The results of one layer of analysis would lead to a new round of interviews and conversations.

The cultural analysis process described in this text assumes a shorter time frame for an exploration of organizational culture. Most of you will be doing projects in which you engage with the culture for two to three months of part-time exploration, applying the same methods an anthropologist uses. Others may use these methods to regularly explore some critical aspects of culture in relation to applications such as progress on diversity initiatives or change leadership. In those cases, data collection might involve an annual, but relatively brief, data collection phase, perhaps relying on surveys and focus groups. Rather than dozens of repeated observations, you might conduct only a few. Instead of hundreds of pages of textual analysis of policies or newsletters, you might focus on a few key cultural artifacts and a meaningful sample of a dozen newsletters. Regardless of the scope of the project, the data collection phase is one where you will come to understand systematic analysis of texts, observation options, interviews, and surveys and how one data collection process often leads back into the other.

The process of systematic data collection may begin with any of the major methods outlined: textual analysis, observations, qualitative interviews/focus groups, and surveys. Some of you might find it more meaningful to begin with observations, move to interviews, and then analyze texts. Still others will find that textual analysis provides a relatively non-obtrusive way to begin the process. Informal interviews may also provide a useful entry point. In addition, a survey might be used to gain perspectives on various elements of culture. Regardless of where you begin, the initial objective of your first round of data collection is to gain a feel for the organization and its players and to notice regularities and/or paradoxes. This information will form the ground for the next phase. For instance, if you begin with observations or textual analysis, you may use that information to aid you in developing meaningful questions in a qualitative interview guide.

In the following chapters, we first introduce various types of textual analysis. Systematic analysis of organizational texts must be approached with a major caution in mind. You should not automatically assume that mission statements, annual reports, employee manuals, or corporate newsletters are the most significant organizational texts to analyze because they may reflect more about the ways that upper management wants to portray the culture but may not reflect the daily interactions of employees and their interpretations of culture. Internal memos, employee e-mails, or even coffee room bulletin boards may be truer reflections of organizational culture. We will suggest a variety of systematic methods for analyzing organizational texts. You may also uncover important organizational texts during the process of observation and interviews. Furthermore, textual analysis will be useful when you analyze your field notes from observations and with your interview transcripts or summaries.

Observations will be the second method we introduce. Some of you may be analyzing an organization you participate in on a regular basis, either as a volunteer or an employee. In such cases, you may decide to begin with observation. As noted in the meeting example at the opening of this unit, we all engage in making observations and then inferring from these experiences about how to interact. The process of taking field notes when you observe will challenge you to reflect on a broader array of organizational contexts. Furthermore, you will be asked to distinguish between events and your interpretation of events.

Ethnographic or qualitative interviews/surveys as well as focus groups, are also introduced. Interviews, like conversations with organization members, will help you understand how they interpret the events you have observed. Even if you are an insider to the organization, you will be encouraged to gain a wider array of perspectives on the events you observe as well as the texts you analyze. Any individual in an organization may have a limited perspective on overall cultural patterns. Focus groups may function in a way similar to qualitative interviews by gaining perspectives that go beyond those of an individual. Surveys with open-ended questions provide a way to invite narrative responses and are, thereby, an effective way to gain interpretive data from a larger sample of organization members. We introduce qualitative surveys in combination with interviews because the types of questions covered in each are similar. For instance, in an interview, you might ask someone to describe a metaphor they would use to explain the organization to an outsider. This same question could be placed in a survey to gain responses from a broader sample of organization members.

We are often asked about the use of quantitative surveys in cultural analysis. We concur with Van Maanan (1979) that "qualitative methodology and quantitative methodology are not mutually exclusive" (p. 520). We have used quantitative surveys in research and consultation with organizations. We have found the Downs and Adrian instrument (2004) to be of value in assessing member satisfaction levels with certain communication practices, such as horizontal or vertical communication. Glaser, Zamanou, and Hacker (1987) assert that organizational culture can be measured by analyzing how members feel an organization communicates on six factors: a) teamwork; b) morale; c) information flow; d) involvement; e) supervision; and f) communication during meetings. This instrument has been used to correlate several of these factors with member identification (Croucher et al., 2009). In addition, highly specified quantitative surveys have been developed, such as one focused on the capacity of an organization to renew through a crisis event (Fuller, McNatt, Ulmer, & Ruiz, 2019). You can also locate commercially available quantitative surveys. Such surveys typically assume the culture as a variable approach. The primary claim is that this survey data can aid the company in identifying ways to be more productive and competitive. These surveys have the advantage of gaining a snapshot of participant views on a variety of culture-related topics. For example, one survey assesses the extent to which participants believe the organization is responsive to change and values an external orientation (Culture Strategy Fit, n.d.). Another examines culture along four dimensions: adaptability, consistency, involvement, and mission (Denison, Hooijber, Lane, & Lief, 2012; Denison, n.d.). Gallop has also produced a set of culture tools including a survey focusing on employee engagement (Gallop, n.d.) with clear connections to organizational culture.

What is our view of these types of surveys? We believe these surveys can be of value. Nonetheless, we introduce other survey options in Chapter 7 with a caveat. As discussed in Chapter 2, organizational culture can and has been explored from the variable, root metaphor, and discursive construction frameworks. Each option provides insights for improving varied organizational outcomes. However, the OCA is based on viewing culture as "discursive construction"—an approach that examines the way organization and organizing processes are constituted in communicative action via cultural elements. We believe that this approach promises to provide a richer, deeper, and ultimately more meaningful analysis. To this end, it is important to realize that quantitative surveys allow input from a broader range of organization members, but such data, by definition, is reduced to quantifiable categories. This quantification allows statistical manipulation, averages, and comparisons. However, the trade-off, if one relies fully on quantitative data, means missing the rich symbolic elements that both reflect and constitute the culture—the stories, metaphors, language, rituals, and other elements. Even when a survey includes open questions, such as "What metaphors best describe your organization?", employees do not share as much in-depth information as they do in interviews. Yet, at the same time, over the past 30 years of engaging students and professionals in this process, we find there are times when well-worded survey questions may be of value. One value in a survey is the snapshot it can provide, for example, on an annual basis, on such areas as participant engagement or diversity initiatives. Such surveys also, if well worded and administered, may become a ritual that meaningfully engages participants in regular reflection on their role in the culture creation process. Thus, in the final section, we have provided Rehearsals that include survey questions as options for use in combination with other methods.

Multiple Methods and Cultural Elements

As you begin data collection, remember that the first analytic step is to connect your data back to elements of culture. The idea is to attend to all elements. The reason for attending to all elements is to gain a rich data set to set the stage for a more ethical and credible interpretation and application. In addition, capturing data across elements is consistent with the theoretic frames underlying the OCA model, such as Structuration and the CCO. The goal is to attend to the dual role of communication in organization and organizing processes. These elements represent both macro practices (structures such as rituals and place, etc.) and micro (conversation rules, stories, etc.). For instance, you may gather organizational texts, field notes from observations, and interview summaries or transcripts. You may then perform a series of analyses to tease out elements such as history, language, symbols, and metaphors that may lead you to an understanding of overarching themes. We will discuss this process of moving from elements to themes in Chapter 8. For now, Table III.1 suggests a place to start with each method; it is not a prescription of what information is necessarily paired with each method.

Table III.1 Methods and Cultural Elements Revealed

Method	*Focus*	*Cultural Elements Revealed*
Observation	Artifacts	Rules Heroes History Values Communication style
Interviews/ Qualitative/ Quantitative Surveys	Interactions Language Symbols	Rules Heroes, villains, and outlaws Rituals, Humor Communication style Metaphors Stories, Humor Heroes Values Metaphors
Analysis of Texts Observations	Place Representative texts Heroes and villains Stories Rules History Metaphors Communication style	Values Root metaphors Thematic Action

Indeed, you can usually find most of the elements of culture revealed across the methods we cover in Chapters 5, 6, and 7.

For example, in observation, you might choose to focus on artifacts such as office arrangement, objects hanging on the walls, corporate dress style, and public meeting spaces such as conference rooms or break rooms. In this analysis, you might especially look for signs of history—pictures of the founders prominently displayed or historical pictures. You might also look for regularities that would suggest formal rules or informal norms, such as a lack of personal items in offices or conformity in the style of dress. You might also find suggestions of heroes—pictures hanging on the wall, prominent office locations, and employees who are frequently mentioned with high regard. You can subtly infer values from the artifacts you observe. How does the organization present itself to insiders and outsiders? In a similar way, interviews or qualitative surveys might serve to follow up on the things you have observed and ask their meaning from an insider perspective. You'd also ask about difficult to observe elements, such as stories, the influence of place, and metaphors.

Connections: Getting the Best Data

The rationale for using multiple methods is that the validity of cultural interpretations can be improved. The idea of multiple methods is called method "triangulation." Geographic surveys use triangulation to find a point by identifying two vectors that intersect. In a similar fashion, method triangulation provides the basis for drawing more credible conclusions about a culture by gaining perspectives using more than one method. Thus, rather than relying on perceptions from a single method, such as surveys, the effective cultural analyst uses additional methods, such as observations, to enrich the data set (Miles & Huberman, 1984). For example, informal "interviews" in the organization may prompt you to take note of a metaphor used by an employee who says, "Working here is like visiting cyberspace." Observations of work teams or the physical setting may be used to determine the pervasiveness and salience of the metaphor (e.g., is it found in company logos, newsletters, or in language used during meetings?). For instance, if space was devoted each week in the newsletter to applications of the latest and best of technology, then support exists for the metaphor beyond the one-time mention by a single employee.

Each of us has used the data collection methods outlined in this unit. We may not have consciously walked backstage and taken on the role of anthropologist or method actor. Whether or not we viewed them as "methods" per se, we have been observers of organizational behavior, we have read documents in our organizations to gain knowledge or insight, and in most cases, we have participated in informal interviews and possibly even completed or sent out formal surveys. Thus, the process of collecting data about culture, like the notion of cultural elements, is not foreign ground. Put differently, to be a member of an organization is to be a "sense-maker," someone who is trying to make sense of his or her environment (Weick, 1995). This process of sensemaking is important not only during the first weeks as a new member of an organization but also during organizational changes and job promotions (Kramer & Noland, 1999). The only ways to gain information to make sense of an organization is to observe, ask questions, and/or ask someone else to observe or ask questions for us.

These naïve approaches to understanding culture can have great practical significance for the organization members. Angi conducted one cultural analysis in which there was one employee in an insurance company that no one could stand. The cultural analysis team had probed to understand why this woman was so disliked and rejected by the majority of other employees. All agreed she was competent and hard-working. When pressed for details, many of the employees gave the same answer about her failure to fit in. "She brings crackers to the office potluck," several explained, assuming that we would understand immediately the significance of this culinary contribution.

Only in analyzing the culture further did they understand the significance. The monthly office potluck embodied several of the organization's defining values and a sense of community and sharing, nurturing, and generosity. All the employees put great effort into bringing creative and tasty dishes. The fact that this employee brought crackers signified to the others that she did not care about the group and that she was cheap. It, of course, signified that she did not share other important group values. The employee probably never grasped the seriousness of her offense or understood why she was disliked by co-workers. She had not picked up on cultural cues about values or the significance of the potluck ritual within the company.

Two "safe" assumptions about our everyday data collection habits prove the value of this approach. First, we tend to draw conclusions about culture based on sporadic, biased, and incomplete information. In short, we can improve the thoroughness and validity of our efforts. And second, incomplete data leads to interpretations that can harm the effectiveness of our communication and thus adversely influence the ethicality and credibility of our leadership efforts. The hypothetical meeting presented at the start of this chapter is an example of one person's observations. Notice how the story contains a mix of descriptive data ("two minutes late") and interpretive data ("they must not respect the boss"). The newcomer made a decision not to ask a question based on everyone else's behavior. It is clear, however, that he has much to learn about the function of these meetings and when, if ever, questions can be asked at meetings. In short, the newcomer's observations, his experience of this meeting, form an important aspect of information that will guide his future behavior.

The question, then, is how can he improve his abilities as an observer? As a participant in the confusing, often ambiguous world of organizations, how can he move forward from this meeting to contribute to an effective and ethical organizational culture? Just as consultants and researchers can be critiqued based on their methods used for data collection and interpretation, so can and should we be. If, for example, from the meeting experience, I fail to ask questions of colleagues even after they present incomplete or inaccurate information at a meeting, then my behavior is no longer simply that of "fitting in"; it can and should be challenged on ethical grounds. Rehearsal III.1 provides a way to reflect on your experiences in this arena. As we will discuss in Chapter 11 on ethics, we must resist two tendencies that surface in research on communication: ethics and upward communication, in particular. One, we tend to think we are alone in our observations and thoughts about ethics in given situations, and thus may tend to be silent, "pluralistic ignorance" because we have a misperception of group norms in which we assume we are the only one holding a particular moral stance (Bisel, 2019). Two, we may fall into the story of the "Emperor's New Clothes," where we, out of fear, do not address an obvious problem. This later concern, as we will explore later, is found in research by Bisel and colleagues as the Hierarchical Mum Effect (Bisel, Kelley, Ploeger, & Messersmith, 2011).

Rehearsal III.1 Introduction to Method Acting: The Last Time I Was Wrong

Purpose: Identify the types of informal data you collect and the consequences of relying on these data.

Steps:

1. Recall a time when you drew an inaccurate conclusion about a work relationship, a company policy, or perhaps a change introduced in your organization.
2. What types of cultural data did you use to infer your mistaken conclusion? From what source?
3. What other types of data might have helped? From what other sources?
4. What other cultural elements might have helped improve the accuracy of your inference?

Miller and Jablin (1991) point out an inverse relationship between risk and information accuracy when seeking information in organizational entry. The less obtrusive ways of gathering information, such as observing the behaviors of others and drawing inferences, may be perceived as "safer" by the average employee because there is less risk of offending someone or appearing stupid. Yet this less direct way of gathering information can lead the employee to draw the wrong conclusions about the behaviors observed. The more direct information-gaining strategy of asking specific questions produces more reliable data but may be seen as riskier by the employee because of fear of loss of face or being perceived as incapable.

Will Multiple Methods Result in Objectivity?

A common misconception is that you can somehow create an objective interpretation if you get the right data. We would point out that even triangulated data do not produce an objective view of organizational culture. A researcher always develops subjective conclusions from a point of view. Triangulation produces data drawn from multiple points of reference but still contains elements of subjectivity. You will need to accept at the outset that your conclusions about the organizational culture may be different from those another individual might draw. These differing conclusions do not mean that either is invalid. It does mean that you need to be explicit about supporting your conclusions with data and explaining why you drew the conclusions you did. This transparency of logic would allow your readers or listeners to compare the ways in which they might draw different conclusions from the same data set. As we stressed in our introductory analogies, whether "painting by numbers" or "putting together a jigsaw puzzle," the key is to create ethical, credible, and useful interpretations.

What about examples of cultural analysis that use a single method or single cultural element focus?

Researchers sometimes use multiple methods to obtain information about one or, at times, two cultural elements. In some cases, however, a more specialized approach (e.g., root metaphor, linguistics, rules) may focus on a particular "element as a method" for interpreting culture. For example, an analysis of stories may be the method used to decipher organizational values (e.g., Meyer, 1995). Cultural research on the role of humor has been used to gain insight into organizational sensemaking practices (Bochantin, 2017). A focus on a single element might be used to gain an understanding of a particular phenomenon, such as metaphors for workplace bullying (Tracy, Lutgen-Sandvick, & Alberts, 2006) or communicative rules used in a virtual organization (Scott, 2013). The goal of this workbook, however, is to help you perform a more comprehensive cultural analysis in order to produce competent individual and organizational performances. The key is to allow researchers who focus on a particular element to spark your imagination regarding the value or importance of a given element. Our goal is to go beyond the study of one element to gain a richer description of the culture than can be obtained from a focus on a single method or element. In the following three chapters, we explore each method in more depth and offer practical suggestions for how you can use each to gain insight into your organizational culture. We begin with the least obtrusive tool for actors seeking to be more effective at directing and leading the communication practices on the stage-textual analysis.

What Steps Should Be Taken to Protect Participants?

We provide a full chapter on ethics and hope you have noted the issue of ethics as a theme throughout this book. As stressed in our introduction of CCOs, theorists using this framework foreground our ethical responsibilities in co-creating cultures. Thus, we also have an ethical responsibility to realize how formal and informal analysis processes impact the culture. Science fiction buffs can cite examples of time travelers who have to be very careful in their visit to the past and not take actions that would alter all of subsequent history. There is a parallel in organizational intervention. We need to realize that the questions we ask, how we ask them, and how we use the data all influence the culture of the organization. For instance, if handled improperly, data may negatively influence an employee's job security. Also, imagine an ill-planned, leading question like, "Don't you think the leaders around here care less about us?" Such questions may lead participants to be dissatisfied or question the motives of management, affecting organizational trust. We cannot stress enough the importance of being diligent about protecting the people in the organization you serve in this analysis process and being aware of how your activities in the cultural analysis can have an effect on the long-term culture of the organization.

Universities require researchers using human participants to seek approval from an institutional research board (IRB). This requirement often applies to student projects as well. An IRB protocol can be informative and encourage ethical research processes for those using the OCA model outside of the university context. For those in the university setting, your instructor can guide you with the particular requirements and processes at your university. At some universities, each student must gain independent approval for each project; others require a "blanket" approval form to cover all the student class projects. Still others use a consent process, but as a class-based project, they are not required to complete a formal IRB.

Protection of human subjects is based on three principles contained in the Belmont Report of Ethical Principles and Guidelines for the Protection of Human Subjects of Research, which was issued by the National Commission for the Protection of Human Subjects of Biomedical and Behavioral Research (previously the Office for Protection of Research Risks) in 1979. These three principles include a) that the study will pose no undue risks to the life, health, or integrity of research subjects; b) that any risks to subjects are outweighed by the potential significance of the study; and c) that subjects have the opportunity to give informed consent about their participation in the study.

An informed consent form must contain information about the purpose and procedures of the study, any risk involved, the voluntary nature of participation and ability to withdraw at any stage of the study, and contact information for questions or concerns. It also must inform subjects of the nature of confidentiality and how their privacy will be protected in the study. It will also inform them about what will be done with the information obtained in the study. An example of an informed consent form is included in Rehearsal III.2. These same guides may be adapted for use by those conducting an analysis outside of the context of a university. Again, the intent is to ensure participants are protected by communicating how the data will be used and how their identity will be protected.

Summary

We are all characters in a story. The challenge and opportunity of cultural analysis is becoming more aware of the parts we are playing or should be playing. Cultural analysis methods are aimed at improving insights for ourselves and our organizations. Before diving into your analysis, you should understand several key ideas in the overview of methods:

1. In conducting a cultural analysis, your aim should be to gather valid and credible data without engaging in the years of data collection that might be involved in an ethnography of an organization.

2. Utilize the methods introduced in the coming chapters in an order that is appropriate to your analysis. We introduce a systematic analysis of organizational texts followed by observation, interviews, and surveys.
3. You have used the data collection methods outlined in this unit, yet your everyday data collection process tends to provide incomplete and biased information that can decrease effective leadership.
4. Less direct or unobtrusive methods of data collection, such as textual analysis, are safer in terms of influencing participants but may lead to inaccurate conclusions. Conversely, more direct information-gaining strategies, such as formal interviews, are more obtrusive but may provide more reliable data because of your ability to gain insider perspectives.
5. Triangulation or using multiple methods will result in more credible conclusions about a culture.
6. One person's conclusions about the organizational culture may be different from those another individual might draw yet again; the main goal is a credible interpretation based on multiple sources of data across varied enacted elements.
7. Be sure to attend to micro (i.e., interpersonal norms) and macro communicative processes (i.e., rituals).
8. Maintain diligence in protecting members of the organization; gain formal written permission from the organization (see Rehearsal 3.3, "Writing a Cultural Analysis Proposal"). For students, you should gain approval from a university institutional review board before beginning your study.

Rehearsal III.2 Sample Informed Consent Form

Adapt the following informed consent form for use in your cultural analysis.
This consent form applies to:
Name: ____________________________________

The following information is provided to inform you about the research on ___________. Please feel free to ask any questions you may have about this study and the information given in it. You will be given an opportunity to ask questions and to have your questions answered. In addition, you will be given a copy of this consent form.

1. **Purpose of the study.** This study is being conducted by [researcher's name and faculty/student status] of the Department/School/College of [subject] at the University of [university name] in order to better understand [research topic]. This research will help [who?] better understand how [process of the issue being investigated]. Your responses in the interview are confidential and available only to the [interviewer/researcher/faculty supervisor].
2. **Description of the procedures to be followed and approximate duration of the study.** Participants in the research will participate in [describe data collection process], which will focus on [research topic]. This [data collection process] will last approximately [length of time].

3. **Description of the discomforts, inconveniences, and/or risks that can reasonably be expected as a result of participation in this study.** Discussing [research topic] may be uncomfortable, and [care services] will [or will not] be available to you as a result of your participation.
4. **Description of how confidentiality will be assured and the limits to these assurances, if any.**
5. **Anticipated benefits resulting from this study.**

   a. The potential benefits to you from participating in the study are [describe benefits]. The study may be helpful to increase your understanding of [the issue being investigated].
   b. The potential benefits to science and humanity that may result from this study are [describe benefits]. This study will provide information to [intended audience of research results] to help them [intended outcomes of the research results].

6. **Alternative procedures.** If alternative procedures exist, please describe them here. Otherwise, include a statement that says: There are no alternative procedures to participation in the interview.
7. **Contact information.** If you have any questions about this study, you can contact these person(s):

Name of Principal Investigator ______________________
Department/School ______________________
Name of Supervisor (if PI is a student) ______________________
Department/School ______________________
Include name, address, telephone number, and e-mail addresses
If you have any questions about your rights as a research subject, please contact the Chair of the Institutional Review Board at [telephone number; e-mail].

References

Bisel, R. (2019). *Organizational moral learning: A communication approach*. New York: Routledge.

Bisel, R., Kelley, K., Ploeger, N., & Messersmith, J. (2011). Workers' moral mum effect: On facework and unethical behavior in the workplace. *Communication Studies, 62*(2), 153–170. https://doi.org/10.1080/10510974.2010.551314

Bochantin, J. (2017). "Ambulance thieves, clowns, and naked grandfathers": How PSE's and their families use humorous communication as a sensemaking device. *Management Communication Quarterly, 31*(3). https://doi.org/10.1177/0893318916687650

Croucher, S., Long, B., Meredith, M., Doommen, D., & Steele, E. (2009). Factors predicting organizational identification with intercollegiate forensics teams. *Communication Education, 58*, 74–91. https://doi.org/10.1080/03634520802450523

Culture Strategy Fit. (n.d.). Retrieved from www.culturestrategyfit.com

Denison, D. (n.d.). Retrieved from www.denisonconsulting.com

Denison, D., Hooijber, R., Lane, N., & Lief, C. (2012). *Leading culture change in global organizations: Aligning culture and strategy*. San Francisco, CA: Wiley & Sons.

Downs, C., & Adrian, A. (2004). *Organizational communication: Strategic communication audits*. New York: Guildford Press.

Fuller, R., McNatt, A., Ulmer, R., & Ruiz, J. (2019). Extending discourse of renewal to preparedness: Construct and scale development of readiness for renewal. *Management Communication Quarterly, 33(2)*, 272–301. https://doi.org/10.1177/0893318919834333

Gallop. (n.d.). *Fortune 500 employee engagement tools.* Retrieved from https://q12.gallup.com/

Glaser, S., Zamanou, S., & Hacker, K. (1987). Measuring and interpreting organizational culture. *Management Communication Quarterly, 1(2)*, 173–198.

Goodall, H. L. (1989). *Casing a promised land.* Carbondale, IL: Southern Illinois University Press.

Kramer, M., & Noland, T. (1999). Communication during job promotions: A case of ongoing assimilation. *Journal of Applied Communication Research, 27(4)*, 335–355. https://doi.org/10.1080/00909889909365544

Meyer, J. (1995). Tell me a story: Eliciting organizational values from narratives. *Communication Quarterly, 43*, 210–224. https://doi.org/10.1080/01463379509369970

Miles, M., & Huberman, A. (1984). *Qualitative data analysis: A sourcebook of new methods.* Beverly Hills, CA: Sage.

Miller, V., & Jablin, F. (1991). Information seeking during organizational entry. *Academy of Management Review, 16*, 92–120. https://doi.org/10.2307/258608

Scott, M. E. (2013). "Communicate through the roof": A case study analysis of the communicative rules and resources of an effective global virtual team. *Communication Quarterly, 61(3)*, 301–318. https://doi.org/10.1080/01463373.2013.776987

Tracy, S., Lutgen-Sandvick, P., & Alberts, J. (2006). Nightmares, demons, and slaves: Exploring the painful metaphors of workplace bullying. *Management Communication Quarterly, 20*, 148–185. https://doi.org/10.1177/0893318906291980

Van Maanan, J. (1979). Reclaiming qualitative research methods for organizational research. *Administrative Science Quarterly, 24*, 520–526. https://doi.org/10.2307/2392358

Vineberg, S. (1991). *Method actors: Three generations of an American acting style.* New York: Schirmer Books.

Weick, K. E. (1995). *Sensemaking in organizations.* Thousand Oaks, CA: Sage.

Chapter 5

Method Acting

Textual Analysis

The fourth step of the OCA model, "Collect data on elements via multiple methods," is introduced by starting with the process of textual analysis. We read texts (reports, e-mails) every day. Systematic analyses of organizational texts are similar to the intense work an actor does with a script prior to crafting a performance. Textual analysis is an unobtrusive research method and can reveal a great deal about an organization. Texts, in themselves, can be understood as having a type of agency that is, like human actors, part of the constitutive process of organizing and organizations. Three systematic ways to analyze organizational texts are introduced: Content analysis, rhetorical analysis, and discourse analysis. Four guidelines for improving the textual process are discussed: a) choose a sufficient sample of credible texts to analyze; b) determine which of the three main analysis method(s) fit your purpose; c) decide on your unit of measurement; and d) tie your analysis back to elements and cultural significance.

Step Three: Use a Variety of Methods to Collect Cultural Data

The following quote reflects the chapter's aims:

> It is easy to create tension by trying a simple experiment. Try lifting something, such as an edge of a piano or a heavy table. At the same time, try to solve a simple mental problem, such as multiplying 75 by 6—an intellectual exercise that would normally involve little difficulty. You will discover it is nearly impossible to do so while lifting the heavy object.
>
> (Strasberg, *A Dream of Passion*, 1987, p. 125)

Objectives

- Understand the significance of texts from a constitutive perspective.
- Distinguish among the major types of textual analysis.
- Explain major guidelines for analyzing a text.

Stage Terms

Textual analysis	Content analysis	Rhetorical analysis	Critical linguistic analysis

DOI: 10.4324/9781003482529-8

Textual Analysis

> *"So, Jane, are you saying you read the company newsletter? Really?"*
> *"Yes, Jamal, and you would do well to pay attention to it. The HRD department takes a lead role in writing it, and they often have the inside scoop on what is happening. They have a way of dropping hints in the newsletter that you may not get elsewhere."*
> *Jamal was shocked to learn that in his new organization, the newsletter mattered at all. In his prior experience, the newsletter went into the recycle bin without even a glance. In fact, even e-mails were not considered as important as a text or a post to a social media "App."*

"Textual analysis" is a generic term used for the analysis of any written artifact. Just as an actor in a play must be adept at reading not only the script but also the reviews, biographies of the author, and so on, so also the effective organizational actor must be adept at analyzing texts that give insight into the culture. At an informal level, you engage in textual analysis any time a document (i.e., newsletter, report, contract, checklist, memo, sign, etc.) influences you to respond, discuss, or take any sort of action. What is easily missed is that texts can be understood as having an impact, a type of "agency" of their own. In other words, our focus regarding texts can too easily be on our role or that of management in the creation of texts. In contrast, some theorists with the CCO approach stress the "active contribution of texts (especially documents) to organizational processes; that is, on the ways that texts, such as reports, contracts, memos, signs, or work orders, 'perform something'" (Cooren, 2004, p. 374). For instance, in the preceding example, the text, through the supposed design of the writers, is creating interactions by "dropping hints" concerning possible changes. In addition, texts coordinate activities, as in the case of signage or policy, and guides behavior, such as a pilot's checklist. The significance of texts is further illustrated by attending to the ways they constitute organizations and organizing processes. Think of the following functions of words or speech acts: a) assertiveness such as informing, confirming, indicating, reminding, contradicting; b) commissives such as committing, promising, threatening, assuring; c) directives such as requesting, advising, warning, demanding; d) declarations such as dismissing, approving, legalizing, blessing; and e) expressives such as thanking and apologizing. The power of texts is further underscored by the fact that a "text remains active as long as it is recognized or not destroyed" (Cooren, 2004, p. 385).

These examples illustrate the power and significance of texts. Yet, determining what to read in a more formal textual analysis may not be as difficult as determining how to read. In other words, reading just for a quick update is different from reading for cultural information. Reading for a quick update might provide information about a new policy or a meeting change. Reading for cultural information, however, will also guide you in discerning the *culture creating* roles certain texts play. For those conducting a cultural analysis, reading a newsletter for general updates while also trying to analyze it for cultural meaning may be like lifting the corner of a piano while doing a math problem. Such a process creates tension one must learn to respond to in constructive ways. This chapter is about learning to still attend to the math problem (or the need to attend to meeting notices) while also focusing on the heavy lifting of textual analysis. This heavy lifting or attending to the cultural creation process, is not only important for textual analysis of newsletters and company webpages, but also for analyzing field notes and interview transcripts or summaries.

We first review three methods of textual analysis before providing five guidelines. Regardless of the type of textual analysis selected, we see value in beginning a cultural analysis with this method. The reason for this encouragement is that much can be learned from texts in an unobtrusive manner. By unobtrusive, we mean you are less likely to influence or draw attention to your efforts to understand the culture. Texts from web pages, artifacts, and newsletters, for example, provide insights into various elements of culture, such as rituals, norms, and history. These types of texts do not reveal all you need to know, but they hold rich information. In addition, while some texts may hold primary information about the way corporate leadership wants to portray the culture, they may also contain hints at the informal (e.g., postings about informal events, etc.). In the process of attending to texts like these, you gain data you can then explore further through observations, interviews, and/or surveys. You may, for instance, wonder about the significance of a plaque on the wall about a founding member of the organization. She may be recognized on the plaque, yet it will take additional data perhaps from an informal interview to discern if she is a hero in the organization. Therefore, in the coming chapters, we provide guides for conducting observations, as well as interviews and surveys. For now, we review three different means of textual analysis.

"Content analysis" is a method of developing categories from the text (e.g., newsletters, interview transcripts, e-mail correspondence, etc.) and developing a method of counting material related to each of the categories. We will discuss specific data interpretation procedures in Chapter 8, but here, we want to be sure you grasp the basics of the analysis process.

For purposes of illustration, you might have examined several newsletters and picked up on multiple elements of culture (e.g., stories, rituals, and humor) as well as several possible themes cutting across these elements. Imagine you then jotted down four plausible categories related to these themes: risk-taking, public image, innovation, and profitability. You might then systematically sample additional newsletters as well as the web page (and in time interview transcripts) to count the number of times each theme is mentioned. At the end of your categorizing, you might conclude that profitability had been mentioned twice as often as any other value. You might also have picked up on a fifth category or the need to reword and clarify one of them based on attending more closely to the data. For instance, in a study on employee engagement, one team of researchers explored the expanded role of Public Relations professionals with regard to employee engagement. They conducted a content analysis of responses to interview questions sent via e-mail as well as transcripts from face-to-face interviews. Their analysis allowed them to glean insight into a public relations sub-culture that viewed their primary function as "building trust through dialogue" through "employee engagement" and owning "all channels of communication" (Mishra, Boynton, & Mishra, 2014, p. 195). These themes were based on a content analysis involving first looking for the frequency of themes, then for clusters of terms related to these themes, and then finally, "patterns of association" to discern the most important clusters (p. 189). As such, like the other types of textual analysis, the goal is to be intentional and systematic in order to create a more credible and ethical interpretation. This same focus on intentionality and systematic processes is true as well in the second type of content analysis.

Rhetorical analysis is typically more qualitative and less quantitative than content analysis. Thus, rather than counting based on categories, the researcher examines the author, background, purpose, strategy, and effect of written or oral texts. Examples of this type of textual analysis in organizations can be found in the study of apologies and crisis management responses made by corporate figures as well as public officials. For instance, scholars have used rhetorical analysis to study Planned Parenthood's response to the release of controversial videos (Brandhorst & Jennings, 2016). In another instance, a university leadership's response was analyzed as they addressed a plagiarism crisis in the context of revoking the former Minister of Science and Education's dissertation (Fähnrich, Danyi, & Nothhaft, 2015). Specific "image-response" strategies to the Gulf oil spill have also been explored (Smithson & Venette, 2013). Others focus on organizational renewal involving ethical and effective rhetoric in response to a crisis (Ulmer, Sellnow, & Seeger, 2009, 2015). In these and other studies, the rhetorical scholar might investigate the public attitudes or climate in which the apology is offered, the nature of the person offering the apology, the characteristics of the message (Does it take personal responsibility? Does it contain excuses?), and the effect on the intended audience. Although this method of textual analysis is quite involved, it may be appropriate with certain important organizational texts that are cited as the moment of major cultural change, after a crisis, and/or mission redefinition.

A third type of textual analysis is "discourse analysis." This method may involve a variety of practices, including language and grammatical structures of messages (linguistic analysis) and/or attending to sequences of sentences, turns at talk, and propositions. For instance, the researcher may pay attention to why a corporate leader chose one term rather than another, why one word was repeated over and over in a text, or the intent or effect of passive verb use, which tends to deny responsibility. In addition, if analyzing a conversation pattern in a meeting, attention could be given to who speaks first and the functions of patterns that emerge. For instance, in a study of communication during organization-wide meetings in a Danish firm, researchers discerned three ways participants legitimized decisions: a) pointing to the abnormality of a strategic situation; b) attending to socio-economic factors; and c) utilizing idiomatic expressions (Aggerholm & Asmuß, 2016). This type of analysis may also surface paradoxes. Wasson (2004) examines the use of marketplace or enterprise metaphors. Her analysis provides insight into how these metaphors created irony and paradox for employees. One interviewee reflected on how the "enterprise ideology" should have prompted her to feel confident and take control of a project. However, the reality is that the success of the project was not under her direct control. Thus, this employee was ironically "disempowered by being forced to speak as if she were empowered" (Wasson, 2004, p. 190). In another example, Angi, in her study of a church conflict (Brenton, 1993), examined two major texts: a statement by a dissident at the church, read ostensibly as an apology to the congregation, and the second a response from the church leaders. She found that the statement by the dissident used active voice, stressed agency by specific references to individuals, and used language related to change 14 times in the message. On the other hand, the statement from the church leaders used passive voice, did not include any references to specific people, and used language related to order and stability 24 times. The linguistic features of the message displayed the different reactions of the two parties in their orientation to change and responsibility.

Perhaps the most powerful argument, as mentioned previously, for using textual analysis is the unobtrusive nature of the method. You can, without influencing reactions from anyone, read and gain useful cultural data. Much can be learned from organizational documents and artifacts such as memos, written histories, newsletters, or even oral texts such as speeches or videos. Textual analysis could also be used to investigate a culture that no longer exists or to analyze the past of a current organization through archival material. So, as you might imagine, wise leaders and consultants who want to be effective directors will do their homework at this stage. To make the most of a textual analysis, follow these four guidelines:

1. Determine Credible "Text(s)" for Analysis

Locating a credible text involves several key factors. First, consider the salience or importance in the life of the organization. For example, if you examine newsletters, a salient sample may need to include newsletters from both before and after a major change. Salience may mean samples from various stages or important periods in the history and annual event calendar of the organization. Second, gain a representative sample. It is dangerous to draw conclusions from a single artifact or even from a small sample. The danger is much like that to be found in basing your understanding of an organization on one person's views. Recall a major goal in shifting from informal to more formal cultural analysis is to engage in practices that will catch our tendency to base conclusions on limited data. Third, it is also important to consider official and unofficial samples of written artifacts. In one organization, we had done an extensive analysis of a large sample of employee newsletters only to find that most employees considered the newsletter to be corporate propaganda and never read it. We then sought what culture members considered to be more authentic examples of corporate texts as viewed by culture members. You need to ask yourself who produced a particular text and for what reason in deciding whether it is a credible text for cultural analysis. A fourth consideration involves organizational communication style. Organizational communication style was one of the cultural elements described in Chapter 4. If an organization has a written culture, you should have an abundance of texts to choose from—from policies and procedures manuals to memos to annual reports. If an organization style is more oral or interpersonal, you may have to focus on different types of texts. You may be able to find copies of speech texts or be able to find videos of corporate interactions. In fact, if there is a major focus on face-to-face communication, you will need to discern whether texts are going to be an important source of cultural data at all. Conversely, in an organization whose communication style is electronic, texts to analyze may include e-mail records, Facebook, or other electronic system transactions. In virtual organizations, the primary texts may be from e-mail threads and chats. Consider completing Rehearsal 5.1 to aid you in identifying texts.

Rehearsal 5.1 Selecting Texts for Analysis

Purpose: Identify relevant texts for analysis.

Steps:

1. Review the list of possible organizational texts that follow.
2. Put a check mark by those that you have access to in the organization.
3. Put check marks by those that observation and interviews suggest are salient, representative, official vs. unofficial.
4. Jot down the type of cultural elements present (values, heroes, rituals, humor, etc.).

Type of Text	*Access*	*Salient*	*Representative*	*Official or Unofficial*	*Element*
Newsletter					
Annual report					
Web site					
Mission statement					
Bulletin boards					
Employee handbook					
E-mail					
Speech Transcripts					
Social Media					
Other					

2. Choose Your Method of Analysis

Your selection of a text will also influence the type of analysis method that best fits. Here, we further explore the three types to aid you in discerning the ones most appropriate for your analysis.

Content Analysis

As reviewed previously, you will probably also use this method, not just for organizational texts such as a newsletter, but also for analyzing your field notes and interview transcripts or summaries. The basic technique of content analysis is to let categories emerge from the elements of culture or from your data and then use those categories to count some features of the text. You might have a sense after 10 to 15 interviews that you have heard three values most frequently: teamwork, excellence, and accountability. You will go back through the interview notes and summaries with these categories in mind and perhaps a fourth category of "other." You will count the number of times each of the three values was mentioned and place a tally mark beside that category for each time it was mentioned. When you encounter other values in addition to the three you have chosen as categories, you will place a tally mark by the "other" category. If, at the end of the process, you find that "other" is larger than any of the three categories you started with, you might need to go back through the notes and decide whether there is another category you need to break out of the "other" category to represent the data accurately. Content analysis is often a trial-and-error process in which you may need to revise the category structure one or two times until you find the categories that fit your data best (see Rehearsal 5.2). Researchers also have the option to use software to aid in content analysis. Thus, if your texts are in electronic format (newsletters, typed field notes, etc.), programs such as *Diction 7.2* (Diction, n.d.; Hart, 2000, 2001) enable you to process 30,000 words in one minute. This type of software can examine texts for such features as "commonality"—language highlighting the agreed-upon values of a group, or "certainty"—language indicating resoluteness, inflexibility, and completeness.

Rhetorical Analysis

Although there are many systems of rhetorical analysis, its simplest form involves an in-depth analysis of a specific speech or text given by an identifiable cultural figure. Since the process is so involved, you would use this only on a very significant organizational text. For example, an exploration of a web page might surface videos and/or texts of major speeches by the current (or founding) CEO. A rhetorical analysis might be useful to discern the various elements of culture present, such as values, heroes, language, and history. In one instance, a class analysis of a university website surfaced a former Chancellor's speeches on addressing and improving race relations in the community. The Chancellor, over a ten-year period, used the phrase, "You have to face it to fix it." In subsequent analysis, effort was made to discern if other elements of culture on the campus echoed this language and value set. Students learned of ongoing community surveys related to race, the forming of an Institute on Race and Ethnicity, as well as weekly faculty and staff meetings (Anderson Institute on Race and Ethnicity, n.d.).

A rhetorical analysis might also be useful to explore the communicative function of serving both individual and organizational interests. For instance, Mynster and Edwards (2014) present a rhetorical analysis of a non-profit, Amnesty International Denmark (AID). Their analysis revealed how members, relying on AID moral positions, construct a view of the world that offers them a sense of collective identity and certainty. This same high moral ground creates a broad basis for support. This type of analysis can also be useful if you are studying an international corporation's public communication. For instance, one might study United Airlines' CEO Oscar Munoz's statements to Congress and stockholders in light of the 2017 incident involving the forced removal of a passenger from a plane. In rhetorical analysis, you would find out more about Munoz and the events leading up to his appearance on Capitol Hill. What factors provide context for his appearance? Then, with that appropriate background information, you would analyze the message itself. What was the purpose of the speech? What arguments or persuasive appeals were made? How were they supported? What type of evidence was offered? What cultural elements were woven into the speech—History? Values? Metaphors? Symbols? Finally, you will analyze the results of the speech. How effective was he in providing an apology? How did employees respond? What stories are still told about United and this event? In brief, some of you might use a form of rhetorical analysis to gain insight into values and history in relation to a speech or statement made by a leader.

Discourse Analysis

This method of textual analysis, as reviewed previously, may involve a focus on speech acts, turns in a conversation, or patterns of responses. Thus, you may focus on meeting notes, speeches, corporate apologies, and/or mission statements. For instance, if a theme emerged in newsletters about a value set on the environment, attention could be given to discourse to determine if the environment is indeed viewed as a significant "stakeholder." Lischinsky (2015), in a study in this vein, determined that the organizational value claimed in relation to the environment was not present in actual practices. Your use of this method might also explore minority groups. In a study by Jones (2017), attention was given to the discourse of minority business leaders. The analysis enabled her to identify the way these leaders resisted dominant discourses concerning black businesses. Such an analysis takes a critical turn in that attention is given to how power structures are challenged. Following Fowler (1986), a critical turn may involve identifying a small but culturally significant text and analyzing the language and grammatical patterns to reveal an underlying system logic. Although Fowler includes a number of linguistic features in his system, the following are particularly relevant to cultural analysis:

- Pronoun use: As corporate leaders talk and write, do they talk about "we" or "I"? Do they refer to employees as "them"? Do they use pronouns such as "you" that have the effect of finger-pointing?

- Active or passive verb use: Do decision-makers accept accountability for their actions by using names and active verbs, or do they hide behind passive verbs that fail to identify agents of actions? (The decision was made to eliminate 600 jobs.)
- Overuse or underuse of certain words or types of words: For example, in a public statement Angi analyzed, leaders in one embattled organization used the terms *rational, orderly,* and *proper* more than 17 times. This was indicative of their resistance to cultural change led by the members of the culture.
- Verb tense: Do public statements talk more about the past with past tense or more about the future with future tense?

Like other textual analysis processes, the key is to discern various elements of culture and then patterns that emerge that provide insight into what is being created in communicative processes (see Rehearsal 5.3).

3. Determine Your Unit of Measurement

As you perform content analysis on a text, either by hand or by computer, you must decide your measurement unit. What are you counting? In the previous example, your unit of analysis was "mentions" in a newsletter or an interview. In analyzing printed texts, different measurements might be more appropriate. You could count the number of pictures featuring management versus employees, men versus women, or Caucasians versus African Americans. You could count the number of stories on certain subjects or the number of column inches devoted to various topics. If you were analyzing a smaller document such as a speech, you might focus on counting actual words—how often the word *excellent* appeared in a 10-minute speech, for example. Within a lengthy newsletter, you may want to focus on one area, such as messages from the president or on member spotlights. You can analyze a written artifact at a micro or macro level. You might, for example, count the number of stories in an overall newsletter on various topics (macro analysis) or analyze specific words used in a representative paragraph (microanalysis). You may actually measure square centimeters or inches or do a word count; however, the percentage of an entire newsletter devoted to the issue in comparison to other topics is perhaps more telling. The key here is to use this analysis as *one gauge* of what is important to the organization based on the amount of space allotted in publications.

4. Link the Results of Your Analysis Back to Cultural Elements and Cultural Significance

Like the interview and observation processes, this step is about summarizing your data into a form that is usable. For instance, you might have entries that state the following:

Heroes: Three of the four newsletters gave one-eighth of their space to discussing the ex-CEO. This amount of space was about two times as much as for any other person or issue. Interview summaries and articles written by this ex-CEO all suggest that he remains a hero and perhaps a legend of sorts for this organization.

Values: One value was mentioned 43 times in interviews, four times as often as any other value discussed by employees.

Language: Certain terms are used repeatedly when discussing employee pay and benefit concerns. Such terms as *tenure, earned*, and *seen potential* are words used by management to explain a policy change that reduces benefits for employees who have less than two years of history with the organization.

5. Check Your Interpretations of the Text

At the informal level, as we began this unit, we indicated that all of us engage in informal analysis. We read various texts and draw conclusions. This more intentional, formal process is intended to aid us in checking our first takes or initial interpretations. To that end, in this final step, take time to reflect on your analysis. You might find, for example, that your initial thoughts about the way a change was talked about in newsletters were not congruent with what was experienced on the ground. You should make a list of questions about confusing or contradictory issues. For example, you might find an espoused value in the written documents that is different from the values expressed in employee interviews. The mission statement, for example, might stress the importance of sustainability or community engagement, yet there is not one picture or story in the newsletter that reflects these values. Thus, you should ground interpretations from textual analysis back into the native perspective by asking organizational members about their interpretations.

Summary

Systematic analyses of organizational texts are similar to the intense work an actor does with a script prior to crafting a performance. Textual analysis is an unobtrusive research method and can reveal a great deal about an organization. Texts, in themselves, have a type of agency that is, like human actors, part of the constitutive process of organizing and organizations. This chapter stressed the following points:

1. Three systematic ways to analyze organizational texts:
    - Content analysis
    - Rhetorical analysis
    - Discourse analysis
2. It is vital that you: a) choose a sufficient sample of credible texts to analyze; b) determine which of the three main analysis methods(s) fit your purpose; c) determine your unit of measurement; and d) tie your analysis back to elements and cultural significance.

Rehearsal 5.2 Content Analysis

Purpose: To gain experience in noting the types of cultural elements that can be found in various organizational artifacts.

Directions:

1. Identify an artifact for analysis (newsletter, etc.).

2. Analyze the artifact using content analysis.
    - Determine the unit of analysis or your focus within the text.
    - Pay attention to the amount of space devoted to certain issues from one document to the next.
    - Identify and give examples of specific cultural elements.
    - Make a list of questions about confusing or contradictory issues.
3. Write a brief summary of insights about at least three of the elements.
4. Write down specific challenges and questions you faced in the process. These issues can be shared with a colleague or instructor who is working with you in this process.

Rehearsal 5.3 Discourse Analysis

Purpose: To gain experience in using critical linguistic analysis in cultural studies

Directions: Compare the following language features in two organizational texts. You may identify your own or consider mission and company information from similar and/or different types of organizations such as Tom's Shoes—(www.toms.com/en-us/impact) versus Nike Shoes (https://about.nike.com/en/impact); GM Automotive (www.gm.com/commitments/overview) versus Toyota (www.toyota.com/about/our_values/); Tacos4Life (www.tacos4life.com/10meal-ion) vs. Taco Bell (www.yum.com/wps/portal/yumbrands/Yumbrands/impact/).

As you examine mission statements and corporate philosophies, pay attention to such language features as:

- Pronoun use
- Passive or active voice
- Words that are overused or underused
- Verb tense—past, present, future

What differences do you note in these texts? Commonalities? What tentative inferences might you draw about how the corporate cultures differ?

Discussion Questions

1. Make an argument about why observation is a logical starting point for a cultural analysis, and then make an argument about why textual analysis is the best starting point.
2. Why should you make sure that a text is meaningful or salient to organizational members before you draw conclusions from it about the culture? Brainstorm about texts that would be most meaningful in the organization you are studying.

3. What are the advantages and disadvantages of using written surveys in the analysis of organizational culture?
4. Brainstorm about artifacts you could observe that would reveal important things about the organizational culture.
5. How can our involvement with an organization in performing a cultural analysis actually affect the organization and the individuals in it?
6. Give an example of a situation in which you might want to perform a rhetorical analysis of an organizational text. A discourse analysis?
7. How might the process of a formal textual analysis aid you in becoming a more ethical and credible member of the culture?

References

Aggerholm, H. K., & Asmuß, B. (2016). A practice perspective on strategic communication. *Journal of Communication Management, 20(3)*, 195–214. https://doi.org/10.1108/JCOM-07-2015-0052

Anderson Institute on Race and Ethnicity. (n.d.). Retrieved from http://ualr.edu/race-ethnicity/archive-our-beginning/

Brandhorst, J. K., & Jennings, F. J. (2016). Fighting for funding: Values advocacy and planned parenthood's right-to-life. *Public Relations Review, 42*(*4*), 723–733. https://doi.org/10.1016/j.pubrev.2016.06.002

Brenton, A. (1993). Demystifying the magic of language: Critical linguistic case analysis of legitimization of authority. *Journal of Applied Communication Research, 21*, 227–244. https://doi.org/10.1080/00909889309365369

Cooren, F. (2004). Textual agency: How texts do things in organizational settings. *Organization, 11*, 373–393. https://doi.org/10.1177/1350508404041998

Diction. (n.d.). *Published materials: Scholarly research using the diction program*. Retrieved from https://dictionsoftware.com/

Fähnrich, B., Danyi, C., & Nothhaft, H. (2015). The German plagiarism crisis: Defending and explaining the workings of scholarship on the front stage. *Journal of Communication Management, 19*(*1*), 20–38. https://doi.org/10.1108/JCOM-11-2013-0081

Fowler, R. (1986). *Linguistic criticism*. Oxford: Oxford University Press.

Hart, R. P. (2000). *DICTION 5.0: The text-analysis program*. Thousand Oaks, CA: Sage.

Hart, R. P. (2001). Redeveloping DICTION: Theoretical considerations. In M. D. West (Ed.), *Theory, method, and practice in computer content analysis* (pp. 43–60). New York: Springer.

Jones, N. (2017). Rhetorical narratives of black entrepreneurs: The business of race, agency, and cultural empowerment. *Journal of Business and Technical Communication, 31*(*3*), 319–349. https://doi.org/10.1177/1050651917695540

Lischinsky, A. (2015). What is the environment doing in my report? Analyzing the environment-as-stakeholder thesis through corpus linguistics. *Environmental Communication, 9*(*4*), 539–559. https://doi.org/10.1080/17524032.2014.967705

Mishra, K., Boynton, L., & Mishra, A. (2014). Driving employee engagement: The expanded role of internal communications. *International Journal of Business Communication, 51*(*2*), 183–202. https://doi.org/10.1177/232948841452539

Mynster, A. S., & Edwards, L. (2014). Building blocks of individual biography? Non-governmental organizational communication in reflexive modernity. *Management Communication Quarterly, 28*(*3*), 319–346. https://doi.org/10.1177/0893318914530673

Smithson, J., & Venette, S. (2013). Stonewalling as an image-defense strategy: A critical examination of BP's response to the Deepwater horizon explosion. *Communication Studies, 64*(*4*), 395–410. https://doi.org/10.1080/10510974.2013.770409

Strasberg, L. (1987). *A dream of passion: The development of the method*. Boston: Little, Brown.

Ulmer, R., Sellnow, T., & Seeger, M. (2009). Crisis communication and renewal: Understanding the potential for positive outcomes in crisis communication. In R. Heath & D. O'Hair (Eds.), *Handbook of risk and crisis communication* (pp. 302–322). New York: Routledge.

Ulmer, R., Sellnow, T., & Seeger, M. (2015). *Effective crisis communication: Moving from crisis to opportunity* (3rd ed.). Thousand Oaks, CA: Sage Publications.

Wasson, C. (2004). The paradoxical language of enterprise. *Critical Discourse Studies*, *1*(*2*), 175–199. https://doi.org/10.1080/1740590042000302067

Chapter 6

Method Acting

Observation

The fourth step of the OCA (Organizational Culture in Action) model, "Collect data on elements via multiple methods," is introduced by starting with the process of observation. Like the other methods, the intent is to improve the processes we use each day. Four observation roles (i.e., complete observer, observer–participant, participant–observer, complete participant) are discussed in terms of advantages and disadvantages, including ethical consideration. Seven guidelines to improve the observation process are discussed: 1) make like an alien by making use of various techniques to become a "stranger"; 2) take notes while observing or reserve time immediately after observations; 3) observe both formal and informal and formal interactions; 4) use brackets to help you distinguish description from interpretations; 5) check understandings of elements with insiders; 6) review notes to draw inferences about other cultural elements; and 7) categorize notes by elements to guide additional data collection.

1. Articulate cultural analysis goals and benefits
2. Explore culture as co-construction
3. Reflect on enacted elements
4. Identify enacted elements via multiple methods
5. Interpret thematic action and OCA
6. Co-create positive communication applications

Step Four: Collect Data on Elements Via Multiple Methods

Objectives

- Identify four major observation roles.
- Describe ways to enhance the validity and reliability of observation data.
- Practice recording observations in field notes.

Stage Terms

Obtrusive observation	Complete observer	Participant observer	Field notes
Unobtrusive observation	Observer participant	Complete participant	Bracketing

DOI: 10.4324/9781003482529-9

The following quote reflects the chapter's aims:

> To concentrate, one must have an object of concentration; one cannot concentrate abstractly. The simple presence of an object will not induce concentration. If you look at a chair and try to concentrate, nothing will happen. If you start asking yourself simple questions—How wide is the chair? How tall is it? and so on—simple concentration will take place.
>
> (Strasberg, *A Dream of Passion*, 1987, p. 131)

Everyday Interactions

Imagine an actor (or a director) who never took the time to go behind the scenes, attend to the ways others interact on the stage, or observe stage props and backdrops. We would quickly judge such an actor as incompetent. However, we all have moments when our observations are incomplete, skewed, and/or biased. For example, based on one interaction with a colleague or observing one meeting with a new team, we may form an inaccurate and/or overly negative or overly positive impression. However, even with such awareness, it is often easier and more comfortable to maintain our casual observation and interpretation habits. We may not ever make time to pause, reflect, and develop a greater level of mindfulness about the organization. We may not be in the habit of asking, "What are we co-creating here?" The goal in this chapter is to improve our understanding of and our ability to reduce bias by enacting effective and ethical observer roles—the core or foundation of method acting and cultural analysis.

Observation is critical to method actors, as expressed by Lee Strasberg (1987). He describes training actors to concentrate on the particulars of a process that has become automatic, such as drinking a beverage. Only by concentrating on each element of the habitual behavior can the actor master the subtleties of re-creating a common behavior on stage. The actor must spend hours analyzing and practicing a behavior in order for it to appear natural and compelling on stage. Strasberg writes, "The ability to interrupt the automatic functioning of the nerves and muscles in order to create an object's presence for oneself . . . is part of the process of creating reality rather than imitating it" (p. 133).

What is the significance of Strasberg's comments for our analysis process? One value of engaging in formal cultural analysis is that we become more aware of the way our everyday interactions construct and reconstruct culture. We see, in other words, what we are creating. One way to enhance our capacity for concentration, that is, seeing what we are co-creating with others, is through improving our capacity for observation. Observer roles can be categorized by examining the degree of "obtrusiveness" or the degree of influence the observer has on the members of organizations. "Obtrusive" behavior is that which calls attention to the observer, affecting the flow of behavior being observed. Different behaviors may be seen as obtrusive depending on the organization. For example, extensive note-taking during a meeting may be the norm in certain organizations; thus, taking notes during a meeting would be unlikely to influence the flow of the meeting. Conversely, such note-taking during a ritual morning coffee break would be likely to trigger responses from other members of the organization. Reviews of four observation roles followed by observation guidelines are presented as ways to consider the implications of each type of observer role.

Selecting a Method of Observation

There are four major observer roles. Each role involves trade-offs based on such factors as objectivity, insight into interactions, and ethics. As you review these, be mindful of the fact that you already have engaged in these sorts of roles. Also, realize that it is not uncommon to move between different roles. In other words, entering into one type of observation role does not preclude your engaging in another type of role at some other point in time. For example, we have had students begin observation of a given nonprofit as a complete observer and switch to a participant observer as they begin to identify with the mission of the nonprofit and get to know the staff and volunteers.

1. Complete Observer

In this role, you observe the culture with or without the organization's knowledge and without direct interaction with members. (Please note, however, that your instructor may require you to gain permission from the organization, even if you are studying your own organization.) To use the drama metaphor, you would be an actor doing research for a role, observing the behavior of people similar to the character you are to portray. Assuming this role carries several implications:

- In traditional research terms, the researcher may have increased objectivity due to the lack of involvement with organization members who might bias his or her judgment.
- On the other hand, qualitative researchers would argue that the researcher would possibly also have fewer and less valid insights due to the distance from the experience of members.
- The role of the complete observer can raise possible ethical problems if you observe individuals without their permission, depending on the purposes of the research. If the organization studied is a professional football team, for instance, and performances are public, then the ethical concerns are less of an issue. In all instances, ethical guidelines must be observed.
- The complete observer role may be best when you do not have full access to the organization, when you have organizational permission to observe the organization, and/or when members' knowledge of your presence would be likely to harm research objectives. For example, individuals considering a career move who are trying to learn more about a particular type of organization may find this method appropriate. If, for instance, they want to learn more about the automotive industry, they may find it useful to show up at a public event or simply to walk through public areas of the organization to learn what they can from the setting and artifacts on display.

2. Observer–Participant

In this role, you would let members know they are being observed, and you would participate partially with them in the organization. This role carries different implications:

- This role somewhat reduces objectivity due to involvement, yet possibly increases validity by interacting with organization members and gaining their insights.
- Some would question validity when members are aware of your involvement.
- You may find adopting the observer–participant role places you on more solid ethical ground due to member knowledge of your involvement.
- This role is best when you have access to the organization and/or when member knowledge of your presence would be unlikely to harm research objectives; for example, observation of meetings to understand norms and interaction patterns for the purpose of enriching the current employee handbook.

3. *Participant–Observer*

In this role, you let members know they are being studied, and you become fully involved in the organization. The implications of this role include the following:

- According to a traditional research perspective, it produces reduced objectivity due to high involvement in the organization.
- This role produces increased access to the views and insights of organization members, and the researcher herself begins to understand the organization from both internal and external perspectives.
- This role places similar constraints on you as an observer–participant in relation to member awareness of your involvement, yet the more organizational members accept you as a participant, the less they are aware of you as an observer.
- Since organization members are aware of your dual role (researcher and participant), you are on fairly solid ethical ground.
- This role is best when you have longer-term access to the organization and/or when member knowledge of your presence would be unlikely to harm research objectives; for example, observation of day-to-day communication to understand positive and negative patterns that would affect training interventions.

4. *Complete Participant*

In this final role, you become fully involved without letting members know of your observation efforts. The implications include the following:

- You have reduced objectivity due to high involvement, yet may have a high level of insight due to identification with members.
- Possible ethical problems would ensue because of the lack of notification of research subjects, depending on the purposes of the observations. For example, if you dropped in on meetings without informing those present that you were also there to evaluate and report their behaviors, then your efforts would be judged unethical because of the potential harm that could result to those present. This approach might also be inconsistent with the protection of human subjects if you did not allow informed consent for your observation.
- This role is best when you have access to the organization and/or when members' lack of knowledge of your presence would not influence the ethicality of your research purpose. For example, as a human resource department (HRD) manager, you could serve and lead more effectively if you gleaned insights about norms and rules through observation of meetings and rituals.
- This role, regardless of unit or position, can be undertaken ethically. In fact, whether part of a class assignment or your own professional undertaking, you can rely on the OCA model to improve the way you attend to culture as well as your role in co-construction. You would not report your findings, but you would use them to develop a final self-reflection. You could write up a summary, but your primary audience is, of course, yourself and anything reported in class should not include any identifying information.

Standards of protection of human subjects, presented in the overview of this section, are critical in cultural research, as well. If you present a cultural study to the CEO of an organization, and your study inadvertently reveals rule-breaking or violation of cultural norms, it could have serious career implications for the individuals you study.

One of the observation role options, "complete participant," should stand out as the form of observation we engage in every day. If you do not inform others in the organization of your analysis efforts, you are a complete participant. As a complete participant, you are doing something external analysts and researchers are challenged to justify—"clandestine data collection." The ethical justification for an insider is based on the reality that your observation is doing what all members of organizations do but simply doing it in a more systematic and planned manner. Nonetheless, realize that, for some, it will be appropriate to seek the permission of a supervisor to inform others of your analysis plans. For example, you may be a trainer in your organization or work in a role that has made you aware of the need for a cultural analysis. After reviewing the value of the study with those you decide to inform, you may want to move ahead with a formal analysis that would involve a participant observer role. Regardless of the role you select, the key is to be aware of the specific issues related to objectivity, validity, and ethics.

Conducting Observations

Once you have decided on the most appropriate role, review the following guides for help in the process of conducting the observation and taking notes. You need to have a rationale for what you notice and record. Rehearsal 6.2 provides questions to ask that guide you to places to observe. As a way to focus, approach the observation process with the OCA (Organizational Culture in Action) framework in mind. Recall this framework, based on constructivist theories, encourages our attention to the way enacted elements of culture (e.g., artifacts, stories, rituals) constitute the organization. Recall from Chapter 4 on these elements the need to attend to macro and micro communicative processes. We suggested in the introduction to the section on methods (see Table III.1) that your observations could focus on artifacts, interactions, language, and symbols. We also suggested cultural elements most closely tied to each of these observable organizational representations (e.g., history, values, norms, heroes). Follow these seven guidelines to enhance the quality of your observations. At the end of this chapter, we summarize these guidelines in a checklist to review as you conduct a practice observation in a rehearsal.

1. Make Like an Alien by Making Use of Various Techniques to Become a "Stranger"

The observational ideal of "being a stranger" is, of course, most relevant to those studying an organization as an insider. So much is taken for granted that you may tend to overlook facets of the culture. We suggest three strategies to aid you.

a. *Write notes on the mundane, seemingly unimportant events.* Improving the quality of our observations involves seeing things with new eyes. We encourage this process in Rehearsal 6.3, "Alien Culture Observation." The first step in this process is taking notes that record information that you take for granted. For example, if you were an "old-timer" in the case study that began this unit, you would take notes on the setting, the seating arrangement, and when and how the meeting began and ended. Such detailed notes force you to see situations with new eyes.
b. *Mutate metaphors* by drawing comparisons or making analogies between things that you normally do not compare (Weick, 1979). Mutating metaphors involves merging or synthesizing two metaphors to capture conflicting values or rules. For example, imagine

if you frequently heard members of the organization in pre-meeting talks discuss two metaphors: "fast track" and "outer space." As you listened, you got the sense that "good" employees were expected to be on the fast track. However, you also heard sarcastic statements about working in outer space, with the implication being that there was not a clear sense of what was up or down since, in outer space, "up and down" and "north and south" are arbitrary. To capture these two metaphors, you might mutate them to create a new metaphor, like "working at Organization Z is like being on a corporate ladder without ever knowing which direction is up or down." This mutated metaphor captures a paradox that members may be aware of but have not clearly articulated—"We hear about the expectation to move up the ladder, but we do not know which way is up!" Such comparisons may clarify or serve to identify a problem in the organization. Metaphors and the mutation process may also lend insight to insights related to communicating change.

Smith and Eisenberg (1987), in their now classic study on Disneyland, for example, indicated that the root problem in employee relations might have begun when employees began seeing their work through the family rather than the drama metaphor. Rules and actions that might have been easily accepted through the drama metaphor became inappropriate when viewed through the lens of family. For example, you might replace a cast member who is incompetent in a role, but you do not fire "family." If you were consulting with an organization that had operated primarily through a family metaphor, what implications would a change in that metaphor have for employees? Customers? Helping the organization manage change, as shall be discussed further in Chapter 10, might involve a metaphor mutation—if employees were able to mutate metaphors, they could envision the change in a new way. For example, the mutation might involve both metaphors, "an acting family," that has to determine who is best for what role.

c. *Ask "why" and "what function" questions of everything.* Though you will have to decide the appropriateness of asking others these types of questions, you should, at the minimum, reflect on them yourself. For example, you might observe an organization's annual retirement banquet and assume that it indicated a culture in which employee contributions were valued. However, if you asked a member of the organization about it, she might say that there is great pressure for older employees to take early retirement so that less expensive younger employees can be hired. Or she might note that it is a sign that the company values seniority more than excellent performance since the only significant award banquet in the organization is to honor retirees rather than high performers. Once you have made your own possible interpretations, you can make notes to ask organizational insiders how they would interpret the regularities you have observed. This focus on understanding function is of added importance in multinational contexts. You may, for example, assume you understand the meaning of a closed door (e.g., privacy) versus an open door (e.g., no need to knock) but fail to realize that the function of these nonverbal cues is impacted by culture. Zeisal (2006), in the context of exploring observation guidelines for design engineers, stresses the influence of national culture in the observation process. National culture may mean that an open door actually should be interpreted as "do not disturb." He goes on to stress that "to see behavior from a cultural perspective other than one's own" involves being aware of your own cultural biases, as well as knowledge of the other culture often gleaned from members of that culture (p. 211).

2. *Take Notes While Observing or Reserve Time Immediately After Observations*

Note-taking has the potential advantage to improve the quality of the information you collect on the organization. For those who rarely take notes or keep journals, the process will be awkward and feel like a waste of time. Still, the key is to make time for this process of describing what you see. You may think you will remember details later, but chances are you will forget many important details. Doing a thorough cultural analysis requires noting fine details of language, artifacts, and interaction. These are best captured in detailed field notes (see Rehearsal 6.4). Another value of the process of writing involves not just putting words on paper but taking the time to capture events, reflect on them, and, in time, make sense of them. An enhanced or improved cultural analysis depends on your seeing all the possible "dots" in a connect-the-dots worksheet. Sometimes, you draw conclusions—connect dots—without adequate attention to details that could change the shape of the picture. To use the drama analogy, note-taking may force you to see a way to interpret the language being used in the play in a different light. For example, a review of notes might reveal a pattern you had not seen concerning the way certain types of conflicts were not discussed. This newly emerged pattern might then shed light on other practices, such as premature closure on decisions to avoid conflict. As shown in this example of conflict, your notes should reflect your observation of things that did *not* happen that one might have expected. For example, why did no one ask questions? Why did no one talk about anything that was not on the formal agenda? Why don't employees have any personal items in their offices?

3. *Observe Both Formal and Informal and Formal Interactions*

The tendency, for example, may be to take notes of a ribbon-cutting ceremony or a company picnic but fail to record observations of communication at the coffee pot. Culture, as previously noted, reflects how members experience daily life in the organization. A weekly office meeting or daily coffee pot ritual provides just as much insight into organizational culture as an annual awards banquet. It may be that those coffee pot interactions include significant relationship development rituals that an insider may not see immediately. For instance, Mirivel and Tracy (2005) researched pre-meeting talk and found it carried important agenda and relationship-building functions. Such insights may help current employees do more to engage new employees, especially as will be discussed in the application chapter on diversity, to ensure the latter are not forced to catch on to the importance of the informal interaction rituals on their own.

4. *Use Brackets [] to Help You Focus on Descriptions Instead of Interpretations*

"Bracketing" refers to the idea of putting your first impressions, questions, reactions, initial definitions of the culture, and inferences or insights inside of brackets. Recall that the goal is to be descriptive. For example, your first weeks spent in observation might bring to the surface the way the lounge area has rituals you did not hear in other places in the building. Thus, after describing the ritual, "Members greet each other, and then one person gets up to serve coffee as another enters." You might then bracket: [What is the history of this ritual? Who is the person serving? Might they be an informal hero?]

These bracketed questions might prompt you to ask questions in a later interview, but they might also be the seed for an insight into interpreting cultural themes. Strong personalities in interviews or meetings can also prompt a researcher to draw conclusions early in the process. Indeed, our own ambiguity or uncertainty in a new organization will often prompt us to develop premature ideas. *The key is to bracket these conclusions until you have used other methods and explored all of the elements.*

These premature conclusions, if not set aside, can prompt you to slant your future data collection toward supporting these views. They help you separate descriptions from your tentative interpretations as you process your observation. For example, in participant observation research on a community-building organization, Gerald is regularly challenged to bracket his reactions, biases, and questions due to the varied political and theological positions that surface. The focus on description while bracketing, indeed, gave insight into the way leaders used stories and rituals to reframe dialectic tensions to work together despite historical ethnic and denominational barriers (Driskill & Camp, 2006; Driskill, Meyer, & Mirivel, 2012) as well as best practices for improving race relations (Glazier, Driskill, & Haynes, 2024).

In the following, relying on Gerald's field notes from a study of a collaborative network hub organization, four different types of bracketed information are provided. Under each type of bracketing, you will first see an example of a brief field note.

a. *Questions to ask (other) insiders:* There were several new faces today, including two guests. [How would you compare and contrast what happens in a meeting when visitors or newcomers are present versus those times when just the old-timers are there?]
b. *Possible paradoxes, contradictions, root metaphor(s):* The meeting facilitator briefly introduced the guests, who spoke about a recent statewide political initiative. [In past interviews, I recall hearing discussions about being cautious about inviting political guests to make presentations. I am not clear on the criteria being used.]
c. *Later comparisons—see how your perceptions change:* The meeting ended with a ritual prayer and then with an additional prayer over a leader who was moving to another state to take on an international role in the unity movement. [The send-off made me think about other meetings that included a special send-off. This particular send-off makes me want to compare the differences in that a value emerged that I had not heard before—a global vision of cooperation among faith leaders. The member seems to be in a position to be a hero for this movement.]
d. *Personal reactions/differences:* The guest speakers talked about positive and negative reactions to their political initiative. [I was not fully comfortable with the presentation. I am not sure why; perhaps it was that I did not get to hear the full story or the rationale of their opponents. Has this group ever considered inviting those with divergent views to their meetings? This insight makes me consider business organizations that end up with groupthink because they do not have someone or charge someone to voice divergent views.]

5. Check Understandings of Elements with Insiders

If you are a newcomer or an outsider, rely on insiders to check your understanding of jargon and your inferences about cultural elements. Recall the pros and cons of being an insider vs.

an outsider (Table 1.1). You may oversimplify a simple ritual like the talk that happens after a meeting. An insider may be aware that post-meeting talk is where the real action happens. Thus, consider using informal interviews to check if your understanding is accurate. We will discuss the role of interviews in greater depth; this guide is a reminder that observation alone is not sufficient. Often, your own interpretation of an artifact or event may be quite different from the way an insider (or a different insider) might interpret the same event. For example, in one student culture analysis, conclusions were drawn about an organization's culture from its newsletter, only to discover later that no one read the newsletter; thus, it had little impact on culture at the grassroots level. Another cultural analysis included a conclusion based on the many positive memos that the CEO sent to employees. They inferred that the culture was positive and supportive. When checking this conclusion with employees, they found that the memos from the CEO had become a joke because they were sent so frequently and so indiscriminately.

6. Review Notes to Draw Inferences About Other Enacted Elements

For example, do the notes of a meeting provide enough detail for you to make valid inferences about communication rules? Take a minute to read an edited version of the observation notes used in one of the previous guidelines.

> There were several new faces at the meeting today, including two guests. The meeting facilitator briefly introduced the guests, who spoke about a recent statewide political initiative. The guest speakers talked about positive and negative reactions to their political initiative. [I was not comfortable with the presentation because I did not get to hear the rationale of their opponents.] The meeting ended with a ritual prayer and with an additional prayer over a leader who was moving to another state to take on an eventual international role in the unity movement.

What inferences could you draw from just this brief section of notes? Notice how even a brief section reveals elements of the culture (e.g., meeting opening and ending rituals). However, if the previous passage were the entire entry, what questions would you have? What would you have missed? Details are lacking about how the speakers were introduced, as well as participant interactions or reactions to the speaker. Also, notice how we excluded brackets that were introduced in the earlier example. The lack of brackets around information means that a later review of these notes would be unlikely to resurface the same questions and observations. If you review notes a week or two later and see a lack of detail, make adjustments. Again, remember that the goal is to spend a season being a more careful, note-taking observer. This process will pay off in the form of new insights as well as improve your ability to attend to culture.

7. Categorize Notes by Elements to Guide Additional Data Collection

We reviewed elements of culture in Chapter 4. At this point in your data collection, you should take a first step in analysis by entering relevant data from your notes based on these categories (e.g., rules, heroes, history; c.f. Table 4.2 Categories of Enacted Elements). We provide a Rehearsal activity at the end of this chapter to move you down the road of "performing culture." In particular, as you classify data into elements, you should be aware of two pragmatic goals. First, classifying data into cultural element categories will serve to guide additional data collection by helping you see gaps. For instance, if you have two weeks of notes and have been unable to identify a hero or communication rule, you should let this gap prompt closer and more varied (more times, situations) observations. Second, classifying data into element categories will aid you in the creation/revision of an interview guide or survey. We will cover interviews and surveys in the next chapter. A good set of notes categorized by elements will aid you in gaining the most from these additional data collection practices by helping you identify areas where you need greater clarity or confirmation. For instance, you may have identified what you believe to be a major cultural hero from reading the history of the organization. However, the name of this hero never surfaces in informal discussions or formal meetings. Interviews or surveys may help you determine the relevance of the hero's values and vision for the present.

Connections: Getting More From Rites and Rituals

A frequent and rich object of observation is the organizational rite or ritual—either a special event in the organization or a daily routine with cultural significance. As you stand backstage, consider why something as commonplace as a ritual is worth giving added attention. First, rituals are an expedient way to gain information on other elements of culture. Islam and Zyphur (2009) argue that "[a] focus on rituals expedites the research process because, within these forms, it is possible to examine culturally rich phenomena compressed into relatively short periods" (p. 116). For example, an analysis of an annual retreat or a holiday party may reveal communication rules, heroes, and history. In either of these settings, a speaker (guest or manager) may review past events or honor certain events or employees. As you listen, you will be able to glean something about the espoused values of the organization. Second, rituals function to manage a central organizational tension: stability and change. They aid organizations in transition during a merger or internal change. They also serve to maintain norms and the solidarity of values within the organization. Thus, for instance, rituals provide a way to move ahead in the midst of uncertainty about change while maintaining a semblance of order or progress in the midst of flux (Islam & Zyphur, 2009). In addition, in the context of crisis communication, the ritual of offering an apology, while in need of nuanced application, is argued as critical to effective responses and renewal strategies (Coombs, 2013).

Six major categories of rituals (Trice & Beyer, 1984) are listed in Rehearsal 6.1. As you reflect on examples in your cultural analysis and/or in your organization, be sure to decipher manifest as well as latent meanings. For instance, the manifest or obvious "surface" meaning of a retreat for organizational development might be the value the organization places on strategic planning. In contrast, the latent meaning, or the hidden, less obvious meaning, might relate to the value placed on renewing and reinforcing friendships in the organization. Notice how, in this example, based on Trice and Beyer's (1984) categories, one ritual can serve two functions. For example, the retreat may include a time for play and interaction that serves to bind members together—an integration function. During the same ritual, a renewal function may be served if the key speaker recognizes and reaffirms the current structure of the organization by honoring members who have "climbed the ladder." Yet, even the richness of such an analysis should only underscore an earlier point made. If your analysis focuses on a single element, even an element that holds insights for other elements, you are likely to leave the organization with a skewed or inaccurate understanding of the culture.

Rehearsal 6.1 Identifying Six Types of Rites/Rituals

Purpose: Identify various types of rituals in your organization and the elements of culture embedded in each.

Direction: State your example and then include possible other elements found in the ritual. For example, a ritual of "passage" in the university might be the "tenure" process. Other cultural elements in this ritual include roles (power structures), language (title changes), and communication rules (how you talk to colleagues and superiors about the process).

1. Passage: facilitates transition into new social roles and status (e.g., Army basic training)
   Example: ______________________
   Other Elements: ______________________
2. Degradation: dissolve social identities and power (e.g., firing and replacing)
   Example: ______________________
   Other Elements: ______________________
3. Enhancement: enhance social identities and power (e.g., training certification program)
   Example: ______________________
   Other Elements: ______________________
4. Renewal: refurbish social structures and improve their functioning (e.g., a retreat for organizational development)
   Example: ______________________
   Other Elements: ______________________
5. Conflict reduction: reduce conflict and aggression (e.g., collective bargaining)
   Example: ______________________
   Other Elements: ______________________
6. Integration: encourage and revive common feelings that bind members together and build commitment (e.g., office holiday parties)
   Example: ______________________
   Other Elements: ______________________

Summary

Observation is about paying attention to what we often take for granted. This cultural analysis tool is about taking a step beyond what you do every day. The key is to be more observant, more aware of *what* and *how* you *see*. The intent, as with other methods, is to improve our mindfulness and effectiveness in asking the question, "What are we co-creating here?" In systematic observation, we encourage a formal recording of detailed field notes. At the end of this chapter, we will provide additional rehearsals to help you in the observation process in general and the note-taking process in particular. As you engage in these activities and other observation efforts, you should have a better sense of how to apply the major ideas presented in this chapter.

1. There are four observation roles (i.e., complete observer, observer–participant, participant–observer, complete participant). Each has advantages and disadvantages.
2. Seven guidelines should aid you in the observation process:

   a. Make like an alien by making use of various techniques to become a "stranger."
   b. Take notes while observing or reserve time immediately after observation.
   c. Include observations of formal meetings, rituals, and the like, as well as less formal interactions.
   d. Use brackets to help you distinguish descriptions and interpretations. Bracket items such as questions, possible paradoxes, later comparisons, and personal reactions/differences.
   e. Use insiders to check your understanding of jargon and your inferences about cultural elements.
   f. Review your notes to draw inferences about the cultural elements.
   g. Categorize notes by elements to guide additional data collection and fill gaps; create interview guides or surveys based on your analysis of data in element categories.

3. Rites and rituals are particularly rich sites for gathering observational cultural data; however, you should remain aware of the need to explore and gather information about all of the elements of culture.
4. As an actor with a renewed commitment to observation, if you enact the various guidelines we have suggested, you should become more adept at competent cultural performance.

Rehearsal 6.2 A Potpourri of Things to Observe in Cultural Analysis

Purpose: Practice observing a variety of organization settings and events that provide insight into elements of culture.

Directions: Review the following list of questions. Select two or three and attempt answers to these based on the organization you are analyzing.

1. What kind of building houses the organization? What impression does it convey to employees? Visitors?
2. What kind of parking is available? Is there any reserved parking? For whom? Is there any pattern of vehicles in the parking lot?

3. What does the entry look like? What kind of security? A receptionist?
4. Is there a waiting area for visitors? Does it have chairs? What kind of furniture? What kind of reading material? What is on the walls?
5. How is office space configured? Are there "premium" offices like corner spaces or windows with a better view? Who has these offices?
6. Are there offices or cubicles? Are office doors open or shut?
7. Is the workspace nondescript, or are there personal items? What type of personal items do employees have in their spaces?
8. Do people seem to be working alone or in groups?
9. Are there any items on the walls depicting the history? Photographs of founders? Pictures of early physical locations?
10. Are there pictures of anyone in public office spaces? Of whom? Why?
11. What types of common areas are present? Conference rooms? Break rooms or lounges? Does access to these spaces seem to be restricted?
12. What is in the break room? Do people seem to use it?
13. What is on the bulletin boards?
14. What type of technology do members use? Are there computers on every desk? Recent or vintage? Do employees carry PDAs? Pagers? Cell phones?
15. What do people wear? Do there seem to be status differences indicated by dress? Is the dress formal or casual?
16. How do people address one another? First names? Level of formality?
17. Observe a meeting. Where do people sit? Who speaks at the meeting, and who does not? Do there seem to be cliques supporting different points of view? Is conflict expressed openly? How long do meetings last?
18. Are there awards on the walls? Corporate awards? Individual awards? Team awards?
19. Is there anything in this office to indicate uniqueness based on geographic area, or could this office just as easily be located in Boston as in Santa Fe?
20. How much diversity do you observe by race/ethnicity, gender, age, or dress?

Discussion Questions

1. Discuss the advantages and disadvantages of various observational roles (complete observer, observer/participant, participant/observer, or complete participant).
2. Why is it important to adopt an "alien" perspective when doing cultural observation? How do you accomplish this as a cultural insider?
3. Why is it important to observe daily routine rituals within an organization as well as more formal events and celebrations to understand the organizational culture?
4. Why are rituals a rich source of cultural data?

Rehearsal 6.3 Alien Culture Observation

Purpose: To develop skills in qualitative data collection and analysis through observing an unfamiliar culture and to become experientially familiar with the concept of seeing a culture through "alien" eyes. The process followed here is a short version of each of the steps of a cultural analysis. In Chapter 7, we provide a follow-up activity designed to support the process of developing interview and possibly survey questions in relation to the observation process that follows.

Steps:

1. **Identify a culture that:**

   a. You consider "alien" to your own.
   b. You have limited or no existing knowledge about.
   c. Would not be dangerous to observe (!).
   d. You would most likely not observe if not encouraged to by this Rehearsal.

2. **Arrange a time to visit the culture.**

   a. Allow a minimum of one to two hours.
   b. Be sure to gain permission if needed.
   c. Take a friend with you if needed for comfort or "fun."

3. **Be as unobtrusive as possible.**

Remember that unobtrusive behavior depends on the organization. For example, if you visit an open Weight Watcher meeting, unobtrusive might mean keeping things on a first-name basis and not inquiring too much about the background of other participants. In contrast, unobtrusive at an accounting firm might be quietly taking notes during a meeting with the partners.

4. **Take field notes during and/or after the observation.**

   a. Jot down descriptive information related to both verbal and nonverbal communication.
   b. Bracket [-] information that relates to your own personal reactions, feelings, and interpretations.
   c. An example field note entry from an observation of the UK Day Care might look like this:

The corner of the room is blocked off from the rest of the larger room. The children in the area are in the 2-year-old age group. [I find it strange that they spend most of their day away from older and younger kids]. In the morning, all of the children are greeted with a hug; some children stand limply and did not return the hug, while others squeeze back tightly. [Why don't they ask if the child wants to be hugged?] A teacher runs from one side of the area to catch a child who is about to hit another child with a block. He makes it in time, and after removing the block, he takes the little girl's hand and has her softly touch the little boy she is about to hit. The teacher says, "Remember, hands are for touching softly, not for hitting and hurting." [Why didn't he say anything about the boy taking the block from the girl?!]

5. Develop a summary that:

a. Provides example data related to at least three of the elements of culture.

For example:

1. **Rules:** Redirect aggression by verbally and nonverbally demonstrating appropriate use of hands. Several teachers were observed telling a child how to touch.
2. **Physical Setting:** The setup of the room provides a way for age-specific teaching and interaction to occur.
3. **Rituals:** Morning hugs are part of daily activities.

b. Interprets the data (organized by elements) by stating an overall theme.

For example: Positive use of touch is a mandated and encouraged behavior. Rules and rituals indicate that teachers should initiate touch often during the day and encourage children to touch each other in appropriate ways.

c. infers an overall definition of the culture based on themes and elements

Examples: A paradox: *The UK Day Care restricts inter-age touching but mandates adult–child touching*. Or a root metaphor, *The UK Day Care is like. . . .*

6. Prepare a summary to discuss with a mentor, a colleague, or an instructor.

Rehearsal 6.4 Note-Taking Guidelines

Purpose: Enhance observation abilities by reviewing guidelines.

Action steps: A review of note-taking guidelines is provided in a checklist to assist you. Use this checklist to review the field notes you compiled in the "Alien Culture" assignment to be sure you followed all the guidelines about systematic observation.

_____1. Make like an alien by making use of various techniques to become a "stranger":

a. Write notes on the mundane.
b. Mutate metaphors.
c. Ask "why" and "what function" questions of everything.

_____2. If you do not or cannot take notes while observing, reserve time immediately after observation to jot down notes.

_____3. Attempt to include observations of meetings, rituals, and so on, as well as observations of less formal interactions, events, and more.

_____4. Use brackets [-] to help you focus on descriptions instead of interpretations.

Use brackets for the following:

a. Questions to ask (other) insiders.
b. Possible paradoxes, contradictions, root metaphors.
c. Later comparisons—see how your perceptions change.
d. Personal reactions/differences.

_____5. If a newcomer or outsider, make use of insiders to check your understanding of jargon, your inferences about rules and values, and so on.
_____6. Review your notes to determine if you can draw reasonable inferences about most of the cultural elements from your notes.
_____7. Categorize notes by elements to:

a. Guide additional data collection to fill gaps.
b. Create interview guides or surveys based on your analysis of data in element categories.

References

Coombs, W. (2013). An overview of challenges facing collective apologies: Their use in the corporate world. *At the Interface/Probing the Boundaries, 86*, 229–247.

Driskill, G. W., & Camp, J. (2006). The Nehemiah Project: A case study of a unity movement among Christian churches in central Arkansas. *Journal of Communication and Religion, 29*, 445–483.

Driskill, G. W., Meyer, J., & Mirivel, J. C. (2012). Managing dialectics to make a difference: Tension management in a community-building organization. *Communication Studies, 63(2)*, 243–261. https://doi.org/10.1080/10510974.2011.634476

Glazier, R., Driskill, G., & Haynes, O. (2024). Linking Community-based Research and Faith-based Racial Justice; Sociological Focus.

Islam, G., & Zyphur, M. (2009). Rituals in organizations: A review and expansion of current theory. *Group & Organization Management, 34(1)*, 114–139. https://doi.org/10.1177/1059601108329717

Mirivel, J. C., & Tracy, K. (2005). Premeeting talk: An organizationally crucial form of talk. *Research on Language and Social Interaction, 32*, 1–34. https://doi.org/10.1002/9781444303094

Smith, R., & Eisenberg, E. (1987). Conflict at Disneyland: A root-metaphor analysis. *Communication Monographs, 54*, 365–380. https://doi.org/10.1080/03637758709390239

Strasberg, L. (1987). *A dream of passion: The development of the method*. Boston: Little, Brown.

Trice, H., & Beyer, J. (1984). Studying organizational cultures through rites and ceremonials. *Academy of Management Review, 9*, 653–669. https://doi.org/10.5465/AMR.1984.4277391

Weick, K. E. (1979). *The social psychology of organizing* (2nd ed.). Reading, MA: Addison-Wesley.

Zeisal, J. (2006). *Inquiry by design: Environment/behavior/neuroscience in architecture, interiors, landscape, and planning* (Revised ed.). New York: W. W. Norton & Company, Inc.

Chapter 7

Method Acting

Interviews and Surveys

Asking questions is part of everyday organizational life. Improving the formal interview process can aid us in our everyday interactions. The interview is an essential tool in gaining cultural knowledge because of its ability to allow you to learn from members about their interpretations and meanings. Several key factors, principles, and guidelines relevant to the process are introduced. Interviewers need to adapt to the varied levels of consciousness about why members think and act as they do. Furthermore, the quality of interview data is dependent not just on rapport or technique and preparation but on one's ability to evaluate data in light of other cultural data gained from observations and texts. Six interviewing principles are covered. A few examples include the role of building rapport, avoiding common problem questions, and the role of probing questions. The value and option of combining qualitative methods with quantitative surveys are explored in light of a constructivist framework.

1. Articulate cultural analysis goals and benefits
2. Explore culture as co-construction
3. Reflect on enacted elements
4. Identify enacted elements via multiple methods
5. Interpret thematic action and OCA
6. Co-create positive communication applications

Step Four: Collect Data on Elements Via Multiple Methods

Objectives

- Describe the challenges involved in the qualitative interview process.
- Apply six general interviewing principles.
- Explain the factors to consider when interviewing as a member versus as an outsider to the culture.
- State the five principles for conducting ethnographic interviews.
- Describe basic features of qualitative and quantitative surveys.

Stage Terms

Ethnographic interviews	Open and closed questions	Rapport
Communication competence	Leading questions	Surveys

DOI: 10.4324/9781003482529-10

The following quotes reflect the chapter aims:

> The power to question is the basis of all human progress.
>
> —Indira Gandhi

> The most serious mistakes are not being made as a result of wrong answers. The true dangerous thing is asking the wrong question.
>
> —Peter F. Drucker

> The way a question is asked limits and disposes the ways in which any answer to it—right or wrong—may be given.
>
> —Susanne Langer

All About Better Questions

Method actors, like effective observers of culture, become adept at making observations. They also rely on informal interviews as part of rehearsal. Communication between actors in a scene, including natural reactions and questions of each other, is at the core of the type of interviewing we introduce in this chapter. In the same way, we rely daily on informal interviews when we ask questions, for instance, in a meeting about a new product or change in structure. These questions are often taken for granted as just what "needs to be asked." Yet, even our determination of what "needs to be asked" is part of what constitutes the culture. We may not even consider asking certain questions because they are not the kind of questions deemed normal or allowed. As we explore in greater detail in Chapter 11 on ethics, Bisel (2018) presents a compelling research-based model for organizational moral learning that indicates ethical behaviors are more than individually determined decisions about what to say or not say, do or not do. Rather, they are constituted in the practices we create with others. Thus, for instance, in organizations where explicit talk, especially by supervisors, does not include ethical reflection, then the probability of subordinates asking about and/or addressing ethical issues is reduced (Zanin, Bisel, & Adame, 2016). Therefore, we find the process of asking better cultural analysis questions, as an insider or outsider to the organization, to be more than simply an effort to learn about the culture.

This chapter introduces you to ways to sharpen your informal and formal interviewing practices. We then move to discuss the option of developing surveys. In this process, in agreement with the opening statements, *learning to ask better questions is critical to the process of discovery. Questions guide both researchers in the way they draw attention to and way from new understandings*. Like observations, interviews can range in their degree of formality and obtrusiveness. "Ethnographic interviews" are, by definition, best when both participants view them as a "friendly conversation" as opposed to an actual interview. In fact, if an informal interview with a co-worker became a series of direct questions fired one after another, your colleague might shut down at some point by saying, "Hey, what is this, an interview?" To return to the director metaphor, if the actors on stage sense you are "after them" or out to put them on the spot, they will be less likely to help you understand what is going on in their world, in the very play you are seeking to guide and direct.

Interviewing organization members about organizational culture is grounded in several assumptions:

- Organizational culture is constructed by organization members and woven deeply throughout organizational sense-making. It is not the property of organizational leaders.

The values and views of leaders are not culturally defining unless members of the organization share the interpretations of leadership.

- Organization members can talk knowledgeably and authoritatively about their own organizational experiences and meanings. Harre and Secord (1973) refer to this as the "Open Souls Doctrine," which states that one unique attribute of human beings is their ability to reflect and comment on their own behavior. However, organization members vary in their degree of consciousness about communicative and organizing practices. Harris (1979) and others (Pearce, 2007) have found that individuals range in their mindfulness of and ability to discuss and reflect on their own communication. We provide examples of these differing ranges or levels of competence (minimal, satisfactory, and optimal) later in this chapter. Thus, in your interviews, be aware of the need to adapt questions and to rely on other methods.

We first review seven general interviewing principles before delving into the particulars of cultural interviews.

Principle 1: Rapport Is Critical to Gaining Valid Information

What would it take for you to respond in a candid way to questions about what you really think or believe?

Trust. As you might suspect, the interview process, like all relationships, requires trust building. As such, a three-step formula for creating this type of relationship does not exist. However, there are essential practices that must be woven together as you adapt to individual interviewees.

- *Provide a full description of your purpose.* If there has been conflict or change in the organization, interviewees may suspect your motives or purpose. We have both had interviewees tell us they feared the interview because they believed management would use the data as a way to pave the way for further job layoffs or reorganizations.
- *Create motivation and engagement.* Review the benefits of a culture analysis (e.g., improving coordination, communication, conflict management, ethics, and inclusion). Be sure to indicate that the results will be shared with all involved. In addition, discuss a commitment from leadership on the time frame for sharing results, along with ways data will be used. Finally, and perhaps most overlooked, it is important to understand that the greatest motivation to participate is intrinsic for the interviewee. Few employees are asked about their views or experiences in the organization. Therefore, it is not surprising that being asked to comment on the organization confers a sense of significance and inclusion. We, along with our students, are continually surprised at how much participants enjoy the process of the cultural interview and how much information they are willing to share. Furthermore, we have found when we have been in the role of the interviewee, the process of reflecting on questions has a subtle way of influencing our awareness of issues or concerns and various communication processes. For instance, in one interview, as Gerald was reflecting on the way conflicts were managed in his organization, he became more aware of his ethical responsibility to more openly discuss conflict stories with new members that foregrounded positive communication practices.
- *Stress what will be done to maintain confidentiality.* The promises you make of confidentiality must have a basis in fact. We always indicate in advance that no raw data or other data with identifying information will be available to the organization. We also obtain agreement in advance that we will not reveal the source of interview comments or the identity

of employees in organizational stories that are selected for a final report. These assurances are critical to your credibility. Table 7.1 captures various stages of rapport building. These stages serve to heighten awareness of normal aspects of the process and factors to keep in mind at each stage. Notice how the higher or more developed the rapport, the more the interview is like a partnership in the cultural analysis process. While such levels of rapport are not necessary for an effective cultural analysis, we see the value of making time to develop such relationships.

Principle 2: Create Culture Based Questions

Question wording and construction are critical to eliciting the information you want. Put differently, questions point toward answers. You have to ask the right question in the right way to gain an understanding of the interviewee's experiences and perceptions. Question construction, clarity, and organizationally appropriate language are all keys to effective cultural interviewing. As you prepare and interview, consider the following four guides.

- *Develop open questions.* Interview questions range across a continuum from open to closed. *Closed questions* ask for a short, specific answer. They include yes-no answers or questions that ask for a specific piece of information, such as, "What is your title?" "Who is considered a hero in this organization?" "When was this organization founded?" Closed questions in an interview (or survey) may have value, especially if they are then followed by secondary or probing questions. So, for instance, if I asked the date of the founding of the organization (a closed question), I might then ask probing and more open questions such as: "Tell me what you have heard about the founding. When is the history of the organization talked about? For what purposes?" On the other hand, *open questions* such as, "What is it like to work here?" or "Tell me about something that could get you in trouble here" require more expansive answers. Cultural interviewing calls for a reliance on open-question construction because you are seeking stories, metaphors, explanations,

Table 7.1 Stages of the Rapport Process

Apprehension is a normal first stage experienced by most interviewees. To put interviewees at ease, focus on low-risk descriptive questions such as describing their job or how they came to work at the company. Adapt to each person. The key rule is to keep them talking.

Exploration is the second stage of rapport in which interviewees may test boundaries to ascertain if they can trust you. You can help them in trust building by

- repeated explanations of your role, confidentiality, the analysis process, purpose of questions, and the recording process
- restatement of information in their language; speak as you would to someone in their culture

Cooperation is the third stage of rapport building, in which interviewees begin to see a shared purpose for the interview. You can enhance their motivation to cooperate by describing the constructive uses of the interview and by giving attention and significance to the information they are providing.

Participation is the final stage of rapport building. The interviewee becomes an active participant in helping find ways to assist you in learning about the culture. In this stage, the control and direction of the interview are shared, and it becomes more of a conversation.

and other rich data to understand the organizing and communicative practices that constitute the culture. Some questions, however, are too open to offer sufficient guidance to the interviewee. A question like, "Tell me about this organization," may be open but can also be intimidating to an interviewee who doesn't know where to begin. Midrange open questions, like the ones mentioned previously, are the most effective.

- *Revise to create clarity*. Using cultural terms may seem like jargon to the average organization member. For example, instead of asking about "recognition rituals," you might ask, "How do employees get recognized here? What kinds of honors or awards are given to employees?" Or instead of asking about symbols, you might say, "What can you tell me about the signs predominantly displayed near the opening doors?" or "Describe the communication behavior of the employee who is a perfect example of what Company A stands for?" Sometimes, a question in the first draft of an interview guide is confusing in its wording or hard to answer. As part of your interview preparation process, it is good to "pilot test" your interview questions with one or two employees or colleagues who are typical of the participants who will be interviewed. This piloting process ensures you will then have revised questions that maximize the value of the data collection process.
- *Adopt language appropriate to the culture you are studying.* As you analyze texts and/or observe the organization in your first step of data gathering, you need to pay attention to organizational titles, acronyms, and unique terms. Being able to use these terms appropriately in your questions gives you credibility and taps into cultural organizing practices more easily. For example, if salespeople are called associates, that is culturally significant. You should use the term *associate* in your question and ask what it means to them, when and how it is used, etc.
- *Adjust questions based on your interviewee's awareness of organizational practices.* If the interviewee has minimal awareness or communication competence, he may respond to many of your questions with, "I don't know when or even why we talk about decisions. We just do." Or "I don't know exactly what that term signifies. That is just what we call it." With such a response, adjust your questions to, "Tell me about a time when . . ." With an interviewee with more awareness, you could expect more explanation and interpretation, but such a person could not offer comparative judgments, such as explaining why one way of making decisions was in place over another. Questions for this type of interviewee might ask for an interpretation of what this means within the organization or why something is considered inappropriate. A person with a greater level of awareness, perhaps someone who has experience in several different cultures, is a gold mine for an interviewer. This person can understand the culture from multiple viewpoints and often can provide rich cultural interpretations and explanations (see descriptions of cosmopolitan communication, Pearce, 2007; Pearce & Pearce, 2000). The key is to adapt to your interviewee.

Principle 3: Gain a Thick Description with Probing Questions

Thick description is all about rich, meaningful, and detailed cultural data. Recall that the way we think about or define organizational culture requires more than just a list of varied enacted elements. For example, an interviewee might have said that Mr. Jones is a hero in the organization because he is so compassionate. You might ask, "Can you think of an example that illustrates this compassion?" The response may involve the interviewee sharing a specific story about a time Mr. Jones loaned a car to an employee who had recently lost his car in a wreck. Such stories will tell you more about how compassion is enacted and defined in this culture. Follow-up questions require listening carefully for small clues in answers that should be explored further. For example, let's say you hear an answer like, "Mr. Jones would be seen as a hero by some but not others." You need to follow up by asking: "Help me understand what you have heard or seen that explains these different perceptions." Probes are different in cultural interviewing from strict research protocols in which every question must be asked in the same manner and order for each respondent. In a cultural interview, you learn most by following up on the particulars of each answer; thus, the probes may be quite different in one interview than another, even when the initial interview protocol is the same. Table 7.2 gives examples of probe questions. Notice how each follow-up or probe allows for richer and thicker descriptions.

Principle 4: Avoid Common Interviewing Errors

The art of interviewing is just that, an "art." Thus, it is about practice, about improvement, not perfection. Give consideration to three common errors to be avoided.

- *Avoid asking leading questions.* A leading question points the interviewee to a desired response (e.g., "Don't you think more transparency is a good thing?"). Often, interviewers make this mistake by giving an example when they ask a question in order to make the question clearer. Unfortunately, the example offered tends to direct interviewees' responses in a way they might not have gone without the example. If you say, "What are values shared in this organization? Like, is responsibility an important value?" This switch from an open and leading question to a closed question forces the interviewee to either agree with you or think of responsibility as the primary value to be discussed. In contrast, a non-leading question might be: "What are the values you believe are important to this organization?" This question is more likely to elicit other values (e.g., diversity, profitability, creativity, etc.) that might not have been introduced due to the closed and leading question.
- *Avoid rushing into pauses while the interviewee is answering.* It is not uncommon for an interviewee to take time to respond. Silence can be uncomfortable. When there is a gap in conversation, we are tempted to rush in with another question or a summary that puts words in the interviewee's mouth. Good interviewing takes patience. One of the best interviewing techniques is to remain silent while being nonverbally attentive and connected. This use of silence often encourages the interviewee to say more or to go into an answer more fully, revealing rich cultural information. One simple technique, if you tend to rush into pauses, is to quietly count to the number five to ensure you have given time for reflection. If a longer amount of time passes, perhaps 10–15 seconds, then a follow-up question might be of use. Rehearsal 7.1 provides a process for practicing catching various problem questions in order to reword them.

Table 7.2 Sample Probe Questions

1. Tell me more about that.
2. Help me understand why you see it that way.
3. Please provide an example of _______.
4. What views might other members of the organization have about this story (or rule, etc.)?
5. Why is this (ritual, history, etc.) important here?
6. How might a supervisor interpret this (interaction, metaphor, etc.) versus a subordinate?

Rehearsal 7.1 Revising Problem Questions

Purpose: Sharpen your ability to catch problem questions to reword them into effective and ethical questions.

Directions: Note if the question is leading, loaded, and/or closed, and then reword it to make it an open question likely to glean information on elements of culture.

1. Weren't their strange or different practices you noticed when you joined this organization?
2. Is there anyone here a newcomer could learn the ropes from?
3. Does a family metaphor best describe the organization?
4. Would you say this is a positive or negative culture?
5. Aren't meetings generally a waste of time here?
6. Don't you think leaders here are just after profit?
7. Do you get tired of hearing gossip?
8. Just how diverse is this organization?
9. Have you ever wanted to leave this organization?
10. Are there any negative rumors you want to tell me?

- *Be careful not to underestimate the significance of nonverbal communication.* Interviewer nonverbal communication has a huge impact. Making eye contact, leaning forward, using encouraging facial expressions, and nodding give the impression of interest and attentiveness. Distracting gestures such as checking your wristwatch or drumming your fingers can quickly shut interviewees down or cause them to shorten their answers. You also need to pay careful attention to the interviewee's nonverbal communication, such as when facial expressions or physical tension do not match the interviewee's response to a question. We find it helpful to see the cultural interview process as giving the gift of listening. Participants value such a gift if you practice a level of nonverbal attentiveness that sends a clear message of your level of commitment to listening.

Principle 5: Consider the Implications of the Way You Record the Interview

Choosing to audio-record an interview can have implications for interviewee comfort and for data analysis. You also may need to get interviewees to sign consent forms when you record interviews, using forms such as those we presented in Chapter 5. Table 7.3 demonstrates the advantages and disadvantages of recording interviews. We generally ask the interviewee whether they mind if we record the interview. We have also used the technique of setting the recorder beside the interviewee and showing him how to turn it off. The control over the taping reduces discomfort, yet we find that few interviewees actually turn off the recorder, and in fact, they often lose consciousness of the recorder once they become engaged in the interview.

Another recording issue is whether you choose to transcribe an interview or summarize it with detailed notes about the answers. Transcribing means you write down word for word what was said in the interview. In fact, free applications allow you to gain a transcription while recording. In contrast, a summary means that you capture the main ideas. A summary might contain a few verbatim quotes of expressions that seemed particularly important, but it contains mostly conceptual summaries. The advantage of transcripts is that you can do more sophisticated analysis with the exact language that an interviewee uses. The disadvantage is that transcripts are extremely time-consuming to prepare and analyze (see Table 7.3).

Principle 6: Consider the Advantages of Interviewing with a Partner

There are advantages to interviewing with a partner. Each of you may notice different things about the interviewee's answers and nonverbal elements. One can take notes while the other asks questions and notices nonverbal elements. The main downside of having a partner is the possible negative impact on interviewee rapport. Interviewees might feel "double-teamed," or it might be more difficult to build a trusting relationship than they might have with an individual interviewer. It is also easy to inadvertently compete for leadership during the interview in a way that is confusing to the interviewee unless you have carefully planned your roles and interactions prior to the interview.

Principle 7: Consider Focus Group Interviewing

A focus group is a cross between a group discussion and an interview. A focus group usually consists of five to ten members. The interviewer asks broad questions, and members are asked to discuss them. The interviewer plays the role of facilitator, constraining members who are too talkative, drawing out more reticent members, summarizing, and playing devil's advocate. A focus group is a rich source of data because participants are stimulated by one another's answers to think of things they would not have thought of in a one-to-one interview. In addition, a one- or two-hour focus group can then gather a great deal of rich data that may mirror some of the same insights that would have been gained from a dozen one-to-one interviews. Disadvantages include the greater complexity of scheduling, the potential for a few members to dominate the discussion, the reticence some have in talking about sensitive cultural issues before others, and the "bandwagon effect" in which members agree with a dominant member instead of thinking of ways their own perceptions might be different. There are various forms of groupware that allow group interaction while avoiding some of the pitfalls of oral group discussion. One product we have used is facilitate.com. This web-based software allows groups

Table 7.3 Recording Interviews

Advantages	*Disadvantages*
Captures more detail about interviewee answers; allows you to analyze actual language patterns	May inhibit free and open communication and cause mistrust
Frees you from taking notes and allows you to give more attention to the interviewee	Takes more time to listen to interview tapes, transcribe, or summarize
You can focus on the interviewee's nonverbal communication	You may not record impressions gained during the interview; they may be hard to recapture listening to the tape

to brainstorm, react to one another's ideas, and prioritize. The facilitator can choose whether to make all comments anonymous or allow participants to see the identity of individuals who offer comments. A key in making the decision about interviews in place of one-on-one interviews may be the communication style of the organization. For example, a student learned that the large engineering firm had bi-monthly meetings that were natural times for focus groups. At the same time, she also learned that the organization was spread out over so many locations that the pragmatics of one-on-one interviews was problematic.

Special Considerations of Interviewing as an Insider or Outsider

In Chapter 2, we discussed the considerations in deciding whether to do an analysis of a culture of which you are a member or a culture of which you are an outsider. In Chapter 6, we discussed various observer roles and how each role influences your strategy and the type of data you collect. Your relationship with an organization and its members will also impact your interviewing strategy.

Insider Considerations

If you are a member of the organization, you come to each interview with a relational context. The interviewee already knows you or at least knows you are a member of the organization. Hopefully, you have a good relationship with the interviewee, so you will need to spend less time building rapport at the start. However, there are times when you may bring baggage. You may be part of management, and that could create social distance if you are interviewing a line employee, for instance. You may be a member of quality control, which has a perceived adversarial relationship with production. The biggest hurdle to overcome as an insider is the necessity to ask questions about things you think you already know. You must ask others about their perspectives, and you may find different parts of the organization have different conceptions of the culture than you do. It also is sometimes difficult for the interviewee to answer questions fully and directly from a fellow employee. If you ask them what employees are rewarded for, they will say, "Oh, you know that," and you will not harvest the rich stories and details that might be shared with an outsider. It is necessary for insiders, in the introduction to the interview, to ask interviewees to treat them as if they knew nothing about the organization and for insiders to prompt and probe during the interview just as if they did not know anything about it.

Another advantage of interviewing as an insider is that you may know more specifics to ask about and be able to start at a deeper level of questioning than an outsider could. You might be able to ask an initial question that would take an outsider two or three probes to reach. You also have more context for interpreting answers. Another negative to being an insider, however, may be confidentiality. Interviewees may be afraid that you would share answers with others in the organization or that their answers would affect your perception of each other and your continuing work relationship. Giving assurances of confidentiality is especially important for an insider.

Outsider Considerations

Outsiders will find it easier to adopt a genuinely naïve position in the interview on organizational culture. They will think of questions that the insider may not think to ask because the insider's cultural knowledge takes certain features of cultural practices for granted. The outsider will have to work harder to develop rapport and trust with the interviewee. Another disadvantage to overcome is substituting your own interpretation for the meaning within the culture. An interviewee might tell you that a stag is the representative symbol for an insurance company, and you might assume you know the reasons why without finding what the symbol means to culture members. Therefore, probes and paraphrasing are especially important when you are an outsider interviewer to be sure that you are checking your interpretations for cultural accuracy.

Connections: Linking Observation with Interviews

In addition to the seven general interview guidelines, it is important to keep in mind the specific considerations for interviewing based both on the unique characteristics of the ethnographic interview and on the data you have already collected. Four guides are provided that should be considered as you prepare.

1. Review Data You Have Gathered on Elements of Culture to Guide Question Development

As a general rule, it is best to rely on interviews, focus groups, and/or surveys after you have gathered data via textual analysis and/or observation. This guide is based on the typical sequence of sense-making: We notice something, and then we ask about it to gain more detail or check our interpretations. Thus, be sure to make notes about elements of culture in which your textual analysis and/or observation notes resulted in an incomplete and/or confusing description. Then, draft questions that might aid you in gaining clarification. In particular, review your notes to check the following possible issues:

a. Confusing or unclear data.
b. Data that lacks confirmation from multiple elements.
c. Your interpretation needs to be checked to see if it is shared by organization members.
d. Cultural significance of texts or artifacts that you observed but perhaps overlooked in earlier textual understanding.
e. Elements not readily apparent through observation, such as metaphors, stories, history, and so on.

2. Determine Members to Interview Who Represent a Variety of Perspectives (Position, Tenure, etc.)

Our information sources—who we select to interview—may bias our interpretation of culture. At times, random interviewing can have value in ethnographic interviewing. When you choose respondents for a specific reason, you may overlook other important sources. In cultural interviewing, every member of the culture has a perspective that may be valuable. The janitor may be in a position to overhear hallway conversations throughout the building. A part-time employee may have a boundary-spanning role that would be valuable to explore.

It is important to remember in interpretive research that every interviewee "counts." In quantitative survey research, you may treat a statistical deviant (e.g., one or two persons strongly agreeing or disagreeing with a statement on the survey while everyone else tended toward the other end) as simply an aberration to be dismissed. However, the interviewee who presents information that diverges from the mainstream might be telling you something important about the culture or subcultures within the organization.

One question our students often ask is, "How many interviews are enough?" The answer, of course, varies. It depends on the size and complexity of the organization. In small organizations (25 or fewer members), it makes sense to interview everyone or perhaps conduct two or three focus groups. In larger organizations, time constraints often necessitate sampling. The key is to aim for a sample that is as representative as possible. For example, once you know the structure of the organization, you would seek to gain representatives from each main unit or department. Then, within those departments, you would aim for meaningful representation based on demographics such as age, tenure, ethnicity, and gender. Furthermore, projects may focus on a unit in a larger organization. One student examined a specialty clinic in a hospital. The hospital was home to thousands of employees, yet this clinic, while part of the larger culture, had a unique subculture among its 40 employees. This focus still required attention to gaining meaningful representation in the sampling process.

Recall that ethnographic interviewing focuses more on depth than breadth. It is important to generate "thick" and rich descriptions from fewer people rather than having more superficial data from a larger sample, as we might do in quantitative surveys. In a practical sense, we often know we've done enough interviews when we conduct three or four interviews without hearing anything new, anything that we haven't fully explored in previous interviews. Yet, if these three or four interviews did not come from an accurate sample of the organization, then the results would not be accurate.

3. Develop and Focus on Descriptive Questions

We provide six types of descriptive questions in the following. We encourage you to experiment by using several of these during the interview process. As open questions, they also have a way of helping the interview by providing a context for exploring organizing and communicative practices.

- *Grand tour questions*: Take me on a tour of the company by walking me through the doors at the start of a new day.
- *Mini tour*: Take me on a tour of . . . (a specific department or a particular event, such as a meeting).
- *Example questions*: What are the kinds of questions that are typically asked (by certain people, positions, times, settings)?
- *Experience questions*: Give me an example of experiences you have had (with, at, and/or when).
- *Native language questions*: *What does the title "Associate" mean here?* Asked to gain cultural definitions/uses of specialized language.
- *Hypothetical language*: If I were to be late to a meeting, how would it be interpreted?

4. Use Contrast Questions to Understand How Interviewees Construct Meaning

Like the previous descriptive questions, a contrast question invites an exploration of meaning. For example, you might ask, "*What is the difference between a new employee labeled as a 'player' and one who is called a 'gunner'?*" Such questions, as indicated previously, should flow naturally from data you have already gathered. The contrast question, therefore, provides a way to gain insight into language and, in this case, metaphors rich with cultural meaning. Depending on the response and the cultural competence of the participant, you might then probe with questions about when they have heard this term used, such as stories told about a "gunner" versus a "player."

In all, these four guides should give you a sense of not only the ethnographic interview process but the content of certain types of questions you might elect to ask. Explore Rehearsal 7.2 as a resource for possible questions.

Rehearsal 7.2 Sample Interview Questions for "Reading" a Culture

Purpose: Develop an interview guide based on the following suggested questions. In Chapter 8, guides for interpreting data will be provided (c.f., Tett, 2021).

1. When you were a newcomer to the (name of organization), what was strange, or different, or unexpected about the way things were done here?
2. If you wanted to explain or illustrate to an outsider the essence of (name of organization), what incident(s) would you describe? Tell me more about what happened. What was said? Done?
3. What should visitors see or observe if they want to understand this organization? What would they need to understand to "get along" and feel comfortable here?
4. To whom should visitors speak if they want to understand this organization? What would you expect them to hear from this person?
5. When compared with similar organizations, what is special or distinctive about this organization?
6. What are the principal images or metaphors that people use to describe the organization? Give an example of a time or setting when you have heard this image mentioned. What was said? Done?
7. What physical impression does the organization and its artifacts create? Does this vary from one place to another in the organization?
8. What kinds of values are represented in the way members talk among themselves? What is said?
9. What could limit a person's career success here? What kinds of talk might you hear to encourage success?
10. What are the ceremonies/rituals? Describe one of these. What is said? Done?
11. What are members recognized for? How is this done?
12. What language dominates everyday conversation? What words do you hear in this organization that you wouldn't hear at other organizations?
13. What are the dominant stories that members tell about how to get work done here?
14. What reward systems are in place? What "messages" do they send in terms of the best way to get things done around here?
15. What are the favorite topics of informal conversation?
16. What do you know about the history of this organization? When, if ever, are references made to the past? Has work here changed in significant ways in recent years? In what ways?

17. Think of three influential people in the organization. In what ways do they enact the values of the organization?
18. What, if any, identifiable subcultures exist in the organization? What makes them identifiable?
19. What written sources about this organization would really tell you something about what the organization is like?
20. How do people prefer to communicate here? If there were a new policy, how would you expect to hear about it? If your boss wanted to thank you for a good job, would you prefer him or her to tell you in a face-to-face meeting or in a note? What, if anything, would you say should not be communicated via electronic media?
21. If you heard a rumor about layoffs or a major change, how would you check it out for accuracy?
22. What kinds of talk, if any, occurs that includes reference to the surrounding environment, such as the neighborhood, community, and/or city?
23. When do you hear the word "diversity" around here? Who uses this term? What groups typically are considered part of diversity? What groups, if any, would feel uncomfortable being a part of this organization? Explain situations where they might feel uncomfortable.
24. When, if ever, do members of this organization interact outside of work hours? Who? What do they do?
25. What are special activities or events this organization sponsors for its members? What role do they play in creating the culture of the organization?

Now select the ones that best fit your interview goals and consider developing a few of your own:

____

____

____

____

Qualitative Surveys

The process of creating effective qualitative interview questions is almost identical to that of creating qualitative survey questions. In what follows, we discuss blending qualitative and quantitative questions, but here, the idea is to use the primary qualitative interview questions in a survey format. For example, imagine not being able to catch a colleague in a "friendly conversation" or even a formal interview and instead sending an e-mail survey with your questions. We have had students who have not been able to coordinate an interview time with several participants use this approach. The important point is that just as in an interview, you have to be sure that you gain data that you then check against other information you have gathered about communicative behaviors that constitute the culture. In this way, though you may not gain the same depth of information you would have via probes in an interview, you remain focused on gaining an in-depth understanding of the culture. A grounded analysis takes an inductive approach, as opposed to a deductive approach that assumes an existing set of categories in advance (Strauss & Corbin, 1990). Furthermore, a grounded analysis challenges you to devise your own interpretation of the culture rather than one constrained by factors already loaded into a standardized survey. Four reminders for survey development that parallels interviews include the following.

- Establish appropriate rapport in the written opening by stating the value, purpose, and length of the survey as well as your means for ensuring anonymity and plans for how the data will be used.
- Include an explanation of the flow and types of questions to make sure interviewees understand your reason for asking for examples via open-ended questions.
- Develop questions based on prior data as well as various question options (i.e., structural, contrast) so as to gain needed cultural information.
- Develop question clarity and appropriateness through piloting.
- Be prepared to adapt to the competence level of the interviewee.
- Engage participants who represent a variety of perspectives (position, tenure, age, gender, etc.).

On a final note, remember that writing responses to open questions is time-consuming; thus, it is best to narrow your survey to focus on a handful, typically eight to ten, of the most important questions. In addition, you might find that an electronic survey of even fewer (four to six) key questions will glean more cultural information from a wider array of members than attempting a long list of a dozen questions from a handful of respondents. As a general rule, we find face-to-face interviews will glean more cultural data than what is provided from an on-line, open-response question. However, if the primary communication style of an organization is electronic and/or you are studying a virtual organization, this format might be your best option.

Quantitative Surveys

Based on data from textual and/or observation methods, as well as your project goals and time frames, a quantitative survey may be of value. This decision should be influenced by such factors as the needs of the organization and perhaps also the time frame. As already indicated, we encourage using multiple methods to glean reliable and valid cultural data. Our experience with such projects is that blending open-ended questions with quantitative, closed-ended questions is the best route. In the opening to this section on methods, we mentioned survey options that are commercially available. These options rely on frameworks that may hold value depending on the focus of your project. Our one caveat—be sure that the net caste by the survey provides the cultural data you seek. In this section, we review options grounded in the constructivist approach we are attempting with the OCA model. Thus, recall that from such theories as CCO or Structuration, rather than examining variables or ways to surface the culture, we are looking for the ways the culture is enacted through varied communicative and organizing practices. The questions, thus, reflect this focus on communicative action.

Enacted Elements

The OCA model assumes the value of multiple methods in order to gather data for both macro- and micro-level elements. We have encouraged a primary focus on using qualitative methods for gathering cultural data and then categorizing these data based on various elements. In Chapter 8, we explore a process of interpreting these enacted elements to determine what we label as "thematic action" and an "overall characterization" of the culture. The assumption is that the move from cultural data to enacted elements to thematic action and then an overall characterization effectively attends to micro and macro constitutive organizing practices.

Over the past decade, we have noted how project goals and parameters may suggest the value of including a quantitative survey. For example, one organization wanted a cultural analysis focused on diversity (see Chapter 11). In the process of developing a data collection plan, it became clear that gaining a wide range of perspectives with this organization, given the time frame, would only be possible via a quantitative survey. The first step was to build this survey after first analyzing key organizational texts and conducting observations. These data were coded based on the elements of culture. Then, following the guides presented in this chapter, areas where information on certain elements was missing, incomplete, or unclear became the basis for wording survey questions. In addition, key concepts in Chapter 11 on Diversity were utilized to ensure the exploration of communication practices relevant to this topic. Closed-ended questions were also designed to be paired with a probing or secondary question. Several example questions from this survey are provided in Table 7.4, followed by a rationale for the approach taken. Each question fits a certain type or category of question. The first question in each pair of questions utilized a strongly agree to strongly disagree response. One benefit of this type of survey is that it can also be used as a benchmark and perhaps returned on an annual basis to discern progress.

The following factors should be kept in mind when developing questions:

- *Explore intertwined elements of culture.* Notice how *Question #1* focuses on rituals as they enact values. The intent is to check data that may have surfaced in an observation. For example, you may learn of several ceremonies but do not have a clear sense of how they constitute the culture. This type of question provides a venue for a wide array of participants to "weigh in" on their perceptions of the presence of such rituals.

Table 7.4 Example Diversity Survey Questions

1. Organizational leaders utilize events such as ceremonies or meetings in order to recognize individuals who embody core values.
    a. State an example of a recognition event that functioned in this way.
2. Communication during times of transition includes what will change and what will not change.
    a. Provide a story about change that demonstrates the previously mentioned commitment.
3. Organizational processes, norms, and expectations are intentionally introduced and explained to minority members to aid in their adjustment.
    a. Provide an example of one of these mentoring efforts. How is it talked about by minority members?
4. Discussions about hiring and development practices include talk and action focused on improving and/or enhancing leadership diversity.
    a. Provide an example of statements made during these discussions.

- *Gain an understanding of perceptions of communication related to common dialectics.* Question #2 represents an effort to gain perceptions on communication related to *the change and stability dialectic.* Imagine learning through observation and/or textual analysis that members were concerned about how changes were being communicated. The goal is to gain perceptions of how members frame inevitable dialectic tensions. For example, you might ask about the extent to which leaders engage others in rituals that celebrate the past while anticipating a positive future (see Chapter 12).
- *Measure experiences with positive practices.* Questions 3 and 4 are based on the positive practices found in the application chapter on diversity (Chapter 9). Recall the second of the three main questions carried throughout the OCA analysis process, "What do participants want to create?" Exploring enacted elements of culture with questions like these aids in surfacing data about the desired culture.
- *Include a secondary question to gain examples.* While participants will not consistently provide the same sort of detail with an open-ended survey question as they might in an interview, we have found that rich cultural data can be gained that provides context and a grounding for interpreting the statistical data. For example, simply knowing that 70% of the respondents agreed or strongly agreed that rituals enact core values is better comprehended if we learn something about those rituals—the specific ones on their minds when they responded to the question. In the same way, those providing a low response rating need to be heard and included as well, and thus, the open, follow-up question gives them a voice.

In summary, a quantitative survey based on elements of culture and, when appropriate, on concepts from an application such as diversity, change, or leadership may be a valuable tool. To that end, we provide Rehearsal 7.3, which will jump-start this process by guiding you through creating qualitative questions from the view of an "alien" that can then lead to follow-up quantitative questions.

Rehearsal 7.3 Alien Culture Interviews/Surveys

Purpose: Recall that one goal in this process is to develop questions that will give you an outsider or "alien" viewpoint, that is, to see your organization with a new set of eyes. Thus, the purpose of this activity is to develop this capacity to see your organization as an outsider. This activity focuses on developing skills in qualitative data collection and analysis by interviewing a member of an unfamiliar culture and then developing possible survey questions as well.

Steps:

1. Review your notes from your visit to the alien culture from the previous Rehearsal 6.3. If you did not conduct observations as an "alien," you should still take time to reflect on your knowledge of this culture. If you did not conduct observations as an "alien," you should still take time to reflect on your knowledge of this culture. To take this step, reflect on elements that might seem strange or taken for granted.
2. Determine areas in which you have confusion or lack data on a given enacted element.

3. Prepare for your interview by creating a rapport section in your interview guide. Include ways you might build rapport through greetings, description of the purpose of the interview, explaining your role in the organization, assurances of confidentiality, general topics of the questions you plan to ask, analysis and note-taking explanation, expressions of cultural interest and ignorance, and incorporating and restating informant's terms.
4. Create the following types of questions for your interview guide, but remember you will need to adapt to the interviewee by providing more detail in the question, repeating the question, and so on.

   One grand tour question; one native language question.
   One structural question; one contrast question.

5. Provide a closure/leave-taking section on your guide (appreciation, reminder of purpose and what is ahead, ask for any questions, etc.).
6. Like the observation assignment, develop a summary section that incorporates triangulated and new data and that:

   a. Provides example data related to at least three of the elements of culture.
   b. Interprets the data organized by elements by stating an overall theme.
   c. Infers an overall definition of the culture based on themes and elements.

7. Reflect on the strengths and limits of observation and interviewing. What did you understand differently/in more depth after the interview? What did you observe that would have been difficult to understand solely through an interview?
8. Now consider the value of creating a quantitative survey follow-up based on your findings. For example, you may have picked up on the significance of stories in relation to multiple elements (e.g., rituals, values, heroes, communication rules). These stories may also suggest communication applications that merit exploration, such as leadership, diversity, change, and/or ethics. Thus, consider questions such as: "Stories in this organization consistently introduce shared values." "The stories I hear around here encourage awareness of communication expectations." The key is to develop survey questions in a way that flows from areas that merit further exploration as well as questions that provide open-ended secondary questions to encourage respondents to provide examples grounded in communication.

Summary

We engage in question-asking and responding every day. Method actors, like those interested in enhancing the quality of an informal interview process, must become more aware of their questions and how they interpret and respond. The interview process is an essential tool for gaining cultural knowledge. Developing best interviewing practices allows you to learn from member interpretations and meanings. This chapter covered several key factors, principles, and guidelines relevant to the process.

1. Members vary in their levels of awareness about the reasons for varied cultural practices and communication behaviors.
2. The quality of your interview data is dependent not just on rapport or technique and preparation but on your ability to evaluate data in light of what you have learned from other participants and through observations.

3. Interviewers must be conscious of six interviewing principles:
    - Rapport is critical.
    - Question wording is important for eliciting the information you want.
    - Probes are critical for getting deeper cultural information.
    - Avoid the common problems of leading questions, rushing into pauses, and discounting nonverbal communication.
    - The interviewer should carefully consider different methods of recording.
    - Interviewing with a partner has advantages.
4. Be aware of special considerations about interviewing as a culture member or as an outsider.
5. Be sure to review the four specific ethnographic interviewing guides: a) review data you have gathered on elements of culture to guide question development; b) determine members to interview who represent a variety of perspectives; c) develop and focus on descriptive questions; and d) use contrast questions to understand how interviewees construct meaning
6. Explore the value and option of combining qualitative methods with quantitative surveys grounded in a constructivist framework.

Step Four Review: Collect Data on Elements Via Multiple Methods

The major methods of textual analysis, observation, interviews, and surveys each provide a useful means of gathering cultural data. You should consider the following guidelines as a way to provide a credible and valid interpretation. These methods and the call to integrate them into our cultural data collection process are provided as a way to combat a natural tendency we all have. Each of us tends to rely on initial impressions based on a limited number of observations, a few interactions or discussions with a limited number of employees, and perhaps a cursory look at a newsletter. Optimal cultural performance is achieved when we sharpen our ability to collect and analyze data more systematically with each of these methods. If we have a clear grasp of the following guidelines, then we will be more effective in the culture interpretation process covered in the next chapter.

1. Use method "triangulation" to obtain credible and valid data.
2. Conduct textual analysis using one or more of the methods outlined: content analysis, rhetorical analysis, and/or textual analysis.
3. Select a method of observation and write field notes with bracketed inferences and questions.
4. Adopt the curiosity of an outsider (i.e., act like an alien), especially when you observe your own culture.
5. Apply important principles in the conduct of interviews and surveys, such as selecting interviewees, developing rapport, wording questions in an open and clear fashion, using probes to dig deeper into answers, choosing effective recording methods, and negotiating the special roles of cultural insider or outsider.
6. Draw and bracket initial inferences from each of the methods about cultural elements.

Discussion Questions

1. Discuss why interviews are an especially rich source of cultural data.
2. How do you approach the interview differently if you are an organizational insider or outsider? What are the advantages and disadvantages of each status to the interview process?
3. What are the limits to the ability of organizational actors to talk meaningfully about their own culture?
4. How is a focus group different from individual interviews? What are the advantages and disadvantages of focus groups compared to individual interviews for cultural interviewing?

References

Bisel, R. (2018). *Organizational moral learning: A communication approach*. New York: Routledge.

Harre, H., & Secord, P. F. (1973). *The explanation of social behavior*. Totowa, NJ: Littlefield, Adams.

Harris, L. (1979). Communication competence: Empirical tests of a systematic model. Unpublished Doctoral Dissertation. Amherst: University of Massachusetts.

Pearce, W. (2007). *Making social worlds: A communication perspective*. Malden, MA: Blackwell Publishing.

Pearce, W., & Pearce, K. (2000). Combining passions and abilities: Toward dialogic virtuosity. *Southern Communication Journal, 65*(2), 160–175.

Strauss, A., & Corbin, J. (1990). *Basics of qualitative research: Grounded theory procedures and techniques*. Thousand Oaks, CA: Sage.

Tett, G. (2021). *Anthro-Vision. A new way to see in business and life*. Nueva York: Avid Readers Press.

Zanin, A. C., Bisel, R. S., & Adame, E. A. (2016). Supervisor moral talk contagion and trust-in-supervisor. *Management Communication Quarterly, 30*(2), 147–163. https://doi.org/10.1177/0893318915619755

Chapter 8

Getting Inside the Character

Interpretation

Ethical and credible data interpretation, step four of the OCA model, requires not only immersion in the data but also interpreter creativity. At this point, if an array of data on enacted elements has been collected, the consultant, researcher, or insider of the organization has already gained a richer, more credible understanding of the culture than they had before. Like an actor who has hung out behind the scenes to interact with an array of other actors, one who has studied not just their script but the full script, this chapter assumes you are now in the position to discern larger patterns of communicative practices that constitute the organization. These larger patterns are introduced as thematic actions. Discerning thematic action involves identifying enacted elements that constitute various organizing processes. The final step of discerning a general characterization of the culture is possible. This step involves interpreting thematic actions as they constitute the overall culture in action in the form of paradoxes, master rules/values, or root metaphors. Guidelines for drafting your cultural analysis report are provided.

Step Five: Interpret Thematic Action and OCA

1. Articulate cultural analysis goals and benefits
2. Explore culture as co-construction
3. Reflect on enacted elements
4. Identify enacted elements via multiple methods
5. Interpret thematic action and OCA
6. Co-create positive communication applications

> I must have at least a dozen pages or more of just notes and more notes. Of course, I also have draft after draft of cultural elements. The process has been interesting, but it is not realistic. No one can really spend this much time. The pay-off just cannot be worth it!
>
> Anonymous, Cultural Analysis Student

DOI: 10.4324/9781003482529-11

Objectives

- Explain the interpretive nature of cultural analysis.
- Determine ways that enacted elements constitute thematic action.
- Create an overall characterization of the culture constituted in thematic action.
- Explore basic guides for drafting a report that connects with others.

Stage Terms

Pervasiveness	Salience	Thematic action	Characterization

A Time to Interpret

Data overload! TMI! We have all been there. Our day-to-day lives involve a bombardment of information. To what extent has the cultural analysis process added to what was already too much? The opening statement about data overload reflects a common experience at this stage of the process. Making sense of varied data based on texts, observations, interview notes, and survey results can be overwhelming. In fact, one reason we may defer from engaging in this process is the simplicity and ease of drawing conclusions about culture based on limited data. Perhaps the sense of being overwhelmed can be compared to a dress rehearsal of a play when you have doubts about all the pieces coming together, about those watching the performance being drawn in and compelled to trust the story being enacted and the characters believable. This phase of the OCA model is like the process of "getting inside the character." In short, you move to an actual interpretation of the script—all of your data. Until this time, the method actor has been devoted to rehearsing the elements, but the time comes to put it together. It is natural to feel overwhelmed at this stage. Miles (1979) discusses the issue of rich data in his article "The Attractive Nuisance of Qualitative Data." He notes that while qualitative data allows richer interpretations and explanations, it is also more time-consuming and complex to analyze (c.f., Van Maanan, 1979). If you gathered quantitative data as well, then making sense of the numbers can add to the challenge.

The move from description to interpretation is no doubt daunting. One way to gain perspective is to return to the reality that we engage in data collection and interpretation on an informal basis each day. We may not formally ask the big question: "What kind of culture is being co-created?" Nonetheless, it is present each time we interact with others and make sense of organizational life. Reflect on the following statements and consider adding to these words that we interpret every day.

- The meeting went the way I predicted—nothing was accomplished. Why can't leadership get its act together?
- I love the way we work together—the synergy makes me want to be here.
- Did you hear what Terry said the other day? He is just that way—nothing can be done.
- I heard today about Justin and Meg actually working through a tough conflict. Glad to know.

Notice how each statement is an interpretation—a take on life in the organization. The statements reflect meeting rituals—patterns or norms of communication formed or being formed.

Our goal in using the OCA model is to enhance our ability to ethically collect and interpret data. The interpretation stage is about being mindful of ways to improve the cultures we are creating with others. Also, recall we began by noting that the six phases in this process are not linear. We likely enter the process, especially if we are insiders, with our varied interpretations and perhaps even recommendations. In fact, we have read first drafts of student analyses that contain findings and implications that read less like a credible interpretation and more like someone seeking to support positions they already held. Put differently, one of the most common challenges is not simply data overload but failing to check our biased interpretations and applications at the door. Put differently, ***imagine a character on stage acting or responding to one story that everyone knows to be incomplete or filled with lies. As we watch, we know that unless something changes, a bad outcome is likely.*** The key at this point is to check and revise our interpretations by systematically analyzing a wider array of data. The following comments from a few alumni on the value of the process may help give perspective and enhance motivation.

- Evaluating the organization's culture adds another dimension. Although the culture of the organization may not seem to have a direct impact on the immediate, short-term profit or bottom line, it does play a big part in the long-term effectiveness of the organization.
- The basic idea that an organization has a culture was an eye-opener. Since then, I've seen the importance of personal fit with the culture. "Problem employees" are often those who won't/can't adapt to the culture and have a conflict with those who identify closely with the culture.
- I learned to ask questions in an interview to find out about the culture when I was considering making a job move. I also ask questions of people I'm considering hiring to see if they'll fit with our organizational culture.
- Just simply realizing that an organization has a definable culture has been helpful in dealing with the changes that have been and are continuing to occur at the medical facility I work for.

At this point in the process, if you have been collecting data on multiple enacted elements, you likely have more information about the culture than may seem reasonable or "normal." Three factors should help you keep this data overload in perspective:

1. **A formal analysis is usually appropriate only at certain points in time** (e.g., seeking to improve hiring or orientation practices, a desire to improve responses to organizational crises or change, and/or as part of an annual cultural analysis focused on some aspect of the culture you desire to continue to improve such diversity initiatives). Thus, the practice of conducting a formal analysis should be framed as time well spent, but not time you give beyond those instances when an analysis is indicated.
2. **Managing the overload of data has meaningful pay-offs.** You began this process (recall Chapter 2) by learning to articulate the value of a cultural analysis before taking the step to enrich your understanding of the concept of culture. At this point, you may need to pause and review the factors that motivated your engagement as well as the OCA framing of culture as co-construction. To that end, a few questions merit reflection:

    - How would you explain the benefits of this process to yourself, a co-worker, or organizational leadership? (e.g., the need to see my role in creating better processes,

managing change more effectively, improving diversity efforts, aiding in leadership development, or addressing ethical challenges?
- How would you explain to someone the value of focusing on communicative practices that constitute the culture for your own professional development?

Recall again that the aim is to benefit you and others, yet sometimes. Given our mental shift on seeing organizations as intertwined networks, we trust one of the biggest takeaways is based on the insight gained about your role in co-creating a more positive social world (i.e., in and beyond a given organization). Recalling these benefits is important to maintain motivation in sorting through the data. The final encouragement seeks to enhance the pay-offs.

3. **Improve positive communication practices by returning to the three big questions.** "What are we creating here? What should we be creating? What kinds of communication will get us there?" These big questions are not reserved for formal analysis but aid in daily informal analysis and communicative action. For instance, one student commented: I asked these questions on my way to a meeting where I was at first intended to "give someone a piece of my mind." These questions gave this student reason to hit a mental pause button: *I realized such a move would not create what I truly wanted—or should want—a positive working relationship.* This student was able to pivot and tap into options, such as asking better questions to discern common ground (Mirivel & Lyon, 2023). These same questions should also function to hit a pause button as we attend to our interpretations of multiple elements of culture. This analysis serves to develop the art and skill of being a better interviewer, observer, and interpreter—one who listens intently with ears, eyes, and heart. Therefore, perhaps the most meaningful outcome, one worth wading through the data for, is the potential insight for our role in co-creating a more effective and ethical culture in our day-to-day interactions, not just at work but at home, in places we volunteer, worship, and play. From the varied constructivist approaches informing the OCA, such as Structuration, CCO, and CMM, we must be aware not only of our role in communication behaviors we are enacting as well as those we should enact (e.g., the kinds of questions we ask, stories we disclose) but also the processes that are not in our direct control and/or are challenges to influence (e.g., the interpretations of others, entrenched conflict patterns). This awareness requires a mindfulness of what is in our communicative control and what is not. We may not be able, for example, to immediately and/or directly change an entrenched conflict. However, we can discern positive communication practices that may aid self and others in making such changes.

Not a Video Recording

What do you recall about this statement? "Culture does not exist." We introduced this statement in Chapter 1 as a way to remind all of us that not only does the construct of culture have varied definitions and applications but also as a way to develop caution and humility in making claims. To that end, be cautious when you hear yourself or others saying (or thinking) things like:

- "That is just the culture around here, the way things are."
- "If we could get employee values to align with leadership, productivity would go up."
- "What else was I supposed to do? Staying silent is the only option around this place."

In this phase of the OCA model, the interpretive process should be about pushing back against the tendency to make claims that are not valid, not reliable, and not grounded in research. Recall that causal links between some aspects of culture and organizational outcomes are limited at best (Barends & Rousseau, 2022).

We find it helps at this fifth phase of the OCA model to return to the drama metaphor. Consider the drama metaphor as a way to remind you that when opening night finally occurs, when the curtain is being raised, the performance the audience sees will vary depending on the way a director has set the stage, cast the characters, and interpreted the tone and theme of the script. A cultural analysis is not an objective or neutral video recording. Indeed, such a recording is impossible. Instead, the individual researcher (or team) works to provide a meaningful, valuable, and valid interpretation. ***An interpretive researcher's work is driven by plausibility rather than making claims of absolute objectivity*** (Weick, 1995). The goal is to create an interpretation or reading of the culture based on connecting numerous data points. To reach this goal, however, we need to return to review the varied approaches one may take in the cultural analysis process.

Recall our introduction in Chapter 3 of varied approaches or assumptions regarding the cultural analysis process: a) culture as variable; b) culture as root metaphor; and c) culture as discursive construction. As we stressed before, each approach has value. Consultants in the "variable" mode may focus on the congruence of formally held values versus those members actually hold and recommend changes based on such an analysis. In a "root metaphor" approach, rituals and stories become a way to discover and then describe the culture. In each case, an organization may benefit from the insights gained. The OCA model is grounded in the "discursive construction" approach. In this approach, we are challenged to go beyond identifying variables or uncovering various depictions of the culture revealed by rituals or stories. Instead, the OCA model views symbolic forms such as rituals and stories as enactments of a culture constituted in communication. What does such a shift in thinking mean at a practical level for the consultant, student, and/or researcher? How might we visualize this analysis process?

The following three-stage interpretive model, shown in Figure 8.1, captures a process that is not easily systematized. The process of interpretation is difficult to delineate because interpretation involves insight and intuition. The idea of interpreting constitutive processes by moving from a) enacted elements to b) thematic action to c) an overall characterization of the culture in action may not happen in a linear fashion. There may be points at which the process is much less linear and systematic than is portrayed in the model. Nonetheless, it is important that you cover each of the steps with the understanding that you will need to move back and forth among the steps. The first stage in this process takes us back to Chapter 4 by focusing on the way culture is constituted in enacted elements. We provide additional data analysis instruction with coding examples and exercises in our online resources.

A. Creating the Actor's Script: Enacted Elements

Each time you collect cultural information through any one of the methods, you should sort that data into summary sheets based on the cultural elements. Recall from Chapter 4 that when cultural elements were introduced, we used the term "enacted elements" to create a mental shift from a "culture as variable" or "culture as metaphor" to a "culture as discursive co-construction" approach. The idea is to view these elements as communicative processes

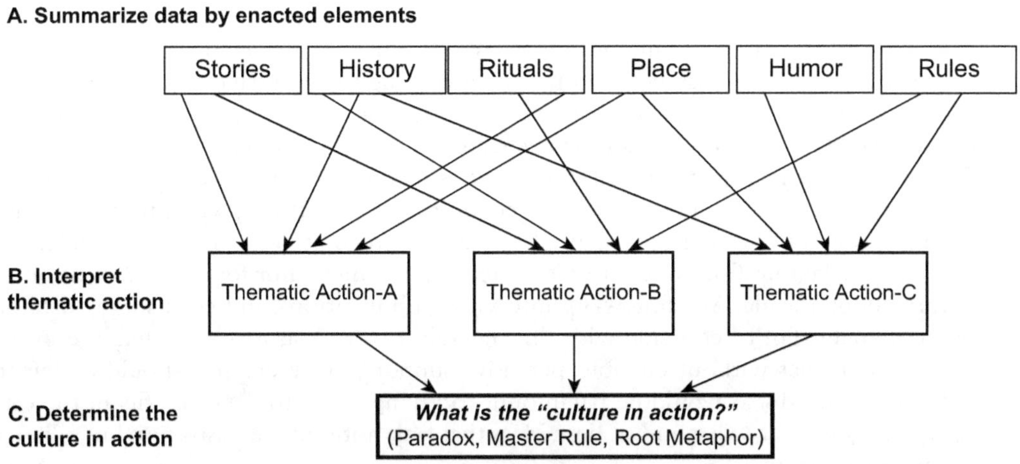

Figure 8.1 OCA Model: Interpreting the Culture in Action

that enact or constitute the culture. Thus, these summary sheets can be seen as a first step in creating the script—a set of notes that influences the way the director interprets the overall performance or culture in action. In order to create these summary sheets, take one pass through your interview notes, your observation notes, and/or your textual analysis to consider references to one of the elements, such as place or history. You might place each reference to history on a separate note card or in an electronic document with a column labeled history. As you look across all those different references to history, you may find patterns or even contradictions. You would then move to another element, such as heroes or rituals, and repeat the process. In this process, recall that a "discursive construction" perspective does not view elements as variables to manipulate or as a way to unearth varied representations of the culture. Instead, as communicative co-created, they constitute the culture or enact the culture. A few specific guides in this process include the following:

1. *Return to the same data set more than once to identify overlooked elements.* For example, if you focused on communicative rules in your first analysis of the interview data, return to your data again to discern stories or rituals, and so on. Remember to reflect on elements of culture embedded in one another. A story, for example, might introduce you to communication rules, rituals, and/or a hero. A ritual, in the same way, will likely contain values and communication norms or rules.
2. *Review data in each category to be sure you have collected micro and macro data.* A primary goal, based on the OCA framework, to attend to macro- and micro-level elements as they constitute the culture. Why is such a step so critical? Congruent with CCO (Communicative Constitution of Organization), a sole focus on either micro-level (i.e., "here and now" or in momentary elements such as interactions) or macro-level ("then and there" or elements that transcend time, such as policies, signs, history) misses a full understanding of organizing processes (c.f., Cooren & Fairhurst, 2009). For example, the initial analysis of your observational data might indicate a lack of information on communication or interaction rules (micro level). You may need to return to observation notes from a meeting and attend to patterns on what is said (or not said), how decisions are made, who speaks and does

not speak, etc. Deciphering how participants create and invoke communication rules is challenging. Recall that communication rules or norms are rarely explicit. Thus, returning to guides in Chapter 4 may be important in discerning the ways rules are co-constructed and constitute a varied organizing process. As you discern these practices, be sure such macro-level data, such as place and artifacts, are understood as well.

3. *Leave out unclear, incomplete data.* Ideally, if data is incomplete or a given element, such as a ritual or metaphor, you return to collect additional data. If not, when in doubt, leave it out. This step of leaving out incomplete data is also an ethical one. For example, you may have picked up from one interview the idea of a metaphor for the organization or a story about a leader. Yet, follow-up interviews, observations, and even survey data on other elements fail to coincide with this metaphor story. You may even like the metaphor or story, yet without credible, pervasive support, this metaphor should be left to the side. To not do so would be paramount to giving voice to data that fits in the category of "gossip" at worst and, at best, ideas that lack not only pervasiveness but salience in the organization.
4. *Conduct a reliability and validity check.* In the process of data collection, whether as an insider or outsider, you have interacted with others. You have listened, observed, and developed insights to varied elements being enacted. At this juncture, having someone check your coding of elements will further enhance the credibility of the process. We provide an activity (Rehearsal 8.3 Reliability/Validity Check) as one suggested step. You may rely on a member of the organizational development team if you are an insider or perhaps a colleague or fellow student. The ethical standard is to be sure your list of elements does not include data that might identify individuals, or in the case of an outsider, you may need to conceal the name of the organization. This step not only serves to check on the accuracy of your process, but this coding check might inform you as to the need to collect additional data and/or clarify the recording of the data.
5. *Engage in a "back and forth" iterative process.* The intent is to engage in movement between elements and your initial interpretations of constitutive processes while also reflecting on relevant research (Tracy, 2013). For example, you might note the way certain stories, rituals, and communication rules all involved references to laughter and humor. Thus, it would be useful to reflect on research that reviews the various functions of humor (Meyer, 2015) and specific studies that reveal the impact of positive humor. For instance, one study suggested that the role of positive humor introduced by supervisors, in turn, impacted satisfaction and effective recruitment of interns (Sobral & Islam, 2015).

In all, engaging in these five guides has two benefits. First, it reduces the anxiety tied to data overload. Next, and perhaps more importantly, it prepares you for the second phase of interpretation.

B. Sorting Subplots: Thematic Action

A list of elements does not constitute a final cultural analysis any more than a list of characters empowers you to interpret or enact the play. Capturing these enacted elements is foundational for understanding the organization and gaining a valid interpretation, but without the next step, all you will have is a list with partial insights. This second step, discerning "thematic action," is about discerning instances when enacted elements combine to constitute an organizing process such as cultural performance. Put differently, think back to the OCA mental shift concerning the construct of culture. The shift involves moving from culture as a variable (e.g., values predicting an outcome) or as a root metaphor (e.g., elements revealing the culture) to culture as an ongoing construction (***What is being created here?***). To turn back to White's (2021) take on culture, you may think of thematic action as "underlying logics" that are co-creating the culture. The goal is to identify enacted elements merging or coalescing. Such mergers suggest thematic action or constitutive processes that create the organization. Here, we discuss two options or approaches to discerning thematic action, the Four Flows Model and the pervasiveness and salience of enacted elements.

Four Flows Model

One of the more established CCO approaches was introduced by McPhee and Zaug (2000). They argue that organizations are constituted in four flows or organizing processes. As you review your data on enacted elements, you may notice how several merge into a particular flow or patterns relevant to one or more of these flows. We consider instances of such mergers as thematic action. Here, we review each of these flows with the understanding that two or more flows are, from the theorist's perspective, what is required for a group or movement or gathering to actually constitute an organization.

1. "Membership negotiation" refers to communicative processes that make one a member of an organization. Recall our suggested interview questions: "What does it mean to be a member here?" Or "When you were a newcomer to this organization, what was strange, or different, or unexpected about the way things were done here?" Participant responses likely referenced stories, rituals, and varied communicative norms. What patterns emerge that suggest membership negotiation practices? You might find, for instance, and then capture thematic action in terms of "membership involves upward mobility by enacting service." This phrase may then be discussed in terms of norms and rituals that reflect the way membership negotiation is being constituted in certain enacted elements. For example, a norm is observed for listening to others and promotion rituals celebrating the service of a member.
2. "Self-structuring" addresses "internal relations, norms, and social entities . . . for connection, flexing, and shaping work processes" (McPhee & Zaug, 2009, p. 36). Thus, beyond yet interconnected with membership negotiation, this flow involves enacted elements that capture formal or informal policies, charts, accounting, and control regarding such things as how labor is divided, member rights and responsibilities, and decision-making. These all form a sort of meta-communication that ultimately steers all or part of the organization. Your textual analysis, for instance, may have picked up on enacted elements related to clear and/or ambiguous policies about family leave. Informally, you may have heard stories about the best way to "get things done" around here when you have a problem with the boss. Self-structuring is, however, not inherently consistent, coherent, or successful. One way to represent self-structuring is the various communicative practices that are inherently part of responding to a dialectic of clarity—ambiguity. On the one hand, clarity in accounting procedures may ensure accuracy and a certain level of ethical responsibility in communicating the financial pictures. Yet, sufficient ambiguity in decision-making norms may be useful in allowing greater member autonomy to get work done in more than one

way. Thus, you might imagine a thematic action capturing some aspect of self-structuring in your organization, such as: "Creative collaboration around a clear core."

3. "Activity coordination" refers to adjusting work processes and addressing immediate problems that arise from self-structuring. In short, members develop ways to make adjustments, albeit coordination might involve seeking power over others for self or group advantage, collaborative communication to improve ethical decision-making in the midst of a crisis response, or other forms of coordination. If you asked a question, "What are the dominant stories that members tell about how to get work done here?" you would pick up on rituals, stories, and norms related to this flow. Thematic action might then emerge from these enacted elements. You might note, for instance, that past crisis events are featured in stories told in meetings to encourage continued efforts to collaborate to improve product quality and customer communication. You might then capture these enacted elements as thematic action in the phrase, "Collaboration is encouraged in re-told crisis stories."
4. "Institutional positioning" refers to communication with those outside the organization, which may include governmental agencies, regulators, potential buyers, customers, suppliers, and partners. Recall our discussions on defining organizations in Chapter 1, in which we foregrounded McPhee and Zaug's (2009) definition of organizations with the following three features: a) communication and coordination—organizations or organizing processes are created or constituted in communication; b) interconnectedness and boundaries—organizations or organizing processes are not limited to a building or place thus a focus on intertwined networks is important; c) goals and outcomes—vary at individual and group levels, but are never neutral, that is decisions are influenced by certain goals being honored over others. We concur with this focus on intertwined networks, interconnectedness, and boundaries that ensure that we do not focus on organizations or organizational communication in terms of a building or some entity that exists in isolation. A compelling and provocative instance of research on this flow is found in a study conducted on ISIL (Islamic State of Iraq and the Levant). In their study, Bruscella and Bisel (2018) explore the way members of this terrorist organization position themselves through various communicative practices. One practice they document is "cooptation" or "the adoption of a rival's messaging for a purpose different from its original use" (p. 11). For instance, they refer to texts in every issue of an ISIL publication that has a section labeled "In the Words of the Enemy." In this section, they take words from Western leaders and use them to substantiate the success and strength of ISIL as a resource-rich organization.

While your study may not focus on this type of organization, you may have attended to enacted elements relevant to communicative practices surrounding risk and crisis communication, both of which involve external organizations. In all, these four flows comprise a theoretically rich way to frame and discern thematic action. We also provide an option for an analysis that is not tied to a specific framework.

Pervasiveness and Salience

Thematic action can be thought of as involving both "pervasiveness and salience" (Saffold, 1998). Pervasiveness has to do with the extent to which the thematic action is relevant to various units in the organization. Limited pervasiveness refers to those cultural enactments that are relevant to specific departments, while extensive pervasiveness refers to organization-wide enactments. For example, in one organization, enacted or performed rituals, norms, values, and rules might be captured by the phrase "Work hard, play hard." This thematic action, however, might only relate to just one or two departments, for example, sales or marketing. It may, however, have limited pervasiveness in the rest of the organization for the majority of the other units, such as Human Resources or Research and Development. In contrast, thematic action involves extensive pervasiveness that cuts across all units.

Salience, on the other hand, has to do with the importance of the thematic action or its "weightiness." The assumption is that the analysis of varied performances or enactments of varied elements suggests their significance, not just the extent to which they are widely shared (i.e., pervasiveness). Salience is more than the number of times an element is enacted. Salience is indicated when numerous elements of culture constitute the thematic action. For example, thematic action may emerge from significant symbols identified in textual analysis and interviews, rules from observations of meetings, and metaphors from interviews. Across each of these elements, you learn something about what appears to be a pattern of withdrawing or avoiding disagreements. You might at first word the thematic action as "silence is the best policy." However, you may find other elements that indicate a more nuanced communication process. For example, you may learn of other rules that conflicts, and disagreements are handled in indirect ways, and thus, you reword the thematic action as "work out your differences without causing a scene." Again, the key here is to make an interpretation that is supported by your data—enactments of the culture that emerge as significant. Just as a director checks to ensure the subplots are being born out on stage, so must our analysis attend to thematic action. Your discussion of thematic action should give the reader a sense of pervasiveness as well as salience. Rehearsal 8.1 provides a space to draft a theme based on enacted elements.

Here, though, it is right to pause and ask—"Should a final report include themes that hold true in some units but not in others?" Put differently, what is the value of reporting thematic differences that surfaced across the organization? Our answer is yes. Yes, there is value. As in the preceding examples, it should not be a surprise that differences emerged based on what it takes to get the work done in a given unit (e.g., the degree of collaboration needed in HR vs. Sales). We would encourage careful wording of these themes to capture the complexity and the contrasts. For instance, following the previous example, the uniqueness of the HR department might coalesce into a theme like, "Listen well, serve well." Thus, my report could go one of two routes. I could simply note these as unique thematic actions and label them as such. Conversely, I might capture an underlying commonality based on the data (e.g., "Serving and working both hard and well").

Regardless of whether you report themes that are unique or not, it is of value to give time to editing and revising so that the wording of the theme reflects the richness of the data. Let's return to the earlier example concerning how hard one should work. Your first pass might have led to the wording—"Work hard, play hard." Yet, as you again review data, you find consistent instances tied to communication norms of how members negotiated their roles and positions based on work-life balance. Based on these enactments, you now revise this thematic action as: "Work hard, but not too hard." To support this co-constructed performance, you should be able to summarize data from the enacted elements relevant to this thematic action. You might note, in your support of the enactment, statements like the following: Of the ten people interviewed, all but one made some reference to maintaining a healthy work-life balance; images and symbols in newsletters include members both at work and play; a CEO speech references the value he places on family as well as work. Informal member interactions include talking about how to best interpret and enact the company policy on work-life balance. A daily ritual was observed—a flex, two-hour break (leave early, come late or mid-day) for members to be with children, exercise, or have a long lunch.

Notice how, in the example from earlier, at least three enacted elements cut across more than one method. Support from these multiple sources provides a credible reading of pervasive and salient thematic action. Support like this is also about finding data that will challenge or check your biases in an organization. Of course, as you develop support by reviewing field notes, realize that other examples and relevant observations may occur to you that you failed to record in your notes. If this happens, be sure to document these important observations. As you discern instances of thematic action, remember that your analysis does not end there. As indicated earlier, this "back and forth" iterative process should include reflection on relevant research tied to the thematic action. Thus, in the preceding example, you might explore research on work-life balance. For instance, Hoffman and Cowan (2010), in a study of 96 employee requests for accommodation on work/life balance, relied on a structuration analysis to discern resources and rules that both reproduced and challenged the system. Their study aids us in seeing the challenges involved in change. They argue, based on the "principle of the duality of structure," "that to employ a rule or resource is to reinforce its power." The voices of participants pointed toward rules that dictated that "employees should only make requests they know will be granted" or that are in the best interest of the organization. The reproduction of structure, of a thematic action, "continually limits the pool of potential requests because few new requests are offered for consideration" (p. 219).

This "back and forth" process between your data, revising themes, and relevant literature ensures that the way you capture varied thematic actions is not isolated from common organizing processes. In addition, as several instances of thematic action emerge, you may be able to identify an overall characterization of the organizational culture in action.

Rehearsal 8.1 Finding Thematic Action

Purpose: Practice discerning the ways enacted elements combine to suggest thematic action

Steps:

1. Briefly state examples of three enacted elements (e.g., heroes, rules, and stories) from your observations, interviews, and/or textual analysis that merge to constitute an organizing process.

   Element A:

   ____

   ____

   ____

Element B:

Element C:

2. Identify connections across these enacted elements as they constitute thematic action—how might you word this co-construction?

3. Determine the relative pervasiveness of this thematic action. How widely spread is it in the organization? You may determine this by checking the sources you used for the various elements (e.g., organization-wide meetings vs. interviews in one department?).

4. Determine the relative salience of this thematic action. How important is it to organizational outcomes (e.g., productivity, employee engagement, work-life balance, community connection)? How often was it mentioned? How many enacted elements?

C. The Defining Plot: "What Is the Culture in Action?"

You walk out of a play, an art gallery, or a music performance hall and think about what you just experienced. The effort of translating the symbolic forms of music or art into words is difficult: something is always lost. For example, a book/opera like *Les Misérables* might leave you with a mix of feelings and ideas, as various enactments merge to suggest "the power in love," "the mystery of mercy," and "the self-destruction of evil." These word pictures capture thematic action in the play. Yet another step can be taken if you reflect across varied thematic actions and attempt to answer the question, "So what is the *Les Misérables* story about, anyway?" The process of distilling thematic actions into a clear statement about what constitutes or characterizes the overall culture is the third interpretive step in the OCA model. This step provides another way to respond to the question, "What is being co-created here?" Thus, when we consider "defining the plot" in an effort to reflect a constitutive approach, we use the phrase "organizational culture in action." This phrase is intended to stress the dynamic enactment of culture or how culture is being produced and reproduced by overlaps of varied thematic actions (i.e., organizing processes, multiple flows, salience/pervasiveness of enacted elements). Recalling the metaphors introduced in our discussion of the meaning of "constitutive" (see Chapter 2), it may be helpful to imagine this analysis process as deciphering communicative actions that have the power to "institute or enact" the culture (i.e., Communicative Constitutive of Organization); "flow like a river" constrained by the banks, but able to make changes through such processes as erosion (i.e., Structuration); or "building with Legos" by which you discern if participants are limited by their understanding of resources available in the "Lego box" and perhaps by the instructions included, or the extent they sense the option to locate additional Legos and directions outside of the box (i.e., Coordinated Management of Meaning). These varied images share in common the challenge of capturing a process—an organization in action or in the process of organizing. We will provide options for this interpretative step, but first, we need to consider a critique of this effort to capture an overall characterization.

An overall characterization of an organization or organizing processes may appear to fly in the face of the convention that organizations cannot or should not be reduced to specific labels or monoculture characterization (Martin, 1992). However, a general and overall characterization does not necessarily mean an oversimplification. Indeed, the answer to the question, "What is the culture in action?" may take a number of forms, each of which provides room for characterizations that are complex and creative. Furthermore, an answer to the question "What is being co-created here?" has value for organizational development as well as potential insight for internal and external communication. We provide three options to aid you in this process. Each of these options for characterizing a culture in action should be seen as a tool for reflecting on ways to capture the way thematic actions are suggestive of organizing processes that constitute the whole organization. Rehearsal 8.2 provides guides for practicing this process.

1. Is There a Central Paradox Co-Created Across Thematic Actions?

A paradox is a contradictory statement that is nevertheless true. By a central paradox, we mean a contradictory true statement that captures the core of the culture in action. Thinking about paradoxes in the organization can help you and your members make sense of varied enacted elements that may be constructing high levels of uncertainty. For example, "Chaotic Order" might capture a number of elements relevant to an organization characterized by standard policies and procedures that guide creative endeavors, discussed as the reason for chaos in the organization. Often, the crux of the culture is best depicted in tensions and contradictions, for example, the contradiction between espoused values and actual organizational practices. The OCA model, consistent with CCO and other constructivist approaches, assumes contradiction is a central part of the organizing process (Putnam, 2013). Thus, while attending to a given contradiction, the idea is to discern how this paradox is being enacted or constituted in various thematic actions and enacted elements. Here again, as we recommended in the process of bringing in relevant literature in your discussions of thematic action, the same holds true in this section. For example, Meisenbach and Feldner (2019), analyze the constitutive nature of reality TV in terms of workplace identity. In their analysis of "Undercover Boss," they capture several contradictions or paradoxes. The boss as a superhero is simultaneously about "Empowering Disempowerment." In addition, the superhero boss uses language that complicates who is to blame or responsible by capturing his discourse tied to "I Am/They Are/No One is Responsible" (p. 415). Perhaps most challenging is the contradiction or paradox of "Solving/ Not Solving," which introduces a narrative of how the boss truly helps a few individuals but is powerless to impact larger structures that maintain low pay wages.

2. Is There a Master Rule/Value Co-Created Across Thematic Actions?

The notion of a master rule or value implies that thematic actions merge to suggest an overarching guiding principle that permeates and is recreated across varied organizing processes. For instance, using the preceding example, if a paradox or contradiction is not the sense you get from your reading of the culture, you might note that the culture can best be captured by drawing attention to the way employees are expected to follow an implicit communication rule in all that they do. The rule, more than tied to one meeting or one decision-making process, is present across settings, including conflict management, self-structuring, and even membership negotiation. In each flow or thematic action, the role and value given to novelty and new ideas is present. Thus, an overall characterization of the culture might be: "Introduce new ideas always and everywhere." Research might then be reflected in positive communication practices that use the opening 15 minutes of each meeting to ask an open question such as, "What is the latest craziest idea you have had about improving our organization?"

3. Is There a Root Metaphor Co-Created Across Thematic Actions?

The idea of a root metaphor, like a master rule or value, suggests that one thing serves as the source for describing varied thematic actions. It may be thought of as a metaphor "that lies underneath the understanding of something (e.g., organization) and is thus the 'root' for our understanding of it" (Örtenblad, 2017, p. 58). Root metaphors can capture multiple elements and provide a valuable way to examine an organization (Morgan, 2006). Thus, one option for characterizing the culture is to explore your enacted elements and thematic actions in light of the eight metaphors provided by Morgan (2006) (introduced in Chapter 3): machines, organism, brain, culture, political systems, psychic prison, flux and transformation, and instrument of domination. The idea, for instance, would be to examine enacted elements, such as language, and discern if a root metaphor best captures multiple constitutive practices (e.g.,

"Getting promoted around here is like trying to win an election suggests a political root metaphor"). In one organization, a wide array of diversity initiatives were evident across elements and thematic actions. The student studying this organization sought to capture the uniqueness and unanticipated breadth and depth of these communicative practices, which included intentional efforts to diversify the ethnic make-up of leaders by including the ethnicity of a candidate as part of the qualification to hire, a mentoring program for minorities, and the use of more than one language in meetings. In the process of reflection, this student was creative in extending the organism metaphor described as tied to images of adaptation and survival (Morgan, 2006). He used the metaphor of a "duck-billed platypus." Historically, the first stories of this creature were not even believed because of their uniqueness and unexpected appearance. As a root metaphor, this creative take on the organization allowed for a depiction of the uniqueness of their approaches to co-create a multi-ethnic organization. These approaches were then reflected in light of research showing the uniqueness of such organizations, with only about 10% of churches that are 90% diverse (Emerson, 2006). Just as the duck-billed platypus is novel, this organization was unique in their shared focus on diversity found across enacted elements.

Despite the power of discerning a root metaphor, caution is in order. If not used cautiously, foregrounding a root metaphor may promote or disguise problematic power relationships. Thus, another factor to consider in your interpretation is to ask yourself, "What is not here that I would expect to see?" Martin (1992) refers to this type of analysis as probing silences and empty spaces. Angi once served as a consultant to a children's home, trying to survive a leadership transition. As she questioned the board members about the strengths and weaknesses of the organization, she was struck by the absence of any language about the care of children. Board members talked about the strength of leadership, the business plan, the endowment, and the new facilities, but no one talked about the children. The silence made it clear that the non-profit organization had drifted from the clarity of its original mission and values. In this instance, while members might have introduced a family metaphor, the lack of enacted elements that included children is problematic given their goals. In other instances, a metaphor, such as a "family," may fail to attend to the way a pattern of paternalism continues (Putnam & Boys, 2006). Thus, again, macro- and micro-level enacted elements should be attended to, and thus, the goal would be to discern more nuanced metaphors. Thus, rather than a simple "family" metaphor, a closer reflection on multiple elements may suggest a particular type of family (i.e., dysfunctional or blended).

Drafting Your Report: Writing to Connect

We encourage you, at this juncture, to draft the main sections of your report, which are absent in the applications section. Rehearsal 8.4 provides a format for this process. These guides, while general in nature, stress a central theme of this process—relational and ethical connection. You have connected with a leader of this organization from the proposal process and others throughout the data collection process. You have observed and listened in a way that shows respect and ethical concern for others and the quality of the data you collect. You have also shown care and caution in the interpretation process, realizing that data that is not accurately represented is not just an issue of personal interpretation but ethics. The next goal is to discern a format that will best aid others in connecting with this interpretation. Recall that while other interpretations are possible, you have based your interpretation on a richer, more diverse data set than most take the time to gather. At the same time, this drafting step is one meant to prompt careful reflection on creating not only a credible but compelling and ethical account of the culture. The writing process can be daunting. What language? What tone? What details to include? What format? All of these are critical questions and will be explored further in the final chapter. At this point, consider the following encouragements as you draft:

1. **Plan on multiple revisions.** Writing and rewriting is a form of reflection. This reflection process allows you to see the flow and the way ideas can be worded more clearly in a way that will connect with others.
2. **Involve others.** Gain feedback from colleagues, team members, and the person who conducted the coding check. Recall that a coding check and referencing this step in the report adds credibility due to the high bar you are setting for engaging in an ethical analysis process
3. **Remember the big question.** At the heart of the drafting is making sure you are clearly answering the big question, "What is being created here?" To that end, we discourage presenting your findings in terms of a list of elements. These can be provided in an Appendix. Instead, as indicated in Rehearsal 8.4, you will move directly to phrases that capture "thematic action" in the Results or Findings section. The idea of "thematic action" is to paint the picture of subplots or "grounded in action" (Fairhurst & Putnam, 2004) processes based on the four flows (McPhee & Zaug, 2009) and/or the concepts of salience and pervasiveness. These constitutive processes can then aid you in discerning an overall characterization of the culture.
4. **Create a compelling narrative.** When you write your analysis, experiment with creative forms. A cultural analysis should read more like a short story than a formal research paper. Yet, it should be a short story with credible data captured in a compelling manner. You may think about this process as data with a soul or data telling a story. Thus, you may include extensive quotes or narratives from interviews with culture members to illustrate thematic action. You may also include narratives of key episodes you observed. Thus, the resultant statement about the "plot" or overall characterization is made more compelling by including the stories you heard and the places you observed.
5. **Blend quantitative and qualitative data in an ethical and credible manner.** You may have heard the phrase "statistics lie." We would add that data of any type can be misrepresented and, perhaps unconsciously, presented to support a bias. Thus, simply stating a percentage or the quotes from interviews should be avoided. The three-phase process of moving from enacted elements to thematic action to an overall characterization is about a careful process of reflecting on data that creates a credible, compelling account. To that end, if you used a quantitative survey, avoid simply stating a mean, average, or percentage. Numbers alone will not tell a story that is supported in an ethical manner. For instance, if you found that 80% (16/20) participants agreed that the stated values were talked about in terms of creating space for both *continuity and change*, you need to then provide context. You may have picked up on a story that echoes this finding, a ritual that celebrates the role of history as a continual, as well as a discursive thread that honors the introduction of new goals. Thus, your thematic action might be something like: "Keep the old and bring in the new." This thematic action would then be discussed in light of the data points mentioned previously. On the other hand, if you find other elements that contradict this find, you have options. You might need to return to a focus group to explore this finding.

You might find that your survey data was skewed. In fact, the 20 who responded from an organization of 50 were all from one unit. Thus, you would need to consider wording the thematic action as: "Contrasting stories of continuity and change." Conversely, you might find that the sample was valid, but participants only agreed with the statement at a general level. In the focus group, they express concerns about the execution of this value set. Thus, the thematic action might read: "The challenge of living out continuity and change." This wording then allows you to explore the seeming contradiction in light of the stories told versus those being lived out.

Rehearsal 8.2 Practicing Interpretation

Purpose: Develop interpretive skills in light of the OCA constitutive approach.

Major Steps:

1. Complete two weeks of observation notes.
   a. A minimum of three to four hours a week in observation.
   b. A variety of observation settings (e.g., meetings, informal interactions, setting).
   c. Notes that include bracketed information (about inferences and questions).
2. Use interviews or qualitative surveys to explore cultural interpretations of organizational actors.
   a. Choose a representative sample of interviewees.
   b. Develop rapport.
   c. Use relatively open questions to elicit accounts, stories, and explanations.
   d. Follow up answers with probes.
3. Content analysis of a representative text or texts.
   a. Choose representative and credible texts that match the communication style of the organization.
   b. Use content analysis, rhetorical analysis, or linguistic analysis.
4. Create a document summarizing data by enacted elements of culture.
   a. Be sure to make clear reference to observation notes (date, etc.) and/or content analysis text (date of newsletter, section, etc.); the key here is to have summary data that can easily be traced back to notes.
   b. Be sure you have several examples of most, if not all, of the elements.
5. Analyze your summary of enacted elements to determine thematic action.
   a. Thematic action attempts to capture organizing processes from three or more of the enacted elements.
   b. State the thematic action and enacted elements. Be specific.

For example: In a daycare organization, thematic action might be: "Supportive touch is a mandated and encouraged behavior." Rules and rituals indicate that teachers should initiate touch often during the day and encourage children to touch each other in appropriate ways. Furthermore, during a weekly staff meeting, a story was told of a teacher's aide who was fired because he did not take time to hug and encourage children through positive and appropriate touch.

  c. Aim for a minimum of three phrases that capture thematic action.

6. Create an overall characterization of the culture based on thematic action and enacted elements.
   a. An overall characterization is a general statement that attempts to capture the core of the culture.
   b. An overall characterization does not mean that subcultures do not differ or that the culture is unified across all levels and divisions of the organization.
   c. Thematic action and relevant enacted elements provide support for the characterization you have developed.
   d. Review Chapter 8 for options in developing an overall characterization of the culture.

7. Checklist for reviewing major steps of the Rehearsal:

_____ Interpretation section with thematic actions and an overall characterization.
_____ Appendix with a paper trail (for validity and reliability/consistency checks).
_____ A copy of your field notes.
_____ A description or copy of the text you used for content analysis.
_____ A copy of notes from any other method used (survey, interviews).
_____ A copy of your summary data for each enacted element.
_____ A completed reliability check by a trusted colleague, a mentor, a classmate, or a member of the organization to make sure your account is consistent with how organizational members interpret the culture.

Note: Though the idea of a reliability check seems at first "too academic," it should be part of our interpretive processes—we check our perceptions with others. The following guide sheet can be used by a trusted colleague, mentor, or classmate to review your work.

Summary

Data overload? We trust that with these guides to support from colleagues and co-researchers, you have moved past being overwhelmed. At this stage of the analysis, your immersion in the data and your own creativity as an interpreter are all important. You should have a sense of seeing the organization you are studying in a new light or with a clearer understanding. Like an actor who has hung out behind the scenes to interact with other actors, who has studied the script and gotten inside the character, you should know more than the other actors about the set, the stage, the relationships among the players, and what makes this particular troupe and performance unique. The thematic action you have already discussed as well as other relevant data should support your overall characterization of the culture. Before moving to the application section, be sure you have a clear grasp of the following aspects of the interpretation process:

1. Cultural analysis is an interpretive process; characterizations of the culture will likely vary from person to person.
2. Thematic action involves enacted elements that constitute organizing processes via multiple enacted elements. These may be captured with words based on the pervasiveness/salience of enacted elements that coalesce or emerge as one of the "four flows."
3. A characterization of the culture is constituted by insights that involve more than one thematic action and may take the form of a paradox, master rules/values, or root metaphor.
4. Begin the process of drafting a credible and compelling account of your findings.

Rehearsal 8.3 Reliability/Validity Check

1. Observation process:

______ Clear rationale for the observer role that was selected.
______ Clear understanding of ethics involved in the choice of roles.

2. Check field notes: Check for improvement (from weeks one to three) in the following:

______ Detailed descriptions.
______ Use of brackets.

3. Check text analysis:

______ Clear rationale for choosing this set of documents.
______ Representative sample.
______ Credible.
______ Method of analysis documented and explained.

4. Review summary of each enacted element:

______ Are there gaps that indicate the need for more data?
______ Can you trace examples back to field notes, text, and interviews?
______ Does it focus on descriptions? Free of judgment?
______ Examples clearly fit each element according to the characterization of elements.
______ Missing details? (Is information sufficient, makes sense?)
______ Method triangulation on most enacted elements: examples from text analysis and observation and/or interviews/surveys?

5. Check thematic action for:

______ Method triangulation: examples from content analysis and observation and/or interviews/surveys?
______ Data triangulation: examples from three or more enacted elements?

6. Check an overall characterization for:

_____ Thematic triangulation: support based on two or more thematic actions (may include other well-developed enacted elements).
_____ Method triangulation: support from text analysis and observation and/or interviews/surveys?

Discussion Questions

1. At what points in an organization's history and life cycle would it be especially important to engage in in-depth cultural analysis?
2. Discuss the process of working to create interpretive order from a mass of cultural data (identify enacted elements, develop thematic action, draw an over-arching cultural characterization).
3. Give examples of cultural assumptions that lie beneath the surface of organizational events and processes and are often unconscious.
4. What do the authors mean by probing silence and empty spaces in your cultural data, trying to pay attention to what's not there?

Rehearsal 8.4 Cultural Analysis Drafting Guides

Directions: This final checklist should guide rather than dictate your writing process. These suggestions are intended as guides to develop a highly credible and compelling report. Of course, who your audience is (members of one department vs. executive leadership team) will dictate the format. Remember, the goal is to "tell the story" of your analysis in a credible and convincing manner. In this suggested outline, you are focused on enacted elements, thematic action, and your overall characterization of the culture. After we cover application topics, we will discuss ways to develop the implications of your findings as a final section of this report.

Introduction

_____ Draw interest to your analysis.
_____ Discuss the importance of your analysis.
_____ Develop credibility—references.
_____ Preview main sections.

Body

1. Overview of analysis

_____ Background of organization (mission, structure, brief history).
_____ Methods (discuss data collection, rationale, time spent).
_____ Refer to Appendix with notes on each enacted element.

2. Thematic Action

_____ Minimum of three; each supported by data from three or more enacted elements.
_____ Clear, convincing support from Appendix of enacted elements.
_____ Clear tables/data summaries (e.g., examples, frequency counts, quotes, paraphrases).
_____ Written to capture the richness of cultural data.

3. Overall characterization of culture

_____ Supported by thematic action and enacted elements.
_____ Clear articulation of the rationale for the characterization.

4. Implication/Application

_____ Preview subsections (limits/future research, implications, and comm. recommendations).
_____ Identifies limitations of methodology and tying them to suggestions for future research.
_____ Identifies one communication and theoretically-informed implication from data analysis ["*so what*"—value claims—what it means for the context—what we learned about theory/context]-integrating relevant literature.
_____ Three communication recommendations are clearly tied to cultural data as ethical feedback.
_____ Positive communication practices tied to application chapters & references using ethical feedback guides (e.g., "*now what*"—communication-action plan for organization integrating relevant literature with a positive focus by noting what is working and building on current practices).
_____ Address potential communication barriers to implementing recommendations (identify, clearly explain, and support each with relevant literature). Stating barriers might be include acknowleding:

- diverse perspectives on goals.
- the challenges of accomplishing goals for various audiences.
- the positive and negative consequences of accomplishing potential goals for various audiences or stakeholders.

___ Transition to next section.

Conclusion

_____ Restate major goals, major conclusions, and benefits.
_____ Review the process (strengths of analysis, lessons learned).

References (complete; consistent format)

Appendix

_____ Synopsis of inferences on all elements (e.g., list all the rules).
_____ Copy of interview/survey guide if used.
_____ Copy of Executive Summary (when applicable).
_____ Field notes.
_____ Texts used for analysis.

References

Barends, E., & Rousseau, D. (2022). Organizational culture and performance: An evidence review. *Scientific summary*. London: Chartered Institute of Personnel and Development. Retrieved from www.cipd.org/en/knowledge/evidence-reviews/evidence-culture-climate

Bruscella, J., & Bisel, R. (2018). Four flows theory and materiality: ISIL's use of material resources in its communicative constitution. *Communication Monographs, 85(2)*, 1–26. https://doi.org/10.1080/03637751.2017.1420907

Cooren, F., & Fairhurst, G. (2009). Dislocation and stabilization: How to scale up from interactions to organizations. In L. L. Putnam & A. M. Nicotera (Eds.), *Building theories of organization: The constitutive role of communication* (pp. 117–152). New York: Routledge.

Emerson, M. (2006). *People of the dream: Multiracial congregations in the United States*. New York, NY: Oxford University Press.

Fairhurst, G. T., & Putnam, L. (2004). Organizations as discursive constructions. *Communication Theory, 14*, 5–26.

Hoffman, M., & Cowan, R. (2010). Be careful what you ask for: Structuration theory and work-life accommodation. *Communication Studies, 61(2)*, 205–223. https://doi.org/10.1080/10510971003604026

Martin, J. (1992). *Cultures in organizations: Three perspectives*. New York: Oxford University Press.

McPhee, R. D., & Zaug, P. (2000). The communicative constitution of organizations: A framework for explanation. *Electronic Journal of Communication, 10(1, 2)*. Retrieved from www.cios.org/ejcpublic/010/1/01017.html

McPhee, R. D., & Zaug, P. (2009). The communicative constitution of organizations: A framework for explanation. In L. L. Putnam & A. M. Nicotera (Eds.), *Building theories of organization: The constitutive role of communication* (pp. 21–47). New York: Routledge.

Meisenbach, R. J., & Feldner, S. B. (2019). Constructing the ideal worker identity: The rhetorical construction of discursive resources in *undercover boss*. *Western Journal of Communication, 83(4)*, 403–422. https://doi.org/10.1080/10570314.2019.1566564

Meyer, J. (2015). *Understanding humor through communication: Why be funny anyway?* Lanham, MD: Lexington Books.

Miles, M. B. (1979). Qualitative data as an attractive nuisance: The problem of analysis. *Administrative Science Quarterly, 24(4)*, 590–601. https://doi.org/10.2307/2392365

Mirivel, J., & Lyon, A. (2023). *Positive communication for leaders: Proven strategies for inspiring unity and effecting change*. New York: Rowen & Littlefield.

Morgan, G. (2006). *Images of organization* (updated ed.). Newbury Park, CA: Sage.

Örtenblad, A. (2017). Approaches to using metaphors in organizational analysis: Morgan's metaphors and beyond. In A. Örtenblad, K. Trehan, & L. L. Putnam (Eds.), *Exploring Morgan's metaphors: Theory, research, and practice in organizational studies* (pp. 54–86). Thousand Oaks, CA: Sage.

Putnam, L. (2013). Primary and secondary contradictions: A literature review and future directions. *Management Communication Quarterly, 27(4)*, 623–630. https://doi.org/10.1177/0893318913504139

Putnam, L., & Boys, S. (2006). Revisiting metaphors of organizational communication. In S. R. Clegg, C. Hardy, T. B. Lawrence, & W. Nord (Eds.), *The Sage handbook of organizational studies* (2nd ed., pp. 541–576). London: Sage.

Saffold, G. (1998). Culture traits, strength, and organizational performance: Moving beyond "strong" culture. *Academy of Management Review, 13*, 546–558. https://doi.org/10.2307/258374

Sobral, F., & Islam, G. (2015). He who laughs best, leaves last: The influence of humor on the attitudes and behavior of interns. *Academy of Management Learning & Education, 14(4)*, 500–518. https://doi.org/10.5465/amle.2013.0368

Tracy, S. J. (2013). *Qualitative research methods: Collecting evidence, crafting analysis, communicating impact*. Malden, MA: Wiley.

Van Maanan, J. (1979). Reclaiming qualitative methods for organizational research. *Administrative Science Quarterly*, *24*, 520–526. https://doi.org/10.2307/2392358

Weick, K. E. (1995). *Sensemaking in organizations*. Thousand Oaks, CA: Sage.

White, D. (2021). *Disrupting corporate culture: How cognitive science alters accepted beliefs about culture and culture change and its impact on leaders and change agents*. New York: Routledge.

Part IV

Cultural Analysis Application

An Introduction to Step Six

1. Articulate cultural analysis goals and benefits
2. Explore culture as co-construction
3. Reflect on enacted elements
4. Identify enacted elements via multiple methods
5. Interpret thematic action and OCA
6. Co-create positive communication applications

Step Six: Co-Create Positive Communication Applications

Diversity

Stage Terms

Diversity	Symbolic leadership	Organizational effectiveness
Change leadership	Ethics	

> Corporate social responsibility is measured in terms of businesses improving conditions for their employees, shareholders, communities, and environment. But moral responsibility goes further, reflecting the need for corporations to address fundamental ethical issues such as inclusion, dignity, and equality.
>
> – Klaus Schwab, Founder of the World Economic Forum

Answering "So What?" and "Now What?"

Actors undertaking the rigorous training of method acting must ask themselves at some point, "Will this really make me a better actor? Will it pay off in the final production?" As they focus on drinking a cup of orange juice, channeling emotions from previous experiences, and increasing concentration on stage, they have to wonder about their ability to transfer these activities into the creation of better performances. "Will this focus of attention matter?" In the same way, we may wonder if the rigorous effort necessary to understand organizational cultures has a payoff. At such junctures, we find it helpful to return to the big picture, just what we are after with the OCA model. Recall our focus is on *fostering the co-creation of positive*

DOI: 10.4324/9781003482529-12

organizations by developing implications through the analysis of enacted elements that both shape and are shaped by communication.

We have, until now, focused on the first part of this definition by answering the question, "What is being created here?" The goal was to engage in ethical and effective data collection and interpretation processes. Now we turn to the later part of this definition, which responds to the other questions we had at the start of the process: "What kind of culture should we co-create?" and "What forms of communication will co-create the culture we want?" These big questions provide a tool to encourage reflection on ways to co-create ethical communication implications (Step 6) grounded in your analysis. Like other "steps" in this process, this one is not linear. Therefore, we need to be aware of five organizational cultural analysis realities.

1. **Application contexts overlap.** Just as organizations exist as part of intertwined networks, so also do the varied applications. For instance, if you focused on "diversity" (Chapter 9) in your data collection or themes surfaced tied to diversity, it is incumbent to reflect on units such as "change" (Chapter 10) since the communication practices related to change will be critical to efforts you make at introducing diversity initiatives. If your data, perhaps due to recent conflicts and/or high turnover rates, points toward the need to explore application guides in the chapter on Leadership (Chapter 12), key ideas in the "Ethics" (Chapter 11) should be considered
2. **Explore additional communication applications.** For instance, the chapter on "effectiveness" includes potential applications such as crisis communication, conflict management, and mediated communication. Thus, there may be a need to reflect on your data in ways that go beyond any one chapter (tie back to other points?).
3. Engage in a **data check** as you develop communication applications. It is critical that you have support for your recommendations. In more than one student paper, the implications section had only a limited connection to the data. The reason was clear—as insiders, the assumed need for certain changes skewed data collection and interpretation.
4. **Shift from a problem, deficit orientation to positive communication.** Rather than a "problem-solution" focus, it is more effective to capture what is working. In one study, Gerald found that the vast majority of the communicative practices were creating what they hoped to create. The organization, however, had never had that sort of validation.
5. **Explore ways to co-create applications.** As you develop communication implications, we encourage you to see these as drafts. Chapter 14 guides you in translating your applications into an execution plan. This plan encourages wording recommendations that focus on the process and recommending dialogue. For example, rather than stating, "Create a training plan for . . . ," a recommendation might state, "Engage the leadership team in co-creating training options grounded in listening to members."

Before moving to the application context focused on diversity, we review our rationale for these five application contexts.

Five Application Contexts

Chapters 9 through 13 introduce five application contexts: diversity, change, leadership, ethics, and organizational effectiveness. It is valid to ask, "Why these five?" Each application chapter is:

- *Significant across boundaries of nations, organizational type, and time.*
- *About discerning enacted elements of culture as pathways for co-creating positive organizations to improve all our social worlds.*

What, Then, Is the Focus of Each Application Chapter?

- Chapter 9, "Casting Against Type: Diversity," explores the linkage between organizational culture and processes that support and encourage various forms of diversity.
- Chapter 10, "Improvisation: Leading Change," captures best practices ("small wins") focused on tapping into elements of the culture rather than changing in opposition to the culture.
- Chapter 11, "An Honest Portrayal: Ethics," introduces communication practices that co-create highly ethical organizations with a focus on "here and now" ethics talk.
- Chapter 12, "The Director's Chair: Symbolic Leadership," offers opportunities for you to evaluate leaders in your organization as well as your own symbolic leadership abilities.
- Chapter 13, "Reading Reviews: Organizational Effectiveness," identifies ways the previous application topics contribute to co-creating positive organizations by offering tools to assess your organization in light of cultural data.

We anticipate each of you having useful insights during this final step. We are confident you will develop practical and meaningful applications for organizations. Diversity is the first application context.

Chapter 9

Casting Against Type

Diversity

This first of five applications introduces the final step in the OCA model by focusing on how to co-create positive communication applications for organizational diversity. The challenges and opportunities presented by the diversity paradox are explored. The choices made in response to cultural data may result in improving the quality of life and creative outcomes for participants whose voices have been muted. Five communicative practices are introduced: a) ask to discover lived experiences with diversity; b) disclose to deepen commitment to diversity values; c) engage in dialogue about the meaning of diversity; d) assess progress on the diversity journey; and e) co-create multi-level action plans.

Step 6: Co-Create Positive Communication Applications

Objectives

- Understand the challenge of the diversity paradox.
- Apply five positive communicative practices to co-create diversity.
- Explain communicative strategies to empower minority subcultures.

Stage Terms

Diversity	Diversity Paradox	Cosmopolitan Communication	Dialogue
Multiculturalism	Hegemony	Mentoring	Marginalized groups

The following quotes reflect the chapter's aims:

> [The] way we handle our differences, more than the positions we take or even who wins the arguments, will shape the evolution of our social worlds.
>
> (Pearce, 2007, p. 216)

> Thus, creativity has come to be the most highly prized commodity in our economy .... Hiring for diversity, once a matter of legal compliance, has become a matter of economic survival because creativity comes in all colors, genders, and personal preferences.
>
> (Florida, *The Rise of the Creative Class*, 2002, p. 5)

DOI: 10.4324/9781003482529-13

An Assessment Plus a Challenge

Please take a few seconds to complete this mini-assessment. Rate your level of agreement from high to low with the following four statements. My organization:

1. Places a high value on diversity, evidenced in recruitment and retention practices.
2. Has a clear vision for diversity, equity, inclusion, and belonging practices.
3. Equips members to improve intercultural competence.
4. Engages in meaningful measures of progress on the diversity journey.

Regardless of your rating level, in our consulting, research, and leadership roles, we have seen cause for hope. We hear from alumni and community members whose goals are congruent with our focus in this workbook. Recall the overarching goal of a cultural analysis is to *provide insight for improving positive communication practices that result in meaningful personal, professional, and organizational culture development and growth.* Such a vision demands attentiveness to power and identity dynamics enacted, established, and constituted in communication (Allen, 2011). To set the stage for this application chapter on diversity, reflect on the following challenge:

> Create a positive and vibrant culture in which values are shared, members are socialized into a common way of creating meanings and engaging, and at the same time, maintain a diverse organization with enough tension to promote creativity, innovation, and a sense of belonging.

This challenge captures the essential paradox of culture. The question, then, is *how do we manage this paradox?* In this chapter, due to the significance of this paradox, we further describe the paradox before exploring the challenge of engaging in DEI+ (Diversity, Equity, and Inclusion, plus Belonging). We then focus on five positive diversity practices we argue constitute the best path forward.

The Diversity Paradox

As implied in the opening, strong cultures tend to reproduce themselves. New employees are hired because they are a "good fit" with existing employees. Cultural values and norms are so strong that employees are socialized to accept the "company way," or they leave. The diversity paradox is an example of value tension, creativity, and constraint (LeGreco, Eisenberg, Tretheway, & Goodall, 2024). The very cohesiveness forces woven into the fabric of a strong culture can be a constraining force on diversity and, thus, creativity. The flip side also can be true. If a company strives for diversity in hiring and consciously chooses individuals quite different from the existing employee base, changes in the way elements enact culture are likely. Stories may no longer carry shared historical meanings, and discourse surrounding rituals may not include the newcomers.

Subcultures and divisions likely emerge. These divisions may be positive in the long run as new ideas and ways of organizing become valued, but they are disruptive and difficult at the start, including possible impacts on short-term productivity (Julian & Ofori-Dankwa, 2017). For instance, in an ethnographic study, Zak (1994) explored a blue-collar organization newly diversified by race, gender, ethnicity, and class due to legal mandates. Veteran employees sought to maintain cultural identity and hierarchical position through linguistic strategies such as inside humor, exclusive language, and horseplay. Frequent conflicts between newcomers and veterans prompted management to step in to increase control and enforce punishments, leading to cultural fragmentation and resentment. This same pattern surfaced in the Asian context, where research identified a "double-edged sword." In brief, "workforce diversity was positively related to negative affect, which in turn, increased interpersonal conflict" (Liu, Zhu, & Wang, 2023, p. 8). Such a finding indicates that efforts at diversity do not come easily.

Beyond workplace organizations, efforts to move away from the norm of segregation in religious organizations face additional challenges. These organizations, unlike public or federal ones required by law to address inequities, are increasingly driven by an ethical vision rooted in their faith. As one national-level faith leader commented in the context of a community forum on faith, "If heaven is not segregated, why on earth are we?" (Driskill, Arjannikova, & Meyer, 2014). However, the challenges are complex. The pressure toward homogeneity in voluntary organizations is evidenced by the shorter durations of minority members. One explanation, akin to what may happen in the workplace, is that integration can be experienced as a loss of identity and ethnic culture (Scheitle & Dougherty, 2010). Another homogeneity force is the lack of intentionality in diversifying leadership (Emerson, 2006) as well as the lack of diverse worship styles (DeYmaz, 2007). In addition, low awareness of and/or acceptance of differences in communication practices creates barriers (Jenkins, 2014). Yet, in the midst of these challenges, trend data shows continued increases in the number of multi-ethnic congregations (Dougherty, Chaves, & Emerson, 2020).

The Challenge of DEI+ Initiatives

This diversity paradox is real, regardless of organizational context. The challenges involved in the diversity paradox and doing this work are daunting. Consider these three challenges. First, there are continued changes to the legal and political context, especially in the US. In 2023, the US Supreme Court ended Affirmative Action in college admission. While military academies may be able to continue, the only caveat for other universities is that nothing prohibits them from considering an applicant based on how race affects his or her life (Totenberg, June 29, 2023). In addition, major organizations are scaling back or removing DEI programs (e.g., Walmart, Ford, Harley Davidson, Google, and Lowes). As such, organizations are left with continued challenges to enact practices that are just and fair while responding to political pressures. Discerning a meaningful scope of diversity will likely continue to challenge us all at the individual, organizational, and societal levels. Second, the term diversity, when placed in a historic context, may miss what was intended by earlier initiatives. The 1960s Civil Rights movement and related initiatives "constituted a social justice approach." Beginning in the 1980s, growing from political shifts, "managing diversity" surfaced as a way to create a competitive advantage based on such factors as cost saving, marketing, and creativity (Villamil, Branton, & Meisenbach, 2024, p. 297). As such, while having other motivations for diversity than "social justice" is not problematic, they mean diversity initiatives miss a core value—justice.

A third and final challenge regards the development of intercultural competence. Efforts to improve competence involve more than motivation, language, and cultural/diversity awareness and knowledge. Those taking on this challenge must navigate contradictory and conflicting dialectics such as individual–cultural, personal–contextual, and privilege–disadvantage (Martin & Nakayama, 2015). For example, Schein and Schein (2021) foreground a case in which a US organizational culture's norm of "lengthy talks" at breaks about family made a worker from India "extremely uncomfortable" since it went against the norm in India. As such, the concept of friendliness in the workplace can, paradoxically, create a sense of "over-exclusion" (p. 75–76). Multiple questions arise from these challenges:

- "How can people work and live together" in diverse settings and interact in authentic and productive ways "while maintaining valued identities?"
- "How can collectives use their differences as a source of benefit both to individual members and the whole?"
- How do we navigate differences in how equity, fairness, and effective leadership are defined?
- How can diversity goals be "clarified" and "implemented" to co-create "sustainable changes"?
- What "individual qualities" and "interactions that support finding" and "implementing answers" to these questions?

(Ferdman, 2021, pp. 4–5)

AI and Best Diversity Practices

Given these challenges, and in response to these questions, perhaps like us, you wondered if perhaps the best option might be to let AI do the work of generating best practices. We did take that step and found one article that caught us off guard. Consider this somewhat promising AI forecast. A Forbes article suggests the role of AI may, in time, improve efforts to address bias in hiring and promotion. For instance, Uber is cited as using AI to create a culture of meritocracy—performance-based retention and promotion, not bias (Chamorro-Premuzic, 2024). Given the major challenge in diversity initiatives in addressing hiring and promotion biases, such a tool may be useful. Yet, another paradox emerges. Western conceptualization of leadership tends to focus on short-term profit, individual effort ("anyone can get to the top"), and a. high value on participatory decision-making. In contrast, non-Western conceptualizations focus on long-term goals and collective needs and value social status and titles (Enarsi & Riggio, 2021, p. 29).

However, as we reviewed research summaries captured (and not captured) by AI and also spoke with DEI professionals, we found ourselves revising our list of practices. As before, they are not organized as a set of exhaustive steps in a linear process. These practices, consistent with a CCO perspective, respond to the big question, "What forms or kinds of communication will create what we should create?"

Our first practice is foundational to the ones that follow. What they all share in common are three defining attributes: a) a challenge to model this practice regardless of your role in the organization; b) a focus on relationship building and connection, not just on accomplishing a DEI checklist; c) a formal practice (top-down) practice but not at the expense of the informal. (c.f., Turi et al., 2022). After a brief definition and rationale, we identify varied ways each practice can be put into action. Again, we provide reflection questions and/or Rehearsals as additional ways to explore and apply these practices.

1. Ask to Discover Lived Experiences with Diversity

Defined: Asking open questions to develop relationships based on understanding diverse and common experiences.

Rationale: Progress on the diversity journey is co-created by relationships that model the positive communication practices of asking to discover the unknown. This process relies on sharing stories that, on the one hand, might surface differences that create a sense of exclusion, but on the other hand, learning of those differences may also create a sense of trust and inclusion (c.f., Schein & Schein, 2021).

In action: Discovering lived experiences with diversity takes varied forms. For example, Gerald ends a class now and then with a "non-assignment" assignment by stating: *Here is an optional assignment, no credit, don't even tell me you did it.* One such assignment is to connect with someone you think is different in some way from you (politically, socially, religiously, etc.). He then encourages them to focus on open questions, on listening, and on paraphrasing what they think they heard. In short, to listen well, to connect across differences. This first practice is about relational connection. You may already have a network of diverse, deepening relationships. In existing or new relationships, we provide questions later that are inspired by positive practice from Julien's "Model of Positive Communication" by focusing on asking open questions. The questions are ones that you can weave into conversations with colleagues, friends, and other members in and outside your organizations. For instance, given research on the exclusionary role of humor experienced by minorities (Wolfgruber, 2023), a question might be: "What has your experience with humor been around here?" Or, borrowing from such questions, if part of developing a trusting relationship, can deepen awareness of minority experiences. Imagine, in response to that question, your minority colleague shares the following statement that his supervisor shared with a group during a coffee break.

> The one who is often taken for a ride, and he doesn't really know it, is the regional manager of my company. A Persian.*chuckles* We call him the carpet dealer or his car is the flying carpet. So we always say that he came to work with the flying carpet. Or we also call him the caraway dealer.*chuckles* I think we only do that because he's our boss and because he doesn't seek much private contact with us.
>
> (Wolfgruber, 2023, p. 45)

Imagine as well that when your colleague said something about not being comfortable with what was said, he was told, "It was just a joke."

Learning from such experiences is a powerful step. At the same time, as a leader, you can not only model this type of informal engagement but also look for the right timing to support listening forums in a formal way—company lunches, roundtables, and coffee chats. In the context of congregations, a research team explored national and local level best practices. Relationship building, both through formal table talks and informal discussions, was one key way to improve race relations (Glazier, Driskill, & Hanson, 2024).

Questions to Discover the Unknown

1. What experiences have you had in connecting with others who you considered different in some way from you (culturally, ethnically, etc.)?
    a. What did you learn from such connections? What was meaningful to you?
    b. What makes such connections important to you? To this organization?
    c. What questions do you wish I or others would ask to understand your experiences more fully?
2. What experiences have you had with diversity initiatives in this and/or other organizations?
    a. What is beneficial? Not helpful? Why?
    b. What, if any, complexities, contradictions, or misconceptions surfaced?
    c. What might we do to improve/develop such efforts?

3. What aids you most in being aware of inequities in your organizations?
   a. What success stories have you heard, if any, in making progress?
   b. What barriers still exist?
4. What actions might we take individually and then collectively to improve equity, inclusion, and belonging?

2. *Disclose to Deepen Commitment to Diversity Values*

Defined: Understand motivations or reasons to co-create a value for diversity, equity, inclusion, and belonging by disclosing relevant agency-honoring experiences.

Rationale: Disclosing positive as well as negative experiences tied to diverse contexts has the potential to co-create commitment to work through the challenges.

In action: Notice we did not say disclosure of any kind is beneficial. Disclosure can too easily be a catch-all term that focuses on the benefits of "being authentic self" in the workplace. Notice that in our definition, we used the caveat—"relevant agency honoring experiences." Thus, first, an explanation of this caveat is provided before discussing examples and additional prompts.

To disclose or not disclose? Research is plentiful in terms of the positive influence, such as group cohesion, of disclosure (Pettigrew & Tropp, 2006). However, attending to the challenges involved in diverse settings is important. Dumas, Rothbard, and Phillips (2008) provide several key implications drawn from their review of these varied challenges. First, realize that across diverse groups, there are individual preferences on when and how they choose to segment or integrate their personal and professional lives. In short, agency should be respected. Second, when considering agency, introduce prompts to encourage disclosures tied to team-related successes rather than personal information. If personal information is considered important to the team and individual, prompts might allow individuals to share what they have in common with the larger group while also sharing unique experiences such as education or work (Crane, Thomas-Hunt, & Kesebir, 2019). Lastly, a tendency to give a negative interpretation of low disclosure by minority members. Imagine a team meeting where everyone seems to be open about varied home and work experiences. Everyone, that is for minority members. It is critical to check a tendency to view lower disclosure as a sign of withdrawal or commitment to the group. Silence may be due to opinions or experiences that differ greatly from others, a desire not to create discomfort, and/or memories of disclosure that were "misunderstood or dismissed" (Dumas, Rothbard, & Phillips, 2008, p. 159).

Case Examples: In the context of training, Julien was engaged by a multinational organization to aid them in improving their intercultural communication. At one point, a participant disclosed that in his two years at the organization, no one had greeted him. He volunteered this disclosure after other participants voiced some doubt about one element of the training focused on the significance of greetings. Thus, while this organization claimed diversity values, the reality on the ground was that not everyone was engaged in practices, such as greeting one another, that opened the door for relationships. The power of disclosure by this participant created the potential motivation to do more to engage across differences.

In a different context, in our university, the incoming president in 2003, Dr. Joel Anderson, launched his tenure with a speech to an auditorium filled with internal and external stakeholders (business and political leaders, families of students, students, faculty, etc.). He stressed that one of his main goals during his tenure would be to address issues of racism—"we have to face it to fix it." He then held informal conversations with faculty and staff about their motives for addressing racism. These conversations led to bi-monthly meetings that became a formal weekly working group. Over time, these meetings included personal stories about colleagues still facing racial inequity. One faculty member shared, "I cannot tell you the number of times I have been pulled over in my predominantly white neighborhood for no reason." This statement, along with other disclosures about experiences with racism, co-created a deeper motivation to engage in diversity work, especially focused on justice (Anderson Institute, 2003).

These types of disclosures about actual experiences co-create values that shape organizational culture. As a "here-and-now" practice, disclosures may aid in bias reduction. Such disclosures attend to the "intracorporeal and relational nature of difference." Put differently, this practice embodies "the intertwined humanity of organizational members, recognizing this interrelatedness as essential to organizing" (Villamil, Branton, & Meisenbach, 2024, p. 305).

One way to co-create value in addressing race relations is to ask questions that prompt disclosure. In particular, we added questions relevant to four major reasons often cited as motivations to engage in DEI efforts. Consider the following questions as part of an informal and/or formal discussion.

Questions to Deepen Commitment to Diversity Values

1. What drives you to engage with those who differ from you in some way? What stories might you share about times you have been challenged to connect across differences? Or, times you have heard about challenges faced?
2. What have you heard disclosed, formally or informally, about the reason your organization is involved in DEI initiatives?
3. What stories have you heard and/or have to share tied to globalization and demographic shifts (United Nations, 2024; Colby & Ortman, 2015)?
4. What role have technological trends had on your journey with diversity in your organization (Maroccia, 2012)?
5. What experiences have you had and/or stories heard tied to the impact of eliminating minority earnings gaps (Roehrig, 2013)?
6. What have your experiences been related to inequalities in pay/promotion (Hegewisch & Williams-Baron, 2017; Turner, 2016)?

3. Engage Is Dialogue About the Meaning of Diversity

Defined: An exploration of assumptions, mindsets, ways of thinking about diversity, and diversity goals.

Rationale: Definitions of diversity and diversity goals vary and thus merit exploration grounded in both individual and organizational level understanding.

In action: At first glance, the idea of defining "diversity" seems simple. Yet, consider how this one term conjures images of diverse nationalities or ethnic groups as well as diversity represented by age or economic status. Our thinking about diversity may include differences in race, gender, ethnicity, age, cultural background, disability, social class, and sexual orientation (Allen, 2011). Diversity, as we will note later, may also be concerned with personality differences that may impact interactions more profoundly than the first list of classifications. This list, the breadth of diversity, can at times seem to be ever-expanding to the extent that meaning is lost.

We assert that the conversations about how we define and think about diversity are critical. They matter in part because goals are implied in the definition. In fact, you could survey an organization to discern the degree of consensus on any one definition. In one study involving in-depth interviews of communication professionals, Oliveria (2013) found that they tended to define diversity in terms of communicating with a particular ethnic group, such as Hispanics. While this focus on ethnic groups has merit, the limits are clear. Our contention is that co-creating a diverse culture requires us to challenge our assumptions about and meanings associated with the term diversity. This positive communication practice focuses on encouraging and enriching formal and informal discussions by asking the question, "What do we mean when we say we want a diverse organization?" Here, we explore several definitions that can be used as discussion starters and ways to enrich the conversation.

Defined by Cultural Context. Cultural diversity, as defined by Cox (2001), is "the representation, in one social system, of people with distinctly different group affiliations of cultural significance" (p. 6). This definition is useful because it recognizes the role of perceptual identification and cultural significance in defining diversity. For example, an African American female who identifies more with her social class and gender than with her race might not add to the diversity of an organization in which her race is underrepresented. A Caucasian male who identifies more as a disabled person than as a majority male might add to diversity. Cox's definition also stresses the importance of group affiliation. For example, in a traditional religious organizational structure that is composed predominantly of intact nuclear families, introducing a leader who identifies himself as a single or divorced female would have great cultural significance and add to the diversity, while a divorced or single individual in another organization may have limited cultural significance. Conversely, a multinational firm with a dominant Asian Indian culture would enhance diversity more with the inclusion of employees with vastly different assumptions about hierarchy and power distance (Hofstede, n.d.), such as Germany, than a country with similar cultural assumptions, such as Pakistan. Thus, as you seek to enrich conversations about diversity, ask questions about "cultural significance" in light of group affiliation.

Broaden the Definition of Differences and Similarities. An even broader definition may enrich conversations. Thomas (1996) argues that diversity has become understood by many, especially in the US, as a new word for affirmative action, often focusing attention on African American employees. Thomas counters that narrow focus to define diversity as "any mixture of items characterized by differences and similarities" (p. 5). He notes that this broader definition encourages organization members to focus not only on differences but on similarities as well and explore the contours of difference and sameness. He stresses the idea that his definition refers to the collective (all-inclusive) mixture of differences and similarities, using the metaphor of a jelly bean jar. In looking at the diversity, you consider not only the last color added to the jar but also the overall mix of colors and what each adds to the jar. Finally, he states that a broader view of diversity can stretch beyond socially constructed demographic differences to consider functional or methodological diversity as well. Diversity becomes a holistic way of thinking about organizational complexity in a holistic way. His ideas would suggest formal and informal conversations focused on asking questions about commonalities and differences, not only in terms of demographics like gender, ethnicity, or race but also about our approaches to decision-making, problem-solving, and conflict management, for example.

Hays-Thomas (2004) adds additional rationales for a broader definition of diversity, such as Thomas's. She says that when diversity is understood as accommodating only a few legally protected classes of employees, it may engender resistance or resentment from other employees. The broader definition also draws on research from fields like group dynamics and decision-making, noting the superiority of heterogeneous work groups. In addition, the broader definition helps organizations understand that meeting legal requirements is only one rationale for diversity, but more important rationales lie in the potential for innovation and organizational effectiveness. We would add the value of human connection across differences. Consider this quote about conceptualizing diversity based on environmental complexity and change:

> Complexity of thought and flexibility of behavior are required for success in contemporary organizations. An important consequence of this perspective is that diversity management is seen as a form of organizational development and change as well as a set of processes for increasing effectiveness and harmony in a workforce that varies along important dimensions.
>
> (Hays-Thomas, 2004, pp. 11–12)

We concur with the value of these added rationales. In fact, Gerald participated in a book conversation in an organization aimed at enriching thinking about diversity. In this context, a group explored a book, *Far from the Tree*. The author, Andrew Solomon (2012), complicates our thinking about identity tied to disability. From in-depth interviews, the voices of participants ranging from autistic to ex-convicts and dwarfs to transgender people complicate identity based either on a simple binary of a medical model ("We can fix this disability") or a cultural model ("I am this way, I was born this way"). Exploring our motivations for improving diversity practices is thus tied to our understanding of the experience of those with differing identities. Thus, we return to our claim about the need for informal interactions as well as formal gatherings that create relationships. Such explorations set the stage for the next communicative action aimed at gauging progress on our diversity journey.

Consider the following questions, perhaps as part of an informal or formal dialogue and/or self-reflection. As you review these questions, discern the extent to which a particular practice is one that fits as a communication implication from your analysis.

Questions to Engage in Dialogue About the Meaning of Diversity

1. What implicit or explicit references to diversity did you hear?
2. What assumptions were being made about being or becoming a diverse organization?
3. How is diversity being defined in the organization?
4. What diversity goals are stated or implied?

Reflecting on these questions and others that prompt exploration provides critical insights for positive practices. Insights, for instance, on assumptions and goals provide a beginning place for assessment.

4. Assess Progress on the Diversity Journey

Defined: Embed clear goals and ways to measure progress and adjust strategies.

Rationale: Diversity is a journey, not a destination. Thus, organizations need to identify targets and engage in regular dialogue about ways to improve and keep improving.

In action: To set the stage for a model of gauging progress, consider the experience of one student's cultural analysis. The analysis surfaced conflicting and competing views of the value being placed on diversity within one unit of a large organization. Some interviewees boasted about various diversity practices. Others quietly spoke of the surface nature of these practices. What would you do with this data set? Yes, you could note thematic action, such as "An incongruity between diversity values and action." What, then, would be your communication implication?

Unfortunately, the preceding analysis reveals what may too often be the case—widely published or surface-level statements about diversity values and goals, but the lived experience of members indicates a lack of action. Indeed, these incongruities may be part of what Taylor Cox Jr. (2001) calls a "diversity-toxic" culture (p. 13). In "Creating the Multicultural Organization," Cox stresses the importance of deep cultural change in supporting diversity goals. He indicates that the root cause has to do with a misdiagnosis of the problem. The problem is not as simple as not having enough people of certain cultural identity groups or a lack of sensitivity. Rather, he asserts the need to address toxicity. We argue that to address toxicity and/or stagnation, measurement practices aimed at co-creating a learning organization need to be instituted. Thus, we turn to a model and survey to aid in the process to ensure we stay on the journey of growth, of getting better.

A Model of Multicultural Organizational Development (MCOD) developed by Holvino (1998; Table 9.1) provides a place to begin (Holvino, Ferdman, & Merrill-Sands, 2004). The model includes six phases, moving from monocultural to multicultural organizations. We have augmented this model from a meta-analysis of effective DEI metrics (Roberson et al., 2024) that focuses on goals and contexts for interpreting progress. As Dr. Holvino (personal communication, December 10, 2024) indicated, the model can appear to be linear. The reality is that the phases represent back-and-forth, progression, and regression over time. Assessment is not about arriving but recognizing that progress might occur in one unit,

Table 9.1 The Multicultural Organizational Development Model

Monocultural		*Transitional*		*Multicultural*	
Exclusionary	*Passive Club*	*Compliance*	*Positive Action*	*Redefining*	*Multicultural*
Actively excludes in its mission. Practices are not inclusive of members of the dominant group.	Actively or passively excludes those who are not members of the dominant group. Includes other members only if they "fit."	Passively committed to including others without making major changes. Includes a few members of other groups.	Committed to execute strategies to include those in designated target groups. Values the differences that others bring.	Actively works to expand its definition of inclusion and diversity. Examines and changes barriers, creating practices impacting members of non-dominant groups.	Actively includes a diversity of groups, styles, and perspectives. Continuously learns and makes systemic changes required to value and include all kinds of people.
		Seeks to integrate others into systems created under dominant norms.		Integrates diverse perspectives, identities, cultures, styles, and groups into the organization.	
		Leadership communication increasingly suggests a value of inclusion.		Regularly assesses progression and regression and adopts individual, team, and organizational practices to support learning.	

Source: Adapted from Holvino (1998). Used by permission.

not others. At another point, regression may occur, and thus, the value of keeping questions before leaders and members encourages on-going improvement. We can always improve. After the following introduction of the six stages, review Table 9.2 before turning to the survey (Rehearsal 9.1). As you review these sections, recall that at any particular time, a unit or department might be in a different phase or stage than others.

1. Exclusionary—lack DEI goals and explicitly and actively base themselves on the values of one cultural group and explicitly privilege that group in organizational practices and norms.
2. Passive club—less openly exclusionary but still only admits new organization members who are similar in values and perspectives to the dominant group.
3. Compliance—A transitional stage in which the organization may not actively exclude members who are different from the current dominant group but also do not make affirmative changes in management or cultural practices that would seek out diverse new members.
4. Positive Action—A transitional stage in which the organization becomes committed to including others, especially those in legally protected categories, and begins to tolerate differences created by new members.
5. Redefining—The beginning of multiculturalism in which the organization expands its definition of inclusion and diversity. Leaders and members attempt to identify and change barriers to diversity.
6. Multiculturalism—The organization actively includes the diversity of groups, styles, and perspectives and becomes a continuous learning organization focused on enacting positive top-down and bottom-up communication practices.

As you reflect on the previous stages, take time to identify where you would locate your organization and/or unit (see Rehearsal 9.1). Think of the stages as a cycle with back-and-forth elements rather than discrete linear progressive stages. The open-ended questions that follow and others you develop are intended to aid in reflection as part of regular assessment

Table 9.2 Creating Diverse Cultures

Method	*Advantages*	*Disadvantages*
Creating diversity as a central organizational value	Ends duality of culture and diversity Sends clear messages through multiple channels	Difficult to change culture Top leadership must support and lead by example
Encouraging diverse subcultures	Creates pluralistic cultural values and norms	Can erode community and identification Can set up battles for organization identity
Formal mentoring programs	Gives equal access to informal cultural information	Not the same effect as natural mentoring relationships
Organizational orientation, including cultural information	Recognizes the importance of culture Gives all access to cultural information	Much cultural information is tacit
Minority networks for personal and professional development	Empowering	May not have cultural insight to share

and learning. You may, for instance, engage in focus groups or surveys on a regular basis (i.e., every one to two years) to discern progress. Conversely, you might do a mini-assessment with a few questions every quarter that invites reflection and encourages positive practices at an individual or team level. Recall that, like other positive practices, the application of this model suggests progress markers related to each stage of the journey. An online quantitative survey is provided as well.

Rehearsal 9.1

Purpose: To apply the material adapted from Holvino Table 9.2 to your organization.

Directions: First, review Table 9.2 and then respond to the following questions.

1. Which phase or elements of different phases would you place your organization or department? Why?

2. What structural changes in recruitment practices, policies, pay and benefits, holidays, work/family balance, etc., would support multiculturalism?

3. How do employees' communication patterns contribute to or inhibit multiculturalism? Are certain voices muted in the organizational dialogue? Does employee communication about diversity policies limit their impact?

4. What behavioral changes are necessary to promote more effective inter-group relations?

Based on completing Rehearsal 9.1, the final positive practice involves an exploration of CCO processes designed to address micro-interpersonal as well as macro-structural/organizational constitutive actions.

5. Co-Create Multi-Level DEI Action Plans

- What words would you use to capture a vision of a multicultural, diverse organization?
- What is your own dream for organizations you work with and/or serve through this analysis?

You have spent time reflecting on where your organization is on the diversity journey. Now, consider ways to work your own vision. Here is one we find compelling.

> We define a multicultural, inclusive organization as one in which the diversity of knowledge and perspectives that members of different groups bring to the organization has shaped its strategy, its work, its management and operating systems, and its core values and norms for success.
>
> (Holvino, Ferdman, & Merrill-Sands, 2004, pp. 249–250)

These same authors also underscore the ideal of equal treatment, inclusion, and opportunities at all levels and functions. Ferdman (2014) stresses in his chapter on inclusion not only how "well organizations and their members connect with, engage, and utilize people across all types of differences" but also the individual level experience of inclusion (p. 4). These ideals involve weaving diversity into the very fabric of the organization and the community. As such, the ideal is for everyone to continue learning by seeing diversity as an asset, not a problem.

To achieve these ideals, we concur with their call to engage in three types of changes, each involving positive communicative practices: a) structural, such as recruitment, policies, and pay; b) cultural, such as values as constituted in rituals, language, and metaphors; and c) behavioral such as trainings and dialogue groups. While Ferdman's categories miss that structures and behavioral practices are all part of culture, we find the ideas under each category of value due in part to the way they connect with the notion of "third culture building." The idea of third culture building is aimed at moving beyond adapting to another culture or simply adopting the other culture's norms, but instead attending to ways to develop common ground and transcend norms in order to promote positive interpersonal and group interactions (Broome, 2013; Hopson, Hart, & Bell, 2012).

In the following, we provide a checklist of practices that cut across enacted elements. Based on your assessment of cultural data, discern the diversity strategies in place and those that need to be introduced or developed.

Rehearsal 9.2 Checklist of Structural, Cultural, and Behavioral Diversity Practices + = in Place; / = Needs Development; x = Missing

<u>Structural changes:</u>

- ___ Recruitment policies and practices.
- ___ Regular reviews to ensure equality in pay and benefits and opportunities/support for advancement.
- ___ Shift from a "benevolent" relationship to equity to give agency to both parties (e.g., organization, community stakeholders, and individuals).

- ___ Policies on work/family balance (leave, holidays, etc.).
- ___ Mentoring to include conscious culture socialization/orientation processes so that hidden rules shared by a majority culture are made transparent.
- ___ Encouraging diverse subcultures; value "niches" of diversity across the organization.
- ___ Networks formed to advance the interests of minorities.

Cultural changes:

- ___ Rituals (forums, focus groups, lunch discussions) for exploring diversity motives and definitions.
- ___ Ceremonies inclusive of stories and language affirming common ground and diversity.
- ___ History displayed through artifacts relevant to an oppressive past and to the pride of cultural accomplishments and practices.
- ___ Shared metaphors that embedded values related to diversity (tributaries, stew, quilt, jelly bean jar).

Behavioral changes:

- ___ Regular communication training, coaching opportunities, and story sharing on positive communication to counter stereotyping, unconscious bias, and negative inter-group relations (e.g., awareness of marginalized groups, structural racism, dialogic communication, cosmopolitan or dialogic communication).
- ___ Use of dialogue groups to promote and develop third culture building.
- ___ Strengthen leadership accountability and capabilities.

These three categories set both the stage and the script for moving toward an organization valuing and benefiting from diversity. The key is to take this final practice and combine it with the other positive practices: a) ask to discover lived experiences with diversity; b) disclose to deepen commitment to diversity values; c) engage in dialogue about the meaning of diversity; and d) assess progress on the diversity journey. The following "Connections" section provides further insights and applications.

Connections

In an ideal world, all organizations would be in the process of becoming multicultural and developing practices to aid in responding to the challenges of this process. However, in the real world, some organizations are blind to the value of diversity or uncertain as to how to move toward and respond to multiculturalism. Because organizations vary so widely in regard to inclusion, it is also crucial for members of marginalized groups to understand the dominant organizational culture. Being able to read the dominant culture can provide critical information to guide employment choices, as well as promote individual career development. We offer this connection section along with other Rehearsals as a way to improve awareness of the experiences of marginalized groups and to gain insights on discursive practices related to family-leave policies. Both organizations and individuals have responsibilities to enhance cultural awareness. Organizations can develop mentoring, dialogue, and training. Individuals can learn to ask the right questions, participate in informal organizational activities, seek out mentors, and form their own communication networks to enhance cultural knowledge. As you analyze your cultural data, you may find that themes emerge related to the ideas introduced in this section. Tie this back to your data, and you may then find implications and recommendations for your organization. We begin with a reflection on the role of awareness.

Developing Awareness: Minority Experiences and Muted Voices

Marginalized groups are those whose interests and styles are not privileged within the organization. Such groups face a number of challenging obstacles. Rosabeth Moss Kanter (1977), in her classic book *Men and Women of the Corporation*, offered a numerical minority hypothesis that tokens (one of only a few representatives of their category in a larger dominant group) face similar pressures whether it is a woman in a male-dominated profession, an African American executive in a European American—dominated team, or an American manager in a Japanese subsidiary of a multinational corporation. Allen's (1995) research found that one major obstacle is that "persons of color tend to have limited access to social networks, blocked mobility and often do not have mentors or sponsors" (p. 150). Acculturation stressors experienced by Hispanics have also been documented (Amason, Allen, & Holmes, 1999). Again, the limited access to supportive networks contributed to the challenges they faced in adjusting.

One way for the majority culture members to develop awareness is by reflecting along with minority members on their experiences with being marginalized. One colleague and friend found himself in tears during this type of activity (see Rehearsal 9.3 at the end of the chapter) as his close friend and co-worker was left behind.

Another challenge is related to family leave policies. For example, Buzzanell and colleagues (2017) document how women engaged in a contradictory discourse to manage the challenges of workplace communication in light of maternity leave. They note that women simultaneously adhered to and resisted discourses related to time off and disability in order to gain leave. Check our online Rehearsal on Identifying Barriers to Family Leave Policies.

Other minority groups face additional challenges. Meares et al. (2004) examined responses to mistreatment in the workplace. They document various forms of mistreatment that occur both at the interpersonal and institutional levels. Their analysis includes documentation of various ways minorities construct "muted narratives" in response to mistreatment. For instance, minority responses to mistreatment tended to fall into narrative categories such as "muted but engaged," "angrily disengaged," and "resigned." The authors stress that ambiguous policies about mistreatment were a major source. While management had acknowledged problems for several years, no action had been taken to create clear definitions or ways to address mistreatment. In fact, minorities faced a dilemma in how to respond.

> If they work to resist mistreatment, they are placing themselves in a position where they are likely to face more mistreatment. If they react to the mistreatment by becoming disengaged, they are indirectly recreating the power structures and giving up the chance of being heard.
>
> (p. 21)

As this study on mistreatment suggests, the challenges faced by marginalized groups are varied and complex. Thus, give consideration to the quantitative online survey to assess the overall experiences of members.

Strategies for Marginalized Groups: Mentoring, Dialogue, and Multicultural Training

We recognize an ethical dilemma as we propose strategies for marginalized groups to understand the dominant organizational culture. Numerous critical theorists (Clair, 1993, 1998; Mumby, 1997, 2015) have pointed out that when marginalized groups adapt to the dominant culture, they reinforce the legitimacy of unjust cultures that privilege the interests of some groups over others. They call this process hegemony, the participation of marginalized groups in their own domination. In a study focused on the challenges of minority members on a school board, Mease and Terry (2012) introduce a question as part of their analysis: "How do racist organizational structures persist despite what we generally assume to be the good intentions of individual organizational members?" (p. 125). The researchers rely on a CCO approach to "demonstrate how co-constitutive performatives of race and organization create and maintain a hegemonic Whiteness while simultaneously making it difficult to acknowledge the fact that Whiteness exists as an organizing principle" (p. 128). Their study captures the difficulties and challenges minorities face as well as majority culture members who face such a "double-bind."

We concur with the value of addressing these challenging and conflict interactions, not by simply focusing on one strategy but by various micro and macro processes. As these authors note, attention must go beyond rhetorical strategies to "a reconfiguration of the organizational structures through which those rhetorical styles, discursive strategies, and material realities of race are organized" (Mease & Terry, 2012, p. 138). Manzie's (2018) crisis response analysis of the Royal Dutch Shell company in Nigeria documented efforts by this multinational to contribute to local communities. However, their process reinforced patronizing colonial practices by not addressing agency. Thus, the relationship remained prescriptive rather than responsive to both the organizational and community organizing practices. We believe marginalized groups and majority members must understand the dominant culture in order to co-create positive changes with others. Often, the means of domination through unconscious cultural patterns can be the means of liberation when we understand and use cultural patterns to support the interests of equality and fairness. Both organizations and individuals should take responsibility for ensuring that members have the resources to learn about cultural expectations. We explore three such options, recognizing that one strategy alone is unlikely to align a culture with a value for embracing diversity.

Mentoring Program

One strategy is to install formal mentoring programs in which a senior member of the organization is paired with a new employee to "show him [or her] the ropes." These formal mentoring relationships may not produce the same results as naturally occurring mentoring relationships based on perceived mutual benefit and professional attraction. Studies comparing the two approaches found that both groups expressed greater socialization and career progress than employees who had not been mentored at all, satisfaction was much higher in informal mentorships, and those relationships also resulted in higher salaries for mentees (Chao, Waltz, & Gardner, 1992). Beyond traditional outcomes such as satisfaction, pay, or upward mobility, others argue for co-constructing trust in mentoring relationships that also have such positive outcomes as resilience and organizational learning on both sides (Blake-Beard et al., 2016). We provide several examples of how such goals and efforts might become part of the culture.

Kreps (1983) writes of an interesting way that organizations have sought to help all new employees with enculturation. RCA developed extensive video orientation programs, not only telling the new employee about policies and corporate data but also cultural information about history, rituals, heroes, and norms. In a context focused on leadership development and entrepreneurship, community-based mentoring could find resources through insights from a different study. Jones (2017), in a groundbreaking study of empowerment narratives from Black entrepreneurs, explored ways they enacted rhetorical agency to work within oppressive systems as well as to resist damaging, dominant discourses about black businesses. In particular, their stories focused on: a) economic improvement of resources; b) targeted and localized community action; c) legacy leaving or passing on ideals to future generations or passed on from older generations; and d) social justice ideals, focused on poverty, identity, justice, and politics. Tapping into such a leadership network for mentoring is another powerful way to empower future generations.

Such minority mentoring strategies have been formalized by minorities themselves in organizations such as fraternities and sororities, all-female professional networking groups, and communities of immigrant populations. These alternative information networking groups may give the edge that formal programs lack. For example, the CEO of Facebook, Sheryl Sandberg, has launched an international effort to provide mentoring groups for women. Based on her best-selling book, *Lean in: Women, Work, and the Will to Lead*, she promotes the development of varied communicative practices to aid leadership development. According to the "Lean In" website, 33,000 "Lean in Circles" or mentoring groups are now present in 150 countries. Eighty-five percent of the participants credit this experience with a positive change in their lives. This approach has been critiqued by Mumby (2015) from a critical perspective in terms of the assumption that the primary problems women face are "self-imposed." Mumby argues that this individualized approach is based on the agency "framed as personal choice rather than collective action." Rather than an on-going "collective struggle for social change," the focus is on "individual entrepreneurship" in a "neoliberal moral framework in which each of us has a duty to ourselves to cultivate a self-brand" (p. 34). However, this critique does not attend to the other resources and collective actions provided beyond mentoring resources. For instance, the website provides ways managers (both women and men) should change their communicative practices, ranging from challenging interpretations of women who are called "bossy" or "pushy" to ways to create gender-blind evaluations. In addition, this movement is not solely based on individual efforts but creates organizational partnerships at no fee that involve access to and involvement in public awareness campaigns. We see a congruence with such efforts and constitutive processes that cut across micro and macro (CC) elements of culture. Such processes, especially given the inter and intra-organizational and global reach, hold promise for aiding the vision of greater equity and improving social worlds.

African American fraternities and sororities are an especially interesting social networking phenomenon. More than 1.5 million members, predominantly African Americans, are members of nine fraternities and sororities associated with the National Pan-Hellenic Council, according to its website (URIwww.nphchq.org/URI). The fraternities include Omega Psi Phi, Kappa Alpha Psi, Alpha Phi Alpha, Phi Beta Sigma, and Iota Phi Theta. The sororities include Alpha Kappa Alpha, Delta Sigma Theta, Zeta Phi Beta, and Sigma Gamma Rho. Unlike many Caucasian college sororities and fraternities, the organizations of the National Pan-Hellenic Council are formed as lifetime networking groups to give members an alternative to exclusive corporate and social networks. Members of the National Pan-Hellenic Council have become an economic, political, and social force. The organizations also create a strong and effective alternative networking structure. Recently, we interviewed an African American applicant for a tenure-track teaching position at the university. Angi was fascinated when her associate dean greeted the young man and proceeded to tell him about every member of his fraternity on campus and leading members of the community who were also "brothers." Listservs for the fraternity offer opportunities to seek career guidance, re-establish connections after moves, or offer social support.

Such constructive efforts provide alternative networking/mentoring structures to counteract the exclusion of many women, racial/ethnic minorities, international employees, and other marginalized groups from informal communication networks in many organizations. They may offer the best long-term opportunity for learning cultural information in alternate ways.

Dialogue Groups

Mentoring programs provide a key strategy for empowering marginalized groups. However, the need also exists to do more to engage employees in discussing their experiences through regular feedback systems. Such experiences may happen in settings in which conflict is embedded by the nature of the identity of the organization. In one Christian-based hospital in the US, an ethnic and religious minority was hired to work in a context of Christian values, language, and practices such as praying for patients. The new member was conflicted from the start and faced the challenge of realizing the culture was in place by design, based on mission, history, and values. She realized that such norms would not change, yet she was not comfortable with the practices. In time, others sensed her disrespect for these norms, yet there was not a process in place to negotiate these conflicts.

Imagine a different scenario. During the interview process, the nature of these norms was made clear so you could discern if this is a place you wanted to serve. Then, you learned from a mentor and from the orientation that quarterly discussions and monthly dialogue groups were held to learn about minority concerns. These dialogue groups gave time to explore ways to navigate differences. Then, over time, you discover that information from these sessions is being integrated into management training. In fact, Meares et al. (2004) call for such a process based on a case analysis of a large, 1,000-member research and development organization that had a history of reports on mistreatment. One issue was the ambiguity of defining mistreatment. Their case study makes it clear that engaging members in dialogue groups should not be undertaken in a casual way. We concur with Barnett Pearce and Kim Pearce (2004) with the following list of six core assumptions that should influence dialogue initiatives:

1. Dialogue is a form of communication with specific "rules" that distinguish it from other forms.
2. Among the effects of these rules are communication patterns that enable people to speak so that others can and will listen and to listen so others can and will speak.
3. Participating in this form of communication requires a set of abilities, the most important of which is remaining in the tension between holding your own perspective, being profoundly open to others who are unlike you, and enabling others to act similarly.
4. These abilities are learnable, teachable, and contagious.
5. There are at least three levels of these abilities, including the ability to respond to another's invitation to engage in dialogue, to extend an invitation to another to engage in a dialogue, and to construct contexts that are conducive to dialogue.

6. Skilled facilitators can construct contexts sufficiently conducive to dialogue so that participants are enabled to engage in dialogue in ways they would not without the work of the facilitator.

(p. 162)

The promise of dialogue groups, if implemented based on the stated guiding assumptions, is that they co-create communication practices that begin to shape the culture. Stories, for instance, begin to be told of employees finding their voice and of leaders willing to address problems before they get out of hand. In crisis response, for instance, dialogue groups should also consider widely distributed or communal modes of leadership, as suggested by Manzie (2018). Multinational leaders need to discern ways to truly empower decision-making by and with community stakeholders.

Multicultural Training

Dialogue groups, however, suggest the need for developing intercultural or multicultural communication competency. Earlier in this chapter, we discussed the growing reality of diversity in the USA. Beyond the growing diversity in the USA, we have stressed throughout this book the rapidly expanding number of multinationals. Friedman (2005), in his best-selling book, *The World is Flat*, recounts his experiences in connecting with business leaders in India. As he reflected on those experiences, he concluded that contrary to popular belief, the world is flat. Indeed, a typical day mirrors the experience of an increasing number of individuals. For instance, in the relatively small city of Little Rock (about 190,000), Gerald and Julien interact with faculty and students from different nations, ranging from Brazil, Slovenia, and Senegal to Pakistan, Taiwan, and Cameroon. Furthermore, within the city, it is now common to learn of diverse cultural connections. Neighbors speak of working for French- and Dutch-owned companies based in Little Rock.

An additional driver to improve training resources is found in the communication practices and assumptions that may be operating at a hidden level. For instance, Aritz and Walker (2014) studied leadership practices across diverse problem-solving groups. They noted that "East Asian language speakers reported that they did not feel as included, valued, or supported as their American counterparts" (p. 78). They explain this difference by noting the varied assumptions about important leadership characteristics. US team members identified "decisive and task oriented" as the most important leadership characteristic, whereas,

> Japanese and Chinese valued status-conscious and procedural style over being decisive and task oriented followed by involving others in decision-making processes (listed as second by both groups) and modesty, compassion, and support (in the case of Japanese). Koreans identified "involving others in decision-making process" as the most important attribute of a leader.
>
> (p. 78)

In another study of three countries, research found differences in managers and non-managers in the United States, India, and Malaysia in relationship to preferred listening behaviors (Roebuck, Bell, Raina, & Lee, 2016). These types of findings and the diversity of our organizations remind us of the reality of the "flat world" and indicate the need to go beyond mentoring and dialogue groups. We also encourage organizations to take the initiative in developing intercultural communication training. Such training should be adapted to the experience and needs of participants. Training activities and assessment practices should also attend to models for developing intercultural competence (Driskill & Arjanakova, 2010). One central practice is to engage participants in an increased awareness of cultural identity. Jameson (2007) provides one valuable resource in this area. She stresses the importance for the field of business communication to develop professionals with insights concerning the hidden forces of culture:

> To help achieve this goal, (we) should more strongly emphasize how to understand one's own individual cultural identity: the sense of self derived from formal or informal membership in groups that impart knowledge, beliefs, values, attitudes, traditions, and ways of life.
>
> (p. 200)

Beyond integrating aspects of improved insight into identity and communication, effective training should go beyond awareness to include affective training as well as skills or behaviors. Training should also reflect on the challenges of responding to the inevitable dialectic tension introduced earlier. Martin and Nakayama (2015) introduce six dialectics: individual–cultural, differences–similarities, past/present–future, personal–contextual, privilege–disadvantage, and static–dynamic. Including these dialectics in training moves beyond a focus on the individual to connect "individual agency with larger, structural constraints" in a way that reveals "the complexities of culture, as well as the various interests at work in driving cultural hierarchies" (p. 19). However, beyond model-based training, more needs to occur to further encourage progress in this arena.

In one stellar example of going beyond "just training," Heifer International, a non-profit working to address poverty in over 30 countries, took major strides to enhance the capacity of its employees to work in a diverse environment. As part of a larger diversity initiative, Gerald developed full-day training on intercultural communication. Heifer leadership, consistent with their process-focused culture, then took three additional steps. They a) transferred the training to employees to empower them to conduct the training in the future; b) integrated intercultural competency expectations into job descriptions; and c) invited employees to occasional lunches to discuss progress in their development of cultural competencies.

If done well, such training initiatives can be part of a set of practices that reflect a commitment to empowering employees from diverse backgrounds. Such training should focus on the types of diversity present in the organization. Generational diversity training programs, as well as gender and national or ethnic training, indicate another level of commitment to creating a culture where the diverse backgrounds of individuals truly enrich the culture of the organization.

Summary

We summarized a variety of approaches for assessing and integrating the value of diversity into organizational culture. These various approaches, along with their advantages and disadvantages, are summarized in Table 9.3. The challenges and opportunities presented by the diversity paradox are real. The choices you make in response to cultural data may result in improving the quality of life and creative outcomes for your organization and beyond. We provide Rehearsal both in the book and online to assist in the diversity journey.

Table 9.3 Creating Diverse Cultures

Method	*Advantages*	*Disadvantages*
Creating diversity as a central organizational value	Ends duality of culture and diversity Sends clear message through multiple channels	Difficult to change culture Top leadership must support and lead by example
Encouraging diverse subcultures	Creates pluralistic cultural values and norms	Can erode community and identification Can set up battles for organization identity
Formal mentoring programs	Give equal access to informal cultural information	Not same effect as natural mentoring relationships
Organizational orientation including cultural information	Recognizes the importance of culture Gives all access to cultural information	Much cultural information is tacit
Minority networks for personal and professional development	Empowering	May not have cultural insight to share

In all, we trust that you have found practical tools for using cultural data in the context of diversity. Four major ideas were stressed in this application section.

1. The "diversity paradox" suggests that strong cultures can prevent organizations from embracing diversity because of hiring biases and expectations for new employees to embrace cultural norms and expectations; conversely, diversity can create a lack of shared communication norms that create barriers.
2. Five communicative practices can aid organizations:
    - Ask to discover lived experiences with diversity.
    - Disclose to deepen commitment to diversity values.
    - Engage in dialogue about the meaning of diversity.
    - Assess progress on the diversity journey.
    - Co-create multi-level action plans.
3. Women, racial/ethnic minorities, international employees, and other marginalized groups are often disadvantaged because they are not part of informal communication networks that transmit cultural norms and values.
4. Working toward pluralistic cultures in which diversity is a central organizational value seems to be the best long-term solution. In the meantime, mentoring or conscious culture socialization processes can help to level the playing field.
5. Naturally occurring mentorships have advantages over formal mentoring programs. Networks specifically formed to advance the interests of women and minorities also show promise in creating cultural change.
6. Enhancing the experience of minorities should also involve well-designed dialogue or feedback groups as well as intercultural training that equips employees for a diverse workplace and thereby creates a culture that embraces diversity.

Rehearsal 9.3 Are You a Privileged Member of Your Organizational Culture?

Purpose: To develop an awareness of your relative position of advantage over members of marginalized groups.

Guides: Besides completing this as individuals and then moving to reactions and discussion, another option is to have participants line up on one side of a room or a parking lot (e.g., some open space). Then, indicate as you read each question that if their response to the question is "agreed," they are to take one step forward. The idea is to visually capture the impact of varied experiences on minority groups. Then, process this experience by asking what they observed and experienced and what positive communication practices they would recommend for themselves and the organization.

1. I have never left an employment interview wondering if my race or sexual orientation was a factor in not getting a job.
2. It is very likely that my direct supervisor in most organizations is of my race and/or gender.
3. I never have to use two languages or idioms, one for social and the other for professional.
4. It is rare for me to walk into a meeting in which I am the only member of my representative group.
5. It is unlikely that someone of my ethnic or social identity group will be available as a mentor within my organization.
6. Holidays associated with my religion are standard organizational holidays, such that I do not have to ask special permission to observe them or take personal vacation days.
7. I am asked at times to speak for all members of my race or gender in a business conversation.
8. No questions would be raised if I chose to select or promote a member of my race or gender.
9. I am never invited to a club or restaurant for an organizational function at which I feel uncomfortable as a member of my minority group.
10. I do not have to rely on laws to ensure equal treatment of my minority group.
11. I never have to seek assistance or alternatives to be able to enter an office or to use a restroom because the facilities are not designed for me.
12. I never feel like I have been chosen for committees or assignments, not because of my qualifications or interests but to represent my minority group.

Discussion Questions

1. What factors prompt you to value diversity?
2. Which of the five positive practices do you see as most relevant to your data?
    - Ask to discover lived experiences with diversity.
    - Disclose to deepen commitment to diversity values.

- Engage in dialogue about the meaning of diversity.
- Assess progress on the diversity journey.
- Co-create multi-level action plans.

3. Why is a broad definition of diversity like Thomas's ("any mixture of items characterized by differences and similarities") helpful? Unhelpful?
4. How do generational differences pose a challenge for organizational cultures?
5. What is the danger in creating and fostering subcultures in an effort to support diversity?
6. What are ways in which organizations can mute the voices of marginalized groups?

References

Allen, B. J. (1995). "Diversity" and organizational communication. *Journal of Applied Communication Research, 23(2)*, 143–155. https://doi.org/10.1080/00909889509365420

Allen, B. J. (2011). *Difference matters: Communicating social identity* (2nd ed.). Long Grove, IL: Waveland Press.

Amason, P., Allen, M., & Holmes, S. (1999). Social support and acculturation stress in the multicultural workplace. *Journal of Applied Communication Research, 27(4)*, 310–334. https://doi.org/10.1080/00909889909365543

Anderson Institute. (n.d.). Retrieved from http://ualr.edu/race-ethnicity/

Aritz, J., & Walker, R. (2014). Leadership styles in multicultural groups: Americans and East Asians working together. *International Journal of Business Communication, 51(1)*, 72–92. https://doi.org/10.1177/2329488413516211

Blake-Beard, S., Murrell, A., Krothapalli, V., Halem, J., & Kweder, M. (2016). Mentoring as a connecting competency builder. In L. Wooten, L. M. Roberts, & M. Davidson (Eds.), *Positive organizing in a global society: Understanding and engaging differences for capacity building & inclusion* (pp. 110–116). New York: Routledge.

Broome, B. (2013). Building cultures of peace: The role of intergroup dialogue. In J. G. Oetzel & S. Ting-Toomey (Eds.), *The Sage handbook of conflict communication* (2nd ed., Chapter 28, pp. 737–761). Thousand Oaks, CA: Sage.

Buzzanell, P., Remke, R., Meisenbach, R., Liu, M., Bowers, B., & Conn, C. (2017). Standpoints of maternity leave: Discourses of temporality and ability. *Women's Studies in Communication, 40(1)*, 67–90. https://doi.org/10.1080/07491409.2015.1113451

Chamorro-Premuzic, T. (October 23, 2024). How benevolent tribalism hurts meritocracy and fuels biases at work. *Forbes*. Retrieved from www.forbes.com/sites/tomaspremuzic/

Chao, J. T., Waltz, P. M., & Gardner, P. H. (1992). Formal and informal mentorships: A comparison of mentoring functions and contrast with non-mentored counterparts. *Personnel Psychology, 45*, 619–663. https://doi.org/10.1111/j.1744-6570.1992.tb00863.x

Clair, R. P. (1993). The use of framing devices to sequester organizational narratives: Hegemony and harassment. *Communication Monographs, 60(2)*, 113–136. https://doi.org/10.1080/03637759309376304

Clair, R. P. (1998). *Organizing silence: A world of possibilities*. Albany: SUNY Press.

Colby, S., & Ortman, J. (2015). Projections of the size and composition of the U.S. population: 2014 to 2060 population estimates and projections. *Current Population Reports*, pp. 25–1143. Retrieved from www.census.gov/content/dam/Census/library/publications/2015/demo/p25-1143.pdf

Cox, T. H. (2001). *Creating the multicultural organization: A strategy for capturing the power of diversity*. San Francisco: John Wiley & Sons.

Crane, B., Thomas-Hunt, M., & Kesebir, S. (2019). To disclose or not to disclose: The ironic effects of the disclosure of personal information about ethnically distinct newcomers to a team. *Journal of Business Ethics, 158(4)*, 909–921. https://doi.org/10.1007/s10551-017-3714-0

DeYmaz, M. (2007). *Building a healthy multi-ethnic church*. San Francisco, CA: Jossey-Bass/Leadership.

Dougherty, K. D., Chaves, M., & Emerson, M. O. (2020). Racial diversity in U.S. congregations, 1998–2019. *Journal for the Scientific Study of Religion, 59(4)*, 651–662. https://doi.org/10.1111/jssr.12681

Driskill, G.W., & Arjanakova, S. (2010). Assessing intercultural communication: Models and methods. In P. Backlund & G. Whitfield (Eds.), *An assessment primer: The role of assessment in the life of a communication department*. Washington, DC: National Communication Association.

Driskill, G. W., Arjannikova, A., & Meyer, J. (2014). A dialectic analysis of a community forum on faith: The "most segregated" or separated hour? *Journal of Applied Communication Research, 42(4)*, 477–496. https://doi.org/10.1080/00909882.2014.880938

Dumas, T. L., Rothbard, N. P., & Phillips, K. W. (2008). Self-disclosure: Beneficial for cohesion in demographically diverse work groups? In *Diversity and groups* (Vol. 11, pp. 143–166). Emerald Group Publishing Limited. https://doi.org/10.1016/S1534-0856(08)11007-6

Emerson, M. (2006). *People of the dream: Multiracial congregations in the United States*. New York, NY: Oxford University Press.

Enarsi, N., & Riggio, R. (2021). Exclusion of inclusion in leadership theories. In B. M. Ferdman, J. Prime, & R. E. Riggio (Eds.), *Inclusive leadership: Transforming diverse lives, workplaces, and societies* (pp. 23–38). London, England: Routledge.

Ferdman, B. (2014). The practice of inclusion in diverse organizations. In B. M. Ferdman & B. R. Deane (Eds.), *Diversity at work: The practice of inclusion* (pp. 3–54). San Francisco, CA: Jossey-Bass.

Ferdman, B. (2021). Inclusive leadership: The fulcrum of inclusion. In B. M. Ferdman, J. Prime, & R. E. Riggio (Eds.), *Inclusive leadership: Transforming diverse lives, workplaces, and societies* (pp. 3–24). London, England: Routledge. https://doi.org/10.4324/9780429449673

Florida, R. (2002). *The rise of the creative class and how it's transforming work, leisure, community, and everyday life*. New York: Basic Books.

Friedman, T. (2005). *The world is flat: A brief history of the 21st century*. New York: Farrar, Straus, & Giroux.

Glazier, R., Driskill, G., & Hanson, D. (2024). Race and faith: The role of congregations in racial justice. *Journal for the Scientific Study of Religion*. https://doi.org/10.1111/jssr.12943

Hays-Thomas, R. (2004). Why now? The contemporary focus on managing diversity. In M. S. Stockdale & F. J. Crosby (Eds.), *The psychology and management of workplace diversity*. Malden, MA: Blackwell Publishing.

Hegewisch, A., & Williams-Baron, E. (April 4, 2017). The gender wage gap by occupation 2016; and by race and ethnicity. *Institute for Women's Policy Research*. Retrieved from https://iwpr.org/wp-content/uploads/2017/04/C456.pdf

Hofstede, G. (n.d.). *Country comparison*. Retrieved from www.hofstede-insights.com/country-comparison/

Holvino, E. (1998). The multicultural organizational development model. Unpublished Training Materials. Brattleboro, VT: Chaos Management.

Holvino, E., Ferdman, B. M., & Merrill-Sands, D. (2004). Creating and sustaining diversity and inclusion in organizations: Strategies and approaches. In M. S. Stockdale & F. J. Crosby (Eds.), *The psychology and management of workplace diversity*. Malden, MA: Blackwell Publishing.

Hopson, M., Hart, T., & Bell, G. (2012). Meeting in the middle: Fred L. Casmir's contributions to the field of intercultural communication. *International Journal of Intercultural Relations, 36(6)*, 789–797. https://doi.org/10.1016/j.ijintrel.2012.08.008

Jameson, D. A. (2007). Reconceptualizing cultural identity and its role in intercultural business communication. *Journal of Business Communication, 44*, 199–235. https://doi.org/10.1177/0021943607301346

Jenkins, J. J. (2014). A "community" of discipline: The paradox of diversity within an intercultural Church. *Western Journal of Communication, 78(2)*, 134–154. https://doi.org/10.1080/10570314.2013.845793

Jones, N. (2017). Rhetorical narratives of black entrepreneurs: The business of race, agency, and cultural empowerment. *Journal of Business and Technical Communication, 31(3)*, 319–349. https://doi.org/10.1177/1050651917695540

Julian, S. D., & Ofori-Dankwa, J. C. (2017). Context matters: Diversity's short- and long-term effects in fortune's "best companies to work for". *Strategic Management Journal, 38(7)*, 1557–1565. https://doi.org/10.1002/smj.2576

Kanter, R. M. (1977). *Men and women of the corporation*. New York: Basic Books.

Kreps, G. I. (1983). Using interpretive research: Development of a socialization program at RCA. In L. Putnam & M. Pacanowsky (Eds.), *Communication and organizations: An interpretive approach* (pp. 243–254). Beverly Hills, CA: Sage.

LeGreco, M., Eisenberg, E., Tretheway, A., & Goodall, H. (2024). *Organizational communication: Balancing creativity and constraint* (9th ed.). New York: St. Martin's.

Liu, J., Zhu, Y., & Wang, H. (February 9, 2023). Managing the negative impact of workforce diversity: The important roles of inclusive HRM and employee learning-oriented behaviors. *Frontiers in Psychology, 14*, 1117690. https://doi.org/10.3389/fpsyg.2023.1117690. PMID: 36844330; PMCID: PMC9947786. Retrieved from www.ncbi.nlm.nih.gov/pmc/articles/PMC9947786/

Manzie, V. (2018). Applying the rhetoric of renewal model in a contemporary African context: Lessons learned from the royal Dutch shell oil crisis in Nigeria. *Journal of International Crisis and Risk Communication Research, 1(2)*, 201–224. https://doi.org/10.30658/jicrcr.1.2.2

Martin, J., & Nakayama, T. (2015). Reconsidering intercultural (communication) competence in the workplace: A dialectical approach. *Language and Intercultural Communication, 15(1)*, 13–28. https://doi.org/10.1080/14708477.2014.985303

Meares, M., Oetzel, J., Torres, A., Derkacs, D., & Ginossar, T. (2004). Employee mistreatment and muted voices in the culturally diverse workplace. *Journal of Applied Communication Research, 32(1)*, 4–27. https://doi.org/10.1080/0090988042000178121

Mease, J., & Terry, D. (2012). [Organizational (performance] of race): The co-constitutive performance of race and school board in Durham, NC. *Text and Performance Quarterly, 32(2)*, 121–140. https://doi.org/10.1080/10462937.2011.653390

Maroccia, M. (2012). The internet, intercultural communication and cultural variation. *Language & Intercultural Communication, 12*, 353–368. https://doi.org/10.1080/14708477.2012.722101

Mumby, D. K. (1997). The problem of hegemony: Rereading Gramsci for organizational studies. *Western Journal of Communication, 61*, 343–375. https://doi.org/10.1080/10570319709374585

Mumby, D. K. (2015). Organizing power. *Review of Communication, 15(1)*, 19–38. https://doi.org/10.1080/15358593.2015.1015245

Oliveria, M. (2013). Multicultural environments and their challenges to crisis communication. *Journal of Business Communication, 50(3)*, 253–277. https://doi.org/10.1177/0021943613487070

Pearce, B. (2007). *Making social worlds: A communication perspective*. Malden, MA: Blackwell Publishing.

Pearce, B., & Pearce, K. (2004). Taking a communication perspective on dialogue. In R. L. Anderson, L. Baxter, & K. Cissna (Eds.), *Dialogue: Theorizing difference in communication studies* (pp. 39–56). Thousand Oaks, CA: Sage.

Pettigrew, T. F., & Tropp, L. R. (2006). A meta-analytic test of intergroup contact theory. *Journal of Personality and Social Psychology, 90(5)*, 751–783. https://doi.org/10.1037/0022-3514.90.5.751

Roberson, Q., Avery, D. R., & Leigh, A. (2024). Lights, camera, action: Moving beyond performative diversity management to drive change. *Academy of Management Perspectives, 38(2)*, 197–213. https://doi.org/10.5465/amp.2021.0188

Roebuck, D., Bell, R., Raina, R., & Lee, C. (2016). Comparing perceived listening behavior differences between managers and non-managers living in the United States, India, and Malaysia. *International Journal of Business Communication, 53(4)*, 485–518. https://doi.org/10.1177/2329488415572789

Roehrig, C. (August, 2013). *Economic impact of closing the minority earnings gap*. Ann Arbor, MI: Altarum Institute.

Schein, E., & Schein, P. (2021). The problem of inclusion from a multicultural perspective. In B. M. Ferdman, J. Prime, & R. E. Riggio (Eds.), *Inclusive leadership: Transforming diverse lives, workplaces, and societies* (pp. 70–80). London, England: Routledge. https://doi.org/10.4324/9780429449673

Scheitle, C., & Dougherty, K. (2010). Race, diversity, and membership duration in religious congregations. *Sociological Inquiry, 80(3)*, 405–423. https://doi.org/10.1111/j.1475-682X.2010.00340.x

Solomon, A. (2012). *Far from the tree: Parents, children and the search for identity*. New York: Scribner.

Thomas, R. R. (1996). *Redefining diversity*. New York: American Management Association.

Totenberg, N. (June 29, 2023). Supreme court guts affirmative action, effectively ending race-conscious admissions. *NPR*. Retrieved from www.npr.org/2023/06/29/1181138066/affirmative-action-supreme-court-decision

Turi, J., Khastoori, S., Sorooshian, S., & Campbell, N. (2022). Diversity impact on organizational performance: Moderating and mediating role of diversity beliefs and leadership expertise. *PLoS One, 17*(7). https://doi.org/10.1371/journal.pone.0270813

Turner, A. (2016). The business case for racial equity. *National Civic Review*, (Spring), 21–29. https://doi.org/10.1002/ncr.21263

United Nations Department of Economic and Social Affairs, Population Division. (2024). World Population Prospects 2024: Summary of Results (UN DESA/POP/2024/TR/NO. 9).

Villamil, A. M., Branton, S., & Meisenbach, R. J. (2024). Piecing together inclusion: A critical overview of organizational inclusion research and praxis. In *Organizational communication theory and research* (Vol. 8, pp. 295–314). De Gruyter, Inc. https://doi.org/10.1515/9783110718508-016

Wolfgruber, D. (2023). I'm only joking!(?) the role of disparaging humor in the communicative constitution of inclusion/exclusion in organizations. *Equality, Diversity and Inclusion*. https://doi.org/10.1108/edi-08-2022-0223

Zak, M. W. (1994). It's like a prison in there. *Journal of Business and Technical Communication*, *8*, 282–298. https://doi.org/10.1177/1050651994008003002

Chapter 10

Improvisation

Leading Change

Improv theatre involves implicit scripts and structure. Change leadership also requires attending to implicit rules, norms, and values that constitute the culture. Guiding and promoting change through collaborative processes is a critical change leadership skill. Five assumptions about culture and change are reviewed as foundational for developing ethical and effective change leadership scripts: a) not all change involves cultural change; b) change, like culture, is symbolically constructed; c) not all cultural change is purposeful; d) a strong culture may create resistance to change; and e) change leadership is not just about leaders.

Regardless of the type of change (merger, resizing, yo-yo-ing business cycles), a constitutive approach to change informs five communication practices: 1) collaboratively create a transparent positive change process; 2) develop and enact a communication plan that foregrounds the recursive learning loops; 3) adapt communication to the varied emotions and responses to change; 4) respond dialogically to tensions inherent in the change process; and 5) ethically utilize cultural elements during the change process (e.g., rituals, stories, values, humor). These positive communication practices empower us to *foster the co-creation* of positive organizations by *capturing their unique qualities as constituted in enacted elements such as rituals, stories, and history that both shape and are shaped by communication.*

1. Articulate cultural analysis goals and benefits
2. Explore culture as co-construction
3. Reflect on enacted elements
4. Identify enacted elements via multiple methods
5. Interpret thematic action and OCA
6. Co-create positive communication applications

Step Six: Co-Create Positive Communication Applications

Leading Change

Objectives

- Identify language embedded in the discourse of change.
- Describe five assumptions about the relationships between change and organizational culture.
- Reflect on cultural data in light of five change practices as a way to develop positive practices.

DOI: 10.4324/9781003482529-14

Stage Terms

Substitution	Evolution	Loss
Integration	Differentiation	Fragmentation

The following ideas heard from students, colleagues, and clients reflect the chapter's aims:

- "This merger was tougher than others in that we were expected to do a full banking computer conversion in 12 hours."
- "Things change so often around here that we do not even call it change."
- "If it were not for a supervisor really listening to our gripes, I am not sure I would be handling these changes so well."
- "We are learning to align our internal communication with our external communication in order to be more ethical and adaptive to our clients."

Improvisation

Training method actors involve improvisation—creating scenes and characters without the security or structure of a script. Characters draw on their creativity and inner experiences to create a reality with one another when neither knows what is coming next. They must adapt to twists and turns and changes. To the outsider, the actors simply have a knack for being creative in the moment. However, there is more going on than meets the eye. The reality is that improv acting operates within certain implicit rules. For instance, one improv rule is that of "yes and . . ." in which the actor responding to another must first validate their statement by agreeing to it. They are then to add information to it in "the form of detail, feeling, or consequence such as turn taking or staying on topic that guide the conversation" (Quinn, 2007, p. 4). For example, one actor might begin an improv scene by saying, "You lied to me." In response, the other actor might say, "Yes, and the truth is the lie is what you need to hear." In short, they learn patterns involving constitutive rules. Somewhat akin to improv jazz, where players rely on structures, these actors are not simply making up what they say or do next (Hatch, 1999).

This analogue is useful for change leaders as well as other organizational members initiating and/or navigating change. If we attempt, for instance, to introduce or navigate changes without an awareness of unspoken scripts or assumptions, then no amount of strategy will aid us. Perhaps you have experienced times when you or others in the organization have attempted and/or experienced changes without being tuned into organizational history, assumptions, and values. The constructivist assumptions underlying the OCA model stress the need to attend to history, communication norms, and values. Such attention is not about history or norms as part of culture or as variables to analyze. Rather, the intent is to understand the way the past is brought into the present, like an "improv cue" that members can use to co-construct theory framing of change. Put differently, think about times when history is referenced to encourage or discourage a particular change in organizing practices. You might have said or heard: "Let me tell you about a time when we tried what you are suggesting." Such phrases underscore a critical insight: change leadership poses challenges, yet an awareness of how performances are enacting culture provides a way to navigate those challenges.

This constructivist perspective provides a unique viewpoint on organizational change in three ways by:

- Focusing on how organizations are constituted in varied communicative processes such as membership negotiation and activity coordination (c.f., McPhee & Zaug, 2009).
- Helping organizational leaders understand resistance to change (or at least what they may interpret as resistance) and helps them co-create successful change strategies.
- Suggesting collaborative and symbolic strategies necessary for successful organizational change.

This viewpoint then is responsive to the overall vision we maintain in each of these application chapters. Thus, regardless of the type of change being considered, when asked, "What should we co-create?" Our response is that we should engage in a *cultural analysis process fostering the co-creation of positive* organizations by *capturing their unique qualities as constituted in enacted elements such as rituals, stories, and history that both shape and are shaped by communication.* This chapter focuses on communicative practices that aid in adapting to and introducing change in ethical and effective ways. We argue that leading organizational change is a co-constitutive process that cannot be escaped by linear thinking.

We first review the forces or language often featured in the discourse surrounding change before discussing major assumptions regarding culture and change. These practices answer the third big question, "What forms of communication will create what we should create?" We also provide Rehearsals to guide the application of your cultural data. We conclude with a "Connection" focused on tapping into humor as a resource for introducing and leading change.

The Discourse of Change: It Is Not What It Is

Begin thinking with us about phrases found in the rationales and talk about change or proposed changes. What comes to mind? What phrases are used when changes are proposed or made in your organization? Jot your top three responses in Rehearsal 10.1.

Rehearsal 10.1 The Discourse of Enacting Change

Purpose: What phrases are used when changes are proposed or made in your organization?

1. ______________________________
2. ______________________________
3. ______________________________
4. ______________________________

Your list probably includes such things as competition, changes in the environment and technologies, government regulations, economic conditions, generational changes, globalization, and/or rapid growth. What did we miss? Our list of rationales is often part of the discourse surrounding restructuring ("right-sizing"), labor force reductions, and mergers. Regardless of the rationales, it is critical to pause and reflect on assumptions about culture and change. The tendency can be to think in terms of "forces that drive change" rather than language or discursive moves that constitute the change process. What value is there in viewing these as constitutive of change rather than "forces or factors?" First, the tendency can be to think of them as unmediated, that is, as "facts" that do not involve interpretation or framing. If, for example, I represent globalization as a bare fact, it may be assumed to be a sort of external variable that mandates certain responses. A tendency might be to assume the rightness or logic of the larger discourse of the need to "right size" our labor force. "It is what it is." Communication may then be relegated to tips found in popular literature, such as "communicate a clear, meaningful vision" or "celebrate and reward successes during the change." Furthermore, the assumption that changes such as labor reductions or "right-sizing" are the best moves can get lost in automatic responses to "forces" without being mindful of our ethical responsibility in co-creating change. In sharp contrast to "It is what it is," we invite you to simply state, "No, it is not. It is what we make it." This is a phrase borrowed from Dr. Mike Hemphill, Director of Leadership Development at the Clinton Foundation and Co-Director of the Presidential Leadership Scholars program. Gerald can still hear him repeat the phrase as part of a workshop on co-creating better social worlds. "It is what we make it." "It is what we make it."

Dr. Hemphill's phrase is one at the heart of this chapter. Before discussing change leadership practices, we review five assumptions about change and culture to ensure we rely on wisdom guided by theory and research on change processes.

Check Assumptions About Culture and Change

Just as we might hear and/or say, "It is what it is," and miss our role in co-creating change, so also assumptions we may hold can be blinders that create barriers to leading change efforts. Thus, we offer five assumptions about the relationships between culture and change.

- *First, not all change involves cultural change.* Changes in technology, leadership, business or DEI strategy, or even the competitive landscape may not alter the flow or direction of organizing practices. At times, we even talk about how an organizational change is going to "re-shape" the culture when, in fact, it does not. For example, Coulson-Thomas (2015), based on a five-year study, foregrounds changes in "performance support" processes for front-line work groups. He found that groups and individuals may maintain certain values and practices while still learning "critical" behaviors important to organizational effectiveness. Even though not all organizational changes are cultural changes, employees tend to view changes through the lens of their lived experiences and values. A bureaucratic culture trying to become more service-oriented may still view customer service as following correct procedures. Traditional faculty members may still remain threatened by on-line instruction and the evolving use of AI. They may express conviction that the best technology cannot produce the highly ethical and effective educational quality of face-to-face instruction (Mirivel, 2012). We are convinced that the reason why many organizational change efforts such as those related to improving diversity or ethics, are not ultimately successful is that they are not co-constructed in a way that attends to the lived experiences of members. For example, a leader might mandate diversity training or implement a policy in isolation from the members. The outcome may be surface-level change but not substantial changes in behaviors or culture. On the other hand, while not all change involves cultural change, attention must be given to anticipated and unanticipated cultural changes tied to technology. Chapter 12, on "Symbolic Leadership," explores the role of generative

AI. This quickly evolving technology change has implications for both positive and negative shifts in managerial control systems and thus goes beyond surface-level change.

- *Second, change, like culture, is not controllable due to being symbolically constructed.* When leaders initiate an organizational change, they may have a rationale in mind. However, they cannot control the ways in which organization members will interpret or react to the change. Jian (2007) refers to employee sense-making as one factor creating unintended consequences of planned organizational changes. For instance, change often produces a reassuring sense of order and control for corporate executives but cognitive disorder, stress, and lack of control for rank-and-file employees (McKinley & Scherer, 2000). Employees may engage in resistance strategies and attribute different motives for the change or superficially comply (Ford & Ford, 1995). Resistance is also influenced by informal networks. For example, in a study of the introduction of government-mandated electronic medical records (EMRs), Barrett and Stephens (2017) found that participants able to create "workarounds" to implement the new system were also more likely to have lower levels of resistance. Deetz, Tracy, and Simpson (2000) offer a timeless insight into the different reactions of management and employees to major change:

> Business leaders rarely anticipate the extent of the resistance to planned changes. One reason for this is that the leaders have had more time to think about the change and more fully understand the reasons for it. But equally important, leaders often have less to lose from it. Employees, on the other hand, are surprised, do not understand the reasoning, did not participate in the choice, and see themselves as having much to lose.
>
> (p. 39)

The uncontrollable, symbolic nature of change surfaced in a case study in Indonesia. Research gave insight to the way corruption was framed by members of this developing country. Rather than viewed as disruptive or illegal as the West frames it, Indonesians framed corruption as part of caring for each other, as necessary, due to the constraints placed on them by multinationals (Pertiwi, 2022). These different perspectives get at the heart of how change practices may be framed in radically different ways. Consider the following two cases and how they were managed in terms of what was controllable and not controllable.

Case 1: Overcoming an Impasse In a prior role as a dean of the college, Angi called together two departments to suggest that they explore the idea of a merger to create a professional school. She stressed that she was proposing the idea only as a proactive investigation that might enhance the position of both departments and that the decision rested totally with the faculty and staff of the two departments. However, in response, the faculty and staff developed their own rationales for the impetus for the action—the desire to reduce budgets, political motives about the leadership of the two departments, or other rationales. Only through consistent and open discussion did some of these attributions subside. These open discussions co-created a new organizing process where members developed a better understanding of the complexity of decision-making and, in turn, a greater trust in each other to maintain faculty control of final decisions.

Case 2: Contradictory Framing of Integration. Framing practices suggest that one-way leaders symbolically accept or reject cultural change. Perhaps you have heard the phrase, "The most segregated hour in America is Sunday." This quote is often attributed to Martin Luther King, Jr. However, congregational leaders frame this statement in opposing ways. Leaders may embed their talk in the national-level discourse surrounding the removal of barriers to integration in congregations (DeYmaz, 2007; Jenkins, 2014). These leaders stress that they have a textual mandate to create pathways for integration as a way to improve race relations (Driskill & Jenkins, 2019; Glazier, Driskill, & Hanson, 2024). In contrast, others frame "segregation as separation" based on choice; that is, since it is no longer mandated to segregate a higher value is placed on a shared ethnic history and culture (Driskill, Arjannikova, & Meyer, 2014).

- *Third, cultural change is both intentional and unintentional.* As we discussed in Chapter 3, cultures are enduring and dynamic. They are always being created and re-created in the interactions of their members. Kuhn and Corman (2003) claim that cultures evolve in a subtle process as new organization members construct values, assumptions, and practices that slowly create and re-create the culture. Sometimes, these changes are adopted by consensus, and sometimes, they develop through political wrangling and conflict. In contrast to what may seem to be a purposeful, albeit messy process, Alvesson (2002) argues that change may be organic. At times, cultures can follow the same laws of entropy as other social systems, with values that were once functional for an organization becoming dysfunctional over time. For example, in a case reported by a former student in a home health nurse staffing agency, a pattern slowly developed that involved an acceptance of twice the industry standard in employee turnover rates. The organization remained sufficiently profitable despite this decline. One new supervisor took the initiative to show the increased rates in light of national-level data and also indicated the cost of the high rates of hiring and training as well as the negative impact on employee and customer satisfaction. Yet, higher-level leaders had come to accept the turnover rate as part of the cost of doing business. The increases in turnover rates had been gradual, and the overall impact on their profit was manageable, such that the dysfunctional pattern had become ingrained in them as "the way things are." This potential for a dysfunctional pattern to emerge is indeed a major reason to explore the discourse constituting the culture.
- *Fourth, a strong culture may create resistance to change.* In light of the example just provided, this assumption is an important consideration. As you might anticipate, some cultures are built on a strong assumption that continuous change is essential. However, for other cultures, the more ingrained and entrenched the cultural assumptions and values, the harder they are to change. We have found in our work with religious organizations, universities, and government bureaucracies, particularly entrenched ideologies, which are difficult for members to change even when they are dysfunctional. Lyon's (2007) analysis of Merck concurs with the problems of a strong culture. Entrenched patterns at Merck contributed to unethical communication practices, resulting in the death of approximately 60,000 patients taking Vioxx. A closer analysis revealed a pattern of unethical practices that obscured physicians' ability to engage in significant choice—voluntary choice based on relevant, complete, and reliable information (Lyon & Mirivel, 2011). Put differently, a strong culture is not necessarily a good one or an effective one. As we will discuss in Chapter 13 on Organizational Effectiveness, the notion of a strong culture as an effective one is incomplete. *Strong* can be about norms that limit ethical decision-making.
- *Fifth, change leadership is not just about leaders.* Executive management tends to initiate most planned organizational change (Keyton, 2005). This may be due to their belief that new practices or strategies are necessary for corporate success or survival. Yet, since ethical and effective culture and change are constituted through co-constructed and enacted elements, leaders increase the likelihood of success when engaged in a cooperative process. Eisenberg and Riley (1988) claim that cultural change efforts may fail because leaders are pushing an ideology that conflicts with strongly held cultural assumptions and values. We

concur with Jian (2007), who advocates the critical role of dialogue in leading change processes. He offers a process model of organizational change that "emphasizes that both senior management and employees are change agents positioned in different roles: initiation and implementation, respectively" (p. 24). He writes:

> To facilitate system integration and manage tensions, senior managers should be able to create opportunities of employee participation in change initiation, attend to critical communication events by emphasizing dialogue and negotiation, and participate themselves in change implementation among local employee groups. Such two-way participation will foster shared interpretive schemes and transform tensions into constructive energy.
> (p. 25)

Willett (2018) provides a case study on the successful introduction of a major wellness program. Care for others, trust, and the approachability of management resulted in change management initiatives that manifested as more implicit than explicit. The success of this change was closely linked to leadership transparency about "costs, finances, and business operations," which developed trust. In addition, employees were treated as "partners throughout the process of communicating and implementing the wellness program," creating a sense of care (p. 124).

In contrast, another case study focused on a non-profit introducing a sustainability program. Deline (2019) investigated framing processes in three stages: 1) Change Message (e.g., Issue frames: significant/insignificant; Process Frames: Formal/Informal; Reciprocal/Non-Reciprocal); 2) Resistance Interpretations (e.g., disagreeability, conflict stakes); and 3) Coping Behaviors (e.g., role protection or threat). The analysis surfaced management or implementer framing of resistance practices versus employees. For example, implementors framed "disagreeableness" as "grumblers" due to resisting and thus hindering "positive attitudes" (Deline, 2019, p. 52). Employees who were not disagreeable framed fellow employees as "non adaptable and unable to change" (p. 53). Implementers, in terms of role performance, were concerned with the social costs of not being able to make changes to meet resistance demands. In contrast, employees who resisted change spoke in terms of "resistance as an acceptable way to be productive and perform well in their regular jobs" (p. 54).

These case studies echo ideas introduced in Chapter 3. Recall again that *culture creation is both a top-down and bottom-up process*. It is difficult to sustain a change effort in any part of the organization if there is no leadership support and commitment, but at the same time, leaders will fail in change efforts without the active participation and commitment of members and stakeholders. Viewed from this perspective, cultural change cannot have an endpoint. It is not something you do one time. This challenge is illustrated when multinational corporations miss the opportunity to enact change from the bottom up. Manzie's (2018) crisis study of the Royal Dutch Shell company, as introduced in Chapter 9 on Diversity, provides further insight here. In non-Western communities, local leadership is often spread across village groups, community associations, youth groups, and/or women's groups. Engaging these varied groups is an example of how change could occur from the bottom up.

The critical nature of being aware of this assumption is captured in Rehearsal 10.2. This rehearsal challenges you to review three contrasting perspectives in light of the jungle metaphor that members may hold about change (Martin, 1992). Being aware of and listening to these differences may aid in dialogue that connects leaders and members in meaningful ways to aid in the change process.

Rehearsal 10.2 Perspectives on Culture and Change

Purpose: Understand the way an organization views change and change processes in light of a constitutive framework.

Steps:

- Review your data to determine the extent to which a member's talk reveals one of the organizational perceptions of change. To what extent does talk about change reflect integration, differentiation, and/or fragmentation perspectives? Constitutive?
- Determine your own as well as participant awareness of a constitutive understanding of change. To what extent do you, as well as the organization, grasp the way these three perspectives each involve their own language and practices that actually constitute change processes?
- Develop a communication strategy appropriate for the organization in light of a constitutive approach. While attending to the way change is understood, find ways to introduce the way change and culture are constituted. For example, the organization may place a high value on consistency and clarity, which suggests certain top management efforts to establish direction. However, there may be subcultures or minority cultures that have a greater acceptance of uncertainty. A constitutive approach (review practices provided in the next section as well) would encourage mindfulness of how these varied discourses are co-creating their experience of change and allow room for discussion and dialogue on the implication for future change initiatives.

Metaphor A: It Is a Jungle Out There
Culture: A stable force with high consistency among manifestations of culture.
Change: Results in a loss of psychological safety if clarity is not maintained.
Subculture Variation: ____________________________________
Strategy: Leadership creates messages to indicate control over the change process and reduces ambiguity by clarifying roles, norms, and processes in place to maintain stability and meaning.

Metaphor B: The Jungle Is Not All Out There
Culture: Stable within units but diverse and unpredictable across units.
Change: Accepted unless viewed as an effort to disturb subculture clarity or autonomy.
Subculture Variation: ____________________________________
Strategy: Leadership stresses and defines sources of change that can be controlled by the organization and those factors that are beyond their control. Organizational responses are developed as a longer-range incremental approach that will be viewed and adjusted as new information is gained. Messages focus on maintaining clarity and meaning in areas most significant to the organization.

Metaphor C: We Are Part of the Jungle
Culture: Cultural manifestations are accepted as unclear and inconsistent.
Change: Not noticed as a problem unless the underlying value system disturbs the perspective of acceptance.

Subculture Variation: ______________________________________
Strategy: Leaders encourage continued acceptance of the reality of the change process. Policies are reviewed to encourage the empowerment of subcultures and individuals to respond to change and serve as catalysts for future change.

Metaphor D: Co-Created Jungles
Culture: Culture is constituted through enacted elements and through co-created practices.
Change: Negotiated through contested and accepted meanings.
Subculture Variation: ______________________________________
Strategy: Leadership encourages dialogue and negotiation on issues of importance to the employees and management. Symbols and rituals surface from the interactions in the process of co-constructing the change. These interactions involve co-creating ethical guidelines for the change process.

In summary, these five assumptions regarding change are foundational to the practices discussed in the next section: a) not all change involves cultural change; b) change, like culture, is not controllable due to being symbolically constructed; c) cultural change is both intentional and unintentional; d) a strong culture may create resistance to change; and e) change leadership is not just about leaders. These five assumptions set the stage for the following five practices. We begin by challenging the way we have presented change leadership in prior editions of this book and the ones most often found in popular literature.

Positive Communication Practices for Leading Change

It is not uncommon in reading books on change leadership to be introduced to a list of steps. In popular literature and in previous versions of this book, we have introduced such lists. In fact, we would ask that you evaluate this list:

1. Establish a sense of urgency.
2. Form a powerful guiding coalition.
3. Create a guiding vision.
4. Communicate the vision.
5. Empower others to act.
6. Create small wins along the way.
7. Consolidate improvements and create more change.
8. Institutionalize the new culture.

What did you notice? Perhaps you picked up on a logical sequence moving from need (a sense of urgency) through strategic involvement of others (a guiding coalition and empowering others to act) along with support for the change (small wins). The reasonableness of these steps is at first appealing. We contend that it is not that the suggested practices are wrong, yet they are inconsistent with the OCA constructivist model. *Are you able to discern what is inconsistent? Problematic?* One way to word the issue is the failure to engage others in the process. We are not saying that change may not involve "a sense of urgency." Nor are we contending that persuasive processes are unimportant. In fact, integrating the idea of celebrating "small wins" across positive practices is introduced in this chapter. Yet, organizational differences in framing change may suggest that urgency may not need to be the driver. Change may be considered, at times, a normal part of on-going organizing processes.

Thus, our contention is that a list like the previous one needs to be revised to focus on co-creating the change process from the start. We concur with Stan Deetz, a leading organizational communication theorist and scholar, about the ethical and practical value of finding ways to engage in "democratizing" practices (c.f., Deetz, Tracy, & Simpson, 2000). In one community, for instance, a need was seen to close the non-profit hospital and then enlarge the capacity of the previously competing for-profit hospital. The size of the community did not necessitate both hospitals. Concerns, of course, were immediately expressed about the impact on patients and the community. Community leaders created a change process that included community members and representatives from the hospitals. They formed a working group charged to listen and discern ways to collaborate. They attended to community concerns about the loss of the other hospital and the perception that the for-profit would not be there for the community. This group was able to find ways to co-create shared values that resulted in launching a community foundation funded by the new hospital. A percentage of annual profits went to this non-profit foundation. In the coming years, the foundation was able to fund a major park that included an amphitheater, a swimming and fishing lake, and walking and biking trails. This collaborative work is one instance of a change process that sought to engage in a process that was a win-win. *What then do we suggest for change leaders other than revising the list to maximize participation or co-creation in the process?* From research and in response to the five assumptions, we derived five positive communication practices. These constructivist practices are intended to prompt reflection on your data for possible applications.

1. Collaboratively Create a Vision and Plan for a Positive Change Process

Defined: Co-create a change process engaging a diverse change leadership team.

Rationale: Attention to co-creating an effective and ethical change process is central to fostering the development of positive organizations in order to counter a tendency to focus on downward communication.

In Action: The default mode for change leadership often focuses on a downward process involving the crafting of leadership messages in isolation from others. Consider phrases such as:

- "We have to find a way to get them on board."
- "You just have to go with this change or leave."
- "We are making this change and ask you to find ways to value it."

These and variations of these statements are grounded in the assumption that change processes are best when developed, decided, and directed from the top. Then, it follows that one must find and build the most compelling messaging to get others to join in the change. The process we envision counters this approach. Instead, we foreground the need to begin and continue with a mental shift that is foundational to the change practices that follow.

In contrast to the previous quotes, recall the "mental shift" from Chapter 1—"Shift from a leader-focused, transmission model of communication, to a constitutive process model." Another way to consider this shift to a focus on process is to stress that the *how* of change is more important than the *what* (i.e., getting the change to happen). It is not so much where you end up as how you get there that will impact organizational outcomes. Even a good change idea that is badly handled will be damaging. Change processes, again depending on the perspective or way change is framed, may be destabilizing and increase uncertainty. For instance, in the context of responding to the COVID-19 pandemic, researchers found that beyond "information disclosure, . . . transparency, consistency, and accountability" were central to providing resources and support to cope with changes (Li, Sun, Tao, & Lee, 2021, p. 8). A case example of a failure to make this shift sets the stage for a way to move in the opposite direction.

Case Example: The Opposite of Co-Construction

An OD professional shared about a change at a major medical institution. The upper management went on a retreat and constructed a list of value statements. The CEO had HR email the list to the employees. The email fell on deaf ears. The OD department was then charged with developing a three-year formal process aimed at helping employees buy into these values. As you might anticipate, the OD team experienced resistance from employees who had been told what to value. Having to "sell" values from the top down is much more time-intensive and less likely to find success than a collaborative process from the start.

Envision Positive Change Outcomes and Processes

How can we enact this collaborative, transparent process? *The primary strategy is to engage a diverse stakeholder group to envision and communicate a positive organizational change process.* Thus, from the start, communication with the larger organization will involve an awareness that a team has been formed to navigate this change. This initial communication co-creates the value of transparency. Furthermore, as will be developed in the second change leadership practice, letting the organization know of the formation of this team should include that a communication plan will be created to provide updates and opportunities for feedback.

The primary charge of this diverse group is to ensure that the change process is based on current and/or desired values they seek to create/recreate during the change process. This team, in contrast to the preceding example, is charged to engage in a collaborative process. Change, regardless of the impetus (e.g., market shifts, downsizing), merits engagement with stakeholders (employees/members, community members, customers, etc.). For instance, imagine learning from a web page that "Excellence" or "People First" were touted as values. Indeed, you learned that these formally stated values had grown from listening to members in terms of "what they liked about working here." If this is the case, then the actions indicated in the following list would flow from these espoused values. For instance, members would likely explore ways to "recreate" or improve the enactment of these values. However, if "People First" was not already a shared value, then the team leading the process would need to discern desired values and how to co-create them in the change process. Thus, beginning with a cross-section of the organization, this first practice is about creating a vision grounded in current values and/or one that aids in identifying desired ones. At the heart of this process is asking open questions in the process of discovery.

Example questions integrated into varied listening venues (focus groups, etc.) and strategies (e.g., liberating structures) might include:

- What is the situation driving this change?
    - What credible data/knowledge might we rely on? Gain?
    - What data collection process will best engage stakeholders to gain needed information? (e.g., interviews, focus groups, listening tours, liberating structures).

- What are the core values we want to co-create/recreate that will then drive our process?
- What are the desirable outcomes tied to being/becoming a positive culture? As a prelude to the chapter on effectiveness (Chapter 13), consider asking a question about what it looks like to attend to a triple bottom line that involves:
    - People: Engagement, Diversity, Equity, Inclusion, Belonging, and Health.
    - Profit: Long-term sustainable profit margins.
    - Planet: Sustainable, equitable practices.

2. Develop and Enact a Communication Plan That Foregrounds Recursive Learning Loops

Defined: A clear plan for how the change will be navigated that provides opportunities for feedback and adjustment.

Rationale: Change processes are dynamic, involving the need for adjustment while also creating a value for transparency of relevant information to aid in member engagement and agency.

In Action: Recall from the first positive change practices that organization members were to be notified of the formation of this team and that a communication plan would be created to provide updates and opportunities for feedback. Thus, the same team creating the change plan or a different team needs to develop a communication plan. At the heart of this effort is to ensure change leadership focuses on transparency in the process. In what follows, we provide an example to illustrate what such a plan might look like, including reminding members of the first phase.

Example Communication Plan

- Goal: With organizational members, we seek to introduce and manage this change in a highly ethical and effective way to foster the co-creation of a positive organization.
- Method: In order to reach this goal, we have developed change practices flowing from multiple meetings with stakeholders. We plan to regularly remind members of the process and ways to give feedback and improve the plan.
- Guiding Values: *Care* for each other in our change practices. *Trust* by being transparent with relevant information. *Innovation* by learning ways to improve the change and change process through regular feedback. *Accountability* by providing up-to-date information on outcomes.
- Our Process will involve the following practices:
    - 24/7 on-line mini-surveys to check in on any overlooked support or adjustment needed.
    - Weekly listening tours by team members that will involve informal visits with members to understand their experiences and gain feedback.
    - Bi-weekly lunch roundtables with senior management to share what we know and what we do not know in terms of the changes underway.
    - Monthly forums with the CEO to hear updates, hear stories of small wins, and gain other feedback.
    - Quarterly debrief sessions to learn what is working, what we are learning, and adjustments needed to focus on progress, not perfection.
    - Co-created events to celebrate small and big wins, including new innovations, as well as spaces and strategies to provide support for experiences of loss and adjustment.

In summary, *we tend to support what we help create*. Involving stakeholder members in every stage of the change effort, including in developing the process and content of the changes, will reduce feelings of being passive victims while creating ownership. However, a warning is needed here.

What could possibly be wrong with such high levels of engagement? Perhaps like us, you have been involved in a process where organizational members were engaged in the process (e.g., focus groups, brainstorming, etc.). Yet, in time, the credibility of the process was damaged as it became clear that upper-level leaders had an agenda. A decision had already been made. They were simply using the process of "collaboration" as a "good practice to reduce resistance." Have you been there? Done that? In contrast, had they been open about their ideas and rationale and engaged others in responding and discerning options, credibility and a more effective implementation of the change would have been enhanced. As you might anticipate, the first practice is foundational to the next practice—one that we view as too easily overlooked.

3. Adapt Communication to the Varied Emotions and Responses to Change

Defined: Varied emotions are part of the change and thus merit attention.

Rationale: Awareness of different ways change is experienced needs to be part of a change leadership plan.

In Action: Imagine your organization is going through a change, perhaps in leadership or structure. What do you hear being said about the change? Positive and/or negative comments? What emotions do you sense? Sadness? Excitement? Anger? Contempt? Gratitude? What have your experiences been? Perhaps you concur with us that "people are more likely than ever to bring suffering to work as the border between the organization and society becomes increasingly blurred" (Lilius et al., 2011, p. 28). Regardless of what you heard, it is important to stress that a "mental shift" to a co-construction process requires listening to and for varied responses. The critical role of listening, central to Mirivel's model of positive communication, is underscored by research exploring the complexity of responses to planned changes. In a nationwide study involving 21 sites and interviews with a diverse group of 151 members, researchers engaged in an iterative metaphor analysis. The research team explored how members "metaphorically frame planned organizational change projects" over time, including perceptions of success (Redden, Clark, Tracy, & Shafer, 2019, p. 505). In addition, they explored members' understandings of resilience in the face of change. What might you anticipate in their findings? Perhaps with us, you might find their results surprising. One finding in particular stood out to us—"change is framed as scary, daunting, and difficult, even when teams are ultimately successful." One implication is that so-called negative framing, such as perceived resistance, provides "crucial opportunities" for improving change projects (Redden, Clark, Tracy, & Shafer, 2019, p. 519).

In all, the need to respond in compassion echoes research on how disruptions in "meaning structures" are what people most resist in change processes, not necessarily the change itself Marris (1974). Put differently, individuals hold different levels of "psychological safety" in response to change depending on how they view or interpret the form of the change. We would add that the way the change is managed and the degree of permeability between the organization and personal/societal lives. Marris's three "meaning structures" are adapted and revised in the following to capture the significance of how each structure is constituted in the discourse of the lived experience of participants.

- **Substitution:** A change in which one item of meaning is exchanged for another. "We have a new boss, but the way things are done around here is pretty much the same."
- **Evolution:** Gradual shifts in values and meanings. "It took a while, but I now see how our family business needed to expand to be inclusive of others."

- **Loss:** Significant change in the avenue a person had used to achieve attachment, success, and competence. "I was moved to a new role and no longer feel my work is valued."

As we explore these forms of change in greater depth with case studies and examples, we integrate Alvesson's (2002) ideas on these different ways of framing change. The focus is on "every-day reframing"—an informal process in which opinion leaders promote new patterns of interpretations of practices or policies.

Substitution

In "substitution," the organization member gives up one cultural meaning for another. Such "giving up" may involve an overall positive framing. As in the preceding example, the new boss represents continuity. However, substitution or reframing does not always occur easily. Smith and Eisenberg (1987), as introduced in our discussion of metaphors in Chapter 4, analyzed a conflict at Disneyland. In this classic study, a conflict was grounded in the management-held theatre metaphor and a family metaphor held by employees. A family metaphor was experienced as inconsistent with "theatre" business decisions management had to make. You don't lay off family members. The authors suggest that these challenges are not unique, as organizations inherently respond to the dialectics of "stability-change" and "autonomy-connection" (p. 377). Disneyland, they argue, could either *substitute* the current root metaphors with a new one that frames employees as "actors" or "children," or they may find ways to enrich the family-theatre metaphor by not seeing them as incompatible. They contend that the theatre metaphor could subsume the family one by focusing on "family entertainment" that also allows for a business orientation (p. 378). At times, when change is perceived as substitution rather than loss, it may be easier for organization members to accept the change because they are not left with a void. When there is a strong ego attachment to the culture, however, even substitution may be difficult to accept.

Evolution

In "evolution," change is framed as gradual rather than abrupt. In the taken-for-granted reality, members may not even be aware of gradual changes. Alvesson (2002) views this type of change as an organic process in which values and assumptions slowly shift and change over time. Those reacting negatively are members with longer tenure who are most likely to remember "the way things used to be." At times, there is a moment of cultural comparison that may make organization members more aware of the change. Such awareness may prompt reflection on whether changes are perceived as positive and/or negative or not fully in the control of the organization.

Loss

In "loss," change is sudden and shocking, and in the lived experience of some involved, it produces resistance and grief. Alvesson (2002) uses the term "revolution," in which important cultural tenets are abandoned suddenly. Consider the experience of "downsizing" or "right-sizing." Recognizing change being experienced as loss can be useful in recognizing normal and expected reactions. Depression, grief, denial, anger, sadness, and holding on to the past are all responses to loss. Thus, in managing changes viewed in terms of loss, communication practices involving reflection and paraphrasing may be more appropriate than arguing with someone to "get over it." In particular, Bridges (1991), in an excellent and practical book on change, offers several communicative practices to guide us in responding to a sense of loss.

- Identify who's losing what.
- Accept the reality and importance of the subjective losses.
- Don't be surprised by "overreaction."
- Acknowledge the losses openly and sympathetically.
- Expect and accept the signs of grieving.
- Compensate for the losses.

These positive practices underscore and enact a relationship focus via "dynamic boundary-permeability." This idea is about "celebrating, bounded playing," and responding to conflicts that "reflect a collective understanding that it is appropriate to both relax and constrict the sharing of information about members' personal lives" (Lilius et al., 2011, pp. 24–25). Put differently, the charge is to be creative in responding to varied responses to the question: "What forms of communication will create what we should create?" An answer to this question may take macro-level approaches, such as a ritual that allows time to laugh, celebrate what is valued, and also hear stories about loss, about what was out of everyone's control and ways individuals are learning to be resilient (Redden, Clark, Tracy, & Shafer, 2019). In addition, communication training could be provided to equip members to respond to others based on supportive and positive communication practices, such as listening and mutual disclosure of concerns and ideas. At the same time, at the individual, informal levels, we can take guidance from Susan Cain's (2022) call to action in her book, *Bittersweet*. She affirms that we all experience loss as part of the human condition, reflecting ancient seemingly incongruous phrases, such as "Blessed are those who mourn." Thus, in responding to loss, we can learn to avoid toxic positivity. Instead, we can connect with what matters and take committed action. Those actions, such as sharing our loss and identifying ways to grow, can move us from bitter to sweet, from loss to love. As such, specific encouragement, training, and modeling of compassionate care include not only noticing the suffering of another but also finding ways to alleviate that suffering (Dutton, Workman, & Hardin, 2014).

In all, a caveat is needed regarding these "loss" categories. Alvesson and Willmott (2002) note that these ways of experiencing change can be complementary. For instance, a new role created in an organization may also prompt experiences of substitution, evolutionary change, and/or a sense of loss. The new role might be framed as substitution in that the functions were simply covered by others in the past who have made needed adjustments. The shift to the new role might, at the same time, have been discussed off and on over time and thus framed as an inevitable evolution. Nonetheless, at times, members giving up certain functions to this new role might experience loss. For example, in our university culture, we have seen changes occur in relation to developing intercultural competency over a 20-plus year time period. Twenty years ago, there were pockets of administration, students, and faculty who valued the development of this competency in the learning process. Over time, interdepartmental, faculty, staff, and student-led collaborations saw substantial growth in the number of rituals (campus events, research projects, community engagement practices) that co-created this value. For example, an annual intercultural education event was formed by a community member, faculty, and staff. Over time, this became a full week of campus events ranging from international job fairs and non-profit volunteer options to intercultural education poster sessions woven into a music festival. This week engaged our diverse student and community organizations and academic units and, over a ten-year period, saw over 500 students engaged (Driskill, 2007).

However, funding shifts combined with COVID, leadership changes, and restructuring saw the disappearance of these varied rituals. In all, this example captures the evolutionary nature of change that may then also involve some experiencing a sense of loss while others, newer to the organization, would not experience this as a loss but perhaps as a substitution as different rituals emerge.

Regardless of how change is framed and experienced, the value of paying attention to change leadership as a symbolic meaning-management process places a greater emphasis on understanding individual framing or responses to change since symbolic ("sense-making") processes are at the core of understanding change. This concern for sense-making is developed further in the fourth constitutive practice.

4. Respond Dialogically to Tensions Inherent in the Change Process

Defined: Tensions such as transparency–secrecy and inclusion–exclusion are embedded in communication during a change process.

Rationale: The inherent nature of dialectics provides an opportunity to identify the best ways to frame a dialectic to ethically and effectively lead a change process to co-create positive organizations.

In Action: As you review enacted elements, thematic action, and the overall culture in action, you are likely to hear experiences related to change. You might have, for instance, heard stories of changes that created a new sense of vision. Alternatively, you might have heard stories about mergers that have caused a residual ill will. Thus, the ways we respond to inherent tensions are interwoven with the positive practice of responding to varied emotions. For instance, Pepper and Larson (2006), based on a case analysis of a merger, argue for identifying and responding to identity tensions. An identity tension is created as individual values are enacted, perhaps as part of identification with organizational values (c.f., Scott, Corman, & Cheney, 1998). For instance, imagine the emotions interwoven with changes in the branding of an NGO. The inherent identity tensions were certainty/uncertainty, transparency/opacity, and participation/restriction. Lower levels of identification were found when transparency and participation were perceived as limited (Gilstrap & Smith, 2016). In a consulting context, one medical specialty organization experienced major difficulties when it expanded to work with a state-run agency. Comments were made about who was to benefit from this new association. It was clear that most of their energy was being used to negotiate the new political territory. Even as they continued to spend energy there, leadership became aware of a higher turnover rate and much lower employee satisfaction. They noticed that employees called on to spend more time in the state agency were experiencing a loss of meaning. Some of them had a strong identity with the smaller, "family" culture of the home organization. They sensed that they were being asked to assimilate into a new culture that meant a complete loss of their own.

Change leadership practices should involve the identification of tensions and framing practices. Based on Pepper and Larson (2006), Rehearsal 10.3 captures questions to identify two different dialectic tensions. The "assimilation-autonomy" tension refers to the extent that participants value communicative practices that encourage members to integrate with a new culture versus maintaining their own. "Consensus-command" refers to communication practices that focus on decision-making rooted in developing common ground and agreement versus being directed or told based on a dictate. Since tensions are "constructed in the daily discourse of organization life," you should reflect on cultural data in ways that will help surface or unveil these tensions (Pepper & Larson, 2006, p. 65). Yet, one should not stop with discerning the particular tension. Listening to the way these tensions are being framed and responded to is essential. So, for example, the group leaving the "family" based organization is likely framing the "assimilation-autonomy" in terms of no option (i.e., commanded to assimilate). A change leader could engage in a dialogic process with these members to discern other framing options that allow for both/and. The significance of this step is in understanding how members may feel conflicted about how to respond (c.f., Barge & Andreas, 2013). For instance, contention responses may lead to conflict spirals that may "escalate or de-escalate a conflict" (Putnam, 2006, p. 16). Dialogue is aided then by leaders modeling micro-level positive communication practices such as asking open questions, listening, complementing, and disclosing self (Mirivel, 2014). For instance, in the context of change prompted by a crisis, Manzie (2018) calls for leaders to attend to the local community's decision-making norms. In the case of the Royal Dutch Shell company oil crisis in Nigeria, leaders needed to carefully address ancestral land claims over oil ownership which required attention to how the past is intrinsically tied to the present. Dialogic, grounded meetings provide an opportunity to reaffirm and give voice and agency to the varied stakeholder cultures. Listening and asking questions has the potential then to constitute a culture sensitive to managing challenges to identity. Tapping into the power of listening is echoed by the power of shared sadness and loss in co-creating resilience. The questions in Rehearsal 10.3 (adapted from Pepper & Larson, 2006), explore varied questions to aid in constructive framing responses.

Rehearsal 10.3 Assessing Cultural Identity Tensions

Directions: Utilize these questions to discern how these two tensions are being managed.

Identity Tension: Assimilation–Autonomy

- What did you value most about your organization before the merger?
- What are you willing to give up and/or change? Not change?
- What will aid us in maintaining aspects of both cultures?

Identity Tension: Consensus–Command

- How do you make decisions here?
- What differences in decision-making norms have you experienced?
- How are those differences being navigated?

Each of the previous tensions provides a resource for discerning sources of conflict. For example, a merger might find two sets of expectations related to how decisions are made. Other dialectics could be explored as well. In the coming application chapters, for example, we will explore the attention Lyon (2017) gives to other dialectics, such as upward–downward communication practices and transparency–secrecy. Regardless of the dialectic, change leaders need to discern the communicative practices that will aid in framing and reframing these dialectics. To that end, the next change principle stressed the value of tuning into various elements of culture.

5. Ethically Enact Elements During the Change Process

Defined: Cultural change is co-created/recreated through enacted elements (stories, rituals, etc.).

Rationale: Leaders (formal and informal) need to be aware of and intentional about ways to tap into enacted elements to effectively and ethically oversee a change process.

In Action: In the book *The Heart of Change*, Kotter (2012) stresses the emotional and symbolic dimensions of change. Concurrent with the pervasive role of emotions, note that too often, leaders approach change through an analytic procedure, assuming that if they produce enough data, organization members will be able to analyze it and understand the need for change. In agreement with this focus, Waldron (2012) captures a list of varied "moral" emotions and their social referents. For example, listening and responding empathically to such varied emotions as hope, shame, pride, and/or scorn co-creates supportive communication during change processes (p. 138). As such, recall that the OCA model assumes cultural elements as enactments that constitute the culture. For instance, a conscious awareness of communication during a change could involve a ritual for expressing emotional highs and lows while celebrating the past, grieving loss, and affirming a vision for what is ahead (Fox & Amichai-Hamburger, 2001). The power of the cultural analysis process is that you already have at least an initial understanding of varied enacted elements in their role in creating organizing processes. Here, we introduce rituals, stories, and values as examples of how attending to these enacted elements can be of value in leading change. We also introduce, in the Connections section, ideas on humor as yet another resource.

Rituals

You may have been in an organization where a ritual was introduced or carried forward to honor someone retiring, unveil a new brand, a workforce initiative, and/or a new company name in light of a merger. Such rituals may be taken for granted. We attend, we listen, we talk with colleagues, receive an award, retire, admit to mixed feelings over a merger, and the list continues. The OCA model is about checking this tendency to take such moments for granted. Instead, we seek to attend to what is being created or constructed in the ritual, in the talk in and around such moments. At the corporate or formal level, the ritual may seem positive, even if predictable. Lines are read to honor an employee or celebrate a productive year. Yet, at the informal level, I may be part of a clique that interprets the event as compulsory, not serving employees. Before or at various points in the event, we may hear sarcastic comments. The point? In the context of change, rituals are complex and merit attention beyond formal functions.

We reviewed varied functions of rituals (Trice & Beyer, 1984, 1993) in Chapter 4: passage, integration, enhancement, degradation, renewal, and conflict reduction. This list underscores the significance and pervasiveness of rituals. Yet, our goal in analysis and in reflecting on change leadership is to go beyond stated functions to ask, "What is being created or constituted based on how the ritual is enacted?" For instance, a ritual during a change may constitute "activity coordination," which is needed during times of changes in "self-structuring" processes (McPhee & Zaug, 2009). Such coordination involves enacting the ritual by "symbolically" acknowledging the past while anticipating the future. This process involves inviting members to share what they will miss about the way things were while also encouraging talk about what they value about the change (Smith & Stewart, 2011, p. 115).

In this same vein, Bridges (1991) suggests three communicative practices that can be part of co-creating rituals to constitute the change process: "Mark the endings"; "Treat the past with respect"; and "Let people take a piece of the old way with them." These practices suggest ways to attend to how a ritual is enacted or the kinds of communicative practices being enacted.

One can imagine introducing a ritual that would accomplish all three of these suggestions. You may plan a pre-launch event to mark the end of a particular practice or structure. During this event, individuals could be prepared to honor what they will miss rather than just assume all that is old or passing was not valued. Furthermore, reminders of the "old way" could be kept in the form of mementos or artifacts. Anniversary celebrations could include reminders of the continuity of history that not only display respect for the contributions of what has been before but note the continuity of specific values in the present. For example, in a major leadership transition in one organization, the ceremony included stories by an array of organizational members as well as community members. The stories featured various ways this leader addressed race relations in the community. In addition, the event included the unveiling of the plans for a commissioned sculpture related to race relations to be placed on the organization's campus. The sculpture captured the values of the outgoing leader. As such, this transition ritual constituted and recreated values that members of the organization desired to carry forward.

Stories

Your data collection involved hearing or reading varied stories. We have stressed that stories are rich with cultural insights. Stories carry implicit references and explicit language referencing enacted elements such as values, history, and heroes. As such, for example, a story may not only function to make a case for the value of a change but also to co-create the change itself. Thus, attending to what stories are created is important for effective and ethical change leadership. Such a practice has the value of potentially engaging "deep smarts" via members with a historically and intuitively developed sense of ways to move forward (Leonard, Swap, & Fraser, 2005). For instance, imagine your role as an insider who listens for stories told about a change that was introduced in an effective and ethical manner. You pick up on one such story from five years ago when a decision was made by leadership to encourage daily small group meetings as a sort of debrief at the end of the day. You hear across units that the change was introduced through dialogue and discussion, and tweaks were made to how the meetings were conducted based on feedback. After you learn about this story, you realize it can become a discursive resource for leading a change process in the future. In fact, in one study of a major culture change, the researchers noted the key role stories played. They found that "stories sent messages both about the way things had been culturally in the past as well as providing justification or proof of the need for a cultural change in the future" (Dulek, 2015, p. 236). In the context of a challenging diversity setting, hiring female engineers, researchers noted the power of storytelling in educational outreach for improving self-efficacy. They noted that when combined with role modeling by senior management, storytelling created a cultural shift (Fogg-Rogers, Sardo, & Boushel, 2017). Stories, in this context, can and should also include "small wins." As referenced in Chapter 11 on ethics, small wins focus on how "culture is changeable (however slightly at first) and that culture shapes behavior" (Bisel, 2018, p. 238).

In another case example from Gerald's department, the story is told of a time when the option of introducing a major change was being considered. Meetings were held, and the pros and cons were weighed. The particular change involved one that would cost customers, in this case students, more money. It would also end an almost decade-long collaborative and creative process, in this case, faculty co-writing a low-cost textbook for their students. The change would also mean a loss of revenue in that the monies for the faculty-published text were used for students in a learning center. It was, at first, hard for anyone to imagine the value of such a change. Then, one member introduced the fact that the faculty had taken on the book writing project because, at the time, it was the only and best option to meet the learning needs of the students. Now, as he indicated, "there are better books on the market." A consensus was developed that other collaborative projects were also available and that the core value—serving the learning needs of their students (not money)—was what should guide them. This story is now introduced to new faculty and at varied junctures when changes are underfoot, and thus, it re-creates decision-making patterns based on discerning what is best for students.

Values

Values are often represented as an obstacle or a resource for change. From a constitutive view, however, values are not simply slogans on the webpage or symbolic forms representing the culture. Rather, they are part of the discourse used to argue for certain actions (e.g., "we value the environment, so we must . . .") and as such are constituted in communicative practices. Daher (2016), in his study of innovativeness in organizations, noted the way values were represented as central to the change process. Enablers of innovation constituted values in communicative practices such as tolerating mistakes, group reward recognition, valuing new ideas, flexibility, being future-oriented, supporting risk-taking, participative decision-making, adaptability, and empowerment. Notice how each of these enablers of innovation involves communicative actions that enact innovative organizing practices.

It is, therefore, helpful to attend to the way communicative practices represent or constitute certain values before engaging in a change process. For example, Angi was a management consultant for a bank for several years. It was known internally and externally for the value employees placed on exceptional customer service. As banking was deregulated to offer more financial services, the bank rolled out what they thought was an innovative plan to encourage employees to sell more products and services to bank customers. They offered significant financial incentives and were surprised when a few employees achieved their selling goals. After interviewing several employees, she concluded that the resistance to selling was based on employees' perceptions that selling compromised the value they placed on service to employees. She encouraged the bank to drop the financial incentives and to focus instead on explaining to bank employees how the new products could serve existing customers, to tell stories about the elderly lady getting 1.7% on a large balance in a regular savings account who could earn 6% with the same money in a mutual fund. Sales soared once employees "reframed" the new practices not as incentive-based sales but within the existing cultural value of service. The drive to take care of customers was already embedded in the discourse of the culture, and thus, the earlier efforts were misguided.

In summary, enacted elements create communicative processes that create and/or constrain change processes. Rituals, stories, and values, from a constitutive perspective, are not variables to be manipulated for a particular desired outcome. However, we can ask ourselves if we are engaging in the forms of ethical communication that co-create rituals, stories, and values that improve change processes. Other elements, such as history, metaphors, and artifacts, as well as other enacted elements, may be viewed as resources for constituted change. The key, from a CCO perspective, is to engage in ethical processes that attend to both micro- and macro-level practices. Thus, for example, in the story told previously about the book decision, micro-level practices related to collaboration and consensus building were represented. What was not mentioned was that, in time, a macro practice was adopted—the department formally wrote consensus building into their policy manual as their preferred way to make decisions. In this way, as new members join the department and/or in moments when conflicts emerge about decision-making, members may represent the text of the policy manual as having force or shared agreement on the preferred mode. We now introduce another element of culture that we have typically overlooked in our writing, research, and consultation.

Connections: Humor and Sarcasm as Change Resources?

Consider times you have made or heard an ironic or sarcastic statement. Often, such statements are made when an individual or a group believes something needs changing but doesn't see the likelihood of it happening. As such, irony is one way that change is framed and constituted. See if this mix of ironic and sometimes sarcastic phrases resonates with your experience (some original to us, others cited):

- Yeah, right, so we get raises just by telling the boss we are underpaid.
- "Most of what we call management consists of making it difficult for people to get their work done." – Peter Drucker
- I could bet my first child on the odds of that (fill in the blank) happening around here.
- "I will just reduce the quality of my work until my pay feels better." – *Dilbert*
- "If heaven is ethnically diverse, then why on earth aren't we?" (Driskill, Arjannikova, & Meyer, 2014).
- "Pride, commitment, and teamwork are words they use to get you to work for free." – Anonymous

As you read over the preceding statements and perhaps think of your own examples, we want to draw attention to how humor is enacted constitutively. First, let's consider the role of irony before introducing a close cousin, sarcasm. Irony can be viewed as "a form of non-literal language in which the speaker means much more than what is said" (Dews & Winner, 1995, p. 3). An ironic statement might include a shared sense of a contradiction—we may laugh at or notice an incongruity but have not yet moved to a place of contempt, which is central to sarcasm. Irony might serve an expressive function, a way to "improve social interaction" by drawing attention to "clashes in logic" or "absurdity" (Meyer, 2015, p. 28). Thus, an ironic statement may be expressed in a professional, ethical tone to introduce a new level of dialogue or through ritual to provide an alternative symbolic reality, and thus, choice (Hatch, 1999; Sillince & Barker, 2012). For example, in 2007, a community dialogue forum was created to address potential racial tensions at the 50th anniversary of the integration of Central High School in Little Rock, Arkansas. Multiple stakeholders, including community, educational, and business organizations, were present as the issue of integration in congregations surfaced as a major discursive thread. Historically, practices in the U.S., growing from hundreds of years of legalized slavery, resulted in not only segregated schools but also congregations. This pattern continued through reconstruction and Jim Crow. In an analysis of one community forum hosted in a multi-ethnic congregation, an African American leader and panelist indicated that a change to integration would not happen "this side of heaven." In response, a minority Chinese-American leader in the host congregation, comprising over 35 ethnic groups, introduced "dramatic irony." This type of irony requires the audience to detect contradictions inherent "in the characters and their situations" (Brown, 1990, p. 176). This leader stated that in their diverse congregation, they often use a "brainteaser" by asking: "The kingdom of God is not segregated, so why on earth is the church?" The tone and context were not sarcastic, yet there was an intentional effort to use irony to create an opening to challenge the assumption that segregation had to continue "this side of heaven" (Driskill, Arjannikova, & Meyer, 2014, p. 11). Indeed, fast forward from 2007, a trend toward increased integration continues. For instance, in 1998, only 1% of mainline Protestant congregations were multiracial in contrast to 10% in 2019. Evangelical congregations shifted from 7% to 22% multiracial (Chaves, Roso, Holleman, & Hawkins, 2021).

The varied forms and functions of irony may be viewed in terms of discursive enactments that create organizing processes. Thus, in the context of change leadership, attending to such openings created through irony is of value. Ironic statements, however, can take a cynical and divisive turn. Irony, when it contains contempt, becomes sarcasm. Sarcasm may be present for any number of reasons. A group and/or individual may a) perceive they are not being heard; b) experience inconsistency in behaviors; and/or c) learned and carried negative habits of criticism from another organizational culture. A potential danger is present in humor that divides. Research indicates the supervisor humor that differentiates one group from another predicts subordinate dissent, increasing division and reduced trust (Ramsey & Meyer, 2024).

We may tend to think of sarcasm only in a negative light, either deprecating self, other, or some group or organization. Yet, Huang, Gino, and Galinsky (2015), in their experimental study of sarcasm in brainstorming groups, found that levels of individual creativity were enhanced by those sending or receiving sarcasm. While sarcasm did, in some cases, breed conflict, if the other was viewed as trusted, it was a plus. Others have noticed the constructive use of sarcasm to gain support for a union movement (Brimeyer, Eaker, & Clair, 2004). How, then, might sarcasm provide an opportunity for change? Consider how the following example grounded earlier micro and macro communicative practices.

Imagine if you were part of this conversation between two co-workers. One co-worker is convinced it is "about time" for someone to be fired.

BRAD: Jay has had zero sales for months now. It is time for him to go.
MARY: Jay did sell some products this past month. I believe part of the issue is we need a change in our rubric.
BRAD: Well, regardless, the real problem is he poisons the well with others.
MARY: What do you mean?
BRAD: Jay has a habit of being sarcastic and negative. He sends unprofessional and disrespectful emails to me, and I have heard from others about it as well.

The challenge now is for Brad and Mary to discern how to move forward. Jay is perceived as sarcastic. We do not know if he is simply a problem employee seeking to divert attention from his poor performance, or perhaps he is unclear on the best way to introduce complaints. The challenge then is to engage with Jay in a way most likely to tap into his sarcasm in a positive way.

For sarcasm to be an opening for change, at least two communicative moves are needed. First, on the interpersonal level, Mary might encourage Brad to first talk to Jay, co-worker to co-worker. This step would be based on a positive communication approach reminiscent of dialogic communication. Consistent with Pearce and Pearce (2004), the approach would be to avoid judging motives but to ask open questions to seek understanding. Imagine the following conversation.

- Brad: "I am wanting to understand your recent email comments about .... You sounded like you were unhappy about something."
- Jay: "You might say that."
- Brad: "I am hearing frustration. I would like to understand your concerns."
- Jay: "Are you sure you want to hear?"

Quick question: How would you respond if you were Brad? We trust you get the idea. Regardless of the outcome, this positive communication approach (Mirivel, 2014) opens the possibility of improved understanding. Ideally, Brad and Jay could come to an agreement on ways to address concerns (and end sarcastic emails). Check out Rehearsal 10.4 "A Change Plan" and the on-line Rehearsal "A Change Case" to provide further opportunities for application and reflection.

Rehearsal 10.4 A Change Plan

Purpose: Apply change principles by developing a plan. These questions can be adapted to create a survey relevant to change processes.

Overview: Choose a project that would be a significant cultural change within either your own organization, your cultural analysis organization, or another organization with which you are very familiar. Outline a plan for how you would approach leading the change, using principles from your reading. Make sure that your project narrative addresses the following issues:

1. What change is envisioned? Why is this change a cultural change?
2. Discuss how you would prepare individuals in the organization for change.
3. Describe the change process. How long would it take? Who would be involved? What would be the steps toward change?
4. Describe how your plan would accomplish the following:
    a. Shift from a leader-focused transmission model of communication to a constitutive (CCO) process model.
    b. Adapt communication to the varied meaning structures held in response to change (substitution, evolution, loss).
    c. Respond dialogically to dialectic tensions embedded in the change process.
    d. Determine ways to ethically utilize cultural elements during the change process.

Summary

We began with an improvisation analogy. Improv theatre, unlike what we might assume, actually involves implicit scripts and structure. Leading change requires attending to implicit rules, norms, and values within the culture. Guiding and promoting change through collaborative processes will no doubt remain one of the most critical leadership skills. We stressed five mental shifts to address assumptions about culture and change:

1. Not all change involves cultural change.
2. Change, like culture, is symbolically constructed.
3. Not all cultural change is purposeful.
4. A strong culture may create resistance to change.
5. Change leadership is not just about leaders.

These assumptions set the state for five positive change practices.

1. Collaboratively create a transparent positive change process.
2. Develop and enact a communication plan that foregrounds recursive learning loops.
3. Adapt communication to the varied emotions and responses to change.

4. Respond dialogically to tensions inherent in the change process (e.g., assimilation–autonomy, consensus–command, upward–downward, transparency–secrecy).
5. Ethically utilize cultural elements during the change process (e.g., rituals, stories, values, humor).

Attending to these assumptions and positive practices guides us into being more adept at co-creating ethical, diverse, adaptive, and effective organizational cultures that are part of improving all of our social worlds.

Discussion Questions

1. What forces prompting change have impacted you?
2. Review and then select one of the assumptions about change you view as most relevant to your cultural analysis. What implication for the organization do you see from your data?
   - Not all change involves cultural change.
   - Change, like culture, is symbolically constructed.
   - Not all cultural change is purposeful.
   - A strong culture may create resistance to change.
   - Change leadership is not just about leaders.
3. Which of the three ways of experiencing change most resonated with your own experience of change? How might this experience aid you in being a better change leader?
   - **Substitution:** A change in which one item of meaning is exchanged for another.
   - **Evolution:** Gradual shifts in values and meanings.
   - **Loss:** Significant change in the avenue a person had used to achieve attachment, success, and competence.
4. Review and then select one of the five positive practices you see most relevant to your cultural analysis. What implication for the organization do you see from your data?
   - Collaboratively create a transparent positive change process.
   - Develop and enact a communication plan that foregrounds recursive learning loops.
   - Adapt communication to the varied emotions and responses to change.
   - Respond dialogically to tensions inherent in the change process.
   - Ethically utilize cultural elements during the change process.
5. What elements of culture would you find most useful in leading a change effort? Why? Give examples.

References

Alvesson, M. (2002). *Understanding organizational culture*. Thousand Oaks, CA: Sage.

Alvesson, M., & Willmott, H. (2002). Identity regulation as organizational control: Producing the appropriate individual. *Journal of Management Studies, 39*(5), 619–644. https://doi.org/10.1111/1467-6486.00305

Barge, J. K., & Andreas, D. (2013). Communities, conflict, and the design of dialogic conversations. In J. G. Oetzel & S. Ting-Toomey (Eds.), *The Sage handbook of conflict communication* (pp. 609–634). Thousand Oaks, CA: Sage.

Barrett, A. K., & Stephens, K. K. (2017). Making Electronic Health Records (EHRs) work: Informal talk and workarounds in healthcare organizations. *Health Communication, 32*(8), 1004–1013. https://doi.org/10.1080/10410236.2016.1196422

Bisel, R. (2018). *Organizational moral learning: A communication approach.* New York: Routledge.

Bridges, W. (1991). *Managing transitions: Making the most of change.* Reading, MA: Perseus.

Brimeyer, T. M., Eaker, A. V., & Clair, R. P. (2004). Rhetorical strategies in union organizing: A case of labor versus management. *Management Communication Quarterly, 18(1)*, 45–75. https://doi.org/10.1177/0893318904265128

Brown, M. H. (1990). Defining stories in organizations: Characteristics and functions. In J. A. Anderson (Ed.), *Communication yearbook* (Vol. 13, pp. 162–190). Newbury Park, CA: Sage.

Cain, S. (2022). *Bittersweet: How sorrow and longing make us whole.* New York: Penguin Random House.

Chaves, M., Roso, J., Holleman, A., & Hawkins, M. (2021). *Congregations in 21st century America.* Durham, NC: Duke University, Department of Sociology. Retrieved from https://sites.duke.edu/ncsweb/files/2022/02/NCSIV_Report_Web_FINAL2.pdf

Coulson-Thomas, C. (2015). Learning and behavior: Addressing the culture change conundrum: Part two. *Industrial and Commercial Training, 47(4)*, 182–189. https://doi.org/10.1108/ICT-01-2015-0004

Daher, N. (2016). The relationships between organizational culture and organizational innovation. *International Journal of Business & Public Administration, 13(2)*, 1–15.

Deetz, S., Tracy, S., & Simpson, J. (2000). *Leading organizations through transition: Communication and cultural change.* Thousand Oaks, CA: Sage.

Deline, M. B. (2019). Framing resistance: Identifying frames that guide resistance interpretations at work. *Management Communication Quarterly, 33(1)*, 39–67. https://doi.org/10.1177/0893318918793731

Dews, S., & Winner, E. (1995). Muting the meaning: A social function of irony. *Metaphor and Symbolic Activity, 10(1)*, 3–19. https://doi.org/10.1207/s15327868ms1001

DeYmaz, M. (2007). *Building a healthy multi-ethnic church.* San Francisco, CA: Jossey-Bass/Leadership.

Driskill, G. (2007). Using the intercultural class to internationalize the campus. *Communication Teacher, 21(1)*, 6–11. https://doi.org/10.1080/17404620701211485

Driskill, G. W., Arjannikova, A., & Meyer, J. (2014). A dialectic analysis of a community forum on faith: The "most segregated" or separated hour? *Journal of Applied Communication Research, 42(4)*, 477–496. https://doi.org/10.1080/00909882.2014.880938

Driskill, G. W., & Jenkins, J. (2019). The most integrated hour in America: Reframing the organizational discourses of church purpose. *Communication Studies, (4)*, 433–452. https://doi.org/10.1080/10510974.2019.1628083

Dulek, R. (2015). Instituting cultural change at a major organization: A case study. *Business and Professional Communication Quarterly, 78(2)*, 231–243. https://doi.org/10.1177/2329490614554991

Dutton, J. E., Workman, K. M., & Hardin, A. E. (2014). Compassion at work. *Annual Review of Organizational Psychology and Organizational Behavior, 1(1)*, 277–304. https://doi.org/10.1146/annurev-orgpsych-031413-091221

Eisenberg, E., & Riley, P. (1988). Organizational symbols and sense-making. In G. M. Goldhaber & G. A. Barnett (Eds.), *Handbook of organizational communication* (pp. 131–158). Norwood, NJ: Ablex.

Fogg-Rogers, L., Sardo, M., & Boushel, C. (2017). "Robots vs. animals": Establishing a culture of public engagement and female role modeling in engineering higher education. *Science Communication, 39(2)*, 195–220. https://doi.org/10.1177/1075547017696169

Ford, J. D., & Ford, L. W. (1995). The role of conversations in producing intentional change in organizations. *Academy of Management Review, 20*, 541–570. https://doi.org/10.5465/AMR.1995.9508080330

Fox, S., & Amichai-Hamburger, Y. (2001). The power of emotional appeals in promoting organizational change programs. *Academy of Management Executive, 15*, 84–94. https://doi.org/10.5465/AME.2001.5897664

Gilstrap, C., & Smith, S. (2016). Identity tensions during an NGO name change: How managers experience an international organization's rebranding effort. *International Journal of Strategic Communication, 10(5)*, 445–461. https://doi.org/10.1080/1553118X.2016.1225302

Glazier, R., Driskill, G., & Hanson, D. (2024). Race and faith: The role of congregations in racial justice. *Journal for the Scientific Study of Religion.* https://doi.org/10.1111/jssr.12943

Hatch, M. (1999). Exploring the empty spaces of organizing: How improvisational jazz helps redescribe organizational structure. *Organization Studies*, *20*(*1*), 75–100. https://doi.org/10.1177/0170840699201004

Huang, L., Gino, F., & Galinsky, A. (2015). The highest form of intelligence: Sarcasm increases creativity for both expressers and recipients. *Organizational Behavior and Human Decision Processes*, *131*, 162–177. https://doi.org/10.1016/j.obhdp.2015.07.001

Jenkins, J. J. (2014). A "community" of discipline: The paradox of diversity within an intercultural church. *Western Journal of Communication*, *78*(*2*), 134–154. https://doi.org/10.1080/10570314.2013.845793

Jian, G. (2007). "Omega is a four-letter word": Toward a tension-centered model of resistance to information and communication technologies. *Communication Monographs*, *74*, 517–540. https://doi.org/10.1080/03637750701716602

Keyton, J. (2005). *Communication and organizational culture*. Thousand Oaks, CA: Sage.

Kotter, J. (2012). *The heart of change: Real-life stories of how people change their organizations*. Boston, MA: Harvard Business School Publishing.

Kuhn, T., & Corman, S. R. (2003). The emergence of homogeneity and heterogeneity in knowledge structures during a planned organizational change. *Communication Monographs*, *70*, 198–229. https://doi.org/10.1080/0363775032000167406

Leonard, D., Swap, W., & Fraser, B. (2005). Deep smarts: How to cultivate and transfer enduring business wisdom [review of deep smarts: How to cultivate and transfer enduring business wisdom]. *Prometheus*, *23*(*2*), 239–242. https://doi.org/10.1080/08109020500099370

Li, J.-Y., Sun, R., Tao, W., & Lee, Y. (2021). Employee coping with organizational change in the face of a pandemic: The role of transparent internal communication. *Public Relations Review*, *47*(*1*), N.PAG. https://doi.org/10.1016/j.pubrev.2020.101984

Lilius, J., Worline, M., Dutton, J., Kanov, J., & Maitlis, S. (2011). Understanding compassion capability. *Human Relations*, *64*. https://doi.org/10.1177/0018726710396250

Lyon, A. (2007). Putting patients first: Systematically distorted communication and Merck's marketing of Vioxx. *Journal of Applied Communication Research*, *35*, 376–398. https://doi.org/10.1080/00909880701611052

Lyon, A. (2017). *Case studies in courageous organizational communication: Research and practices for effective workplaces*. New York: Peter Lang.

Lyon, A., & Mirivel, J. C. (2011). Reconstructing Merck's practical theory of communication: The ethics of pharmaceutical sales representative-physician encounters. *Communication Monographs*, *78*(*1*), 53–72. https://doi.org/10.1080/03637751.2010.542578

Manzie, V. (2018). Applying the rhetoric of renewal model in a contemporary African context: Lessons learned from the royal Dutch shell oil crisis in Nigeria. *Journal of International Crisis and Risk Communication Research*, *1*(*2*), 201–224. https://doi.org/10.30658/jicrcr.1.2.2

Marris, P. (1974). *Loss and change*. New York: Pantheon.

Martin, J. N. (1992). *Cultures in organizations: Three perspectives*. New York: Oxford University Press.

McKinley, W., & Scherer, A. G. (2000). Some unanticipated consequences of organizational restructuring. *Academy of Management Review*, *25*, 735–753. https://doi.org/10.2307/259202

McPhee, R. D., & Zaug, P. (2009). The communicative constitution of organizations: A framework for explanation. In L. L. Putnam & A. M. Nicotera (Eds.), *Building theories of organization: The constitutive role of communication* (pp. 21–47). New York: Routledge.

Meyer, J. (2015). *Understanding humor through communication: Why be funny anyway?* Lanham, MD: Lexington Books.

Mirivel, J. C. (2012). Communication is the relationship. In C. J. Boden & S. M. Kippers (Eds.), *Pathways to transformation: Learning in relationship* (pp. 31–48). Charlotte, NC: Information Age Publishing.

Mirivel, J. C. (2014). *The art of positive communication: Theory and practice*. New York: Peter Lang.

Pearce, B., & Pearce, K. (2004). Taking a communication perspective on dialogue. In R. L. Anderson, L. Baxter, & K. Cissna (Eds.), *Dialogue: Theorizing difference in communication studies* (pp. 39–56). Thousand Oaks, CA: Sage.

Pepper, G., & Larson, G. (2006). Cultural identity tensions in a post-acquisition organization. *Journal of Applied Communication Research*, *34*, 49–71. https://doi.org/10.1080/00909880500420267

Pertiwi, K. (2022). "We care about others": Discursive constructions of corruption vis-à-vis national/cultural identity in Indonesia's business-government relations. *Critical Perspectives on International Business*, *18*(*2*), 157–177. https://doi.org/10.1108/cpoib-03-2019-0025

Putnam, L. (2006). Definitions and approaches to conflict and communication. In J. G. Oetzel & S. Ting-Toomey (Eds.), *The Sage handbook of conflict communication* (pp. 1–32). Thousand Oaks, CA: Sage.

Quinn, J. (2007). Improvising our way through tragedy: How an improv comedy community heals itself through improvisation. *American Communication Journal*, *9*(*1*), 1–20.

Ramsey, M. C., & Meyer, J. C. (2024). Uniting and dividing: An examination of supervisors' humor use as a predictor of subordinate dissent expression. *Communication Reports*, *38*(TBA). https://doi.org/10.1080/08934215.2024.2432328.

Redden, S., Clark, L., Tracy, S. J., & Shafer, M. S. (2019). How metaphorical framings build and undermine resilience during change: A longitudinal study of metaphors in team-driven planned organizational change. *Communication Monographs*, *86*(*4*), 501–525. https://doi.org/10.1080/03637751.2019.1621361

Scott, C. R., Corman, S. R., & Cheney, G. (1998). Development of a structurational model of identification in the organization. *Communication Theory*, *8*(*3*), 298–336. https://doi.org/10.1111/j.1468-2885.1998.tb00223.x

Sillince, J., & Barker, J. (2012). A tropological theory of institutionalization. *Organization Studies*, *33*, 7–38. https://doi.org/10.1177/0170840611425735

Smith, A., & Stewart, B. (2011). Organizational rituals: Features, functions and mechanisms. *International Journal of Management Reviews*, *13*(*2*), 113–133. https://doi.org/10.1111/j.1468-2370.2010.00288.x

Smith, R., & Eisenberg, E. (1987). Conflict at Disneyland: A root-metaphor analysis. *Communication Monographs*, *54*, 365–380. https://doi.org/10.1080/03637758709390239

Trice, H. M., & Beyer, J. (1984). Studying organizational cultures through rites and ceremonials. *Academy of Management Review*, *9*, 653–669. https://doi.org/10.5465/AMR.1984.4277391

Trice, H. M., & Beyer, J. (1993). *The cultures of work organizations*. Englewood Cliffs, NJ: Prentice Hall.

Waldron, V. (2012). *Communicating emotion at work*. United Kingdom: Polity Press.

Willett, S. L. (2018). The change communications strategy for a wellness program: A qualitative case study. Unpublished Dissertation. North Central University School of Business.

Chapter 11

An Honest Portrayal

Ethics

Organizations with a conscience are a pressing need in our society. The statistics are alarming. They tell a tragic story of ethical abuse related to fairness, safety, bullying, harassment, and our environment. However, enacting an honest portrayal involves more than being aware of these abuses or developing the ability to improve critical thinking regarding moral decision-making. Research on the effectiveness of ethics education and training reveals either no impact or a negative one. Five communication practices are introduced to aid in the process of improving individual and organizational ethical performances: 1) engage in greetings to create connection and trust; 2) ask open questions to reduce the gaps; 3) share stories of positive ethical action; 4) normalize ethics talk; and 5) reframe value tensions. Consistent with each application chapter, we foreground the OCA model as *fostering the co-creation of positive organizations by developing implications through the analysis of enacted elements that both shape and are shaped by communication.*

1. Articulate cultural analysis goals and benefits
2. Explore culture as co-construction
3. Reflect on enacted elements
4. Identify enacted elements via multiple methods
5. Interpret thematic action and OCA
6. Co-create positive communication applications

Step Six: Co-Create Positive Communication Applications

Ethics

Objectives

- Make a mental shift to think of ethics as constituted in communication.
- Enact five communication practices to co-construct organizational moral learning.

Stage Terms

Value tensions	Power aggrandizement values	Organizational conscience
Economizing values	Ecologizing values	

DOI: 10.4324/9781003482529-15

The following quotes reflect the chapter's aims:

> To preserve our deeper desires amid the pressures of the modern corporation is to reserve our souls for the greater life we had in mind when we first took the job.
>
> David Whyte, *The Heart Aroused: Poetry and the Preservation of the Soul in Modern America*, 1994, p. 298

> We have to realize that a true ecological approach always becomes a social approach; it must integrate questions of justice in debates on the environment, so as to hear both the cry of the earth and the cry of the poor.
>
> Pope St. Francis, 5/24/15, *Laudato Si', no. 49*

When the Curtain Is Lifted

When the curtain is raised or when the screen lights up, as audience members, we hope for nothing more and nothing less than an honest portrayal. Method actors are trained to develop a devotion to the "power of truth in acting" (Vineberg, 1991, p. 7). In short, effective acting is not about pretense but honest portrayals.

When the curtain is raised on cultural performances, we hope for the same. In fact, what we deem not only as right and wrong but what should or ought to happen is at the heart of our complaints about life in organizations. Consider your experiences with the following gaps.

- The gap between *CEO versus worker income.*
- *The gap between moral versus legal standards.*
- *The gap between our expectations for a safe place to work and the reality.*
- *The gap between our own moral standards and our actual behavior.*

What experiences with these or other gaps would you add? We will invite you to explore these gaps later in this chapter. For now, they set the stage by foregrounding "the ways ethics are constituted in communication" (McClellan & Sanders, 2013, p. 259). Consistent with our other application chapters, we carry forward the overarching goal of a *cultural analysis process that provides insight for improving positive communication practices that result in meaningful personal, professional, and organizational culture development and growth.* In order to enhance ethical organizing and communicative processes, we argue that five constitutive practices will co-create more ethical organizations. Before discussing these practices, we provide a brief review of the theories underlying these practices, followed by our reasoning for a "small wins" approach. Consistent with our approach in each application chapter, we encourage reflection on your data as well as your own professional and personal life.

Foundational Theories

Consistent with the concept of a "just culture," we focus our attention on organizational learning and transparency. In a just culture, both "the organization and its people are held accountable . . . avoiding retributions and firing while focusing on risk, systems design, human behavior" (Boysen, 2013). As such, a just culture includes keeping the "deep smarts" by not firing or silencing voices that confront unethical practices but instead cultivating wisdom (Leonard, Swap, & Fraser, 2005). The co-creation of just cultures is woven into the heart of organizational moral learning. Yet, to be about creating organizational moral learning, we see value in an orientation toward "small wins," first introduced by Weick (1984), inspired by the work of Peters (1977, 1979). Weick (1984) defines a "small win" as

> a concrete, complete, implemented outcome of moderate importance. By itself, one small win may seem unimportant. A series of wins at small but significant tasks, however, reveals a pattern that may attract allies, deter opponents, and lower resistance to subsequent proposals. Small wins are controllable opportunities that produce visible results.
>
> (p. 43)

Several illustrations of small wins aid us in gaining a sense of the range and importance of this focus:

- The early success of the newly formed environmental protection agency in the 1970s by first gaining a "beach" head in five cities tied to water pollution (Weick, 1984).
- Alcohol Anonymous focuses on staying sober one day at a time.
- Coaching and team success by focusing athletes on "little things" (e.g., celebrating a defensive player moving in the right angle to cut off an offensive player, to learning one-touch passing).
- Reducing gender bias by co-creating performance review research with supervisors that revealed implicit bias in their own processes (Correll, 2017).

In summary, a small-wins approach focuses on how "culture is changeable (however slightly at first) and that culture shapes behavior" (Bisel, 2018, p. 238). The following positive practices each illustrate ways to gain traction in daily "here and now" ethics talks aimed at counteracting the failure of ethics training (Bisel, 2018). After each practice, we provide Rehearsals and/or questions for data reflection and application.

1. Engage in Greetings to Create Connection and Trust

Defined: Greetings are the entry and continuation points for all relationships (see Mirivel, 2014).

Rationale: Regardless of national or ethnic culture, the presence or absence of greetings shapes relational and organizational health, and as such, leaders who model greetings open the door for connection and trust, which are integral to co-creating ethical behavior.

Theory/Research: This first practice is first for a reason. Research has validated this timeless, cross-culture communication practice as critical to all relationships (Mirivel & Lyon, 2023). The practice of greetings is profoundly simple yet central to highly ethical organizations. It is fair to ask what makes greeting so critical. First, consider the dark side or the opposite of greeting others: ostracism—giving someone the silent treatment. Such treatment might take the form of ignoring a greeting, failing to include a colleague in a coffee or lunch gathering, or avoiding eye contact. Each of these practices has been established in research as a form of behavior more acceptable than bullying. However, ostracism is argued as unethical because of the undue harm created. Indeed, the social pain created has been associated with physical pain in neuroscience research. In addition, this failure to greet has also been shown to have an overall negative impact on mental and emotional health. Add to these negative consequences for the victim, research has also documented negative impacts on the perpetrator and on those aware of ostracism (O'Reilly, Robinson, & Schabram, 2013).

Next, consider the positive side. Greetings create connections. They open the possibility of relationships and trust building. As such, they are a daily opportunity to create a "small win" by creating a safe place for the practices that follow, such as "normalizing ethics talk" (Practice #4). Given that ethics talk of any kind may be a source of conflict, trust becomes even more critical. Perhaps you have noticed a tendency to avoid greetings when a conflict is present. The conflict may or may not have to do with a formal breach of ethics, but the perception may involve a missed expectation of something that should have been said or done or not said or done. For example, Gerald learned from a friend in a medical setting of a workplace situation in which an employee no longer responded to greetings due to their unwillingness to engage in resolving a conflict. The result, over time, was not only reduced collaboration but, in time, the person engaged in ostracizing the other, leaving.

We both acknowledge times when we have felt caught on the horns of a dilemma. On the one hand, we are thinking, "I need to talk to this person about something that I think is wrong, yet I am not sure I can trust them to take it the right way. On the other hand, isn't it wrong to not give them the opportunity to respond?" I may, if I am honest, play out the scenario in my mind and think, "I can't handle it if they react, get mad, or blame me for a misunderstanding or causing trouble. There is lots at stake here." This internal dialogue may result in cursory greetings or avoidance, which creates distance and a lessened level of trust. In contrast, maintaining greeting behaviors indicates the opposite of avoidance and creates the possibility of connection.

In action: A quick reality check. What is your norm when you first enter the door of the place where you work or volunteer? At the start of a meeting? When you come home? Did your answer involve a greeting? Did you meaningfully connect? Take a minute to reflect on your experiences with a conflict about something you sensed was not right. Perhaps you sensed that the other person had a different take or wondered if they felt the same. Rehearsal 11.1 provides a way to reflect on and assess your current greeting practices. See our online resources for a Rehearsal focused on re-establishing a connection.

Rehearsal 11.1 Greetings Assessment

Directions: Reflect on your degree of agreement with each of the following statements. Then, discern ways to develop your practices of greeting others in the organizations you serve, work, etc.

- I tend to greet each person at the start of a new day.
- I maintain greeting others even when there is a conflict that needs to be addressed.
- I practice learning greetings from other cultures to provide added connection.
- I follow up greetings to include a moment to check on ways to be supportive and/or how the other person is doing.

In summary, our claim is simple: giving voice to an ethical concern requires a certain level of trust. Trust not just in the other person but in yourself. Such trust can be built by working through conflict. Yet, the trust needed to engage begins with and is maintained through greetings. Greetings create a space for a "small win" by signaling the continuity of the relationship.

Absent greetings, no relationship, no trust. Thus, from the questions listed previously, reflect on current greeting behaviors, both in formal situations, before meetings and hallways, in Zoom, and even in electronic communications.

2. Ask Open Questions to Reduce Gaps

Defined: Open questions are "What?" How?" "Why" questions that invite exploration as opposed to closed questions ("Can't we?" "Don't you think?"), which point toward binary, limited responses that may also be leading. "Gaps" refer to the space or distance between our longings for what is best, right, and good and what we may experience as unethical or immoral.

Rationale: Open questions provide an opportunity to discover (Mirivel, 2014; Mirivel & Lyon, 2023) develop understanding and empathy for the lived experiences of others in their experiences with and concerns with these gaps.

Theory/Research: Our experiences combined with research concur with the reality of gaps. In fact, what we deem not only as right and wrong but what should or ought to happen is at the heart of our complaints about life in organizations. Consider your experiences with the following gaps introduced in the opening of this chapter.

- The gap between *CEO versus Worker Income.*
  - You work a second job to maintain substandard housing.
  - You read that in 2022, USA CEOs were paid 344 times as much as a typical worker.
  - You serve in a developing country, and with Pope Francis, quoted in the introduction, you "hear both the cry of the earth and the cry of the poor."
- *The gap between moral versus legal standards.*
  - "One has not only a legal but a moral responsibility to obey just laws. Conversely, one has a moral responsibility to disobey unjust laws" (Martin Luther King, Jr., 1963, p. 84).
  - "Business is a game," therefore, "business should have its own morality" and "its own rules," such that half-truths, bluffing, and deceit are necessary in order to win (Hamington, 2009, p. 477).
  - "Winning is not everything. It is the only thing" ("Red" Sander, head coach for the 1950s UCLA football team who was given multiple-year sanctions for making payments to players that exceeded the allowable amount; Bolch, August 14, 2018).
- *The gap between our expectations for a safe place to work and the reality.*
  - A friend shares that they were bullied and sexually harassed at work. Threats were made to bodily harm her. The only response from HR was to tell the immediate supervisor that she must stay in her office.
  - You hear about the impact of belittling, rudeness, blatant disrespect, and yelling: 80% lost work time worrying about the incident, 63% lost work time avoiding the offender, 66% said that their performance declined (Porath, Gerbasi, & Schorch, 2015).
- *The gap between our own moral standards and our actual behavior.*
  - You put off saying something to support a co-worker who is having a tough time (c.f., Kirby, Wieland, & McBride, 2013).
  - You remain silent over dishonest budgeting practices out of fear of job loss.

- At a sporting event, another parent glares at you after you tell the official where they can go.
- At home, you react to your spouse and then belittle a child who has not done what you asked.

The list of gaps could go on, but you get the idea. We all experience gaps or, in some cases, a chasm between what your gut instinctively knows as right versus wrong. The practice of asking questions, however, challenges us to make a shift. The shift is one we encourage not only in data collection but in our own communication practices. The shift is from a focus on complaint or criticism to asking questions to understand and to find ways to address the gaps between moral ideals and reality. The shift moves us from assuming we fully understand to realizing we need to understand better. Questions can aid us in creating opportunities for dialogue and improved moral learning. For instance, concerning CEO pay gaps, we have been challenged by Salaszar and Raggiuniti (2016), who explore the reasons excessive CEO pay prevails in the US but not in Japan.

Concerning dialogue, open questions create an ethic of exploration, discovery, and learning. As such, open questions provide a check on the tendency to assume we know all we need to know and/or that we can do nothing to address the gap. In addition, they provide an avenue for understanding and, in the process, develop a critical leadership virtue-humility (Schein & Schein, 2021).

In action: Give thought to the last time you heard (or gave voice) with phrases like the following:

- "That pay gap is just plain wrong."
- "Our supervisor does not treat us like everyone else."
- "I can't believe the CEO did not say anything about the real problem."

Each phrase represents a broken expectation, a gap. Review the examples that follow, which focus on open questions in response to varied gaps introduced earlier. Then, use the space provided to add additional open questions you might ask as well as other gaps and questions you might encourage members of the organization you are studying to explore.

- "That pay gap is just plain wrong."
  - Open Question: "What might help us understand and respond to this gap?"
  - Open Question: ____
- "Our supervisor does not treat us like everyone else."
  - Open Question: Please say more about your experiences in this area. What options do you see for improvement?
  - Open Question: ____
- "I can't believe the CEO did not say anything about the real problem."
  - Open Question: What might we do to understand the issues at hand better?
  - Open Question: ____
- Gap: ____
  - Open Question: ____

In all, reducing the gaps between what we know to be right versus wrong is not an easy task. Asking open questions provides the possibility of a "small win" in what might seem to be intractable. Needed insights might be gained, and improved agency through actionable plans may flow from such interactions. Attending to and giving voice to these gaps by maintaining trust through greetings and asking open questions to understand gaps sets the stage for a third positive practice.

3. Share Stories of Positive Ethical Actions

Defined: Stories that capture "here and now" ethical decision-making in real-time situations. In contrast, "when or if" situations focus on what one might do in hypothetical situations.

Rationale: Research continues to document the importance of "here and now" explicit talk about ethics (Bisel, 2018; Zanin, Bisel, & Adame, 2016).

Theory/Research: You may still ask, why "share stories?" The short answer—stories have a greater impact than training or appeals to moral reasoning. Like other positive practices that focus on ethical co-creation by "acting into," stories do more than present a list of ethical policies or guides. In fact, in the context of practicing medicine, researchers found that doctors again and again reference the power of narrative in developing and learning ethical practices. As one interviewee noted,

> I think storytelling, whether it's a case that happens around the table that you look at a patient, or something that's been more informal in life probably forms part of your memory. Essentially it forms a bank of wise and unwise decisions.
>
> (Paton & Kotzee, 2021)

Thus, stories of those who have foregrounded ethics in their narrative for doing the right thing provide a discursive cue that can empower others. In contrast to a focus on gaps, this practice seeks to affirm untold stories that make us aware that the new is not all back. One such person can be found in the founder and former president of Malden Mills, Aaron Feuerstein. After a fire destroyed his textile plant, he kept employees on the payroll despite the cries of shareholders to do the opposite (Seeger & Ulmer, 2001; Ulmer, 2001). The "1996 Botwinick Prizes in Business Ethics and in Ethical Practice in the Professions" was presented to Feuerstein for his ethical leadership (Columbia Business School, n.d.). Later, despite speculation that bankruptcy could have been avoided had he not been so generous with his employees, he maintained his position of no regrets. The guiding ethical principle for Feuerstein, growing from his religious faith, was that of acting for the larger goal, not for the moment, for doing the right thing (Shafron, 2002).

You might be asking, "What if I do not know of ethical heroes like Feuerstein?" Few of us do. One option is to turn to heroes found in whistleblowers. For example, a scientist and COVID-19 whistleblower, Rebekah Jones, was fired from the Florida Department of Health in May 2020 for refusing to manipulate data and asking her supervisor how to file a whistleblower complaint (National Whistleblowers Center, n.d.). We provide online Rehearsals to reflect on "Whistleblower" heroes, including one Julien heard while traveling on a plane. While of value for co-creating the virtue of courage, the goal of engaging with these reactive stories should be to move toward proactive practices. Table 11.1 illustrates the contrast between reactive vs. proactive.

One approach to focusing on proactive practices is found in "high reliability organizations" (HRO; Weick & Sutcliffe, 2001). These organizations "operate in hazardous and high-risk

Table 11.1 Reactive versus Proactive Social Responsibility Responses

Reactive	*Proactive*
Be a market-driven product and service provider-	Develop and market new "ethical" products and services
Create jobs and ensure health and safety	Invest in education, career development, and diversity
Avoid negative impacts on local communities	Contribute to the community's well-being
Comply with rules and regulations	Move beyond rules and regulations
Maximize short-term shareholder value	Maximize short-term shareholder value

Source: Adapted from Pedersen (2010), Figure 2 Modelling CSR, p. 163

environments with little to no accidents and still maintain high levels of operational capacity or production" (Dwyer, Karanikas, & Sav, 2023, p. 164). As such, HROs move away from what can become a drift toward unethical practices. For instance, a safety culture can drift away from practices at a high societal cost, such as Boeing, in terms of loss of life and injury, where the prioritization of profit corrodes communication (Bohannon, 2024).

Identifying and sharing stories based on HRO's value commitments and/or ethical heroes provides one approach to improving organizational ethics. Recall that ethical lapses as well as times of reaching ethical high marks, are not simply a matter of moral failings or successes of individuals, but reflections of organizing practices that constitute the culture. As Bisel (2018) notes, rather than just focusing on bad apples, "organizational cultures can be 'bad barrels' that exacerbate unethical behaviors over and above the deviousness of any single individual" (p. 58).

In action: The encouragement in each application chapter is to pay attention to your data. For instance, which of the HRO practices may aid in addressing bullying? (Salin & Hoel, 2011) and/or creating civil discourse on divisive issues? Rehearsal 11.2 provides a window for reflecting on HRO practices that you might have found in your data and/or of value in your application in other contexts. As you reflect on HRO practices, give thought to stories you can tell tied to a given practice. Also, check out the online resource, an interview by the "Communication Coach," Dr. Alex Lyon, with Dr. Ryan Bisel (www.youtube.com/watch?v=drWWKqn8PuQ&t=2s).

Rehearsal 11.2 High Reliability Organizational Practices and Stories

Purpose: Reflect on HRO practices that then inspire you to engage in stories that co-create highly ethical cultures.

Directions: Most of us can tell tragic, hard-to-hear stories (harassment, ostracism, bullying, etc.). While these stories are important in terms of confronting wrongdoing, this Rehearsal is based on the claim that we can be proactive by telling positive stories. Review each HRO practice or "value commitments" listed in what follows (c.f., Bisel, 2018). Then, identify a story you could bring up formally or informally to encourage this practice. In addition, consider instances in your data of ethical heroes that merit attention.

1. **Preoccupation with Failure**. "Careful attention to weak signals of failure and define the mistakes that cannot or should not be made explicitly" (Bisel, 2018, p. 196). Example: You hear about a co-worker who said, "We best not minimize this error just because it was rare. Let's discuss what we can learn from this." You decide to share this story at a new employee orientation.
   Story summary and when to share: ______________________________

   ____

   ____

2. **Reluctance to Simplify.** Shift from anxiety-reducing practices that create simple labels for complex situations that require time for problem-solution analysis. Example: You hear a leader say, "Let's avoid blaming this on any one person. That is too easy. What procedures might we analyze?"
   Story summary and when to share: ______________________________

   ____

   ____

3. **Sensitivity to Operations**. Resolving problems when they are small by being "attentive to the front line, where the real work gets done" (Weick & Sutcliffe, 2001, p. 12) as opposed to assuming upper management knows best. Example: As part of a leadership team, when the CEO asks, "What do we need to do to be sure the front line knows they can talk to us before something gets to be a major issue?" You share his question as part of a story about varied initiatives to improve operations.
   Story summary and when to share: ______________________________

   ____

   ____

4. **Commitment to Resilience**. Learning from stressors (i.e., small and big crises) to regain stability by developing redundancy through backup systems, cross-training, etc. Example: You learn about one unit where cross-training and review processes are in place. You also hear and then develop a story that captures how these practices ensure everyone is on the same page when the next challenge emerges.

   ____

   ____

5. **Deference to Expertise**. Empowering members with the best understanding of the situation to make decisions. Example: You share a story about a prior organization where

supervisors and upper management agreed on practices that placed decision-making in the hands of those on the front line holding the right information.

____

____

After reviewing these five practices, reflect on and write about a commitment to share and co-create one or more of these HRO value commitments.

____

____

____

____

In summary, this storytelling practice, like the others, aids in creating "small wins" and making "here and now" ethics talk the norm. In doing so, you co-create highly ethical cultures. Consistent with CCO theorists, we need to attend not just to interpersonal communication practices but also macro structures that shape our practices, such as rituals (Cooren, 2004). One way to think about this move toward improved ethical organizing practices is to reflect on and then share stories informed by HRO practices. This step aids in reinforcing the fourth practice—normalizing ethical talk.

4. Normalize Ethics Talk

<u>Defined</u>: Engaging in small, daily, "here and now" positive communication practices where ethics talk is part of formal and informal interactions.

<u>Rationale</u>: This practice holds promise for creating a "contagious quality" such that members of the organization are more likely to give voice to upward dissent and use ethical terms to talk about everyday situations (Zanin, Bisel, & Adame, 2016, p. 150).

<u>Theory and Research</u>: Bisel (2018) grounds his model for his model of "Organizational Moral Learning" (OML) in neuroscience. This research documents how, from as early as six months old, humans have an intuitive sense of right and wrong. Yet, other research shows that in our organizations, without concerted efforts, these intuitions are not voiced or critiqued. As a result, there is a tendency toward "pluralistic ignorance," defined as "a widespread *mis*perception of group norms by individual group members" (Bisel, 2018, p. 82). This misperception flows from the fallacy in our own thinking that others do not share our concerns over moral discrepancies. Such thinking may lead an employee, for example, to assume that no one else is concerned about bullying. We assume that no one sees a problem, and perhaps we should not see one either or maintain silence (Goodpaster, 2007).

This tendency toward silence, not addressing ethical lapses, has prompted us in our own practices to shift away from training or education tied to models of moral development (e.g., Piaget, 1932; Kohlberg, 1981). As noted earlier, improvements in ethical decision-making require more than improved cognition or critical reflection. In aligning the OCA model with a constructivist approach, we assume the need to move beyond an individual cognitive development model to a holistic approach grounded in organizational learning. We may develop, for instance, at the highest level of Kohlberg's model and only become adept at critiquing the moral failures of others. In addition, we tend to come up with moral reasoning after a decision has been made. Those reasons may, in time, shift or change, and are influenced by others in the organization and thus, in turn, influence future decisions. Bisel's contention, then, is not that verbal reasoning is unimportant, or that training should not occur but that organizational members have private moral concerns and aspirations that they tend to keep private. The goal should be to find ways to draw out these concerns and allow them to shape and improve ethical decision-making. Making the norm to surface these concerns responds to a major thread introduced in Chapter 4 on how a CCO perspective should prompt us to attend to the ways communication processes create and are created by ethics (Meisenbach, 2006).

Bisel (2018) turns to the classic story of "The Emperor's New Clothes" to illustrate research supporting our tendency to remain silent. This story depicts numerous adults who fear speaking the truth about the emperor. The emperor has been tricked into thinking he has grand new clothes when, in fact, he is naked. The cost of speaking the truth is assumed to be too high by those he rules. Indeed, it is a child who gives voice to the obvious—the emperor is naked.

In the world outside of this story, Bisel and colleagues label this tendency to remain silent as the "Moral Mum Effect" (Bisel, Kelley, Ploeger, & Messersmith, 2011). An awareness of the moral mum effect provides an additional rationale to engage in and affirm statements that normalize ethics talk. Research supports the contention that "here-and-now" talk infused with explicitly moralized language makes a difference. For instance, subordinates were more forthcoming with their private moral concerns when their bosses were known to introduce explicitly moralized language (Zanin, Bisel, & Adame, 2016).

<u>In Action</u>: This turn to normalize ethics talk prompts several questions about the organizations you study, work for, and/or serve. Reflect as well on your own practices that co-create "small wins." Place a checkmark if you tend to hear:

- ___ Leaders reference ethics (doing what's right) in meetings or in hallways.
- ___ Members refer to ethics as a major reason for action or inaction.
- ___ Naysayers are affirmed for giving voice to what might be important considerations.
- ___ Encouragement is given to focus on progress and learning rather than perfection.
- ___ Leaders and/or members ask questions about the ethical risks involved in a decision.
- ___ Members talk about the cost of doing the wrong thing.

Continue this reflection by placing a checkmark by the following phrases if they reflect on what you hear in organizations where you work, study, or serve.

- ___"We have to get better at just doing the right thing."
- ___"We do not tolerate abusive language toward any employee."
- ___"My gut tells me something is not right about that idea."
- ___"We need to gain all the relevant information and be transparent about it."

As you review your checkmarks, consider the implications for the organization you are studying and/or are part of now. A high number (seven or more) of checkmarks suggests the need to affirm the value of and continue to focus on making ethics talk part of daily interactions. In contrast, you should consider communication implications aimed at developing "here and now" ethics talk, especially modeled by leaders. Such "here and now" talk should consider inclusivity and belonging practices for the overlooked barriers to veterans developing resilience before and after existing totalistic organizations (e.g., military) (Howe & Wilson, 2024).

We turn now to a final ethical practice consistent with the idea of shifting away from either/or thinking via the practice of reframing.

5. Reframe Value Tensions

Defined: Communication inherently involves responses or ways of framing (interpreting and responding) to value tensions (e.g., long-term vs. short-term; transparency vs secrecy).

Rationale: Developing communication competence in responding to value tensions is an integral part of co-creating highly ethical organizational communication. One critical step in this process is to shift "either/or" thinking/framing by responding with more nuanced options, such as both/and or selecting aspects of each tension that can be integrated.

Theory and Research: Which of the following have you heard, said, or knew needed to be said:

- "This change is just happening too quickly."
- "It is about time someone paid attention to the big picture, what will help us in the long run."
- "Management makes decisions, and we have no clue what was involved and if we were heard."

Each of these statements represents inevitable tensions—"too fast, too slow," or "short term–long term," or "high or low involvement in decision making." A final practice for co-creating highly ethical organizations is about attending to cultural data in light of value tensions. Value tensions are not viewed as a problem but rather an opportunity to improve reflection and dialogue, which are tied to our three big questions: What are we creating? What do we want to create? What forms of communication will get us there? These questions, if applied to cultural data, provide a way to enrich our understanding of and ability to proactively address ethical concerns in the here-and-now.

The research and theory connected with dialectical or "tension centered" approaches are rich, diverse, and expansive. To set the stage for application, we first illustrate a complex national value tension before reviewing three major value tensions and providing a rehearsal. An online updated case on *Google in China* is also provided.

What role might national-level value tensions have on the economy? On contributing to a financial crisis?

A classic study of 16 country cultures by Hofstede (2009) and colleagues indicated that the US values of individualism and short-term orientation contributed to the financial crisis in 2008. They found that US business leaders scored higher than any of the other countries on seeking personal wealth and this year's profits. The practical insight is that a focus on or a framing of individualism (personal profit) over collectivism (what is best for the whole) and a second dialectic, short-term (this year's profits) over long-term orientation (investing profit for the future) created major problems beyond any given organization. The implication is that leaders could and should explore questions that critique decisions, such as "How might we frame these tensions as both/and, not either or?" "How might we address the concerns of stockholders in the short and long term while also addressing larger societal needs while still attending to sufficient individual profit?" (c.f., Li, Sun, Tao, & Lee, 2021; Nicotera & Cushman, 1992; Weaver, 2001).

The preceding study sets the stage for exploring value tensions inherent in organizing: short-term profit–long-term sustainability; centralized–distributed decision-making; macro–micro environment (Frederick, 1995). These tensions involve intertwined issues with ethics. However, the tasks and challenges are considerably more formidable than a simple "discover your organizational culture's values," as popular formulas suggest (Frederick, 1995, p. 5). Reflection on the interdependency of each of the three value sets provides a foundation for understanding and improving our framing practices through dialogic practices (Barge et al., 2008; Tracy, 2004). The goal, therefore, is not to view the tension as the problem but to frame these tensions with ethical mindfulness (Jian, 2007).

Economizing: Short-Term Profit and Long-Term Sustainability

A first set of tensions occurs between short- and long-term sustainability or use Fredericks word-economizing. The economizing continuum involves communicative processes tied to the value tension of short-term profit values and human values of sustainable cooperation. One accepted measure of economizing is monetary profit and loss. However, the bottom line of profits is insufficient as a measure of effectiveness (c.f., Chapter 13). Other measures revolve around the interests of employees, customers, and other stakeholders. Thus, the goal is to avoid framing this tension as an either/or as if attending to one end of this dialectic precludes attending to the other. Consider the problems created by a short-term profit. For example, Enron, before the ethical scandals went public, was a strong culture in a negative sense. A strong value set kept those at the top embedded in a value that focused on short-term profit to the detriment of employees and other stakeholders. The lack of integrity as a core value meant that the company lost its balance in its efforts to place profit as the only value (Seeger & Ulmer, 2003; Ulmer, Sellnow, & Seeger, 2015) and one that contributed to a self-serving value set and unethical practice (Lyon, 2008; Lyon & Ulmer, 2010).

Power Distancing: Centralized-Distributed Decision Making

Power distancing, a term introduced by Hofstede (2003), refers to communicative practices in response to a centralized-distributed tension in decision-making. We use this term, as opposed to Frederick's "power aggrandizing," as a way to get at where decision-making rests. This tension references a political metaphor (Morgan, 2006; Bolman & Deal, 2008) to draw attention to issues of power and communication patterns that may contribute to abuses of power or aid in democratizing decision-making processes (Deetz, 1992). Understanding both poles of this tension places leaders in a position to engage in dialogue on the ethical implications of how this tension is framed.

One end of the pole, "centralized," concentrates power in a hierarchy when a rank order and/or coercive power is imposed. This hierarchical focus is not inherently necessary to be profitable or successful. Giving allegiance to such values may "divert a company from making effective use of resources" (Frederick, 1995, p. 57). Consider, for example, leaders who become too concerned with maintaining position and power and, as a result, cease to adapt strategically to the interests of customers or employees (Kotter & Heskett, 1992). Yet, as noted, hierarchy or high-power distance is not inevitably a problem. Even in low power distance countries, such as in the West, military organizations may have similar structures or chains of command.

In contrast, distributed decision-making refers to various units having a certain level of autonomy over resources and decisions. The assumption is that decisions are often best made by individuals closer to the process or problem they are charged to address. For instance, a case analysis of the Columbia shuttle incident revealed that despite an awareness of the need for changes after the Challenger tragedy, inter-organizational structures were still in place (Garner, 2006). In the case of Korean Airlines (KAL) crashes, Korea is second highest in the world on Hofstede's (2003) power distancing scale, with pilots scoring even higher. In the flight deck context, this meant having "an unchanging routine . . . unchallenged hierarchy" (Helmreich & Merritt, 2000, p. 9). After close scrutiny of the fatal crash of KAL 1997, leaders identified the reticence of first officers to give voice to danger. Training was instituted to give "deference to expertise" versus centralized authority (Bisel, 2018, p. 197). Their safety record has been spotless since 1999.

Ecologizing: Macro and Micro Environment Values

Ecologizing focuses on managing macro environment and micro environment values. On the one hand, the macro environment interweaves values conducive to the perpetuation of an entire community, including the flora, fauna, and physical features that constitute the organization's ecosystem. On the other hand, in tension with the macro values is a concern over the micro environment, which includes allegiance to stockholders seeking sufficient profits. The tendency may be to pit one value against the other. Various organizations have sought to avoid this either/or framing practice. For instance, the opposition of CEOs from over 30 corporations, including General Electric and Exxon/Mobil, to the US pulling out of the Paris Climate Accord indicates a value set on making progress with regard to ecologizing values (McGregor, 2017).

Two key questions need to be asked about this trend toward sustainable practices. First, does the popularity of "sustainability" translate into meaningful and accountable changes that impact the relationship of organizations to the environment? Ihlen (2015), in a study of 76 of the 100 top organizations on the Fortune Global list, found that while they all mentioned being sustainable, their definitions were ambiguous and framed sustainability in terms of business success. She ends by noting that "aspirational talk will not dissolve the discrepancy between business goals and achieving sustainability" (p. 149). Others suggest that a focus on ecological concerns creates a false dichotomy between the environment and the economy (Pal & Jenkins, 2014). Instead, a focus needs to be given to framing processes that ensure accountability or a "license to critique" by multiple stakeholders so that options may be explored to address these conflicts (Christensen, Morsing, & Thyssen, 2017). Indeed, one study of the top 100 Chinese manufacturing companies found CSR practices were "considered as an investment" by meeting the expectations of stakeholders by "maximizing . . . profitability in both the short and long term" (Bai et al., 2023, p. 19). In addition, Hossain et al. (2023) found support for the idea that CEO equity incentives for higher CCR created a better long-term valuation.

One case study exemplifies an organization moving in a proactive direction. "Interface," the world leader in modular carpets, made a major shift in their business practices in the mid-1990s. Until this time, Interface primarily responded to mandated emission controls. Customers began asking what they were doing for the environment. They did not have an answer. A group in their research division decided they should bring together a global task force to discern options. The group asked their CEO, Ray Anderson, to launch this task force and give a kick-off speech with an "environmental vision." However, at that point, he had no vision. Then, in what he describes as "pure serendipity," Mr. Anderson had been sent a copy of Paul Hawken's book *The Ecology of Commerce*. The book was like a "spear in the chest experience—he read it and 'wept.'" His speech challenged the research team to lead the company to sustainability. The end result included impressive accountability measures. The average product carbon footprint has been reduced by 35% since 2008 and about 50% since they first started in 1996. The "Mission Zero" in terms of greenhouse gases has also meant a 95% reduction from 1996 to 2016. These efforts also reduced business costs. Their work has been proactive, including a code of ethics and guiding values. This code resulted in community partnerships ranging from affordable housing projects to creating an ethical supply chain and projects focused on improving school health and safety (Interface, n.d.). Their current CEO, Laura Herd, in the Interfaces 2023 Impact Report, seeks to build on Anderson's legacy with a "desire to push the limit of what was possible" by striving "to be generous to people and the planet" with a "coordinated global operating model" (Interface Impact Report, 2023). This *Interface* story illustrates Goodpaster's (2007) stages of development of organizational conscience, moving from compliance with external laws or standards to an understanding of the interdependence between corporate success and ecological responsibility (c.f., Livesey, Hartman, Stafford, & Shearer, 2009).

In Action: The goal in reframing tensions is to improve not only mindfulness and dialogue but also co-create macro-level processes, such as rituals combined with micro-practices, such as interpersonal communication norms, that will ensure continued learning. The potential for improved ethical decision-making occurs when members learn to talk about ethics in terms of framing options. Three tensions: a) economizing; b) power-distancing; and c) ecologizing, are summarized in Table 11.2 to aid you in completing Rehearsal 11.3 that follows.

Table 11.2 Three Value Tension

Tension	*Defined*	*Measures*	*Goal-Ideal*	*Research Example*
Short Term Profit–Long-Term Sustainability	Communicative processes are tied to the value tension of short-term profit values and human values of sustainable cooperation.	Monetary profit and loss, as well as employees, customers, and other stakeholders.	Values promoting cooperative interactions based on fairness, equality, and caring for both individual, group, and societal needs.	Storytelling to empower female engineers to improve self-efficacy and a culture of engagement (Fogg-Rogers, Sardo, & Boushel, 2017).
Centralized–High power distance) Distributed (Low power distance).	Centralized inequality in decision-making power vs. distributed values equality.	Communication patterns that aid in democratizing decision-making process that also attend to potential power abuses (Deetz, 1992).	Decisions are best made by individuals closer to the process or problem they are charged to address.	Example 1: Safety failure of Korean Airlines in high-power distance context decision making (Helmreich & Merritt, 2000). Example 2: NASA Space Shuttle disasters (Garner, 2006).
Macro–Micro Environment Values	Macro value—conducive to the perpetuation of the ecosystem vs. the micro value—a concern over stockholder profit.	Decision-making involves ecological concerns and profit margins.	Proactive in gauging short and long-term ecological and economic impacts.	Example 1: Short/long term value of CSR (Bai et al., 2023). Example 2: Positive Case (Interface Impact Report, 2023).

As you engage in reframing tensions, recall the goal is to move from either/or framing to a "both/and" perspective. Give thought to the organization you are studying. For instance, for a university, this could be increasing enrollment. For another, it could be fulfilling a mission such as ending poverty or creating technology that connects people. Now, consider additional goals that would increase the organization's ethical stance. For example, a current goal could be to end poverty, but an additional goal could be to protect the environment at the same time. The key then would be to encourage dialogue over questions that would reframe these competing goals as ones that could be both/and. For instance:

- How can we increase enrollment and improve faculty success?
- How can we end poverty and protect the environment?
- How can we sell enhanced social media platforms and help to reduce loneliness?

Rehearsal 11.3 Reframing Value Tension

Purpose: Apply your cultural data by selecting a relevant value tension to gain insight into your organization and personal ethical development.

Directions: Review Table 11.2 and select a value tension that emerged in your data and/or in an organization you work or serve.

1. What enacted element(s) best captured this value tension?

2. What is said (or not said) when members talk about this value tension? How was it framed?

3. How could you frame this tension in ways that avoid either/or thinking?

Personal Reflection: Imagine someone listening to the way you talked about this value tension. What might they conclude about the way you frame this tension? Does your talk reflect selecting one value over the other? Silence over this tension? How might you improve the way you communicate about and frame this value tension?

____

____

____

Connections: Other Tensions

Paying close attention to these value conflicts is not an easy leadership task. Earlier, we indicated that these three value tensions are not intended to be exhaustive. For example, based on Lyon (2017), you could explore transparency versus secrecy. Rather than framing these as either/or, questions should be asked about what is best and right. Furthermore, concerning a different tension, "benevolent patronizing versus agency" surfaced in the context of a multinational relationship with community stakeholders regarding agency (Manzie, 2018). Another value tension could be diversity versus uniformity. A tension could also exist between resistance versus withdrawal in response to mistreatment. In one study, minority members who perceived maltreatment faced a dilemma: resistance might result in more mistreatment, whereas reacting by disengaging might result in strengthening the power structure that kept them from being heard in the first place (Meares et al., 2004). Such a dilemma brings home the types of challenges involved in responding to ethical dialectic tensions, yet such challenges are what, with reflection and dialogue with others, aid us in our growth toward ethical ideals. In a different case study, one focused on the importance of "here and now" ethical dialogue; police officers engaged in a discussion over the challenge of accepting meals as a gift at restaurants. The richness of their discourse revealed the complexity of such situations that may be framed as an ethical dilemma (accepting a bribe vs. rudeness for not accepting a gift) or as a tension between an ethical universal vs. relativism (Jovanovic & Wood, 2006). The authors conclude that the officers explored the complexity of this daily, real situation in ways that went beyond a "then and there" exploration of a case study. Their dialogue revealed the nuanced and challenging nature of daily, mundane, yet ethically loaded events.

As you consider these and other value tensions, we provide an additional online Rehearsal to brainstorm other tensions that you see as critical in the process of making ethical decisions. Again, focus on reflections that will aid in developing small wins that you can enact in your organizations and through applications to the organization you are studying.

Summary

Organizations, members, and leaders with a conscience are a pressing need in our society. The statistics are alarming, as is the significance of ethical abuse in terms of fairness, safety, and our environment. However, enacting an honest portrayal involves more than being aware of these abuses. The OCA model, consistent with constructivist approaches, attends to the power of context. Recall the first mental shift tied to the analysis process: Mental shift 1: *From cultural analysis as identifying variables impacting performance or viewing culture as a metaphor to attending to daily enactments that shape and are shaped by culture.* The five practices introduced in this chapter are all about daily "here and now" enactments that then create a highly ethical culture supportive of organizational moral learning (Bisel, 2018). These practices, though not exhaustive, can at first seem like an overwhelming task. Additional online Rehearsals are provided to support professional and personal development.

1. Engage in greetings to create connection and trust.
2. Ask open questions to reduce the gaps.
3. Share stories of positive ethical actions.
4. Normalize ethics talk.
5. Reframe value tensions.

However, the task need not be daunting. Recall that as early as six months, we share a sense of moral intuition. Thus, we invite you to take a breath. Do the next right thing. As you do so, consider completing the online Rehearsal to prompt further reflection on ethics and culture to co-create "Civic Discourse."

Discussion Questions

1. What are some of the manifestations of an ethical vacuum in organizations?
2. What ethical gaps stand out most to you when you reflect on organizational life?
3. Reflect also on the gaps between your ethical ideals and your communicative behaviors. What gaps do you see there? What do you consider to be the foundational motivation for your ethical framework?
4. Describe the difference between a "surface" attempt to make an organization more ethical as opposed to a cultural approach to engrain ethics deeply within the organizational culture. Can you think of examples of each?
5. How is a values tension approach to ethics different from a rules approach?

References

Bai, K., Ullah, F., Arif, M., Erfanian, S., & Urooge, S. (2023). Stakeholder-centered corporate governance and corporate sustainable development: Evidence from CSR practices in the top companies by market capitalization at shanghai stock exchange of China. *Sustainability, 15(4)*, 2990. https://doi.org/10.3390/su15042990

Barge, J., Lee, M., Maddux, K., Nabring, R., & Townsend, B. (2008). Managing dualities in planned change initiatives. *Journal of Applied Communication Research, 36(4)*, 364–390. https://doi.org/10.1080/00909880802129996

Bisel, R. (2018). *Organizational moral learning: A communication approach*. New York: Routledge.

Bisel, R., Kelley, K., Ploeger, N., & Messersmith, J. (2011). Workers' moral mum effect: On facework and unethical behavior in the workplace. *Communication Studies, 62(2)*, 153–170. https://doi.org/10.1080/10510974.2010.551314

Bohannon, M. (February 26, 2024). Boeing safety culture can be "inadequate and confusing," report finds after 737 max issues. *Forbes*.

Bolch, B. (April 14, 2018). Red Sanders' impact on UCLA football has lasted well past his death, 60 years ago Tuesday. Los Angeles Times. Retreived from https://www.latimes.com/sports/ucla/la-sp-ucla-red-sanders-20180813-story.html

Bolman, L., & Deal, T. (2008). *Reframing organizations* (4th ed.). San Francisco: Jossey-Bass.

Boysen, 2nd, P. G. (2013). Just culture: A foundation for balanced accountability and patient safety. *Ochsner Journal, 13(3)*, 400–406. Retrieved from www.ncbi.nlm.nih.gov/pmc/articles/PMC3776518/

Christensen, L., Morsing, M., & Thyssen, O. (2017). License to critique: A communication perspective on sustainability standards. *Business Ethics Quarterly, 27(2)*, 239–262. https://doi.org/10.1017/beq.2016.66

Columbia Business School. (n.d.). *Aaron Feuerstein and Washington SyCip (MS '43) receive 1996 Botwinick prizes for ethics*. Retrieved from www.columbia.edu/cu/record/archives/vol22/vol22_iss3/Feuerstein_SyCip_Botwinick.html

Cooren, F. (2004). Textual agency: How texts do things in organizational settings. *Organization, 11*, 373–393. https://doi.org/10.1177/1350508404041998

Correll, S. J. (2017). SWS 2016 feminist lecture: Reducing gender biases in modern workplaces: A small wins approach to organizational change. *Gender & Society, 31(6)*, 725–750. https://doi.org/10.1177/0891243217738518

Deetz, S. (1992). *Democracy in an age of corporate colonization*. Albany: SUNY Press.

Dwyer, J., Karanikas, N., & Sav, A. (2023). Scoping review of peer-reviewed empirical studies on implementing high reliability organization theory. *Safety Science, 164*, 106178. https://doi.org/10.1016/j.ssci.2023.106178

Fogg-Rogers, L., Sardo, M., & Boushel, C. (2017). "Robots vs animals": Establishing a culture of public engagement and female role modeling in engineering higher education. *Science Communication, 39(2)*, 195–220. https://doi.org/10.1177/1075547017696169

Frederick, W. (1995). *Values, nature, culture in the American corporation*. New York: Oxford.

Garner, J. (2006). Masters of the universe? Resource dependency and interorganizational power relationships at NASA. *Journal of Applied Communication Research, 34*, 368–385. https://doi.org/10.1080/00909880600911249

Goodpaster, K. E. (2007). *Conscience and corporate culture*. Malden, MA: Blackwell Publishing.

Hamington, M. (2009). Business is not a game: The metaphoric fallacy. *Journal of Business Ethics, 86(4)*, 473–484. https://doi.org/10.1007/s10551-008-9859-0

Helmreich, R., & Merritt, A. (2000). Culture in the cockpit: Do Hofstede's dimensions replicate? *Journal of Cross Cultural Psychology, 31*, 283–301. https://doi.org/10.1177/0022022100031003001

Hofstede, G. (2003). *Culture's consequences: Comparing values, behaviors, institutions and organizations across nations*. Newbury Park, CA: Sage.

Hofstede, G. (2009). American culture and the 2008 financial crisis. *European Business Review, 21*, 307–312. https://doi.org/10.1108/09555340910970418

Hossain, A., Masum, A., Saadi, S., Benkraiem, R., & Das, N. (2023). Firm-level climate change risk and CEO equity incentives. *British Journal of Management, 34(3)*, 1387–1419. https://doi.org/10.1111/1467-8551.12652

Howe, W., & Wilson, S. (2024). Chapter 28 military exit and reentry to family, society, and work. In V. Miller & M. Poole (Eds.), *Organizational communication theory and research* (pp. 565–584). Berlin, Boston: De Gruyter Mouton. https://doi.org/10.1515/9783110718508-029

Ihlen, O. (2015). It is five minutes to midnight and all is quiet: Corporate rhetoric and sustainability. *Management Communication Quarterly, 29(1)*, 145–152. https://doi.org/10.1177/0893318914563145

Interface. (n.d.). Our sustainability journey—Mission zero. *Interface*. Retrieved from www.interfaceglobal.com/Sustainability/Interface-Story.aspx

Interface Impact Report. (2023). Retrieved from www.interface.com/content/dam/interfaceinc/interface/sustainability/global/esg/esg-report/Interface%202023%20ESG%20Impact%20Report.pdf

Jian, G. (2007). "Omega is a four-letter word": Toward a tension-centered model of resistance to information and communication technologies. *Communication Monographs, 74*, 517–540. https://doi.org/10.1080/03637750701716602

Jovanovic, S., & Wood, R.V. (2006). Communication ethics and ethical culture: A study of the ethics initiative in Denver city government. *Journal of Applied Communication Research, 34(4)*, 386–405. https://doi.org/10.1080/00909880600908633

King, Jr., M. L. (1963). *Why we can't wait?* New York: Harper & Row Publishers.

Kirby, E., Wieland, S., & McBride, M. (2013). Work-life conflict. In J. G. Oetzel & S. Ting-Toomey (Eds.), *The Sage handbook of conflict communication* (2nd ed., Chapter 14, pp. 377–402). Thousand Oaks, CA: Sage.

Kohlberg, L. (1981). *Essays on moral development, Vol. I: The philosophy of moral development*. San Francisco, CA: Harper & Row.

Kotter, J., & Heskett, J. (1992). *Corporate culture and performance*. New York: Macmillan.

Leonard, D., Swap, W., & Fraser, B. (2005). Deep smarts: How to cultivate and transfer enduring business wisdom [review of deep smarts: How to cultivate and transfer enduring business wisdom]. *Prometheus, 23(2)*, 239–242. https://doi.org/10.1080/08109020500099370

Li, J.-Y., Sun, R., Tao, W., & Lee, Y. (2021). Employee coping with organizational change in the face of a pandemic: The role of transparent internal communication. *Public Relations Review, 47(1)*, N.PAG. https://doi.org/10.1016/j.pubrev.2020.101984

Livesey, S., Hartman, C., Stafford, E., & Shearer, M. (2009). Performing sustainable development through eco-collaboration. *Journal of Business Communication, 46*, 423–454. https://doi.org/10.1177/0021943609338664

Lyon, A. (2008). The mis/recognition of Enron executives' competence as cultural and social capital. *Communication Studies, 59*, 371–387. https://doi.org/10.1080/10510970802467411

Lyon, A. (2017). *Case studies in courageous organizational communication: Research and practices for effective workplaces*. New York: Peter Lang.

Lyon, A., & Ulmer, R. R. (2010). Ethics in "big pharma": Communicating the risks of medicine. In J. Keyton & P. Shockley-Zalabak (Eds.), *Case studies for organizational communication* (3rd ed., pp. 350–356). Los Angeles: Roxbury.

Manzie, V. (2018). Applying the rhetoric of renewal model in a contemporary African context: Lessons learned from the royal Dutch shell oil crisis in Nigeria. *Journal of International Crisis and Risk Communication Research, 1(2)*, 201–224. https://doi.org/10.30658/jicrcr.1.2.2.

McClellan, J. G., & Sanders, M. L. (2013). (Re)organizing organizational communication pedagogy: Attending to the salient qualities of a communicative approach to organization. *Review of Communication, 13(4)*, 249–268. https://doi.org/10.1080/15358593.2014.886334

McGregor, J. (June, 2017). "Climate change is real": CEOs share their disappointment over Trump's Paris accord exit. *The Washington Post*. Retrieved from www.washingtonpost.com/news/on-leadership/wp/2017/06/01/ceos-make-final-pleas-to-trump-to-stay-in-paris-climate-agreement/?utm_term=.94e79d15c5fa

Meares, M., Oetzel, J., Torres, A., Derkacs, D., & Ginossar, T. (2004). Employee mistreatment and muted voices in the culturally diverse workplace. *Journal of Applied Communication Research, 32(1)*, 4–27. https://doi.org/10.1080/0090988042000178121

Meisenbach, R. (2006). Habermas' discourse ethics and principle of universalization as a moral framework for organizational communication. *Management Communication Quarterly, 20(1)*, 39–62. https://doi.org/10.1177/0893318906288277

Mirivel, J. (2014). *The art of positive communication: Theory and practice*. New York: Peter Lang.

Mirivel, J., & Lyon, A. (2023). *Positive communication for leaders: Proven strategies for inspiring unity and effecting change*. New York: Rowen & Littlefield.

Morgan, G. (2006). *Images of organization* (updated ed.). Newbury Park, CA: Sage.

National Whistleblowers Center. (n.d.). *Meet the whistleblowers*. Retrieved from www.whistleblowers.org

Nicotera, A., & Cushman, D. (1992). Organizational ethics: A within-organization view. *Journal of Applied Communication Research, 20*, 437–462. https://doi.org/10.1080/00909889209365348

O'Reilly, J., Robinson, S., & Schabram, K. (2013). The impact of ostracism on well-being in organizations. In R. Giacalone & M. Promisloeds (Eds.), *Handbook of unethical work behavior: Implications for individual well-being* (pp. 107–222). London: Routledge. https://doi.org/10.4324/9781315703848

Pal, M., & Jenkins, J. (2014). Reimagining sustainability: An interrogation of the corporate knights' global 100. *Environmental Communication, 8(3)*, 388–405. https://doi.org/10.1080/17524032.2014.906477

Paton, A., & Kotzee, B. (July, 2021). The fundamental role of storytelling and practical wisdom in facilitating the ethics education of junior doctors. *Health (London), 25(4)*, 417–433. https://doi.org/10.1177/1363459319889102

Pedersen, E. (2010). Modeling CSR: How managers understand the responsibilities of business towards society. *Journal of Business Ethics, 91*, 155–166. https://doi.org/10.1007/s10551-009-0078-0

Peters, T. (1979). Designing and executing "real" tasks. Unpublished Manuscript. Stanford University.

Peters, T. J. (1977). Patterns of winning and losing: Effects on approach and avoidance by friends and enemies. Unpublished Doctoral Dissertation. Stanford University.

Piaget, J. (1932). *The moral judgment of the child*. London: Routledge and Kegan Paul.

Pope St. Francis. (n.d.). *Encyclical letter Laudato Si' of the Holy Father Francis on care of our common home, no. 49*. Retrieved from http://w2.vatican.va/content/dam/francesco/pdf/encyclicals/documents/papa-francesco_20150524_enciclica-laudato-si_en.pdf

Porath, C. L., Gerbasi, A., & Schorch, S. L. (2015). The effects of civility on advice, leadership, and performance. *Journal of Applied Psychology, 100(5)*, 1527–1541. https://doi.org/10.1037/apl0000016

Salaszar, A., & Raggiuniti, J. (2016). Why does executive greed prevail in the United States and Canada but not in Japan? The pattern of low CEO pay and high worker welfare in Japanese corporations. *The American Journal of Comparative Law, 64(3)*, 721–744. https://doi.org/10.1093/ajcl/avw007

Salin, D., & Hoel, H. (2011). Organizational causes of workplace bullying. In S. Einarsen, H. Hoel, D. Zapf, & C. Cooper (Eds.), *Bullying and harassment in the workplace: Developments in theory, research, and practice* (2nd ed., pp. 227–243). New York: CRC Press.

Schein, E. H., & Schein, P. A. (2021). *Humble inquiry, second edition: The gentle art of asking instead of telling.* Berrett-Koehler.

Seeger, M. W., & Ulmer, R. R. (2001). Virtuous responses to organizational crisis: Aaron feuerstein and milt cole. *Journal of Business Ethics, 31*, 369–376. https://doi.org/10.1023/A:101075931

Seeger, M., & Ulmer, R. (2003). Explaining enron: Communication and responsible leadership. *Management Communication Quarterly, 17(1)*, 58–84. https://doi.org/10.1177/0893318903253436

Shafron, A. (June 29, 2002). Aaron Feurstein: Bankrupt and wealthy. *Aish.com.* Current Issues-Business Ethics. Retrieved from www.aish.com/ci/be/48881397.html

Tracy, S. (2004). Dialectic, contradiction, or double bind? Analyzing and theorizing employee reactions to organizational tension. *Journal of Applied Communication Research, 32*, 119–146. https://doi.org/10.1080/0090988042000210025

Ulmer, R. (2001). Effective crisis management through established stakeholder relationships. *Management Communication Quarterly, 14(4)*, 590–615. https://doi.org/10.1177/0893318901144003

Ulmer, R., Sellnow, T., & Seeger, M. (2015). *Effective crisis communication: Moving from crisis to opportunity* (3rd ed.). Thousand Oaks, CA: Sage Publications.

Vineberg, S. (1991). *Method actors: Three generations of an American acting style.* New York: Schirmer Books.

Weaver, G. (2001). Ethics programs in global businesses: Culture's role in managing ethics. *Journal of Business Ethics, 30.* https://doi.org/10.1023/A:1006475223493.

Weick, K. E. (1984). Small wins: Redefining the scale of social problems. *American Psychologist, 39(1)*, 40–49. https://doi.org/10.1037/0003-066X.39.1.40

Weick, K. E., & Sutcliffe, K. M. (2001). *Managing the unexpected: Assuring high performance in an age of complexity* (1st ed.). Jossey-Bass.

Whyte, D. (1994). *The heart aroused: Poetry and the preservation of the soul in corporate America.* New York: Doubleday.

Zanin, A. C., Bisel, R. S., & Adame, E. A. (2016). Supervisor moral talk contagion and trust-in-supervisor. *Management Communication Quarterly, 30(2)*, 147–163. https://doi.org/10.1177/0893318915619755/REF-LIST

Chapter 12

The Director's Chair

Symbolic Leadership

You influence the organizations you serve, regardless of your role and whether you are an informal or formal leader. This chapter focuses on your role in co-creating better social worlds—organizations that are more ethical, diverse, adaptive, and effective. As such, any leader is called to ethically respond to and interpret organizational events, very similar to the way the director shapes and encourages the meaning of a play carried through the performance of actors. While the leader has an important role to play, organizational meaning is an interactive, co-creation process between leaders and organizational members. Seven positive leadership communication practices are introduced: 1) model the cultural significance of all communicative actions; 2) live and tell stories to co-create ethical values and communication norms; 3) enact rituals to reframe change and continuity; 4) bring history into the present to reframe dialectic tensions; 5) ethically reframe events through language that provides significant choice; 6) co-construct pathways to meaningful and ethical engagement; and 7) rely on multiple frames for productive conflict management and for effective problem/solution identification.

1. Articulate cultural analysis goals and benefits
2. Explore culture as co-construction
3. Reflect on enacted elements
4. Identify enacted elements via multiple methods
5. Interpret thematic action and OCA
6. Co-create positive communication applications

Step Five: Co-Create Positive Communication Applications

Symbolic Leadership

Objectives

- Explain the role of the leader in reframing.
- Explore symbolic forms through which the leader shapes meanings within the culture.
- Recognize ideology and identification as forms of unobtrusive control.
- Develop optimal competence as a leader through multi-frame thinking.
- Evaluate yourself as a cultural leader.

DOI: 10.4324/9781003482529-16

Stage Terms

Framing/reframing	Symbolic leadership	Spin
Vision	Contrast	Unobtrusive control

The following quotes reflect the chapter's aims:

> Good leadership requires you to surround yourself with people of diverse perspectives who can disagree with you without fear of retaliation.
>
> Doris Kearns Goodwin (2018). Pulitzer Prize winner, *Leadership in Turbulent Times*

> Leadership . . . is categorically humbling because it is virtually impossible for an individual to accumulate enough knowledge to figure out all of the answers. Interdependence and constant change become a way of life in which humility in the face of this complexity has become a critical survival skill.
>
> Edgar H. Schein and Peter Schein (2018). *Humble Leadership: The Power of Relationships, Openness, and Trust.*

Imagine This . . .

You are about to enter a job interview (or performance review). You are asked to reflect on and share what you seek to model and practice as a leader. Got it? Now, take a minute to respond to the following prompt. We find it helpful again and again in our learning journey to put down what we already know and seek to practice and develop.

What three leadership communication and culture practices are you seeking to practice and develop?

____

____

____

Next step? First, give thought to what inspired your list. Family? Current or prior leaders? Stories heard? AI? Then, as a next step, review your list with a peer, mentor, friend, and/or family member. Consider asking them:

- What on this list do you agree with about leadership?
- What would you add, clarify, and/or remove?
- Which of the items do you see me as doing well now?
- What areas do you see me needing to develop?

We trust this one activity challenged, encouraged, and inspired you. In full disclosure, we continue to be challenged to discover the best ways to develop and grow in our formal and informal leadership roles. We accept that the analysis and development of our own leadership communication practices and those of the organizational leaders is a journey—we can always grow. We value Schein and Schein's (2018) opening quote, which focused on the role of humility.

In this chapter, we again stress the focus of the OCA model *on* ***fostering the co-creation of positive organizations by developing implications through the analysis of enacted elements that both shape and are shaped by communication***.

In this chapter, we review the power of leaders' shaping meaning through the lens of the acting/theatre metaphor and a core concept of leadership—"reframing." Seven positive leadership practices are introduced. We conclude by returning to your opening reflection on leadership development goals.

Leaders as Directors: The Co-Creation of Meaning

In theater or film, the director plays a critical role in shaping the performance of actors to create a unified artistic vision. To a novice in theatre, then it might seem the director literally sets the stage, ensuring the script is carried out with his or her vision. In this first section, we review the mental shift on co-creation before attending to the influence of gender and national culture and the stage-setting significance of reframing in terms of the kinds of meanings leaders influence.

MEANING AS CO-CREATION

Recall with us the mental shift *from seeing our role as just one actor on the stage to daily enactments with others (including directors/leaders) that create and recreate the culture.* This shift is about challenging leaders/directors to do more than just have a clear interpretation of the play or vision for the organization. In addition, they need to do more than communicate and motivate actors to call on their best efforts to realize the vision. However, the reality is that, in the end, the production is a cooperative venture between the talents of the scriptwriter, director, and actors. In short, the role of a leader is more than planning, controlling, and coordinating organizational resources and systems. Emphasis is needed on the intangible leadership functions of communication and meaning creation. The leader is called to see their role in ethically responding to and interpreting organizational events, very similar to the way the director shapes and encourages the meaning of a play carried through the performance of actors. For instance, Alvesson (2002) notes that there is a symbiotic relationship between leadership and culture. Leaders emerge because organization members see a unique fit between the leader and the culture. As such, the organizing and communicative processes that constitute the organization shape the decision-making related to who to hire as a leader. Consider the following conclusions drawn from research on leadership.

- A person is more likely to be sought out as a leader if they are viewed as being civil, that is, engaged in politeness with regard to others within norms for respect (Porath, Gerbasi, & Schorch, 2015).
- "Discursive" leaders constitute the culture through communicative behaviors that, with others, recreate, maintain, and change organizing processes (Fairhurst, 2008). They "interpret experience to impart meaning and purpose through phrases of meaning and passion" (Bolman & Deal, 2017, p. 353). They illustrate this interpretive role through often-quoted words by President Franklin D. Roosevelt. On a national level, during WWII, he assured citizens, "The only thing we have to fear is fear itself."

- Leaders create and manage culture in direct forms, such as designing systems and procedures for work, allocating resources, and giving or withholding rewards. They also have influence over what they choose to endorse as a rite or ritual (Keyton, 2005).
- Leaders' greatest influence on culture may be through more informal means, such as personal modeling and sacrificial service in their interactions with employees.

Given these findings, consider the online Rehearsal where we provide a survey to gauge your level of commitment to the power of modeling self-sacrificial behaviors. Such a commitment has been shown to influence citizenship behavior for the environment (Qu, Xu, Sun, & Li, 2022). This type of organizational citizenship behavior refers to the "spontaneous performance of work by employees that is not explicitly expressed in their job duties, but is beneficial to organizational effectiveness as a whole" (Chen, Zhang, & Yang, 2024, p. 340).

Whether formal or informal, we need to be aware of the impact of overlooked influences.

LEADER–CULTURE RELATIONSHIP–GENDER AND NATIONAL CULTURE

In previous chapters, we stressed that there are limits to the influence of leaders on culture. Since culture emerges from the interaction of organization members over time, organizational leaders can inspire or shape vision, but the members of the organization must implement the vision before it becomes a reality. Furthermore, the complexity of the leader–culture relationship also needs to be seen in light of leadership practices constructed in gender and national culture-based discursive practices. Concerning gender, Walker and Aritz (2015) found that women were not selected for leadership roles based on differing discursive practices. They note that it is likely that "students and employees hold unexamined stereotypes about the type of talk that may be recognized as 'leadership' in certain organizational settings" (p. 474). Concerning national culture differences, as introduced in Chapter 9, cultures differ in terms of preferences for "power distance" with western norms favoring more direct communication styles, lower power distance, less rigidity in roles (Driskill, 1995; Hofstede, Hofstede, & Minkov, 2010). Our focus in this chapter will be on the direct and indirect ways that formal and informal leaders influence the creation, maintenance, and change of culture. Kouzes and Posner (2017) write that while leaders cannot create or change the culture unilaterally, they can create the conditions for cultural change. This creation process means embracing and modeling new values and assumptions, interacting with and listening to employees, and responding appropriately to resistance to change.

The foundational concept of "reframing" is central to the co-creation of the meaning process.

REFRAMING

The term "framing" or "reframing" refers to adopting a different perspective or interpretation of an event or person. When we refer to reframing as a central function of leadership, we mean that leaders have the opportunity to shape and/or change interpretations of organizational events. However, Bryman (1996) cautions that leaders are not unlimited in their ability to shape meanings in organizations. He notes that organization members are not "passive receptacles but imaginative consumers of a leader's visions and of manipulated cultural artifacts" (p. 286). Some leaders, when facing a financial crisis in their organizations, might frame the emergency as a time to seek out and eliminate weak programs, a perspective that would lead to turf protection and competition. Another leader facing the same challenge could frame the crisis as "a time for the family to pull together and make joint sacrifices for the common good." This framing might lead to stronger ties and a common commitment to making it through the financial crisis. Each of these ways of framing has constraints. The leader who uses the crisis to set organizational priorities may have relational fallout but will also avoid the democratic pitfall of weakening all programs rather than making hard decisions. The second approach will build common ties and commitments but may result in overall weakening. Each framing process then can be viewed in terms of the kind of culture co-created as a result. An effective leader, indeed, may engage in such reflection with their team in the process of discerning framing options.

WHAT KIND OF MEANINGS OR INTERPRETATIONS CAN LEADERS INFLUENCE?

Leaders set organizational perceptions on a number of important areas that affect every other decision within the organization. *Leaders can influence perceptions of external threats.* History is rife with leaders who have used perceptions of external threats to divert attention from internal problems or to create internal unity to deal with a common enemy. Sometimes, employees have become complacent and need to be more aware of potential threats than they currently are. A perception of external threat gives urgency and focus to their work. *Leaders can also influence perceptions of competitors and benchmark institutions.* One university president we observed had a massive impact on his school when he influenced faculty to accept they were no longer competing against small in-state colleges but should consider larger regional universities as their "benchmark" comparisons. This changed views of faculty salaries, research expectations, student admission standards, and many other decisions within the university. *Leaders often create the internal perceptions of primary stakeholder groups to whom the organization should be accountable.* A central question for any organization is: To whom are we accountable? Who has an interest in what we do? An organization that sees itself as accountable primarily to shareholders might focus more on short-term profits. In contrast, one that sees itself as also accountable to employees and customers might stress balanced values of profitability, environment, responsibility, and safety. *A leader, through overt and subtle messages, also shapes what is most valued.* Is it profit? Service? Is it people? Civility? The environment? Too often, the leader may send inadvertent messages about what is most valued by where he spends time, what she talks about, and/or rewards. Longitudinal research documents that organizational founders were influential in shaping both management and worker values and rules (Shockley-Zalabak & Morley, 1994). Finally, a *leader creates meaning by co-creating and casting a vision for the future.* Leaders distill and disseminate a vision of hope by addressing present challenges and future hopes of organizational members. Bolman and Deal (2017) state:

> Vision is particularly important in times of crisis and uncertainty. When people are in pain, when they are confused and uncertain, or when they feel despair and hopelessness, they desperately seek meaning and hope.
>
> (p. 355)

This hope-creating role, however, is not about a leader creating a vision in isolation and then persuading organization members to adopt it. Instead, they co-create the vision by listening to hints throughout the organization. Bolman and Deal (2017) note that they listen for needs, deficiencies, dreams, and goals and then synthesize all the varied input into a compelling image of the future. Deetz, Tracy, and Simpson (2000) contrast mission, strategic planning, and vision. They define "mission" as the direction the organization wants to go and the strategic plan as a roadmap for getting there, but they say that the vision is the compelling image of what it will be like once you arrive at that destination. They conclude that a good vision must be:

> realistic enough to create a recognizable picture of the future, powerful enough to generate commitment to performance, coherent enough to provide coordination, and open enough that others can make it their own. If this is done the vision can inspire and motivate, provide direction and enable benchmarking progress toward the future.
>
> (p. 52)

The power of these various reframing practices should be clear. Rehearsal 12.1 provides an opportunity to reflect on your experiences with these various meaning-shaping practices. We then turn our attention to seven leadership practices informed by research and experience.

Rehearsal 12.1 Identifying Leader Reframing Practices

Purpose: Identify leaders or cultural heroes from your analysis who have engaged in reframing practices.

What was the context/issue involved?

What type of meanings (or perhaps a different one) were influenced?
Perceptions of external threats.
Perceptions of competitors and benchmark organizations.
Perceptions of accountability to stakeholders.
What is valued in the organization?
Co-creating and casting a vision for the future.
What influence did this have on the overall culture?

Seven Positive Communication Leadership Practices

Leaders, like other members, participate in discursive practices that constitute the culture. For instance, Schein (2004), from a "culture as metaphor" perspective, introduced varied "mechanisms" for creating, displaying, and maintaining culture, such as the design of physical space, façades, and buildings; stories, myths, legends, and parables about important events and people. Inspired by Schein, we offer seven leadership communication practices. Though far from an exhaustive set of best practices, we move from a foundational practice to more specific ones, all involving "acting into" co-creating better social worlds. For each practice, we provide reflection questions to encourage you to engage in a mental shift from *the value of engaging in cultural analysis only as an organizational and professional to also personal and community*. Use these questions to journal about insights gleaned from your analysis. The section ends with a Rehearsal 1.2 aimed at application to your own formal and/or informal leadership practices.

1. Leaders Model the Cultural Significance of All Communicative Actions

Defined: Leaders, but what they say and don't say, what they do and don't do, are engaged in shaping organizational culture.

Rationale: Defining culture as co-construction means that leaders enact communicative behaviors that invite others to co-create with them a positive organization or one that moves in the opposite direction.

In action: The first principle sets the stage for the other six. Effective leaders grasp that they are doing something, creating something with all their actions. This first practice recalls a mental shift from *communication as an information exchange to the co-creation of relational networks that create and constrain ethical and effective processes and goals*. We find again and again the need to make this shift in moments when our communication is shaped by thoughts like:

- "If they would just listen."
- "I told them more than once."
- "We e-mailed. We shared in meetings. They just don't want to make this change."
- "I give up. No one gets what I want around here."

Making this shift involves viewing leadership as both about what is said and done as well as what is not said or left undone. Both matter. As Mirivel and Lyon (2023) stress, positive communication rests on commitments to: a) excellence, bringing out people's best, and b) long-term investment in others. For instance, one study foregrounded a particular interactive element of culture—*humor*. Supervisors who engaged in positive humor with interns, increased satisfaction levels and the propensity of interns to accept a full-time role (Sobral & Islam, 2015). In contrast, one leader used sarcasm in meetings. He eventually learned that this practice was a "double edged sword"—creating a bond with some and division with others who viewed the humor as deprecating (Meyer, 2000, p. 329).

From interactive elements such as humor to nonverbal ones such as *space*, an awareness of what we are creating is critical. If the CEO's office is much more opulent and luxurious than the offices of other employees, it sends a message. In particular, gaps between CEO and employee pay are considered a source of shame in certain Eastern cultures such that large gaps do not exist (Salazar & Raggiunti, 2016). If a non-profit manager throws a fund-raiser at an expensive hotel while claiming the non-profit is in dire need of funds, it sends a message both without and within that organization. In sharp contrast, we continue to be inspired by positive communication examples such as:

- A CEO tells his own story of making a major change by stating, "I just want y'all to know that I am the problem. And I'm going to start trying to fix me, and we're going to fix this whole organization starting from the top down. We're going to spend the next few days talking about how we do that" (Morgan, 2015, p. 195).
- A former graduate student of Gerald's took him on a tour of the non-profit. They walk by an office with a missing door. She explains that the new CEO started her first week on the job by removing her office door to bring new meaning to an "open-door policy."
- One large organization hosts a company picnic at which all the corporate officers serve the meal to janitors, secretaries, and other employees.
- At PepsiCo, CEO Indra Nooyi, inspired by practices in her parent's home culture of India, now writes notes of appreciation to the parents of executives on her team. She also took the initiative to provide a daycare on campus to aid in work-life balance.

In short, what the leader spends time doing, what she talks about in public addresses, who she interacts with, what information she asks for, what she spends money on, and a variety of other seemingly insignificant choices send an invitation—"join me in co-create values of humility, support, and care." If you want to show that you value employee input, eat in the company cafeteria. If you claim to value diversity, spend time developing relationships with those different from you. Ensure that hiring practices are equitable, and launch minority mentoring groups and intercultural training. If you want to emphasize customer service as well as civility in an organization and community relationships, serve as a role model yourself; talk about it in every message you give, and appoint the most important members of the organization to a task force you chair yourself. Consider these questions for application:

- *What culture-creating practices have you observed in a leader of the culture you studied?*
- *What practices merit development?*

2. Leaders Live and Tell Stories to Co-Create Ethical Values and Positive Communication Norms

Defined: Leaders, like all humans, are storytellers and, as such, shape culture through their stories.

Rationale: All humans shape and are shaped by the stories we tell and live. Leaders have an opportunity and responsibility to tell and live stories that co-create positive organizations.

In action: From the foundational practice of attending to our roles in co-constructing positive organizations, we move to the power of narrative. Here, we first unpack varied ways of understanding the power of narratives and how they function as counternarratives. We then provide examples before introducing systemic story creation and appreciative inquiry as ways to address the reality of distortion or the dark side of storytelling.

THE POWER OF NARRATIVE

In his theory of symbolic convergence, Bormann (1969) states that when we participate together in telling or hearing a powerful story, we share a common experience that binds and unifies us. Stories are powerful because they are memorable, multifaceted, and dramatic. We can draw multiple messages from a story; thus, the storyteller should recognize that symbolic convergence will vary. Listeners may have more to gain than the storyteller in acting on the implications of the story. Furthermore, they may see cause to confront or challenge the story based on power relations (Olufowote, 2006). Nonetheless, the significance of stories remains due to their power to connect and motivate. In addition, story-telling in organizations has been linked with innovative work behaviors (Halac & Celik, 2016). Recall that stories, like other symbolic elements, reflect and reproduce the culture of an organization, and in the process, they provide the material from which new stories of organizational life can be created" (Barge, 2004, p. 106).

Furthermore, stories can tap into a rich historical legacy to interpret the present or can paint an inspiring picture of the future in imagery to which listeners can relate. The power of the symbolic leader in crafting stories about our past, present, and future is captured by Bolman and Deal (2017).

> The past is usually a golden one, a time of noble purposes, of great deeds, of legendary heroes or heroines. The present is troubled, a critical moment when we have to make fateful choices. The future is a dreamlike vision of hope and greatness, often linked to past stories. (pp. 355–356)

As such, stories can also be a force for change.

COUNTER NARRATIVES

Recall our discussion of counternarratives in Chapter 4. Counternarratives are stories that foreground outliers, individuals, or groups that have overcome the odds. As introduced in Chapter 9 on "Diversity," Jones (2017) captured narratives of Black entrepreneurs discussing ways they overcame oppressive systems. Such counternarratives parallel our discussion of positive deviants in Chapter 10 and, as such, are a rich resource for minority leadership development while also a resource for developing majority culture awareness. The power of counternarrative told about leaders is evidenced by two examples each involving some aspect of "sacrificial leadership" (Qu, Xu, Sun, & Li, 2022).

In one case, Angi heard a university provost of a small university tell an especially poignant story about one of his predecessors. The former president had retired, and on his last workday, unknown to him, every member of the administration and staff gathered in a long line outside the building to wish him well and show their love and respect for him. The provost ended the story by saying, "That's who we are at this university. That's what makes us different."

In a second counternarrative example, during a cultural analysis, the same story about the CEO surfaced in several interviewees. The company had a regional meeting at a hotel in the Southwest. The CEO noticed when one of the regional managers didn't arrive at dinner and called his room. When he didn't answer the door, the CEO got the manager to open the door and found the regional manager barely alive after a heart attack. The CEO canceled an international conference to stay at the hospital with the family for four days until the manager was out of danger. Then, he paid for all medical expenses and travel expenses for the family. He became a legend, and the story did much to create and display the organizational value of caring and responsibility for others. This instance of sacrificial leadership, as evidenced in research, constitutes more than a good story. Narratives like this one have been shown in the context of organizations in China to "inspire helpfulness on the part of employees in various situations" as well as enhance communication between colleagues (Qu, Xu, Sun, & Li, 2022, p. 11).

COUNTERING THE DARKSIDE OF NARRATIVE

Alongside the positives, stories may have a dark side—they may be believed even when they lack ethical or valid support. For instance, Martin Luther King, Jr., Gandhi, and Hitler told stories with starkly different ends. As these historical contrasts suggest, stories told about leaders are often as important, if not more, than the stories a leader may tell. Part of the challenge of determining the veracity of a story is that leaders may focus on what they believe "people want to believe, regardless of historical validity or empirical support" (Bolman & Deal, 2017, p. 356). If organizational members consider them credible, incomplete, or even partially true, stories may be believed. Consider the dark side of political narratives that skew facts to cast a shadow on opponents. However, stories may seem so contrived and manipulative that they not only lose their impact but also may even have a negative impact in that listeners may discount the speaker altogether. An ethical leader, thus, has a responsibility to ensure that a story is not just believable but also true, grounded in the ethical use of supporting data.

SYSTEMIC STORY CREATION

One way to develop stories that are credible and ethical is to engage in what Barge (2004) refers to as "systemic" story creation. Systemic stories involve a process that "values, respects, and incorporates the differing stories other members in a human system have created" (p. 111). At a pragmatic level, this means that symbolic leaders take the time to listen deeply to others. Listening, as a positive communication practice, is about "transcending differences" and, when paired with asking opening questions, provides the opportunity to "discover the unknown" (Mirivel & Fuller, 2024, p. 4). Cultivating these practices creates the virtue of humility by respecting the fact that multiple stories or representations of the culture can and should be woven together. This process means that the resultant stories reflect the inherent tensions in organizational life. For instance, a systemic story about a change would represent the voices of those championing, as well as challenging, the change. Rather than a story criticizing the past or those opposed to the change, leaders weave a story that respects other voices by

> valuing the contributions of others and working with them to create and sustain the collective resources available within a system as opposed to adopting a morally superior position and instructing others in what changes are needed and how to perform them.
>
> (Barge, 2004, p. 122)

Systemic story creation becomes one process or tool you might use. For example, in one meeting, a unit head used the first hour of a six-hour planning retreat to have members share the top three stories of what made them proud to be part of this department. The stories told and shared not only socialized new members into a culture that valued support, transparency, and learning but also fueled the next part of the retreat in terms of vision and direction.

The retreat leader engaged members in a form of storytelling often referred to as "Appreciative Inquiry." This approach assumes effective change leadership must involve positive affect and social bonding (Cooperrider & Srivastva, 1987). Appreciative inquiry resonates with positive organization theory (Cameron & Spreitzer, 2012; Wooten, Roberts, & Davidson, 2016), including positive organizational communication scholarship (French & Holden, 2012; Lutgen-Sandvik, Riforgiate, & Fletcher, 2011; Socha & Pitts, 2012).

As you reflect on your cultural analysis, consider these questions:

- *What stories did you hear about the leader?*
- *What stories did you hear that that leader(s) told?*
- *Where prompt used in meetings and/retreats to elicit stories?*
- *What did you learn about how these stories were developed? Received? Credible? Ethical? Positive?*
- *What stories do you engage in asking about? Sharing? What are they creating?*

3. Leaders Enact Rituals to Reframe Change and Continuity

Defined: Formal and informal rituals are an integral part of leadership and, in particular, the way change is managed.

Rationale: Given the powerful culture-shaping force of rituals, leaders need to be aware of and attend to varied rituals in terms of co-creating a positive culture.

In action: Have you had the experience of a new leader immediately introducing change? Do you have stories, perhaps about the division of those energized by the changes while others were resistant? Recall that, in Chapter 4, rituals were introduced as significant in part because they embed multiple elements constituting the culture. Then, in Chapter 10, rituals were discussed in terms of their role in framing change efforts (Chapter 10). The idea of responding to change in terms of continuity with the past is significant. Rituals, from a constitutive view, are more than windows on a culture, but performances or enactments creating and recreating culture. Recall Mental shift 5: "From culture as a variable or a metaphor, to culture as constituted in everyday communication practices that shape and are also shaped by culture." The mental shift is underscored by CCO theorists who view rituals as "powerful precisely because they cannot be reduced to the actions of individual leaders, but make present the full force of the organization—its values, norms, and relations of power" (Koschmann & McDonald, 2015, p. 247).

In order to more fully grasp the significance of rituals, we first review the importance of value alignment with a case focused on reframing "team versus individual achievement." We end this section on positive practices by stressing the role of rituals in crisis response in which we highlight a case when a process-focused culture experienced unanticipated innovation through a major change.

VALUE ALIGNMENT AND RITUALS

An awareness then of the performative or cultural creation force of rituals is critical. Recall that rituals, as an interactive element, often weave together other enacted elements—stories, communication norms, humor, heroes, artifacts, and history. Thus, it is critical to attend to the extent to which rituals create a consistent alignment with what leaders seek to co-create with members. Recall that rituals can be everyday routines, such as a daily religious observance at a parochial school or a weekly business staff meeting. They can also involve organization-wide events such as family picnics, awards banquets, celebrations of achievements, or retirement rituals. As such, a company with a tradition of rowdy Friday afternoon happy hours is different from a company that only engages in an annual family picnic. An organization that has implemented a rite or ritual that includes mentoring for minority members stands in sharp contrast to one that gives lip service to valuing diversity. In short, an organization's rituals are not just about alignment with the leader's values but rather with shared co-construction with members. The significance of co-creating such an alignment is evidenced in an example when this did not happen at first. One of Angi's clients was in the midst of a cultural transition, shifting to a team-based culture, and was frustrated that employees were still emphasizing individual action over team cooperation. After a review of the culture, she noted that all their corporate awards were for individual achievement rather than team accomplishments.

In summary, symbolic leaders know what you reward says more to employees than the formal mission statement. They reward employees in public ways that emphasize values the culture wants to encourage. Reflect on questions tied to this practice:

- *To what extent did rituals function to aid in continuity and change?*
- *What rituals did the leader of the culture participate in and/or promote? What rewards were presented to employees? What meanings were co-created in these rituals?*
- *How would you describe the culture being created in rituals?*

4. Leaders Bring History Into the Present to Reframe Dialectic Tensions

Defined: Bringing history into the present is about understanding that history is not just about the past but plays an ongoing role in shaping and being shaped by organizational culture.

Rationale: Leadership involves responding to dialectic tensions, such as continuity and change. Understanding an organization's history provides a resource for reframing this and other dialectical tensions.

In action: When was the last time you heard or thought any of the following, either during your analysis and/or at the place you work and/or serve:

- "That will never work. We tried that before!"
- "Why don't leaders ask about what has been working around here?"
- "No one seems to get that our unit is better left to do things our way."
- "I miss the way things used to be."

These phrases capture inherent dialectic tensions that are part of communicative processes. Tensions are not just "part of" but the source or grounding of communication (Bakhtin, 1990). Put differently, we respond to a dialectic in each response, in each utterance made. For example, if I stated, "That will never work," I am responding to inherent tensions such as past–present and "possible–impossible." Recall in Chapter 10, on Leading Change, that dialectic tensions were introduced as part of the challenge and opportunity to be more effective. Rather than seeing the dialectic as a negative or as a source of stress and conflict, we argue that an awareness of dialectics can aid us in avoiding "either/or" framing and moving toward constructive leadership and conflict management practices. After capturing a constructivist perspective on history, we turn to cases that illustrate the power of bringing history to the present.

A CONSTRUCTIVIST VIEW OF HISTORY

We need to catch our tendency to think in terms of history as "that was then" and the present culture as "this is now." Leaders, especially those new to their role, may fall into the trap of bringing change, the new, the ideas they believe they were hired for, and thus determined to move forward—"get on or off the bus." However, a constructivist perspective does not demarcate the present from the past. In fact, history, like other enacted elements, is a discursive resource for the present. Recall the idea in the change chapter from Bridges (1991): "Mark the endings," which could involve a ritual that was about a clear transition from past to future. During such a ritual, he also stressed—"Treat the past with respect." Thus, the ritual might include a celebration of heroes' past, particular moments, or artifacts representing the past, but then also, "Let people take a piece of the old way with them," which captures the idea of continuity. As such, change is also about experiencing together during a ritual what will not change.

CASES: BRINGING THE PAST TO THE PRESENT

Two case studies illustrate the power of this leadership practice. First, an example from our own department captures the power of bringing history into the present. Our department began in about 1970. Founding faculty spent about 20 years constituting a culture valuing students. For instance, a department chair shared in a faculty meeting a semester-to-semester practice in which he sought out and gave extra time to students who were struggling. The department also engaged in an annual assessment practice in the mid-1980s before it was state-mandated.

This practice resulted in faculty agreeing each year on ways to improve student learning, including reframing faculty "autonomy" in light of a dialectic that now included "consensus" on shared teaching practices. In addition, a learning center was introduced, which at the time was the first in the country. This center reframed a dialectic of teacher vs. student-centered learning. For instance, learning center modules were created to aid students in grasping key concepts while the classroom was used for active learning. Fast forward to the early 1990s when faculty realized they did not have a student celebration ritual. Once introduced, the elements of this ritual responded each year to the "continuity–change" dialectic. Faculty and students were empowered to engage in maintaining and changing the event from year to year. Most recently, in 2024, we hosted this "Spring graduation" ceremony in which the 50th celebration of "Communication Skill Center" was celebrated. The event included storytelling from the founding member of this center, Dr. Jerry Butler, as well as other faculty who maintained continuity in this center while introducing changes. The ceremony ended with a relatively new practice of having graduating students tell their own stories in response to the question, "What is one thing you learned that you value most from your time in the department?" Robed in their black graduation gowns, each student captured something from a class, a favorite concept or activity. However, one student opted to use the prompt to bring history to the present. She said, "Well, I know I am not really responding to the question, but, what I took away was how much I was loved and cared for by the faculty." Her statement, further constituted through narrative and ritual, a founding historical value of care and nurturing of students (c.f., Driskill, Chatham-Carpenter, & McIntyre, 2018).

A second case, a university hospital lost its focus on caring for the most fragile and underserved populations through an emphasis on managed care. Medicare reimbursement formulas, funded research, and the bottom line. Few employees knew that the hospital had once been a private charity hospital formed as a healthcare safety net for the poor. Leaders became intentional in including that history in employee orientations, in posting pictures of the first hospital throughout the current facility, and in telling stories about the early heroes. These discursive choices, over time, became part of a culture with a sense of continuity with the past. In a similar situation, another organization hit an impasse on a major decision. Several hours of group meetings and debate over the best route to take proved to be to no avail. The value conflict was seen in the fact that a decision to make a change would mean a loss of profit. Then, one senior member recalled an early life event in the organization. He said something like: "We would not even have this decision to make if we had not originally placed our customers and needs above profit." His statement prompted a discussion that made it easy to develop consensus.

Take a minute to reflect on history being brought into the present.

- *Did the cultural leader you studied integrate organizational history during rituals? To what purpose?*
- *In what ways did leaders introduce talk of history? What role did this knowledge play in creating the culture?*
- *What dialectic tensions were reframed in leadership references to history?*

5. Leaders Ethically Reframe Events with Significant Choice

Defined: Reframing involves providing context that empowers others to have "significant choice," that is, to make informed decisions with relevant information.

Rationale: Highly ethical organizations require leadership who model "here and now" ethics talk involving messages that ensure members are empowered with relevant information.

In action: The idea of reframing is based on the image of providing a context that will aid others in seeing an event, such as a change or crisis, in a different way. Here, the concern is not simply in seeing differently but in providing significant choices. The idea of "significant choice" is concerned with ensuring others have full information to make a voluntary choice in decision making, free from physical or mental coercion, and thus providing all the relevant information available to make decisions (Nilsen, 1966; c.f., Wickline & Sellnow, 2013). However, the challenge in managing change, such as a reduction in staff or leading an organization in crisis response, is in defining "all the available information" and "voluntary choice." Leaders in an organization may not be able to provide information, for example, on the scope and timing of a downsizing situation that may inadvertently harm a client or customer who is a part of the reason for downsizing. An employee may not have a choice in this situation to stay employed. Thus, availability involves an ethical decision about sharing relevant information with those involved. Thus, transparency is central, including sharing reasons certain information is not yet available or cannot be made available and why. For instance, a leader, as part of an update on the process, might indicate: "We are able to use reserves to limit the number of lost positions. We cannot yet share information about the clients we have lost until we are given permission. We will continue to provide updates and our process each week." This approach, then, introduces the question: What might leaders do to better equip themselves? Part of that answer is in the practice of framing or reframing.

Fairhurst and Sarr (1996), in their book *The Art of Framing: Managing the Language of Leadership*, discuss language tools for leaders. They include metaphors, jargon or catchphrases, contrast, spin, and stories. Each of these, if used in light of the concept of significant choice, can aid in discerning options for interpreting events. *Metaphors* a leader uses consciously or unconsciously will shape employee perceptions and meanings. One university president assumed leadership of a university that was second in the state to the "flagship" research campus. In his inaugural address, he said, "I don't care that we're not the flagship. Flagships are an anachronism in today's military. They're large, unwieldy, and difficult to turn. Let's be a starship." This use of metaphor was a discursive choice intended to counter a "second-best" mentality among the faculty, staff, and students. This metaphor also functioned persuasively as a rationale for a number of initiatives during his presidency to create a flexible and technologically sophisticated university. Some metaphors are unconscious and emerge through language patterns. A leader, for example, who talks continuously in athletic terms introduces a metaphor for the organization that has positive and negative implications. It may foster team commitments but may also encourage competitiveness that works against those same commitments.

"Jargon" is defined as "language that is peculiar to a particular profession, an organizational culture, or a well-developed vision or program" (Fairhurst & Sarr, 1996, p. 108). Jargon or "catchphrase" is about using familiar terms to frame a subject (Fairhurst, 2011). In our department, for example, we began to use the term "deep learning" to capture a commitment to "do less, better" by sharing, for example, certain learning outcomes across courses. This focus meant students had the opportunity to learn, for example, effective ways to structure a presentation across multiple courses. Thus, when this catchphrase or jargon is introduced, it provides a shorthand means of encouraging collaborative and focused engagement.

"Contrast" is the opposite of "metaphor." Rather than explaining the common elements of two unlike things through comparison, the leader highlights an essential trait by placing one object, person, or idea in opposition or contrast to another. Just as we talked about the power of a leader to define competitors for an organization or to suggest similar benchmark institutions, contrast can define an organization by what it is not. For instance, the CEO of

Kaiser Permanente used LinkedIn, a professional networking site, to share an internal note he sent to his people reaffirming their commitment to diversity and inclusion. He opens by using contrast. "The recent events in Charlottesville, Virginia and the president's response have been disheartening and unsettling. At times like this, it's important for us to ground ourselves in our mission and reaffirm the beliefs upon which our organization was built." His comments about the organization's 70-year history of inclusivity stand in contrast to his opening remarks contrasting the "disheartening and unsettling" response of the nation's leader (Tyson, 2017).

"Spin" is a term from politics, as political handlers compete to place their own interpretations on speeches, debates, or political contests. As such, the term "spin" easily has a negative and even unethical connotation, yet the intent is to realize that meaning is constructed based on framing or the context given to a particular fact. For example, is finishing third a good or bad thing? Third might be framed in terms of the "top three" finish in the history of the organization versus "we were not first." Is a 10% drop in revenues a crushing blow or, in light of trend data, a normal downturn tied to the economy as well as an opportunity to evaluate which functions are most efficient and essential to the organizational mission? Still, spin has its limits. Organization members are sophisticated enough to see through an obviously self-serving interpretation. Nonetheless, events can be framed in both positive and negative ways. Here, the ethical leader is not about masking or avoiding the need to be real or provide context for statistics. Rather, the intent is to think holistically about other meanings that can be ethically co-constructed to move forward. For instance, the "Discourse of Renewal" theory focuses on communicative practices that aid an organization in learning and growing through a crisis event. An essential element in this discourse is to reframe the crisis in terms of opportunities during the post-crisis phase. This use of "spin" is focused on ethical communication, such that the framing of the crisis as an opportunity does not mask the challenges or information needed for stakeholders to make significant choices (Ulmer, Sellnow, & Seeger, 2015).

However, a need for caution arises concerning framing. There are no simple linguistic recipes or formulas for framing success. No one can say, "Add two parts metaphor, one part story, a master frame, and viola, you will have constructed an artful message!" (Fairhurst, 2011, p. 92). Instead, and consistent with our approach, we invite you to view these options as an artist's palette. The challenge is to ethically and effectively utilize these resources as a leader. For example, Gerald, while engaged in participant observation at a workshop held aimed at creating service-focused and collaborative efforts across congregations, noticed two large (i.e., think mid-size automobile) yet very different, three-dimensional models at the front of the auditorium. For the morning session, there was a model of a country club. In the afternoon workshop, a model of a bridge. Leaders used contrast and metaphor to invite a co-construction of a new vision and different organizing practices within and between congregations. The contrasting images conveyed that a congregation was not intended to be a "country club" isolated from the community for only certain types of people but instead as a "bridge" connecting members to serve diverse people groups. These constitutive practices were part of organizing practices that reframed the collaboration–non-collaboration dialectic tension in a community-based organization (Driskill, Meyer, & Mirivel, 2012).

To that end, reflect on the practices of the leader(s) in the organization you studied. *What types of language behavior did you notice? Can you give examples of metaphor, contrast, stories, spin, or jargon? How were events reframed? How was culture co-constructed through language choice? What was effective/ineffective about these efforts?*

6. Leaders Co-Construct Pathways to Meaningful and Ethical Engagement

Defined: Meaningful and ethical engagement is about a pathway involving progress, not perfection, in the cultural practices aimed at creating a connection with mission and purpose.

Rationale: A major leadership challenge is to engage members through value co-creation that ensures a meaningful connection to the mission of the organization while, at the same time, making sure that such engagement does not undermine their choice to engage or not.

In action: Finding the key to motivation or engagement has long been the quest for the "holy grail" of leadership. We maintain that there are no simple formulas, but rather, the need to attend to ethical co-construction processes. In other words, we argue that engagement or motivation is not something leaders should do to control employees or simply increase productivity, but rather an opportunity for engaging in ethical constitutive practices that bring value and purpose to organizing.

A major goal of these constitutive processes is to attend to the potential ethical problems with unobtrusive control. Tompkins and Cheney (1985) write of unobtrusive control as a "third generation" of organizational control systems. In the first generation, employees were controlled directly by a supervisor who watched every action and corrected errors. In the second generation, bureaucratic rules replaced direct supervision. If we could make rules for every possible situation, then employees would be controlled by rules rather than direct supervision, making possible larger spans of supervision. We suspect we are now in an era of technological control in which software can count and trace every action in a way that monitors performance. Tompkins and Cheney's argument still applies.

Leaders, through unobtrusive control, can influence employee behavior more powerfully through identification with values than with any control mechanism. If you control by supervision, then I will comply only when I am in your line of sight. If you are controlled by rules, you are successful only to the extent I believe you will enforce the rules and know if I have broken them. If you control by technology, I may find ways to modify the technology or to manipulate monitoring systems. Yet, the ability to modify is likely to be increasingly limited. In the third edition, the term AI, much less generative AI, was not part of organizational discourse.

As one student noted in Fall 2024, technology is available to not only monitor employees but to co-create meaning with employees related to engagement. With generative AI, there is the ability for an organization as a whole, or individual teams, leaders, or employees to co-create new processes and control systems. For example, AI systems can currently monitor time spent on Microsoft "Teams." How does this then impact culture? Rachel Berens-VanHeest, a graduate student at the University of Wisconsin-Stout, engaged in some "light hypothesizing" about the future.

> AI is the fourth generation of control systems, and it's one that we don't fully understand and definitely don't always notice. That's why having guidelines around ethical use of AI is so important. My organization is just moving into the intentional use of AI, and trying to create these guidelines, so the idea of a fourth generation of control is very applicable as I help define our approach to AI for employees.

This language of "4th generation" should challenge all of us to engage. What might such engagement look like? One route is to think of AI in terms of algorithms or computation tools to enhance effectiveness and efficiency that are enactments of culture. As such, they engage in problem-solving recipes created by varied actors that "augment and automate" organizational practices that are more opaque than previous generations. These hidden actors may include assessing security risks and potential parolees as well as recommending media optimizing logistical efficiency (Glaser, Pollock, & D'Adderio, 2021, p. 2). As such, this "4th generation" of control systems merits attention in cultural analysis.

Despite these challenges, unobtrusive control is not a concept meant to only paint a potential dark side. For instance, if I believe in an organizational value like service or giving voice to ethical concerns, and that value is strong and unequivocal in the organization, positive practices are present. As such, unobtrusive control is not inherently unethical. Like all communicative processes, the ethical dimension is intertwined with process and outcome. For instance, if leaders have drummed up service as part of the discourse meant to encourage engagement, then it is fair to ask, did members have a voice in the nature of the service and/or the extent to which commitments to service intrude upon work-life balance? The same then would be true in terms of the application of AI. Was there a transparent process for determining the use of AI (and ways to avoid abuse)? Indeed, the dark side of AI, if the prognosis is right, generative AI will become a self-monitoring, self-learning system that can both reduce and replace mundane tasks and then, of course, potentially become the CEO of your nightmares and/or dreams in terms of oversight and control.

Indeed, technology has the power to exacerbate the already present patterns of toxic leadership. Hetrick (2023) defines toxic leadership as requiring "dominance, control, and coercion rather than influence, commitment, and persuasion" (p. 117). Perhaps most disconcerting is her reflection on cultural practices that promote toxicity, including leaders who are unaware of toxicity and toxic behaviors being tolerated. To this, we would add that a toxic leader may be blind to their own behaviors. For example, they may justify control or overlook ethical procedures as necessary, given the situation.

These prognoses encourage us to think more critically about choice and agency. Unobtrusive control should not be oversimplified to mean that supervisors and/or the organization control members who are without agency. In an intriguing study of a Swedish-based multinational research and development firm, Wieland (2011) challenged the position that control operates in a simple way: either the individual is empowered to resist control or the organization controls the individual. Instead, she notes that both "control and resistance operate through powerful normalizing discourses; each discourse provides the material for control and resistance vis-vis the other simultaneously" (p. 178). To be more specific, members experienced times of "domination," when they felt they had to say "yes" to requests to take on projects; but at the same time, they also experienced times of emancipation through a discourse related to moderation and work-life balance.

Many credit Johnson and Johnson's ability to survive an incident of product tampering with strong and consistent organizational values that placed patient safety first. Thus, there was no question that all products would be pulled from the shelves and new product packaging developed. The significance of control via shared values in responding effectively and ethically to the crisis has been documented in numerous case studies (Ulmer, Sellnow, & Seeger, 2015). In contrast, efforts to control through policy and rules may backfire. One of Angi's hospital clients has an employee policy that employees must call in the day before to be eligible for a sick day. Otherwise, if they are absent, they must count the day as a vacation day. The rationale for such a policy is valid since it is critical to public health that hospitals maintain sufficient staffing levels on any given day. However, the effect of the policy was that employees came to work sick and viewed the sick days as an entitlement that they took when they wanted to have a day off. How much more effective would it be if leaders would truly inculcate a value of how important each and every employee is to the hospital's mission, and employees really believed that? They would come to work because they felt their work was important and would take responsibility for making arrangements if they could not come to work.

The power of unobtrusive control should, however, give leaders and members reason for pause. Recent applications of this construct suggest sources of resistance to this type of control (Bisel, Ford, & Keyton, 2007). Unobtrusive control, as indicated in the hospital example, depends on members having a strong sense of identification with the mission of the organization. Yet, individuals typically carry multiple and complex identifications. Thus, certain values of organizational life may be salient to one member but not another. An employee may seek, for instance, to work extra for an ill coworker due to internalizing a value for being a team player but may refuse extra work if they sense it is being placed on them due to a management request to meet certain profitability goals. In short, as we have stressed at various junctures, the leader-follower relationship is complex. Individuals select the types of values that create the level of identification needed for unobtrusive control. Thus, reflecting on core organizational values and aiding members in making informed choices about the importance of these values is an essential leadership task.

- *To what extent do the organizing processes of the leaders seek to engage or motivate members through language focused on values?*
- *What was the effect? How did members respond?*
- *When did they honor them? Negate them?*
- *What AI/Tech policies do you see the need to develop?*

7. Symbolic Leaders Rely on Multiple Frames for Productive Conflict Management and Effective Problem/Solution Identification

Defined: Multi-frame thinking involves using metaphors of organizations that encourage reflection from more than one viewpoint.

Rationale: Effective and ethical leaders need to develop the capacity to reflect deeply and meaningfully on different approaches to improving inevitable conflicts and problems.

In action: Conflicts and problems are part of organizational life. Leaders have a role in developing their communication competence in response to these inevitabilities. One approach to developing competence is to improve our capacity to see from multiple points of view via multi-frame thinking. Lee Bolman and Terry Deal, in *Reframing Organizations* (2017), explain how organizations can be seen through structural, human resource, political, and symbolic frames. If a leader focuses on one frame, they will face added obstacles since each of the frames, as we will discuss, has limits. The key then is to explore your leadership communicative practices in light of all four.

- "Structural leaders" are architects and analysts who are skilled in restructuring the organization to perform more efficiently. They do their homework, are skilled at analysis, and see the connections among structure, function, and environment. They pay attention to the details of implementation and are not hesitant to reorganize if their data and analysis indicate another structure might be more efficient. A downside of this style is that they may lose sight of the human consequences of continual structural changes, they can be micromanagers, and they may not be as adept at seeing the synergy between human and system elements in performance.
- A "human resource frame" leader is a facilitator and catalyst who motivates as well as empowers. Consistent with our discussion on engagement, such empowerment occurs

through participation and inclusion. This process seeks to provide the autonomy and support needed to perform well. Leaders who excel in this way of seeing the organization often adopt a servant-leader model and see their role as supporting organization members to achieve goals. Such leaders would attend to issues of safety and civility in the organization. The strengths of human resource leaders are communication abilities, accessibility, serving as visible role models, and anticipating the impacts of change and motivation on people. Weaknesses can include oversensitivity to how they are viewed by others, insufficient decisiveness, and failure to see that many problems have both human and system components.

- "Political leaders" are pragmatic and realistic. They are adept at analyzing power and determining whose interests are being served by any particular initiative. They are good at developing coalitions to support change and gaining the support of opinion leaders within the organization and external stakeholders. Bolman and Deal (2017) stress that such leaders seek to avoid coercion but focus instead on persuasion and negotiation. Political leaders are effective in getting things done, but they can fall prey to pragmatism over idealism and can be seen as divisive and manipulative.
- "Symbolic leaders" are master image weavers. Organizations are represented as both theaters and temples in this frame (Bolman & Deal, 2017). The authors explain further by noting:

> As theater, an organization creates a stage on which actors play their roles and hope to communicate the right impression to their audience. As a temple, an organization is a community of faith, bonded by shared beliefs, traditions, myths, rituals, and ceremonies.
>
> (p. 353)

Symbolic leaders, as we have stressed in this chapter, exemplify many of the skills we have described, such as framing meaning, considering the importance of symbols, and recognizing the durable fabric of organizational culture. The downside is this framing process may lack substance if the sole focus is on forms that can be empty and meaningless without action.

We concur that each of these ways of seeing the organization can aid us. Multi-frame thinking requires time and attention to communicative practices that will optimize insights to be gained from structural, human resource, political, and symbolic communication and constitutive processes.

We agree with Lyon (2017) that competence across these frames means giving attention to four communicative shifts, which involve moving from: a) control to collaboration; b) top-down to upward communication; c) secrecy to transparent communication; and d) impersonal to engaging communication. These shifts reflect practices required to move away from a toxic culture. Hetrick (2023) provides a list of "Red Flag Behaviors" designed to identify the three corners of the "toxic triangle: toxic leadership, susceptible followers, and conducive environments" (Hetrick, 2023, pp. 163–164). For instance, two of the "red flags" behaviors—"Choosing competition over cooperation" and "Becoming aggressive after negative feedback and devaluing the feedback source"—stand in sharp contrast to the positive practices outlined previously.

In all, when leaders see the organization through multiple points of view, they are better equipped to engage in ethical communication practices. An optimally competent leader is not only able to reframe situations but is adept at reframing events and casting a vision in ways that co-create and, at times, transcend, the diverse national cultures and subcultures within an organization.

- *What frame is the strength of the leader you studied?*
- *What framing practices merit development?*

Summary

You may or may not see yourself as a leader. The descriptive phrases that opened this chapter may not be ones you readily think about when it comes to leadership—"humility," "self-sacrifice," and "interdependence." Recall that we invited you to list your current leadership development goals. We invite you to return to those goals at the end of the summary. For instance, Gerald reflected in particular on a goal of asking process questions (i.e., What might help us move forward on areas we do not have agreement?) to improve decision-making rather than focusing solely on his ideas and suggestions. The ideas in this chapter challenged him, in particular, to model an openness to engaging others in problem-solving and not just being the one with an answer or idea.

Our hope is that whether in informal ways or formal ones, you will grasp the significance of your influence in the organizations you serve. In this chapter, we focused on the leader's role in reaching toward the goal of co-creating ethical, diverse, adaptive, and effective organizational cultures that are part of improving all of our social worlds. As such, the leader is called to see their role in ethically responding to and interpreting organizational events, very similar to the way the director shapes and encourages the meaning of a play carried through the performance of actors. While the leader has an important role to play, organizational meaning is an interactive, co-creation process between leaders and organizational members. Members must identify with the values and vision of the culture to penetrate and guide the organization to desired outcomes.

In this chapter, we have stressed the following main ideas:

1. The most important job of a cultural leader is shaping meaning.
2. The leader can shape many types of meanings:
    - Perceptions of external threats.
    - Perceptions of competitors and benchmark organizations.
    - Accountability to stakeholders.
    - What is valued in the organization?
    - Co-creating and casting a vision for the future.
3. Ethical leaders engage in seven positive communication practices. They
    - Model the cultural significance of all communicative actions.
    - Tell stories to co-create communicative values and communication norms.
    - Capitalize on rituals for culture change and continuity.
    - Bring history into the present to frame the value of change and continuity.
    - Ethically reframe events through language that provides significant choice.
    - Co-construct pathways to meaningful and ethical engagement.
    - Rely on multiple frames for productive conflict management and for effective problem/solution identification.

These seven positive communication practices are guides, not laws for action. We see them as principles upon which to reflect, understanding full well that leadership is a journey and not a destination. Recall that we began this workbook by asking: ***What three leadership communication and culture practices are you seeking to practice and develop?*** Take a minute now to reflect again on what you wrote, review the seven practices we introduced, and refine your leadership development goals by completing Rehearsal 12.2. Also, consider Rehearsal 12.3 on "Leading Virtual Teams" and the online rehearsal—"Case Study of Cultural Leadership."

Rehearsal 12.2 Assessing Yourself as a Leader

Purpose: Assess yourself as a cultural leader or a potential cultural leader. Alternatively, you may adapt these questions to survey leaders in the organization and/or perceptions held by members about leaders.

Directions: Consider each of the leadership practices that follow, and rate yourself on a 1–10 scale, with 10 highest if your leadership style reflects this quality. On items on which you rate yourself 7 or lower, develop an action plan for how you can cultivate this cultural leadership behavior. We state each of the seven symbolic practices along with a secondary question to aid a process of mindfulness in this self-assessment. You should consider having trusted others also share their assessments.

1. I model the cultural significance of all communicative actions.
   Rating:___
   (My verbal and non-verbal actions affirm positive values in the organization.)
   Action plan if your score is less than 7:

   ____

   ____

2. I tell stories to co-create communicative values and communication norms.
   Rating:___
   (I share memorable stories in speeches and remarks that reinforce organizational values, expectations, ways to execute the task, and adapt to changes.)
   Action plan if your score is less than 7:

   ____

   ____

3. I capitalize on rituals for culture change and continuity.
   Rating:___
   (I participate in rituals and give employees rewards that value both change and continuity.)

   ____

   ____

4. I bring history into the present to frame the value of change and continuity.
Rating:___
(I make time to introduce key stories from the past that aid us in maintaining core values.)

____

____

5. I ethically reframe events through language that provides significant choice.
Rating:___
(i.e., I ethically use metaphor, jargon, and/or spin to provide choice in meaning-making.)

____

____

6. I co-construct pathways to meaningful and ethical engagement.
Rating:___
(I use shared values rather than rules to support and encourage effectiveness.)

____

____

7. I use multiple frames for productive conflict management and for effective problem/solution identification.
Rating:___
(I use structural, human resources, political, and symbolic frames to co-create a more diverse, ethical, and adaptive culture.)

____

____

Rehearsal 12.3 Leading Virtual Teams in Organizations

Purpose: Reflect on the leadership implications of research on virtual teams.

Read: Weber and Kim (2015). Virtuality, technology use, and engagement within organization. Journal of *Applied Communication Research, 43(4)*, pp. 385–407. doi.org/10.1080/00909882.2015.1083604

Summary: This study focuses on a multinational organization relying on collaborative technology to enable virtual organizational teams. Collaborative technology provides workers who are distributed by time and space with a way to form relationships and share knowledge, yet this same technology also has complex, interwoven implications for virtual organizing. The researchers consider four key dimensions of virtuality—spatial dispersion, temporal dispersion, dynamic structure (degree of turnover/change on the team), and functional diversity (extent of differences in functional roles and backgrounds as well as priorities, assumptions, and routines). Survey data and analysis revealed connections between two dimensions of virtuality: the use of collaborative technology and peer engagement in the organization. They conclude that understanding interactions in virtual organizations requires a more nuanced approach to virtuality and active management of technology implementation. Leaders need to actively manage the deployment of new collaborative technology by focusing on specific characteristics of work groups.

Questions

1. What have your experiences been with virtual teams? Positive? Negative? Mixed?

___

___

___

2. What steps would you take to ensure a virtual team functioned well?

___

___

___

3. What leadership practices are relevant to introducing a virtual team to an organization and ensuring maximum effectiveness?

___

___

___

Discussion Questions

1. In what ways is one of the most important jobs of a leader "managing meaning"? Give examples. What are the limits and/or potential problems with thinking about leadership as managing meaning?
2. What are the limits on the leader in trying to create or change culture?
3. Why are stories such a powerful force in symbolic leadership?
4. Why do leaders need to understand the power and symbolism of rituals?
5. How does identification of the employee with the values and culture of the organization serve as a form of unobtrusive control? What might a mindful leader do in response to the potential problems with this type of control?
6. Discuss the four frames of leadership from Bolman and Deal (2017)—Structural, Human Resource, Political, and Symbolic. How might these be used to improve decision-making processes?

References

Alvesson, M. (2002). *Understanding organizational culture.* Thousand Oaks: Sage.

Bakhtin, M. (1990). *Art and answerability: Early philosophical works by M. Bakhtin* (M. Holquist & V. Liapunov, Eds.; V. Liapunov, Trans.). Austin, TX: University of Texas Press.

Barge, J. K. (2004). Antenarrative and managerial practice. *Communication Studies, 55(1)*, 106–127. https://doi.org/10.1080/10510970409388608

Bisel, R. S., Ford, D., & Keyton, J. (2007). Unobtrusive control in a leadership organization: Integrating control and resistance. *Western Journal of Communication, 71*, 136–158. https://doi.org/10.1080/10570310701368039

Bolman, L., & Deal, T. (2017). *Reframing organizations* (6th ed.). San Francisco: Jossey-Bass.

Bormann, E. (1969). *Interpersonal communication in the modern organization.* Englewood Cliffs, NJ: Prentice Hall.

Bridges, W. (1991). *Managing transitions: Making the most of change.* Reading, MA: Perseus.

Bryman, A. (1996). Leadership in organizations. In S. R. Clegg, C. Hardy, & W. R. Nord (Eds.), *Handbook of organization studies* (pp. 276–292). Thousand Oaks, CA: Sage.

Cameron, K., & Spreitzer, G. (Eds.). (2012). *Oxford handbook of positive organizational scholarship.* New York: Oxford University Press.

Chen, X. T., Zhang, D., & Yang, X. M. (2024). Is it influence or pressure? A study on the dual path impact of self-sacrificial leadership on employee organizational citizenship behavior. *Open Journal of Business and Management, 12*, 339–349. https://doi.org/10.4236/ojbm.2024.121022

Cooperrider, D. L., & Srivastva, S. (1987). Appreciative inquiry in organizational life. In R. W. Woodman & W. A. Pasmore (Eds.), *Research in organizational change and development* (Vol. 1, pp. 129–169). Stamford, CT: JAI Press.

Deetz, S., Tracy, S., & Simpson, J. (2000). *Leading organizations through transition: Communication and cultural change.* Thousand Oaks, CA: Sage.

Driskill, G. (1995). Managing cultural differences: A rules analysis in a bi-cultural organization. *Howard Journal of Communications, 5(4)*, 353–379. https://doi.org/10.1080/10646179509361676

Driskill, G., Chatham-Carpenter, A., & McIntyre, K. (2018). The power of a mission: Transformations of a department culture through social constructionist principles. *Journal of Innovation in Higher Education.* https://doi.org/10.1007/s10755-018-9449-8; Retrieved from https://rdcu.be/bbNYo

Driskill, G., Meyer, J., & Mirivel, J. (2012). Managing dialectics to make a difference: Tension management in a community building organization. *Communication Studies, 63(2)*, 243–261. https://doi.org/10.1080/10510974.2011.634476

Fairhurst, G. T. (2008). Discursive leadership: A communication alternative to leadership psychology. *Management Communication Quarterly, 21*, 510–521.

Fairhurst, G. T. (2011). *The power of framing: Creating the language of leadership.* San Francisco: Jossey-Bass.

Fairhurst, G. T., & Sarr, R. (1996). *The art of framing: Managing the language of leadership.* San Francisco: Jossey-Bass.

French, S., & Holden, T. (2012). Positive organizational behavior: A buffer for bad news. *Business and Professional Communication Quarterly, 75(2)*, 208–220. https://doi.org/10.1177/1080569912441823

Glaser, V. L., Pollock, N., & D'Adderio, L. (2021). The biography of an algorithm: Performing algorithmic technologies in organizations. *Organization Theory, 2(2)*, 1–27. https://doi.org/10.1177/26317877211004609

Goodwin, D. K. (2018). *Leadership in turbulent times.* Thorndike Press, a part of Gale, a Cengage Company.

Halac, D. S., & Celik, T. S. (2016). The moderating role of organizational storytelling in the relation between organizational memory and innovative work behaviors. *Ileti-S-Im, 25*, 261–285.

Hetrick, S. (2023). *Toxic organizational cultures and leadership: How to build and sustain a healthy workplace* (1st ed.). Routledge. https://doi.org/10.4324/9781003330387

Hofstede, G., Hofstede, G. J., & Minkov, M. (2010). *Cultures and organizations: Software of the mind* (3rd ed.). New York: McGraw-Hill.

Jones, N. (2017). Rhetorical narratives of black entrepreneurs: The business of race, agency, and cultural empowerment. *Journal of Business and Technical Communication, 31(3)*, 319–349. https://doi.org/10.1177/1050651917695540

Keyton, J. (2005). *Communication and organizational culture.* Thousand Oaks: Sage.

Koschmann, M. A., & McDonald, J. (2015). Organizational rituals, communication, and the question of agency. *Management Communication Quarterly, 29(2)*, 229–256. https://doi.org/10.1177/0893318915572386

Kouzes, J. M., & Posner, B. K. (2017). *The leadership challenge: How to get extraordinary things done in organizations* (6th ed.). San Francisco: Jossey-Bass.

Lutgen-Sandvik, P., Riforgiate, S., & Fletcher, C. (2011). Work as a source of positive emotional experiences and the discourses informing positive assessment. *Western Journal of Communication, 75(1)*, 2–27. https://doi.org/10.1080/10570314.2010.536963

Lyon, A. (2017). *Case studies in courageous organizational communication: Research and practices for effective workplaces.* New York: Peter Lang.

Meyer, J. (2000). Humor as a double-edged sword: Four functions of humor in communication. *Communication Theory, 10*(3), 310–331. doi:10.1111/j.1468-2885.2000.tb00194.x

Mirivel, J., & Lyon, A. (2023). *Positive communication for leaders: Proven strategies forinspiring unity and effecting change.* New York: Rowen & Littlefield.

Mirivel, J. C., & Fuller, R. P. (2024). A world of possibilities: Introducing positive communication scholarship to inspire better business and organizational communication research. *International Journal of Business Communication, 61(4)*, 743–759. https://doi.org/10.1177/23294884241264268

Morgan, C. D. (2015). *Matters of life and data: The remarkable journey of a big data visionary whose work impacted millions (including you).* New York: James Morgan Publishing.

Nilsen, T. R. (1966). *Ethics of speech communication.* New York, NY: Bobbs-Merrill.

Olufowote, J. (2006). Rousing and redirecting a sleeping giant: Symbolic convergence theory and complexities in the communicative constitution of collective action. *Management Communication Quarterly, 19(3)*, 451–492. https://doi.org/10.1177/0893318905280326

Porath, C. L., Gerbasi, A., & Schorch, S. L. (2015). The effects of civility on advice, leadership, and performance. *Journal of Applied Psychology, 100(5)*, 1527–1541. https://doi.org/10.1037/apl0000016

Qu, Y., Xu, Z., Sun, H., & Li, Q. (2022). The effect of self-sacrificial leadership on employees' organizational citizenship behavior for the environment: A moderated mediation model. *International Journal of Environmental Research and Public Health, 19(12)*, 7450. https://doi.org/10.3390/ijerph19127450

Salazar, A., & Raggiunti, J. (2016). Why does executive greed prevail in the United States and Canada but not in Japan? The pattern of low CEO pay and high worker welfare in Japanese corporations. *The American Journal of Comparative Law, 64(3)*, 721–744. https://doi.org/10.1093/ajcl/avw007

Schein, E. (2004). *Organizational culture and leadership* (3rd ed.). San Francisco: Jossey-Bass.

Schein, E., & Schein, P. (2018). *Humble leadership: The power of relationships, openness, and trust.* Oakland, CA: Berrett-Koehler Publishers.

Shockley-Zalabak, P., & Morley, D. (1994). Creating a culture: A longitudinal examination of the influence on management and employee values on communication rule stability and emergence. *Human Communication Research, 20*, 334–355. https://doi.org/10.1111/j.1468-2958.1994.tb00326.x

Sobral, F., & Islam, G. (2015). He who laughs best, leaves last: The influence of humor on the attitudes and behavior of interns. *Academy of Management Learning & Education, 14(4)*, 500–518. https://doi.org/10.5465/amle.2013.0368

Socha, T., & Pitts, M. (Eds.). (2012). *The positive side of interpersonal communication.* New York: Peter Lang Publishing.

Tompkins, P. K., & Cheney, G. (1985). Communication and unobtrusive control in contemporary organizations. In R. D. McPhee & P. K. Tompkins (Eds.), *Organizational communication: Traditional themes and new directions* (pp. 179–210). Newbury Park, CA: Sage.

Tyson, B. (August 17, 2017). An important message from Bernard Tyson, Chairman and CEO. *Company Culture, Editor's Picks, Healthcare, Insurance, Social Impact.* Retrieved from www.linkedin.com/pulse/important-message-from-bernard-j-tyson-chairman-ceo-bernard-j-tyson/

Ulmer, R., Sellnow, T., & Seeger, M. (2015). *Effective crisis communication: Moving from crisis to opportunity* (4th ed.). Thousand Oaks, CA: Sage Publications.

Walker, R. C., & Aritz, J. (2015). Women doing leadership: Leadership styles and organizational culture. *International Journal of Business Communication, 52(4)*, 452–478. https://doi.org/10.1177/2329488415598429

Weber, M., & Kim, H. (2015). Virtuality, technology use, and engagement within organization. *Journal of Applied Communication Research, 43(4)*, 385–407. https://doi.org/10.1080/00909882.2015.1083604

Wickline, M., & Sellnow, T. L. (2013). Expanding the concept of significant choice through consideration of health literacy during crises. *Health Promotion Practice, 14(6)*, 809–815. https://doi.org/10.1177/1524839913498752

Wieland, S. B. (2011). Struggling to manage work as a part of everyday life: Complicating control, rethinking resistance, and contextualizing work/life studies. *Communication Monographs, 78(2)*, 162–184. https://doi.org/10.1080/03637751.2011.5646

Wooten, L., Roberts, L. M., & Davidson, M. (2016). *Positive organizing in a global society: Understanding and engaging differences for capacity building & inclusion.* New York: Routledge.

Chapter 13

Reading Reviews

Organizational Effectiveness

A credible, ethical response to research on organizational culture and effectiveness requires a shift from a sole focus on profitability. Problems arise if profit alone becomes the driving rationale for making changes. For example, employees may resist such efforts if they are seen as solely for management's gain. In the wake of corporate scandals, top corporations realize that corporate responsibility in terms of care for the planet and people must be evaluated as well as profitability in determining long-term organizational effectiveness. Several approaches to defining an effective culture are reviewed: a) strong is good; b) strategically appropriate is good; and c) adaptive cultures are good. This final approach finds support in research on long-term, high-performing organizations. We present a set of practices for co-creating an efficiently adaptive culture involving micro- and macro-level organizing and positive communication. These practices are consistent with the OCA model in *fostering the co-creation of positive organizations by developing implications through the analysis of enacted elements that both shape and are shaped by communication.*

1. Articulate cultural analysis goals and benefits
2. Explore culture as co-construction
3. Reflect on enacted elements
4. Identify enacted elements via multiple methods
5. Interpret thematic action and OCA
6. Co-create positive communication applications

Step Five: Co-Create Positive Communication Applications

Objectives

- Describe three major perspectives on the relationship between culture and effectiveness.
- Explore the practices that create an ethical and effective organizational culture.

Stage Terms

Strong versus weak cultures	Strategically appropriate cultures	Adaptive cultures

DOI: 10.4324/9781003482529-17

The following quotes reflect the chapter's aims:

> We forget that the primary function of language, if we have something to say and are not merely babbling, is to uncover something within the world, to bring it into the open.
>
> (Barrett, *The Illusion of Technique*, 1979, p. 158)

> End hunger and poverty in a sustainable way by supporting and investing alongside local farmers and their communities.
>
> (Heifer International, n.d.)

Full Circle

We began the cultural analysis process with the first step of reflecting on the goal and expected payoffs or benefits of conducting a cultural analysis. We noted that the OCA six-phase process of analyzing a culture aids an organization in areas such as hiring and socialization practices and employee engagement initiatives. We also noted how understanding culture is an essential aspect of being an effective and ethical leader. Tools have been provided to link your cultural analysis findings to organizational cultural performances: diversity, change, ethics, and leadership. Each of these areas, along with implications for crisis and conflict management, contribute to overall organizational effectiveness, and thus, our final application will draw together key ideas from the chapters on leadership, ethics, diversity, and change. With this final application chapter on effectiveness, we have come full circle. In this chapter, we argue for the need to re-think the meaning of organizational effectiveness. First, we invite you to reflect on the "review" process in terms of Level 5 leadership as learning and listening.

Level 5 Leadership and Learning

Performance reviews in the workplace, like reviews of dramatic performances, are not always useful. A manager may have already determined "the problem and the solution" without engaging others in discernment, just as a reviewer may critique a performance based on a bias against a particular interpretation of a script. Yet a review of overall organizational effectiveness in light of cultural data should not be discarded or discounted because the process is sometimes flawed. In fact, we would argue that effective organizational performances always involve partial, incomplete reviews. Put differently, a learning organization can always learn. We can always learn. We can always get better. Progress, not perfection.

In the same vein, the OCA model continues to evolve with feedback from our students, who are often working professionals, from colleagues, and our own work in organizational development and training. Concerning overall effectiveness, we want to aim for the fifth level of leadership. As referenced in Chapter 12 on Leadership, humility is central. Level 5 leadership is a concept developed in the book *Good to Great*. Collins (2001) asserts that Level 5 leaders display a powerful mixture of personal humility and indomitable will. Their ambition is for the organization and its purpose, not themselves. Thus, as we consider ways to improve our cultural performances, like you, we have to start with an openness to growth and continuous learning.

This review of organizational effectiveness should provide a perspective on the organization that is convincing, challenging, enlightening, and empowering. The hope is that this process will inspire new insights into the forms of communication that aid in growth and development. Recall our guiding, overarching goal—*a cultural analysis provides insight for improving positive communication practices that result in meaningful personal, professional, and organizational culture development and growth.*

Level 5 Leadership and Listening

This ideal will not be one we always reach, but we can aspire. We can get up again and again each day and move in the right direction. This process provides a clearer sense of how we can each improve our own effectiveness by being an observer of our own thinking (Singe, 1990). Such attentiveness and awareness also provide a greater sense of direction, meaning, and value for your organizational experiences. As one CEO, writing about the process of leadership and organizational success suggests:

Listen
In every office
you hear the threads
of love and joy and fear and guilt,
the cries of celebration and reassurance,
and somehow you know that connecting those threads
is what you are supposed to do, and business will take care of itself.

(James Autry, *Love and profit: The art of caring leadership*, 1991, p. 26)

Our approach to analysis is about listening. Listening not just for problems but listening in a way that seeks to describe the organization in an ethical and credible manner. Listening, then, congruent with Mirivel's Model of Positive Communication, is about discovery. During this listening process via interviews/surveys, observations, and texts, you may have noted important aspects of your own communication that contribute to or distract from certain organizational cultural values. For example, you may realize that you tend to discourage innovation by focusing on failed projects. You may also have interpreted thematic action that revealed inconsistencies between lived versus espoused values. For instance, a web page may have included value statements about community and environmental engagement. However, organizational rituals and employee talk reveal the opposite. Or you may have observed how an organization marginalizes minority populations in decision-making. At the same time, beyond potentially negative cultural enactments, we trust you also attended to positive patterns. The tendency is to believe you have to find problems but, in fact, identifying cultural strengths may be of even greater importance. For example, you might have picked up on the way a unit in an organization consistently enacts organizational learning by discussing failures and lessons learned and then the co-creation of action plans to incorporate this learning into organizing practices. This type of feedback may help members grasp the significance of these positive thematic actions or patterns. Such insights, whether personal or organization-wide, are major payoffs in the analysis process.

Regardless of your organizational role, you are now ready to develop positive communication recommendations. You may be in a position (e.g., a trainer, learning coach, internal performance consultant, or external consultant) to make a formal presentation. For students, the organization may have agreed from the start that you should share your overall findings and implications. However, even if your analysis is never to be formally presented to the organization, this chapter encourages applications of value for your development as a formal and/or informal leader. We begin by reflecting on the concept of organizational effectiveness.

In particular, we focus on three different takes on the relationship between culture and effectiveness. We then introduce varied Rehearsals to prompt reflection on your experiences and your cultural data in light of their relationship to effectiveness. These rehearsals are foundational to the final chapter focused on your plans for professional and organizational development.

Organizational Effectiveness

Terms like "the bottom line," "productivity/profit," and "return on investment (ROI)" are perhaps the most commonly used rationales for making changes or justifying the existence of an organization. You may have said or heard the phrase, "If we don't make a profit, what are we here for?" ROI, return on investment, continues to be a hot topic in the training industry as human resource professionals seek to justify the expense of training and other organizational development (OD) efforts (Jain & Gulati, 2016). Definitions of productivity and effectiveness vary, but the approaches of short versus long-term productivity (Eriksson, Olander, Szentes, & Widén, 2014) or the highest level of performance with the least expenditure of resources (Little, 2016; Mali, 1978) share a common emphasis. Not surprisingly, the concern over maximizing profits and increasing efficiency is either implicit or explicit in most discussions about productivity and performance. Leaders in organizations, like directors bringing a play to the stage, seek a payoff—they want their work to have some sort of success beyond opening night.

We accept the importance of this bottom line; however, there are three problems with making the bottom line of profit the primary rationale to drive changes in culture.

- **First, organizational members and stakeholders typically react to and resist efforts at change that they view as manipulative for management gain.** Employees may actually counter such efforts and resist changes. In fact, it is critical to realize that the cultural analysis process may reveal information that the organization or individuals in the organization are not ready to hear (Deetz, Tracy, & Simpson, 2000). Concerning other stakeholders, such as community members, a "bottom line" approach may result in limited responsiveness to a particular culture. While this unresponsive approach could increase profits, in the long term, there will be resistance from community members whose lived experiences contradict these organizational values (Manzie, 2018). Thus, even if your analysis is a convincing one, grounded in careful consideration of multiple micro and macro elements gathered over time, how you make sense of the analysis and present it to others is a challenging process that merits planning and preparation. Your preparation should take into consideration one particular fact: Cultural change grounded in a profit motive alone is likely to backfire.
- **Second, effectiveness is framed in different ways by organizations.** While everyday discourse suggests a focus on profit, in fact, we see not only trends but new, more complex approaches. Baker and Branch (2002) present three logics relevant to issues of effectiveness and argue that the third logic best represents current trends. Logic 1, "Bureaucratic Control," focuses on the primary value of management with organizations designed around internal functions and hierarchical relationships and processes. Logic II, "Engagement," focuses on leadership with the added value of all employees with the organization designed around external products and customers with lateral relationships and processes. Logic III, "Networking and Collaboration," focuses on facilitation with the value added of partnership and alliances. The design

> tends to be more flexible and fluid. Example adjectives in Logic III reflect ideas referenced in discussing ethics: collaboration, partnerships, alliances, and positioning in an external environment. Logic III has "given rise to the identification of new performance functions, such as change management, organizational learning, knowledge management, organizational partnerships and network formation, innovation and creativity" (p. 10).

A shift in logic from I or II to III is inclusive of discourse that challenges the notion of a single bottom line of profit. One could ask: Was Enron an effective organization? It certainly was profitable over the short run. Yet because of unethical practices and a lack of concern for employees and stockholders, its house of cards eventually collapsed. Organizations are realizing that environmental impact, community citizenship, financial stewardship, global development, and corporate responsibility are as important to evaluate as profitability in determining an organization's effectiveness. For instance, the idea of a "triple bottom line" (people, profit, planet) introduced by Elkington (1998) resonates with the current mission statements (e.g., Tom's Shoes and Nike) that were part of the linguistic analysis exercise in Chapter 5 (Rehearsal 5.3). One other recently launched organization, "Tacos 4 Life," states on its webpage that they "exist to help end childhood starvation around the world through our Meal 4 Meal program" (Tacos 4 Life, n.d.). In addition, several organizations have gained substantial attention for going far beyond the law in terms of improving employee pay rates. Dan Price, the CEO of a Seattle-based company, Gravity Payments, is best known for raising the minimum salary to 70,000.00 a year. Others have followed suit and, in such cases, profits have increased as well as employee engagement (Wheeler, 2017). These organizations are finding that taking care of people is not incompatible with profit. Organizations like these are clearly concerned about multiple bottom lines.

Consider again the case of "Interface" introduced in Chapter 9 on Ethics. Their mission of creating a "planet fit for life" is enacted through micro (e.g., co-creating vision and strategy) and macro (e.g., community engagement practices; benchmarking progress with stakeholders) constitutive of their organizing processes. Their vision statement goes further than the triple bottom line to add two more "p's":

> To be the first company that, by its deeds, shows the entire industrial world what sustainability is in all its dimensions: people, process, product, place and profit.
>
> (Interface, n.d.)

If you completed Rehearsal 5.3 on corporate mission statements, you might have gained additional instances of the latest generation of corporate mission statements as they embed language and other discourse tied to the idea of a triple bottom line.

Beyond instances in the business section, non-profit organizations provide another example of the need to expand the way we discuss effectiveness. Non-profits contributed an estimated $905.9 billion to the US economy in 2013, composing 5.4% of the country's gross domestic product. Added to this, in 2014, giving totaled $358.38 billion, an increase of over 5% from 2013, and 25.3% of US adults volunteered in 2014, contributing an estimated 8.7 billion hours valued at approximately $179.2 billion (McKeever, 2015). As such, non-profits represent a significant sector of the US economy. Non-profits do not exist to make a profit, but they can be examined by a number of other outcome measures, such as social capital (Putnam, 2002). Rehearsal 13.1 provides an opportunity to reflect on this idea of the triple bottom line.

Rehearsal 13.1 How Do You Measure Effectiveness?

Purpose: Reflect on how your organization defines effectiveness in light of the triple (or quadruple) bottom line.

Steps:

1. Select an organization you have worked in or participated in (from business, to non-profit, to faith-based). You may opt to reflect on the organization you are studying in this cultural analysis process.
2. Write down the statements you can recall from members, memos, and so on that best capture how effectiveness is/was measured.
3. What are the pros and cons of the measures being used?
4. Review Table 13.1 (near the end of the chapter). What elements of culture suggest the current logic of the organization you studied? What are the implications you see of this reflection for communication?

- **A third problem with the "bottom line" of profit as the measure of effectiveness is that research/experience paints a complex picture concerning the relationship between culture and performance.** A review of this research provides a backdrop for the model of organizational effectiveness we find useful in the application of cultural data. Research in this area can be captured in terms of three major perspectives on the link between culture and performance.

Perspective 1: Strong Cultures are Good

Early discussions of the link between culture and performance argued for the notion of "strong cultures" being associated with excellent performances. Deal and Kennedy (1982, 2000) popularized this argument by defining strong cultures as possessing the following themes: a) shared vision and values; b) supportive business environment; c) recognized corporate heroes; d) effective rites and rituals; and e) effective formal and informal communication networks. These authors highlighted organizations like IBM and Tandem Computers for their strong cultures. Peters and

Waterman (1982) also popularized certain characteristics of strong cultures based on their study of 62 successful companies. For instance, they noted things like a "bias for action," "close relations to the customer," "simple form, lean staff," and "hands-on value driven or strong core values."

Though dated, the work of Deal and Kennedy (1982) and Peters and Waterman (1982) still resonate. Who can argue against strong core values or effective networks? Still, further exploration of the strong culture concept has shown that some of the organizations identified in these studies have not been strong performers over the long haul. Strong cultures, paradoxically, may honor certain values or communication patterns that are actually detrimental to the organization (Kunda, 1993). In the worst case, unethical practices may become embedded in the culture. As Kotter and Heskett (1992) point out, "the strong culture theory" fails to account for the success of weak cultures. Such organizations as McGraw-Hill and Pitney Bowes, for example, received "weak corporate culture" scores but had impressive performance records.

Perspective 2: Strategically Appropriate Cultures Are Good

A second perspective argues for the notion of "strategically appropriate cultures"—the contents of the culture "fit" the context (conditions of the industry, degree of competitiveness, amount of change, degree of government regulation, degree of uncertainty). This "contingency" notion, like the strong culture, appeals to the logic presented. It makes sense that an effective organization would somehow adapt its strategies to fit specific economic conditions. However, research has shown that while short- and medium-term performance can be predicted by the notion of "fit," prediction of long-term effectiveness remains as elusive to predict with this theory as the "strong-cultures" perspective (Kotter & Heskett, 1992, p. 43). In fact, Collins (2001) based his theory of effective organizations on distinguishing companies that perform well in the short run versus those that have moved from "good to great" over a longer period of time. His analysis indicates that strategic fit is not the key to becoming a great organization. Rehearsal 13.2 provides an opportunity to reflect on this perspective.

Rehearsal 13.2 Finding the Drawbacks of the Best Fit

Purpose: Reflect on the limits of the second perspective, "Strategically appropriate cultures are good."

Steps:

1. Reflect on the discussion of strategically appropriate cultures.
2. Identify an instance in your experience or that you had read or heard about when an organization worked to adapt to its environment yet did not prove to be an effective organization over time.

____

____

____

____

3. Review the facets of the culture that may have contributed to this lower-than-expected performance.

____

____

____

____

Perspective 3: Adaptive Cultures Are Good

A third and final perspective, "adaptive cultures," presents arguments for cultures that can "help organizations anticipate and adapt to environmental change" (Kotter & Heskett, 1992, p. 44). In these organizations, not only is leadership key, but communicative practices are tied to organizational learning. Concerning leadership, organizations such as Hewlett-Packard, Facebook, Golden West, Google, and American Airlines demonstrate the importance of leaders focused on changes needed to satisfy the legitimate interests of stockholders, customers, and employees. In contrast, less adaptive cultures tend to have leadership that is absorbed in self-advancement or protection of position and status.

Collins (2001) documented 11 organizations that made the move from "good to great." He argues that leadership is at the core of this "leap." These organizations, according to Collins's careful market analysis, stood out from competitors in their markets over a 15-year time period. His research team, despite instruction to downplay the role of top executives, found each of these organizations had a type of leadership that blended "personal humility and professional will" (p. 20). In short, their ambition was for the institution, not for themselves. They tended to leave behind an organization that could be great without them. For instance, 75% of the comparison companies, those that did not make the leap from good to great, had executives who set their successors up for failure or chose weak successors (or both).

The adaptiveness of an organization is also seen in its capacity for learning and renewal that extends beyond the typical boundaries of an organization. Organizational learning, in a study of 20 small and medium-sized Pakistani enterprises, revealed the association of four important values: employee empowerment, open communications, employee collaboration, and continuous learning. These values were significantly associated with the perceived goal achievement levels of the firms (Khan & Syed, 2013). In addition, research on effective crisis communication has demonstrated the value not only of message response strategies but also of communicative practices that aid an organization and its stakeholders in learning and renewal (Ulmer, Sellnow, & Seeger, 2015).

For example, in a case study of an education union crisis, the researcher found evidence of learning through renewal processes that increased collaboration between partners (Paquette, 2015). In a case involving the 2009 earthquake in Italy, researchers documented how this crisis proved to be an opportunity for organizational learning and renewal for the international scientific v community (Sellnow, Iverson, & Sellnow, 2017). Manzie (2018) extends the renewal model by documenting the need for organizational learning and renewal to address the dangers of corporate benevolence and neocolonialism through engagement with and respect for local leadership decision-making practices. The significance of organizational learning is explored further in Rehearsal 13.3 in the context of crisis communication.

Rehearsal 13.3 Readiness for Renewal: Crisis Communication

Purpose: Identify thematic action that contributes to the likelihood of an organization's ability to renew through crisis events.

Steps:

1. Determine an organization that you want to assess in terms of its readiness to renew through a crisis.
2. Review current research on the "Readiness for Renewal" inventory (Fuller, McNatt, & Ulmer, 2017) to gain a better understanding of renewal practices.
3. Write down instances when your data indicate implicit or explicit examples of such practices as organizational learning, such as transparency or openness in communication, positive relationships with stakeholders, and collaborative communication.
4. Brainstorm two or more positive communicative implications from this reflection.

In summary, an organization is likely to be effective because of its ability to adapt. While certain traits of strong cultures, such as effective communication practices, make sense, they do not provide sufficient direction. Furthermore, the ability to "fit" current market conditions, while a critical component, fails to account for long-term effectiveness. So, a core question remains: "What, about adaptive cultures, do we need to pay attention to in relation to the data found in a cultural analysis?" Leadership has been mentioned, along with a value on renewal and learning, but what other characteristics might be used to guide the analysis of organizational culture data? From our focus on cultures as discursive constructions, we ask, "What sorts of thematic actions are likely to constitute an adaptive organization?"

Adaptive cultures do tend to share certain characteristics. Table 13.1 highlights a model of organizational effectiveness that captures communicative practices that should be considered in determining the implications of your organizational analysis. This model was co-created through reflection on research and theory, indicating micro and macro positive communicative practices attending to people, the planet, process, and profit. We welcome hearing from you as you discern other practices or revisions/clarifications to these constitutive practices deemed candidates for co-constructing more effective and ethical organizing practices. Remember, however, that any insight or potential recommendation for change needs to be sifted through, researching, finding, and indicating the power of the national culture context. For instance, it would be a mistake to overlook the power of communicative processes that constitute national cultures that also then shape organizations. In the United States, a value is placed on the management of objectives (e.g., working toward clearly established goals). Thus, success is determined and measured by time-efficient goal achievement. In contrast, in other cultures, such as Mexico, business is not conducted until partners have a chance to get to know one another (Varner & Beamer, 1995). Effective organizations find ways to adapt to and manage these cultural differences when engaged in a global environment.

As you review this model, think about the extent to which your cultural analysis contains thematic action that encourages or discourages moves toward being effective through being adaptive. The themes you interpreted in your analysis as well as the overall characterization of culture often give hints about the extent to which an organization is enacting the communication practices indicated in Table 13.1. Embedded in the themes you identified, for example, may be statements about how stakeholders are to be treated or about communication rules regarding customer interactions. For instance, if you identified thematic action related to conflict ("Customers are heard only when they file formal complaints"), you might generate a list of possible applications since this theme has such clear ties to important organizational performance issues. You might note as a strength that this theme makes it clear that customer complaints are important. Yet, in contrast, other important information from customers may be downplayed. Any number of insights and potential interventions might be suggested by such an analysis. Yet, before jumping to recommendations, reflect on aspects of the organization's history that are present in this communicative norm. Furthermore, the exploration of socialization and/or training practices related to customer service merits attention. In all, this process of cultural analysis should be about a willingness to explore patterns that contribute to effectiveness as well as those that are detrimental.

Table 13.1 The Communicative Constitution of an Efficiently Adaptive Organization

Employees

- Participate in informal networks to encourage innovation and supportive change processes.
- Open forum for discussing differences and disagreements.
- Learn from failed efforts without assigning blame.
- Understanding and sharing a vision of what the organization does best.
- Selecting and keeping the best.
- Merit-based (rather than political) rewards and advancement.
- Tapping into strengths of cultural diversity.
- Committed to continual learning of the art of positive communication through greetings, asking open questions, complementing, disclosing, encouraging, listening, and inspiring (Mirivel, 2014).

Customers

- Communicating a clear vision to customers of what the organization does best.
- Channels for receiving customer input and feedback.
- Always listening and changing based on feedback.

Stakeholders

- Balancing demands of stockholders for profits with concerns for the physical environment.
- Balancing demands of stockholders for profits with concerns for employees, customers, and community members.

Leadership

- Practices courageous communication by shifting from: a) control to collaboration; b) top-down to upward communication; c) secrecy to transparent communication; and d) impersonal to engaging communication (Lyon, 2017).
- High value on co-creating vision based on facts/truth.
- Adapts communication to the varied meaning structures held in response to change.
- Responds dialogically to tensions embedded in the change process. (e.g., assimilation–autonomy, consensus–command, upward–downward, transparency–secrecy).
- Ethically utilizes cultural elements during the change process (e.g., rituals, stories, values, humor).
- Enacts symbolic leadership practices (stories, rituals, reframing, optimal competence through multi-frame reflection).

(Continued)

Table 13.1 (Continued)

- Models mindfulness by reflecting on and introducing three big questions ("What are we creating here?" "What should we co-create?" "What kinds of communication will create what we should create?").• Models civil discourse and positive communication through practice and supporting formal policy and training.
- Focus on leadership identification and development.
- Encourage identification of positive deviant practices.
- Plans for leadership succession.

Organizational Structures

- Flexible and dynamic structure to match organizational mission and goals.
- Build in diversity-supportive practices (e.g., dialogue groups, community forums, intercultural training, mentoring, positive communication training).
- Macro-level practices (training, forums, formal policies, etc.) to encourage civil discourse, member safety, and equitable treatment, grievance and conflict management practices.
- Positive external stakeholder relationships with accountability on measurable sustainability goals.

Summary

To return to one of the opening quotes: "We forget that the primary function of language, if we have something to say and are not merely babbling, is to uncover something within the world, to bring it into the open" (Barrett, *The Illusion of Technique*, 1979, p. 158). Research on organizational culture and effectiveness has prompted a revision of earlier, overly simplistic ideas. We agree that sufficient levels of profitability are essential to most organizations, yet we concur that it "should not be maximized at the expense of other equally important social needs, including living wages, sustainable development, quality of work/life, and self-determination" (LeGreco, Eisenberg, Tretheway, & Goodall, 2024, p. 171). We covered two major approaches to defining an effective culture before introducing the one that is best supported by research. We also encouraged your own review process. The following summary points capture the main ideas presented.

1. Problems may arise if profits become the driving rationale for making changes to culture. Employees may resist such efforts if they are seen as solely for management's gain.
2. In the wake of corporate scandals, top corporations now realize that corporate responsibility and values must be evaluated, as well as profitability, in determining long-term organizational effectiveness.
3. The first approach to defining an effective culture is the notion that "strong is good." Reviews of long-term strong performers show they do not always fit this model, and, in some cases, unethical practices can be embedded in a strong culture.
4. A second approach suggests that a "contingency" or strategically appropriate culture is a good one. Again, the long-term high-performance companies that were reviewed do not fit this approach.
5. The final approach, and the one argued for in this workbook, is that efficiently adaptive cultures are the most effective. This perspective supports long-term, high-performing organizational cultures, maintaining and passing on a value set that focuses on changing as needed.

6. We encourage you in Rehearsal 13.4 to review the thematic actions and overall characterization of the culture to gain clues about the extent to which the culture you studied is efficiently adaptive.

Rehearsal 13.4 Gauging Effectiveness

Purpose: Identify thematic action that contributes to or fails to constitute effective organizational communication patterns.

Steps:

1. Review your cultural interpretation, including enacted elements, thematic, and an overall definition(s).
2. Write down instances when your data indicate implicit or explicit examples of effective communication practices relevant to the dimensions of effectiveness based on Table 13.1.
3. Write down instances when your data indicate implicit or explicit examples of ineffective communication practices based on Table 13.1.
4. Brainstorm a list of two or more implications of the observations you made in your data. For example, if you noted effective communication patterns, how might the values inherent in these patterns be further strengthened? Conversely, if you noted ineffective behaviors, how might these be addressed?

Discussion Questions

1. How would you define an effective organization? Give an example of an organization you would categorize as effective.
2. Which of the three approaches to organizational effectiveness seems to make the most sense to you? (strong culture, situationally appropriate culture, or adaptive culture). Explain your reasoning.
3. How can efforts to manipulate culture in order to maximize profits fail for organizational leaders?
4. What makes the idea of a triple (or quadruple) bottom line compelling?

References

Autry, J. (1991). *Love and profit: The art of caring leadership*. New York: Avon.

Baker, K. A., & Branch, K. M. (2002). Concepts underlying organizational effectiveness: Trends in the organization and management science literature. In E. L. Malone, K. M. Branch, & K. A. Baker (Eds.), *Managing science as a public good: Overseeing publicly-funded science*. Retrieved from www.au.af.mil/au/awc/awcgate/doe/benchmark/ch01.pdf.

Barrett, W. (1979). *The illusion of technique*. Garden City, NY: Anchor.

Collins, J. (2001). *Good to great: Why some companies make the leap and others don't*. New York: Harper Collins.

Deal, T., & Kennedy, A. (1982). *Corporate cultures*. New York: Addison-Wesley.

Deal, T., & Kennedy, A. (2000). *Corporate cultures*. Cambridge, MA: Perseus.

Deetz, S., Tracy, S., & Simpson, J. (2000). *Leading organizations through transition: Communication and cultural change*. Thousand Oaks, CA: Sage.

Elkington, J. (1998). *Cannibals with forks*. Gabriola Island, Canada: New Society Publishers.

Eriksson, P. E., Olander, S., Szentes, H., & Widén, K. (2014). Managing short-term efficiency and long-term development through industrialized construction. *Construction Management & Economics, 32*(*1–2*), 97–108. https://doi.org/10.1080/01446193.2013.814920

Fuller, R. P., McNatt, A. M., & Ulmer, R. R. (2017). Extending renewal to organizational preparedness: Development and test of readiness for renewal instrument. Proceedings of the 82 Annual Association for Business Communication Conference. ISSN 2472-0658.

Heifer International (n.d.). About us. *Ending poverty begins with agriculture*. https://www.heifer.org/about-us/index.html

Interface. (n.d.). Our sustainability journey—Mission zero. *Interface*. Retrieved from www.interface-global.com/Sustainability/Interface-Story.aspx

Jain, R., & Gulati, S. (2016). HRD systems and organizational performance: Qualitative review of research. *Journal of Institute of Public Enterprise, 6*(*1–2*), 86–108.

Khan, M. R., & Syed, N. A. (2013). Exploring association of OD values with organizational perceived effectiveness: Case of small and medium enterprises. *Journal of Independent Studies & Research: Management & Social Sciences & Economics, 11*(*1*), 41–55.

Kotter, J., & Heskett, J. (1992). *Corporate culture and performance*. New York: Macmillan.

Kunda, G. (1993). *Engineering culture: Control and commitment in a high-tech corporation*. Philadelphia: Temple University Press.

LeGreco, M., Eisenberg, E., Tretheway, A., & Goodall, H. (2024). *Organizational communication: Balancing creativity and constraint* (9th ed.). New York: St. Martin's.

Little, B. (2016). Benchmark report reveals trends in corporate learning and development. *Industrial & Commercial Training, 48*(*5*), 225–230. https://doi.org/10.1108/ICT-12-2015-0079

Lyon, A. (2017). *Case studies in courageous organizational communication: Research and practices for effective workplaces*. New York: Peter Lang.

Mali, P. (1978). *Improving total productivity*. New York: John Wiley.

Manzie, V. (2018). Applying the rhetoric of renewal model in a contemporary African context: Lessons learned from royal Dutch shell oil crisis in Nigeria. *Journal of International Crisis and Risk Communication Research, 1*(2), 201–224.

McKeever, B. (October 29, 2015). *The nonprofit sector in brief 2015: Public charities, giving, and volunteering, urban institute*. Retrieved from www.urban.org/research/publication/nonprofit-sector-brief-2015-public-charities-giving-and-volunteering

Mirivel, J. (2014). *The art of positive communication: Theory and practice*. New York: Peter Lang.

Paquette, M. (2015). Renewal or re-entrenchment? A case study of the 2011 education union crisis. *Journal of Public Relations Research, 27*(*4*), 337–352. https://doi.org/10.1080/1062726X.2015.1060130

Peters, T., & Waterman, R. (1982). *In search of excellence*. New York: Harper & Row.

Putnam, R. (2002). *Bowling alone: The collapse and revival of the American community*. New York: Simon and Schuster.

Sellnow, D., Iverson, J., & Sellnow, T. (2017). The evolution of the operational earthquake forecasting community of practice: The L'Aquila communication crisis as a triggering event for organizational renewal. *Journal of Applied Communication Research, 45*(*2*), 121–139. https://doi.org/10.1080/00909882.2017.1288295

Singe, P. (1990). *The fifth discipline: The art and practice of the learning organization*. Garden City, NY: Doubleday.

Tacos 4 Life. (n.d.). *Giving-food changes everything*. Retrieved from https://tacos4life.com/

Ulmer, R., Sellnow, T., & Seeger, M. (2015). *Effective crisis communication: Moving from crisis to opportunity* (3rd ed.). Thousand Oaks, CA: Sage Publications.

Varner, I., & Beamer, L. (1995). *Intercultural communication in the global workplace*. Chicago: Irwin.

Wheeler, M. (August 20, 2017). Three years ago, this boss set a $70,000 minimum wage. *Linkedin.com*. Retrieved from www.linkedin.com/pulse/best-boss-america-year-3-michael-wheeler/

Chapter 14

Opening Night

Conclusion

This book opened and now closes by prompting reflection on the span of experiences found in organizations—from the cradle to the grave, from tragic to comic stories as well as stories of hope and transformation. Given the significant time spent in organizations, we have encouraged the use of the OCA model focused on *fostering the co-creation of positive organizations by developing implications through the analysis of enacted elements that both shape and are shaped by communication.* Both the training tools of method actors and the process of cultural analysis foreground an awareness of communication. This chapter focuses on our ethical responsibility to act on this improved awareness. Building on the application chapters of diversity, ethics, change, and leadership, this final chapter invites you to put the final OCA step of *co-creating positive communication applications* into action. Guides are provided for developing a final report that includes an action plan for "acting into" positive professional and organizational communication applications.

1. Articulate cultural analysis goals and benefits
2. Explore culture as co-construction
3. Reflect on enacted elements
4. Identify enacted elements via multiple methods
5. Interpret thematic action and OCA
6. Co-create positive communication applications

Conclusion

Objectives

- Apply your cultural analysis to create professional communication goals.
- Apply your cultural analysis to create a plan for organizational development.

The following quote reflects the chapter's aims:

> The kind of concentration necessary for acting demands the ability to recreate something which is not there. It leads not only to the workings of the imagination, but also the presence of that kind of belief or faith which has often been characterized as the essential element in acting.
>
> (Strasberg, *A Dream of Passion*, 1987, p. 131)

DOI: 10.4324/9781003482529-18

Back to Change

Reflect on the following statements from various individuals involved in this cultural analysis process.

- *I cannot believe all that I am seeing here. I really have a better sense of how to make it in this organization. I realize now why things seem to be going faster than the speed of light. I am not as stressed as I once was, and I am far less critical of management. I began my analysis as I began my second week here, and now I feel like an insider after just a few months. In fact, I was able to make some suggestions on how to manage our recent transitions to a new facility.*
- *I think it was a mistake doing this study. Well, I knew before I started that I held some strong biases, but now I have to face them. The truth is that I would rather not address these issues at this time. It is hard to admit, but it really is easier not to change my communication habits even when I see from my study that they need changing.*
- *I actually went to my boss and said,* "Do you know how my new cultural and communication skill sets can help us?" *He listened, and I have been given new and exciting opportunities.*
- *This analysis has pretty much convinced me that I do not belong in this organization.*

Now, consider this question: What would you add to the list? What might you share with peers, friends, a supervisor, and/or colleagues? As we wrap up this workbook (and this revision), we each have added our own here.

- *Get up and do it again. That is to pay attention in daily informal analysis and positive co-construction. Stay after minute-to-minute small steps of being grateful, greeting and affirming others, and listening between the lines for what someone needs. To share a struggle, a doubt, an unexpected tear at a world that is more beautiful than it has to be. At home, work, and all the places I have breath—Get up and do it again and again each day.* (Gerald)
- *Culture is not something we have; it is something we do. Your actions matter more than you know. As a leader, a practitioner, and a person, your communication does not just transmit information; it helps to create the very reality of your experience in the workplace. Reach out to others, make contact, and stay in a mode of invitation, discovery, and life-long learning.* (Julien)

For now, to set the stage for this final application chapter, we return to a statement we made in the opening chapter when the curtain was first raised.

- Organizations *are the places that carry us from the cradle to the grave.*

We slow to repeat, *cradle to grave. Cradle to grave.*

The two-letter connection "to" and the phrase "carry us" miss the significance, the poignancy, the laughter and tears, the profound and mundane, the bittersweet of all that is in between "cradle to grave." To say "carry" misses how we are shaped and gives shape to identities, relationships, roles, hope, purpose, and meaning in these intertwined networks we call organizations. Recall the mental shift *from organizations as buildings and businesses to a complex communication system that constitutes social reality in ethical and unethical ways.*

Our shared experiences in these complex, connected communication systems motivate our collaborative efforts with friends, colleagues, and students to foster better social worlds. As we move into this final chapter, we contend that change often begins with one single, solitary insight. Insights like the ones listed previously—the ones we added that we hope you add. The challenge of enhancing your own performance or that of an organization is to act on that insight. Put the phone down, close the laptop, the book, the game, and walk down the hall and act into a communication behavior that you know you need to enact. What might that be? Given how connected we are, it might be a conviction that you need to:

- Slow down to affirm a contribution of a team member.
- Get in the habit of visiting each team member's office once a day or a week.
- Let a family member know how much you value their support.
- Offer an apology and/or forgiveness because we are so connected that it can be hard to apologize and/or forgive each other (inspired by author Fredrick Backman).
- Offer to team up with someone to analyze some aspect of the culture.
- ____________________________________

Each of these moments is about co-creating more positive organizations. You may never step on an actual stage or even stand backstage. as mentioned in the opening chapter. Yet, we all, each day, are engaged in varied organizational stages. This final chapter is about such moments when an insight prompts us to step back into our organizations in a new or different way. We trust that such insights occurred as you engaged in the interpretation step of identifying thematic action and the overall culture in action.

Opening night, as we consider the professional and organizational application in this closing chapter, is that moment when an insight, an interpretation of a role, is put into action. After much thought, planning, and rehearsal, a role is enacted, a script is brought to life. As the opening statements suggest, the outcomes of paying close attention to formal or informal culture analysis vary greatly—from aiding in a transition to a new organization to an awareness of a lack of self-motivation in the change process. If these insights are to have value, it is essential to develop and execute both an organizational and professional communication development plan. Perhaps your experience is like ours. We find coming up with strategies to be easy, but execution is often lacking. For instance, Gerald was at a board meeting of a community organization in which members discussed a shared experience. Past meetings had been filled with energy and great strategic plans. Everyone seemed on board with our compelling mission. However, from meeting to meeting, the energy level declined. Execution was lagging behind big ideas. A change happened when we discussed ways to improve execution. This experience and others, both at work and at home, inspired many of the practices outlined in this chapter. The idea is to shift from ideas to action. As the following quote indicates, the challenge of taking responsibility for such action is both significant and meaningful.

> [A] lasting organizational community requires more than commitment and communication. It requires discipline and mastery. This mastery is achieved as each person makes his or her contributions and assumes responsibility for them. Instead of a solitary leader responsible for performance, each member becomes a leader depending on the skills, knowledge, and experience needed in each situation.
>
> (Eisenberg, Andrews, Murphy, & Laine-Timmerman, 1999, pp. 145–146)

Your newly gained knowledge of how to conduct a cultural analysis, as well as the positive communication applications you have identified, place you in the position to make a contribution not only to an organization but also to your own professional and personal development. You have taken time to answer big questions: a) "What are we co-creating here?" and b) "What should we co-create?" This closing chapter guides our response to the final of our three big questions: c) "What forms of communication will co-create the culture we seek to create?"

Flowing from reflections on earlier application chapters, this chapter is about co-creating ethical action plans grounded in positive communication practices. Throughout this chapter, we stress the role of co-creating positive communication action grounded in varied enacted elements of culture, including action steps that can be meaningfully measured, assessed, adjusted, and celebrated as small or big wins. Figure 14.1 captures the OCA model that captures your focus on enacted elements forming thematic action to an overall characterization of the culture leading to the final phase—co-create positive communication applications. Your interpretative process is intended to support you toward professional (Rehearsal 14.1) and organizational application (Rehearsal 14.2).

At this juncture, given the time spent on analysis, all may be tempted to focus on organizational applications in a final report. However, we encourage you to pause organizational applications until you first reflect on your own action plan. Your credibility as a change leader requires intentional effort. Put differently, we hope you will have stories to tell others about the minor and/or major transformations that occurred in the process of your analysis and reflection. Indeed, consider completing Rehearsal 14.1 as an initial reflection on your growth and development.

In fact, we envision some of you having others tell stories about the changes they see in your behaviors. What is the basis for such high hopes? Such hope has grown from several decades of hearing from students, alumni, and colleagues and from our research and consulting with participants as well. We are confident that paying careful attention to culture, to a wide array of cultural elements, as well as the time spent in discerning thematic action, overall characterization of the culture, and varied communication applications (Chapters 9–13), has prompted reflection on your role on the stage. Such reflection results in varied insights, as indicated in the previous statements. Recall one of the statements that echoes more than one

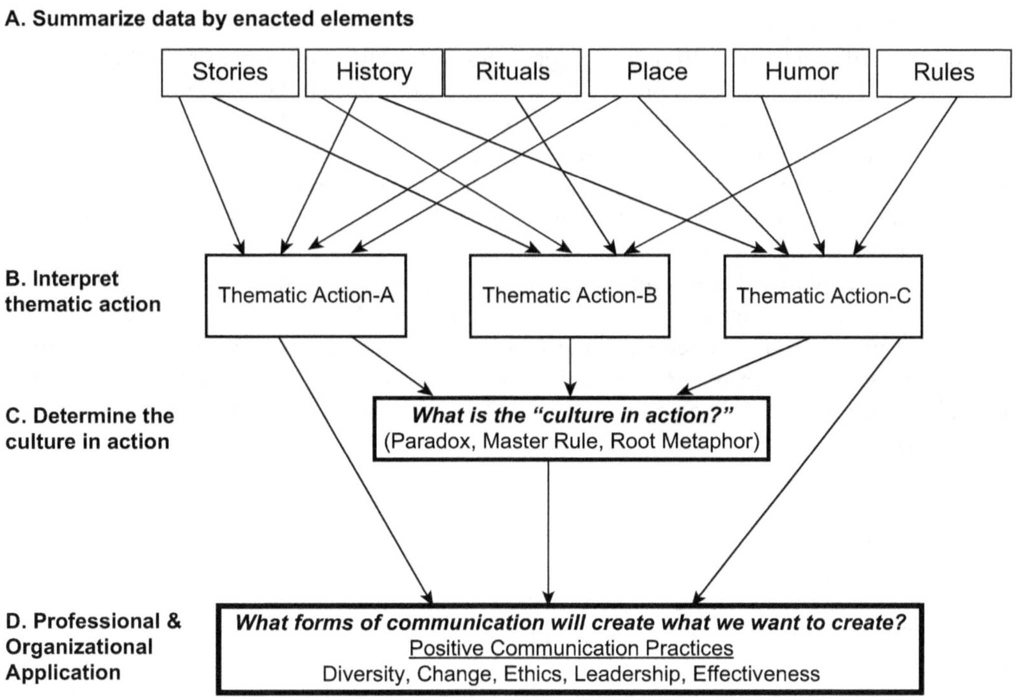

Figure 14.1 From Interpretation to Application

Rehearsal 14.1 Reflective Assessment—Articulate Learning

(Developed by Dr. S. Lynne Willett, University of Wisconsin-Stout)

Reflective Assessment: The idea that reflection provides benefits for learners has been around since the time of Plato, who described reflection as a discourse the mind carries on with itself. At its heart, reflective assessment is a metacognitive and formative assessment strategy that encourages students to think about their thinking. Reflective thinking helps students figure out what they know and do not know and connects their learning to other experiences and information in their world.

Articulate Learning: Compose a brief (150–200 words) reflection to address the following questions. In addition, you may record a video if you would like.

What specific and measurable communication behavior(s) have I learned that I will put to use professionally and/or personally?

How will I communicate to others in my current or future organization to inspire and motivate?

How will I coach others in my sphere of influence to co-create a positive culture?

How has this course changed my perspective, if at all? You may approach the answer from either a personal or professional view or both.

voice—*It is hard to admit, but it really is easier not changing my communication habits, even when I see from my study that they need changing.*

While not all will leave with major insights and/or a willingness to improve their communication, the majority will gain practical insights for professional development. Regardless of the insight or application, we encourage you to connect, share, and listen. Some of you might want to connect with us and others in conversations on "LinkedIn." Conversely, we invite you to connect with the Positive Communication Network—www.positivecommunication.net/. This network, founded by Julien, is dedicated to "communication that improves the human condition."

In all, we trust you will see your role as a leader in paying attention to culture and giving shape to cultures that improve the lives of others. Pearce (2007) challenges us to realize that our diverse world requires effective leaders to become champions of how we communicate and the processes we create through daily interactions. The cultural analysis process framed through constitutive processes enhances this focus on communication. Communication is taken seriously, not merely as a way to share information or get others to line up with some plan, but as a social construction process. As introduced earlier, the OCA model, in conjunction with the varied constructivist theories, shares "the assumption that the organization does not predate communication but emerges and perpetuates itself as a network of interlocking communication events" (Schoeneborn et al., 2014, p. 305). Thus, we need to attend to these constitutive processes again. Do you recall the guiding metaphors from Chapter 2 related to the term "constitutive"? Images of a) atoms or what makes a "thing what it is"; b) political power to "institute, establish or enact"; and c) DNA as a controlling mechanism. These images foreground the fact that communication is more than information sharing or clarity but that it is central, it matters, and it is consequential. Thus, even if you are not formally presenting results to your own organization or to the organization you analyzed, you have gained insights that merit further reflection and application. After discussing an analogy aimed at keeping the planning and change process in perspective, activities designed to aid you in professional and organizational development are outlined.

A Compass, Not a Map

Goal setting and the process of developing an action plan can give the illusion that we know exactly where our plans will take us. The tendency is to think that an action plan is like a map to be followed; for instance, take I-30 west from Little Rock, Arkansas, to Dallas, Texas, or I-67 north to St. Louis or I-40 east to Memphis and Nashville. Using this map analogy, we might think to ourselves: *I know where I am going, and I am not lost.* In contrast, we view action plans as more in keeping with the statement: *I don't know where I am going, but I am not lost.* Action plans are more like a compass than a map. A compass gives you the confidence that you are not lost; you know the general direction you are going, but you may not know exactly where that direction will lead you. You cannot predict all the consequences of all the plans you put in place. You may still gain confidence in moving in the best possible direction with the information you have garnered.

In the art and skill of change leadership, and more particularly making changes in professional or organizational communication, usually, the best that can be done is gaining an awareness of where you are through an analysis and then using an action plan to point you in the direction of the desired change. In fact, there is value in learning to maintain a level of uncertainty about decisions that may flow from plans. Langer (1989) summarizes a study that assessed the level of certainty managers had about decisions they made every day. She and her colleague also evaluated the working relationship of these managers with their subordinates. They found that "those managers who were confident but relatively uncertain were evaluated by their employees as more likely to allow independent judgment and a general freedom of action" (p. 144). Did you catch the paradox? Confidence combined with relative uncertainty? Put differently, there is value in using a compass rather than a map.

The need for both confidence and uncertainty is due in part to the fact that the process of implementing changes involves continual readjustment. For example, you may identify a goal for professional development that involves setting up a conflict management ritual or co-creating a civility policy. Once initiated, this change may make you aware that you have not adequately listened to the issues. You did not fully co-create the goal or plan. Thus, new goals and strategies relevant to co-creating support for effective conflict management may need to be developed. Nonetheless, the process you engage in, a process of awareness, action, and adjustment, is at the heart of enhancing your organizational culture's performances.

> A compass gives you the confidence that you are not lost; you know the general direction you are going, but you may not know exactly where that direction will lead you.

The compass illustration suggests that we have a sense of a desired direction (i.e., a goal to implement an organizational change), and we have an awareness of where we are now (i.e., as a result of the cultural analysis), but even the best action plans cannot predict the future (e.g., what will the actual result of the change be?). Students and practitioners have shared with us the variety of outcomes that have come through their cultural analysis process: promotions and transfers; business as usual; others speak of personal insights or being more effective in adapting to the culture; still others have left their organizations for various reasons. In short, action plans do not guarantee certain outcomes, but they should be developed to make certain desired changes possible.

Professional Communication Action Plan

Rehearsal 14.1 provides a means for reviewing your cultural analysis experience with the intent of helping you visualize results for professional development. The process of writing an action plan is familiar to many of you. Yet, we encourage a process of co-creation, one involving others who have a stake in the organization as well. To that end, the checklists include reminders on writing an effective action plan, but not one done in isolation. This first Rehearsal focuses on professional communication development goals. We provide a space for writing a rough draft. As you develop ideas, note our encouragements to create plans that you can and will execute, as well as plans to continue engaging others along the way. We find the execution of any plan to often be the most challenging, yet also rewarding as we celebrate progress and find support to grow through defeats. The guides are, therefore, intended to integrate positive, constitutive practices to support this journey. To that end, and to encourage a positive communication focus, we encourage you to reflect on Mirivel's (2014) model of positive communication as well as varied levels of positive communication competencies developed by Mirivel and Lyon (2023). His model reflects a growing network (www.positivecommunication.net/) of applied organizational and interpersonal scholarship focused on positivity (Brown, Morris, & Lee, 2012; Lyon, 2017; Pitts & Soya, 2012; Wooten, Morgan, Roberts, & Davidson, 2016). Positive communication practices may serve as a starting point to discern specific communicative actions of value for your professional development. Grounded in constitutive theories of communication (i.e., speech act theory, Coordinated Management of Meaning, Symbolic Interactionism), Mirivel foregrounds seven positive practices. They are listed in the following with possible applications to illustrate how they might become part of an action plan relevant to insights from your cultural analysis.

- Greeting others to co-create relationships.
- Asking questions to discover the unknown about another person as well as varied organizing practices.
- Complimenting to affirm the value others bring to the organization.
- Disclosing to develop trust and deepen relationships.
- Encouraging to co-create networks of social support.
- Listening to co-create dialogic practices during conflicts and negotiations.
- Inspiring to influence and construct meaning and purpose.

Consider integrating and adapting one or more of these positive practices into your action plan. The key here is to reflect on insights from your data about your role in co-creating better, more ethical organizing processes.

Rehearsal 14.2 Action Plan for Professional Communication Development

Purpose: Develop an action plan for at least two communication goals important to your leadership development.

Step 1: Identify two positive communication goals that have the following characteristics.

Specific and measurable communication behavior rather than general attitudes or values. For example, your analysis may have made you more aware of the types of tensions and value dilemmas with a diversity initiative. You might, then, draft a goal related to diversity; something like: "Gain a better perspective on my role in addressing the problems minorities have in our employee engagement program." Then, revise this goal to focus on a specific communication behavior. For example, you might revise it to be: "Explore ideas with my immediate supervisor and team about creating a continuous learning process related to diversity in our engagement program." The key here, as you can see with this last version, is you can see it in action; you can measure if it was accomplished. You can celebrate accomplishments and discern new goals.

Contextualized communication behavior (appropriate setting, purpose, etc.) rather than general statements of what you plan to do. The preceding example does not provide a sense of reflection on the most competent way to approach this topic with a supervisor. For instance, consider the different interpretations and impact of a statement about your awareness of a specific issue made to a supervisor informally spoken over a morning cup of coffee versus a formal discussion during a team meeting. Thus, a revised version should contextualize your plan and might read like this: "Gain approval to add the following agenda item to our next team meeting: 'The creation of a continuous learning process related to diversity in our engagement program.'" This goal then embeds the process in an enacted cultural element—a ritual (meeting) where you are attending to a common norm of introducing items for the agenda.

Your communication behavior rather than something that requires a change in someone else. We have found that a common tendency is for us to see ways a supervisor or co-worker needs to improve quickly. We might say: "If I could just get them to change or if we could just get a decent boss, life would get better around here!" However, this focus is ultimately defeating in that it places the hope for a more productive and meaningful life in the organization on everyone else. In fact, the shift from sarcastic irony (recall Chapter 10 on Change) may grow from assuming you have to wait on others to act. Thus, for example, the goal, "To get my supervisor to provide clearer feedback," would be better worded as: "To provide paraphrases of my supervisor's feedback to ensure understanding."

Inspiring and/or motivating: Remember these are your goals, even as we encourage you to create them with input from others. Go for what is most important—something you know will be good for you to do, something you believe the data indicates would be right and ethical for you to do, something you will be glad you did or at least glad you attempted. We find it valuable to reflect on deeper values and passions that you carry that are transcendent and yet also encompass daily interactions. For instance, a new or renewed commitment to affirming or complimenting others not only impacts others but also your own lived experience. Personal, handwritten notes, for example, to each member of your team place you in the role of constituting a positive, supportive culture. Gerald still recalls the first weeks in a new role in a new department. The verbal affirmation of one colleague is still remembered.

Step 2: Identify a time frame with action steps with space to revise, learn, and celebrate.

For example, one *goal* might be: "During my upcoming review this June, discuss my professional development goals in light of the results of my cultural analysis." We provide an example set of dates and steps. Such details create a level of commitment. Note that in the second step, b, there is the encouragement to include a review with a trusted peer or mentor. Change in communication behaviors happens best in the context of support.

Dates	**Steps**
May 15	a. Summarize data on theme one as it relates to my ability to negotiate differences between work groups.
June 1	b. Review my ideas and goals with a colleague and mentor.
June 15	c. Make revisions in goals and gather resources (books, training, etc., that may be needed).
July 7	d. Present my goals at my performance review.

Step 3: Set a time frame to review the results of your action plan (ideally with a trusted colleague/friend) and evaluate appropriate next steps.

An evaluation step is a way to encourage you to picture desired results and then determine ways to revise and develop a plan. Drafts of this step may actually prompt revisions of the earlier steps. The following example illustrates elements that might be included in this step.

Follow up by October 1.

a. Discuss with key parties the effectiveness of recent meetings that depended on my negotiation skills.
b. Keep a journal of meetings—review the impact of integrating alternative negotiation tactics based on each of the four frames.
c. Celebrate successes and revise goals as needed.

Write a brief follow-up plan that relates to the steps you wrote earlier. Again, remember that a compass allows you to adjust your plan as you gain more information. The adjustments should be considered part of your ongoing commitment to acting on your awareness of ways to enhance your communication in the context of the overall performance of the organization.

Step 1: Communication goals that identify specific and contextualized communication behavior and focus on your own rather than others' behavior.

Goal A: ____

____

Goal B: ____

____

Step 2: Identify a time frame with action steps.

Goal A: ______________________________

Date	Steps
________	______________________________
________	______________________________
________	______________________________

Goal B: ______________________________

Date	Steps
________	______________________________
________	______________________________
________	______________________________

Step 3: Time frame for reviewing action plan results; evaluate appropriate next steps (including revision and celebration).

Date	Evaluation Comments/Revision/Celebration Plan
________	______________________________
________	______________________________
________	______________________________

Organizational Development Action Plan

Beyond your professional development action plan, discerning how to co-create a plan related to positive organizational communication application is equally challenging. The final chapters (diversity, change, ethics, leadership, and effectiveness) provided a venue for reflecting on your cultural data. Each chapter encourages you to draft potential communication implications of your analysis in light of applied research and theory. The intent is to take the next step and discern a way to move forward. This step may involve a focus on one of these application chapters or insights that move beyond any one chapter. Even if you are not being asked by the organization to create a plan of action, you can tailor Rehearsal 14.2 to informal change leadership steps that you plan to adopt.

To that end, pause now to reflect on a poignant, too-often spoken, yet tragic, word. The word we have in mind is "almost."

- "I almost enacted that greeting, and asked that question."
- "I almost spoke to a co-worker about an idea I had."
- "I almost made the time needed to consider how to introduce changes that would help improve work-life balance."

Almost is not a word we want to go to the grave having used often. To motivate "acting into," we find it helps to imagine the sense of loss involved in "almost." Imagine having cultural insights pertinent to organizational effectiveness or change management practices but failing to take action. Imagine the outcome if you failed to translate your insights into action. Such inaction may not only cost the organization money but also reduce levels of engagement and the impact of unchecked unethical practices.

Instead, we invite you to return to the beginning and imagine a different outcome. Recall the proposal process, which involved a commitment by leadership to share results with the organization. Not taking this step may add to a pattern of leaders claiming to listen but then not acting on what was learned. The intent of this final Rehearsal is to co-create a positive pattern of responding to feedback.

This section will guide you through a set of steps intended to make the process comprehensible and more likely to succeed. Remember, however, that this process should not be treated separately from the first section on your own professional development. Recall that formal and informal recommendations are more likely to be received if you have already demonstrated meaningful changes in your own communication behaviors. If, for example, you see the need for improved meeting management skills among all supervisors, and if you have already begun to improve your own skills in this area, recommendations are much more likely to be heard. Because of the breadth of questions reviewed in the next section, space is not provided for all of your responses. We encourage you to draft your ideas, review them, and check them against your cultural analysis before deciding on a final plan of action.

Rehearsal 14.3 Organizational Development Action Plan

Purpose: Develop a process for implementing positive communicative practices that are important for the effectiveness and ethicality of your organization.

Steps for Developing Recommendations

1. *Reflect on insights gained from the application chapters* (Chapters 9–13). Write down specific themes that relate to issues in each of these chapters.

   Chapter 9: Diversity ____________________

   ____

   ____

   ____

   ____

   Chapter 10: Change ____________________

   ____

   ____

   ____

Chapter 11: Ethics ____

____

____

____

Chapter 12: Leadership ____

____

____

____

Chapter 13: Effectiveness ____

____

____

____

2. *Select no more than two themes that you see as most important and most likely to be accepted if translated into communication and culture development goals.* You or another leader may well need to initiate this process, but the key is to let others identify and create goals. Such focus will increase the likelihood of application. The idea is to discern possible goals based on these themes, growing from the relevant chapters. The intent is to brainstorm and envision a communication or organizational development initiative that would enhance or develop a cultural theme that will create what you and others seek to create in the organization. For example, you might have concluded from several elements of culture that the organization's culture is inconsistent in supporting diversity initiatives. However, you did learn that one cultural hero encouraged diversity initiatives and that a diversity strategy was in place. Thus, you might brainstorm a next step that would include additional rituals and training in the area of diversity.

   Possible Areas of Focus:

   ____

   ____

   ____

   ____

   ____

3. *Engage others in translating the draft goal into a meaningful, motivating communication goal.* For example, note the difference between the following goal statements. "To be an industry leader in diversity (or environmental) initiatives by _____." Contrast that

statement with, "To engage 80% of our members in dialogue groups over the next two years." While the first statement may function as a sort of vision statement, the ability to measure it, to celebrate a success, to discern how to move ahead is difficult. The second statement is one that you can then easily imagine creating a plan to execute. More importantly, the plan seeks to integrate ritualized practices of assessing and celebrating progress. Thus, a team might agree to meet each week to celebrate progress and address revised steps.

4. *Decide if these practices would be best presented in a formal manner or introduced informally.* You might have aspects that you present formally and others that are best introduced informally. Here are a few criteria to check to determine if you are in a position to make formal recommendations:

    - Your organization knows of your study and expects you to present your findings.
    - Your position allows you such credibility and thus freedom.
    - Your relationship with leadership makes it possible.

If you are not able to answer yes to at least one of the previous statements, then develop your action plan for this section according to the guides provided in the informal recommendation section. *If you were able to answer yes to one or more of these criteria,* then create your action plan based on the suggestions in the formal recommendations section.

Informal Recommendations

Informal recommendations take on numerous forms. They may, for example, involve talking one-on-one with a colleague or a supervisor. They may involve a team that knows of your analysis and desires to collaborate. In each case, we want to stress that this process should focus on co-constructing relationships with others rather than "telling others" what needs to happen. Still, these recommendations and the process you engage in challenge you to be more than an observer. Wearing the "hat" of a change agent, a leader willing to find ways to reflect on meaningful changes, is invigorating and challenging. The following set of questions, if thoroughly considered, will guide you in dealing with this challenge. You should answer these questions in conjunction with each of the two applications you selected for organizational communication development.

Questions for Analysis: Informal Recommendations

What Are You Presenting?

- What has been the content of past attempts (your own as well as those of colleagues) of making informal recommendations?
- In what ways, if any, does the content of your current recommendation relate to past recommendations?
- Is your recommendation positively worded? Restate one of your recommendations in positive language.

Who Are You Presenting Your Ideas To?

- Is there more than one person who would be receptive?
- What is your relationship like?
- What aspects of diversity or national culture should be considered?
- Who can you rely on to co-create ideas with you that will also champion these ideas?
- Who in your organization is known for implementing change? Who is listened to/respected?
- Who will be reluctant to accept or is against most any idea?
- How can you learn about their reluctance?
- How can you engage them in the process, in co-creating?

Why Should They Listen?

- Why are these changes of value to the organization?
- Are the changes connected with employee, stockholder, and/or customer satisfaction data/issues? Explain.

When Will You Present?

- What time of day will you be best received?
- Is there a time in the week, month, or year when ideas related to change are most likely to be explored?
- Is there a time in the day when the person you present ideas to is most receptive/least rushed?

How Will You Present?

- What are the expectations of those to whom you will present your ideas?
- Do they expect detailed, written support of the ideas?
- Do they prefer to be involved in shaping the idea?

Action Plan

1. Review your responses to each of the preceding questions.
2. Write/rewrite at least two of your *informal* organization-wide communication applications in single-sentence, positively worded statements.
3. Write down the date(s), place(s), and person(s) important to implementing these goals.

Formal Recommendations

Writing and presenting a formal recommendation requires an analysis of your audience, setting, purposes, and so on, in a way much like that of preparing for informal recommendations. Again, we stress that this process, as a communicative one, should focus on relational connection rather than a performance or a set of strategies. Here, what you are seeking to co-create is a relational connection that ensures others know your ethical and credible process and your desire to work with them to discern ways to move forward. The following set of questions mirrors the informal recommendation development exercise with only minor differences. If thoroughly considered, it will guide you in preparing effective recommendations. Each question encourages you not only to examine your own recommendation but the history of past recommendations. The reason for doing this additional history step is so you will be able to determine what was effective or ineffective. You should answer these questions in conjunction with each of the two applications you selected for organizational communication development.

What Are You Presenting?

- What has been the content of past OD recommendations (your own as well as those of colleagues)?
- In what ways, if any, does the content of your current recommendation relate to past recommendations?
- Is your recommendation positively worded? Restate your recommendations in positive language.

Who Are You Presenting Your Ideas To?

- Is there more than one person who would be receptive?
- What aspects of diversity or national culture should be considered?
- Who can you rely on to champion your ideas?
- Who in your organization is known for implementing change?
- Who is listened to/respected?
- Who will be reluctant to accept this idea?
- What can you learn about their reluctance to accept it?
- How can you deal effectively with the reasons for resistance?

Why Should They Listen?

- Why are these changes of value to the organization?
- Are the changes connected with employee, stockholder, and/or customer satisfaction data/issues? Explain.

Where Will You Present?

- Where will you be presenting your recommendations?
- Will media equipment be expected in this setting?

When Are You Most Likely to Be Best Received?

- Is there a time in the week or year that you are most likely to be heard fully?
- Is there a time in the day when the person(s) you present your ideas to is most receptive?

How Does This Organization Define An Effective Presentation?

- How have successful recommendations been presented?
- Formats used? Audiences? Time length?
- Other audience expectations?

Action Plan

1. Review your responses to each of the preceding questions.
2. Write/rewrite at least two of your formal organization-wide applications in single-sentence, positively worded statements.

____

____

____

____

____

____

____

3. Write down the date(s), place(s), and person(s) important to implementing these goals.

Date:	Place:	Contact Names:

Summary

You made it! Regardless of whether you engaged in completing a small-scale analysis involving a few weeks of data collection or a more ambitious one spanning several months, you have improved your grasp of the process. The stage is now set for you to use your analysis in ways that make the most sense to you. Remember, as you discuss your analysis and informal and/or formal communication recommendations, you are involved in the process of shaping communication patterns and, thereby, the culture in an organization. In this process, you have an ethical responsibility to act on your awareness of your culture and to act in ways that improve and enhance organizational life.

Our desire is that both the process and the outcome of cultural analysis will surprise you. The uncertainty you had at the start of the process may be reduced, but the insights and possibilities for future application should provide a sense of curiosity and wonder. We find a sense of meaning and purpose as we learn of other colleagues who are about making better, more ethical social worlds. It is a journey worth our best efforts. We began and now end by reflecting on the span of experiences we have in organizations, from the cradle to the grave, with tragic and comic stories. Given the significant time we spend in organizations, our passion is for each of us to improve the way we co-create organizational stories characterized by hope, joy, love, and purpose. Both the training tools of method actors and the process of cultural analysis encourage an awareness of communication in the foreground. We have found the outcome of this foregrounding process to be no less than greater participation in the meaning-creation process. We concur with Barrett (1979):

> Life is many days, day after day. But it is not, we hope, a mere succession of days. We long that these days will somehow add up to a meaning or a drama that we can call a life.

To Barrett's reflection, we would add a life lived that co-creates better and more ethical organizations for all of those living and participating in them from day to day.

Discussion Questions

1. What insights have you drawn about yourself over the course of this project?
2. What insights have you drawn about your organization over the course of this project?
3. How might you use the three big questions in the future: a) What kind of culture is being co-created? b) What kind of culture do we want to co-create? and c) What forms of communication will co-create the culture we want to create?
4. Which process, formal or informal, will you utilize to share the results of your analysis? Explain why you are taking this route.
5. Based on reviewing the guides for formal or informal presentations, which elements are you most comfortable with at this point? Least uncomfortable? What will help you move forward?
6. What aspects of this process have influenced the way you will evaluate an organization as an employee, member of a faith-based organization, and/or volunteer in a non-profit?
7. How can you see yourself as a change leader as a result of this project/course?

References

Barrett, W. (1979). *The illusion of technique*. Garden City, NY: Anchor.

Brown, L., Morris, G., & Lee, K. (2012). The role of communication in positive organizational scholarship. In G. M. Spreitzer & K. S. Cameron (Eds.), *The Oxford handbook of positive organizational scholarship* (pp. 566–577). New York: Oxford.

Eisenberg, E., Andrews, L., Murphy, A., & Laine-Timmerman, L. (1999). Transforming organizations through communication. In P. Salem (Ed.), *Organizational communication and change* (pp. 125–147). Cresskill, NJ: Hampton Press.

Heifer International (2024). *About us*. Retreived from https://www.heifer.org/about-us/index.html

Langer, E. (1989). *Mindfulness*. Cambridge, MA: Perseus Books.

Lyon, A. (2017). *Case studies in courageous organizational communication: Research and practices for effective workplaces*. New York: Peter Lang.

Mirivel, J. (2014). *The art of positive communication: Theory and practice*. New York: Peter Lang.

Mirivel, J., & Lyon, A. (2023). *Positive communication for leaders: Proven strategies for inspiring unity and effecting change*. New York: Rowen & Littlefield.

Pearce, W. (2007). *Making social worlds: A communication perspective*. Malden, MA: Blackwell Publishing.

Pitts, M., & Soya, T. (2012). *Positive communication health and wellness*. New York: Peter Lang.

Schoeneborn, D., Blaschke, S., Cooren, F., McPhee, R. D., Seidl, D., & Taylor, J. R. (2014). The three schools of CCO thinking: Interactive dialogue and systematic comparison. *Management Communication Quarterly, 28*(2), 285–316. https://doi.org/10.1177/0893318914527000

Strasberg, L. (1987). *A dream of passion: The development of the method*. Boston: Little, Brown.

Wooten, L., Roberts, L. M., & Davidson, M. (2016). *Positive organizing in a global society: Understanding and engaging differences for capacity building & inclusion*. New York: Routledge.

Index

Note: Page numbers in *italics* indicate figures, and page numbers in **bold** indicate tables in the text

For Product Safety Concerns and Information please contact our EU representative GPSR@taylorandfrancis.com
Taylor & Francis Verlag GmbH, Kaufingerstraße 24, 80331 München, Germany

www.ingramcontent.com/pod-product-compliance
Lightning Source LLC
LaVergne TN
LVHW080807011026
849160LV00015B/1557

* 9 7 8 1 0 3 2 7 7 3 3 2 2 *